WARSHIPS
AND NAVAL BATTLES OF THE
CIVIL WAR

WARSHIPS
AND NAVAL BATTLES OF THE
CIVIL  WAR

TONY GIBBONS

Gallery Books
an imprint of W.H. Smith Publishers, Inc.
112 Madison Avenue
New York, New York 10016

CONTENTS

To Rita

This edition first published in the United States in 1989 by Gallery Books, an imprint of W.H. Smith Publishers, Inc., 112 Madison Avenue, New York 10016.

© Copyright: 1989 Dragon's World Ltd
© Copyright: 1989 Color plates, drawings and text: Tony Gibbons of Bernard Thornton Artists, London.

Published in England by Dragon's World Ltd, Limpsfield and London; created and designed by Tony Gibbons.

Gallery Books are available for bulk purchase for sales promotions and premium use. For details write or telephone the Manager of Special Sales, W.H. Smith Publishers Inc., 112 Madison Avenue, New York, New York 10016. (212) 532-6600.

ISBN 0 8317 9301 5

Typeset by The Works, Exeter, Devon, England
Printed in Spain

CIVIL WAR

Before the Republic of America had completed a century of independent national existence, its social and political fabric was torn apart by a terrible civil war that bitterly divided the nation and brought unimaginable havoc, as well as causing the death of over 620,000 men.

The cause of the conflict (which many predicted would last only three months) was the question of Federal versus State rights. When the Union was first created, it was made up of independent states entering into a contract with other states to form a Federal government. This government was expected to look after the interests of the individual states, who were, nonetheless, able to retain their sovereignty. If the government took any action which did not best serve those interests, the state concerned could declare the contract void and resume its independence by withdrawing from the Union.

This is what occurred in 1860 and 1861: eleven states broke away from the Union and formed the Confederacy because they strongly opposed the Union's efforts to ban slavery. At the time, slavery was the very cornerstone of the (mainly agricultural) Confederate economy. Yet of the 5.5 million Whites in the Confederacy, only 346,000 owned slaves, and of these, 69,000 had only one slave.

It must be noted that not all Northerners were opposed to slavery. Many had little interest in the quarrel between North and South; they opposed emancipation of the Negroes simply because they feared competition from them in an open labor market.

During the late 1850s, President Buchanan made attempts to allay the coming split in the Union by formulating policies which allowed the Southern states to continue to manage their own affairs. But as the tempo of secession increased, Buchanan refrained from taking any further action, which may have accelerated the division and ultimately led to bloodshed. Despite this attitude and pressure from Northern members of his own Cabinet, no attempt was made to secure the strongholds in the South. Accordingly, these well-stocked arsenals fell into the hands of the Confederate Army then rapidly being raised.

In manpower the two sides did not bear comparison. The North, with its teeming population (the 1860 national census recorded some 22 million), and its highly developed industrial capacity appeared to be more than a match for the agricultural South whose prime export was cotton.

The South had no real manufacturing capability. Four-fifths of the nation's factories were in the North, as well as the major deposits of iron and coal. Yet, in spite of this tremendous imbalance, the South, helped by a blockade-running fleet which brought in vital supplies, held off conquest for four long, weary years.

In spite of its obvious strength, the North could supply only 3000 regular soldiers from its western borders. The entire army totalled about 16,000 men, and the staff and supply departments were just not up to the demands about to be made of them. Coupled with this was the realization that the South might be almost impossible to conquer. On first taking office in 1861, President Lincoln merely continued the watchful waiting tactic adopted by Buchanan. Indeed, the Federal government seemed feeble by comparison with the activities of various state governments, which rapidly organized large drafts of volunteers, although many of them could not be equipped immediately.

The South simply wished to be left alone, but were prepared to fight in order to preserve its way of life. To this end a special convention was speedily convened in Montgomery in February 1861, and within two weeks a president and congress were elected.

In choosing Jefferson Davis as president, several radical members of the Montgomery Convention who had done most to bring about the Confederacy were passed over. Davis was chosen because he was moderate on secession but a fervent believer in the South; he also possessed the necessary qualities of leadership and experience in government.

However, like so many leaders before and after, Davis made major errors of judgement that would later have dire consequences for the infant nation. His demand that every foot of the Confederacy should be defended threw an impossible burden on the army command. Furthermore, in the period prior to the outbreak of hostilities, Davis had turned down an opportunity to purchase a fleet of merchant vessels which were suitable for rapidly transporting large quantities of cotton for storage in Europe. Had he accepted, a sizable stockpile of this valuable commodity could have been built up and ultimately provided much needed revenue with which to sustain the war. Davis, however, preferred to keep the cotton within the borders of the Confederacy in order to encourage England and France to come to its aid. No such help arrived, and among the ripple effects of the war was the rapid decline of the United

Kingdom's textile industry. Thousands were thrown out of work and many starved to death, in spite of a few earnest efforts to help these victims of an uncaring Victorian society.

Davis knew that invasion of the North was unnecessary; the South had only to resist in order to win. The problem for the North, however, was more acute. She would need to invade a vast area which had massive resources of basic foods. The Confederacy had more livestock than the North, and although her grain harvests were slightly less, these were counterbalanced by great quantities of rice and maize.

The South's weakness lay in poor manufacturing capability. Few factories and foundries had been established within her borders, so many necessities, as well as luxuries, were supplied from outside sources, mainly in the North.

Transportation, or rather lack of it, was another major problem. Of the 30,000 miles of railroad in the entire country, only 9000 were in the South, and as the war progressed these fell into such a poor state that much of it became useless.

The South's major exports were cotton and tobacco, and even these were carried abroad in foreign ships as she had no mercantile marine to speak of. Most of her trade was already in Northern hands and shipbuilding was almost an unknown industry.

Strong on land but powerless at sea, it was, nonetheless, the sea on which the South's prosperity and ultimate survival would depend.

As the war at sea developed, the North attempted to throw a cordon along the 3549 miles of Southern coastline and seal off the 185 harbor and river openings. This blockade was instituted in two stages and, considering the meager resources of the Union Navy in early 1861 — a mere twenty-three vessels fit for service, and another thirteen laid up — it was extremely ambitious. Yet in December 1861 this navy had increased to 264 ships, mostly by purchasing vessels and pressing them into service, and by undertaking a lot of new construction. This was far removed from Congressional discussions of June 1860 when certain senators had suggested that the regular navy be sold off or scrapped!

By the end of the year these units would strengthen the blockade but would still not be entirely effective. During 1861 the chance of a blockade runner being captured was one in ten; by 1865 it was down to one in three, thanks to a vastly increased navy which had captured many Confederate havens.

There would be no major clash of fleets at sea to decide the future of these two nations — only a slow strangulation of the South, in spite of its remarkable achievements in creating a naval service containing many new types of craft from poor resources. Due to weak industrial capability, the conscription of many skilled laborers into the army, and the increasing loss of suitable building yards to Union forces, many of the South's planned warships were not completed in time to be of use. Added to all this, the engines in many ironclads were unreliable, thus negating the great strides made by the Confederate Navy Department under the leadership of Stephen Mallory. Yet, by the end of the war, this man ruled an enormous industrial complex of yards, ordnance factories, forges, powder mills, mines, and smelters — a brilliant achievement, considering it had been created out of a predominantly agricultural country and in the face of constant Union pressure.

While the Union Navy, with its increasing number of warships, slowly strangled seaborne activity along the shrinking Confederate coastline, several Confederate raiders ranged the seas and virtually destroyed the Union merchant marine. This was achieved not just by sinking vessels, but by causing insurance rates to rise alarmingly through depreciations, and thus forcing many Union shipowners to register their vessels abroad. It would take over forty years before the Union could again boast a respectably large fleet of merchant ships.

Time was now running out for both sides, yet in April 1861 Lincoln still hoped that it might be possible to hold the Union together. Although personally opposed to slavery, he was prepared to tolerate it in existing slave-owning states if it ensured those states remained in the Union. Furthermore, Lincoln realized the social problems that would be caused by suddenly freeing 3.5 million slaves.

Although he knew that any false move would drive many of the upper Southern states into the Confederacy and result in hostilities, Lincoln would still not allow Union property in the shape of forts, customs offices, and suchlike to be taken over by the South.

Just prior to Lincoln officially taking office, attention was focused on Fort Sumter, a small, two-story stone fort that stood alone in Charleston harbor on a man-made island. In December 1860 none of the three forts (Sumter, Moultrie, and Pinckney) were properly manned. During this period Northern members of Buchanan's Cabinet urged him to strengthen these forts with more men. However, nothing was done except to warn Major Anderson, senior office in Charleston, to do nothing that might excite the local population and lead to violence, although he could transfer his small force to any fort if he so desired.

On December 26 Anderson moved his men from Fort Moultrie to Fort Sumter as this would place his force in a stronger position if attacked. South Carolina authorities, however, saw this move as an act of aggression and demanded that Anderson return to his former base. Buchanan refused.

Meanwhile, as Anderson's troops were due to be relieved, a relief force was dispatched from New York on January 5, 1861, in the transport *Queen of the West*. (Originally, it had been planned to use a warship, but the orders changed.) Four days later, upon entering Charleston harbor, *Queen of the West* was fired on, so she promptly turned back.

During the period of changeover from Buchanan's to Lincoln's administration, little was done. Lincoln knew that the small fort within a hostile harbor could not last long, yet he was still reluctant to force the issue. It was decided to send in food supplies to Fort Sumter, but before they arrived, South Carolina, fearing a breach of its sovereignty, opened fire on the fort and its small garrison.

Lincoln's dilemma was now solved. Three days later, on April 15, 1861, he called for 75,000 volunteers to enlist for three months. Soon after he called for an additional 42,000 men to sign on for three years, and provided large increases in the army and navy budgets. The purse strings were now loosened, yet lack of planning in the North and poor resources in the South meant that the campaign at sea got off to a slow start. Similarly, time was needed to build up armies from scratch.

The Union Navy received an increase of 18,000 men, and in July, as it became obvious that this was not going to be a short campaign, Lincoln asked for an additional 400,000 men for the army.

Once started, the South organized more quickly than the North as its State militias had been on partial alert since the first states has seceded and President Davis had increased his first call for troops to 400,000. Despite having far fewer men at its disposal — about one-third of those in the North — by midsummer the South had nearly as many men under arms.

It had long been anticipated that Southern shipbuilding facilities would not be able to cope with demand, so by August 1861 Mallory had already contracted for several powerful ironclads in the west. Here again the South was well in advance of the North.

Few Southern shipyards were of sufficient size, and plants for the manufacture of machinery and armor were also inadequate. Of the ten yards belonging to the US Navy in 1860, only two were in the South — one at Norfolk, and a smaller one at Pensacola, which was better suited to refitting vessels, although it had built several large warships.

Norfolk was a far superior facility, having constructed thirteen major warships prior to 1861. But even this potential source of large output would not be enough when compared with the enormous shipbuilding resources of the Union which had many well equipped navy yards and an abundant supply of private companies.

Many small concerns sprang up in the South, but these were often sited on a riverbank in a hastily prepared clearing and frequently lacked adequate facilities. In 1860 there were only thirty-six regular shipbuilding yards in the soon-to-be Confederate states.

Between 1849 and 1858 the volume of ship construction throughout the United States was enormous. More than 8000 vessels were built, 1600 of them in the South. Most of the larger craft in the Southern quota were built at the important coastal towns of Norfolk, Charleston, Savannah, New Orleans, and Mobile. Later, small towns, which were often located miles up twisting, shallow rivers, would play an important part in creating a navy, especially after the fall of New Orleans and Norfolk in mid-1862. By then the main need was for small, shallow-draft, well-protected craft able to navigate Southern waters. As luck would have it, these were the very type of craft that such yards could produce.

When vessels were all built of wood, the South had no problems in finding materials; the difficulties began when iron was introduced. In 1860, from a total of ninety-six foundries and eighty-two rolling mills, only eleven were of sufficient size to meet production needs. In the Union Pennsylvania alone could swamp the entire output of the South.

Similarly, the production of suitable machinery was a constant headache and many Confederate ironclads were lost through inadequate motive power. In 1860 there were nearly 100 engineering establishments, but most of them were small. However, a few larger companies, such as Noble's Foundry at Rome, Leeds & Co. and Clarke Foundry at New Orleans, Skates at Mobile, and Shockoe Foundry at Richmond did their best to cope with the flood of work, but no matter how hard they tried, they were thwarted by the ever-increasing shortage of skilled workers.

Ordnance was another limiting factor in the success of the South, as in 1860 only Tredegar Ironworks could cast guns. (In the sixteen years prior to that date Tredegar had cast nearly 900 guns). Later, other foundries and ordnance centers, such as the one at Selma, were established, but these had to compete for the limited supply of iron and manpower.

New Orleans was the obvious center for shipbuilding in the west, having a well established record going back to 1819 when the first shipyard opened. From then on many of the river steamers were constructed here; by 1860 there were five yards in the city, with five more spread out in Louisiana itself. By the time New Orleans fell in April 1862, more than thirty warships had been built or converted there, but again, these figures are small when compared with the North, where, by the end of the war, several small private companies would have produced almost as many vessels, often of a more advanced design. Such comparisons highlight the tremendous disadvantages faced by the South and make her lengthy resistance to the North even more remarkable and praiseworthy.

Transport caused the South difficulties throughout the war. In October 1861 only a portion of the iron plate rolled for *Merrimack (Virginia)* by Tredegar Ironworks could be delivered as all the railroad stock was in constant use by the army. When Tredegar reworked the main shaft for the *Mississippi*, then being built at New Orleans, it took nearly a month to make the long journey on a specially built flat car and arrived only a few days before the city fell.

For some of the new interior construction sites transport problems were still worse, as they were not even connected to the railroad. Richmond in Virginia, Edwards Ferry and Whitehall in North Carolina, Mars Bluff in South Carolina, Safford and Columbus in Georgia, Yazoo City in Mississippi, Selma, Montgomery, and Oven Bluff in Alabama, plus Shreveport in Louisiana were all yards where it was difficult for supplies to be delivered. These inland yards completed nine ironclads, but another eight ironclads and six wooden gunboats were destroyed before they became operational to prevent them falling into enemy hands.

Like the North, the South could not at first produce 2-inch plate. Eventually three companies were able to produce armor of the required thickness, but it was a lengthy business. At the same time, the Confederate Navy Department tried to start up new rolling mills, but without success.

The poor rail network in the South reflected on the amount of iron produced at the Tredegar Ironworks. Although that establishment could handle 24,000 tons, only 8000 tons could be delivered in a year. In fact, at one time Tredegar was closed down because of lack of iron. Poor transport was not the only reason for this; the Union had made a point of occupying those parts of the South that produced most of the iron ore.

Common to both sides was a shortage of skilled labor, but it was far worse in the South as many of the workers in the machine ships were alien and left in vast numbers once the war started. Much of the remaining skilled workforce was taken into the army. In spite of all the problems, the South did remarkably well to achieve what it did.

One of the North's greatest achievements was to develop a navy almost from zero. It began by purchasing or chartering all suitable vessels, quickly arming them, and rushing them into service with crews who, in many cases, were as fresh to naval service as the ships themselves.

Within a year a vast construction program was under way. About 300 vessels were added to the navy and these started to make the blockade effective. By the end of the war, 418 vessels had been purchased, of which 313 were steamers. An extra 208 warships were built under contract, and over sixty of these were ironclads.

There was great variety in the ships designed for the US Navy, ranging from fast cruisers needed to pursue the Confederate raiders, to shallow-draft ironclads and gunboats needed on the Mississippi and elsewhere. One of the most successful developments was the double-ended gunboat, which was able to maneuver so well in narrow, twisting rivers.

In 1861 US Navy personnel numbered about 1000 officers and 7500 men, and although there was no naval reserve, there were abundant merchant seamen to call on. By 1864 the numbers had risen to 6000 officers and 45,000 men.

It was important for the navy to be seen achieving victories without aid from the army, so Gideon Wells, Secretary of the Navy, insisted that New Orleans be captured by the fleet, and that Charleston should also be taken as the North considered it to be the seat of the rebellion.

Supplying such a large and far-flung navy needed thorough planning, and required the establishment of store ships and well-equipped repair yards. In 1864 coal consumption amounted to over 500,000 tons, and this, together with fresh water, had to be regularly transported long distances to warships, especially the smaller ones which lacked adequate storage facilities.

Viewed against the huge Northern force, the chances of sustained Confederate success were always limited. Nonetheless, they fought on, and although the raiders were not particularly effective in combating the Union blockade, they almost succeeded in driving the Union merchant flag from the sea. However, Union trade itself was not destroyed. When the European harvest failed in the early 1860s, the bumper crops of the Midwest were still sold to eager Europeans and trade generally continued to flourish.

In the end the Union Navy tipped the balance, as the blockade slowly strangled the Confederacy and kept out desperately needed supplies. It took some time, however, before the true effect of this slow process could be seen.

Interestingly, as early as December 1862, the South had asked Emperor Napoleon of France to propose an armistice on its behalf. Although Seward, the Secretary of State, favored the idea, President Lincoln was strongly opposed to any cessation of hostilities.

In the summer of 1864 the Union faced a dark period of the war as the country seemed to tire of the conflict. Battles such as those at the Wilderness and Cold Harbor cost the North over 55,000 casualties against the South's 25,000, but the latter could not so easily make up such losses.

The South was now in dire straits: food was in short supply and morale was low. There had been a major defeat at Gettysburg and Rappahannock when General Lee was unable to force the Union Army back over the river, and the conscription drive in the summer of 1864 had been a miserable failure. Nevertheless, Union forces could not have won that dreadful war if the South had not finally surrendered to the relentless attacks of the Union Army and the subtle but definite pressure exerted by the United States Navy.

NOTE

The ships in this book have been divided into major sections. The first deals with the ironclads which formed the backbone of any fighting force and were usually of the most powerful and well protected type.

Gunboats and sloops were the mainstay of the blockading fleet. They were expected to cope with ships of their own group, while the raiders and privateers preyed on the enemy's merchant marine. Privateers were privately-owned vessels operating with the agreement of their own government, and made their profit from vessels captured and sold in a prize court set up ashore.

Cruisers were mainly used to patrol the ocean highways and hunt down the raiders. In importance they ranked close to the ironclads but were not suited to fight the larger type of ironclad which had superior protection. Cruisers also acted as blockaders along the coasts and deeper rivers.

The section dealing with blockade runners gives a selection of the various types pressed into service, ranging from the standard merchant ships first used and the small sailing vessels able to operate in shallow inshore waters, to the more sophisticated craft specially developed to make the quick dash across an open sea.

Submarines, as we know them today, were first used with some success in the Civil War and their exploits are also recorded.

Vessel names often underwent many changes, but space does not permit them all to be listed. The names given are those carried during the war.

Tonnage is complicated because records give both old tonnage and displacement, but do not always identify clearly which is which. Old tonnage is usually based on burden tonnage and should always be treated with caution as its calculation varied so widely.

Armament listed in the text is usually that carried in the early stages of the war. Before 1850 the smoothbore muzzle-loading gun firing solid cast-iron shot or explosive shells was the weapon in use in the world's navies. When ironclads were introduced in 1860, improved guns were needed to pierce their armor. Larger caliber smoothbore guns were developed which could crush and break up the armor protection. These guns were used exclusively during the Civil War and continued in service for many years afterward in the US Navy. The superior rifled gun, with its greater range and accuracy, was also used, and later this weapon would increase in size and power and eventually replace the smoothbore gun.

Measurements

US measurements are given throughout. Metric equivalents may be calculated as follows:

1 inch	=	2.54 cm
1 foot	=	30.5 cm
1 yard	=	0.9144 m
1 mile	=	1.6093 km
1 pound	=	0.4536 kg
1 ton	=	1.016 tonnes
1 gallon	=	3.7853 lit

CSS *Louisiana*

Displacement: 1400 tons. **Dimensions:** 26ft x 62ft. **Machinery:** Four engines, plus two huge paddle wheels in a center well, two screws and twin rudders. **Armament:** Two 7-inch rifles, three 9-inch shell guns, four 8-inch shell guns and seven 32-pdrs.

By the end of August 1861 the Confederate Naval Secretary, S. Mallory, had authorized the building of three powerful armored vessels. Another ironclad was then contracted for with E. C. Murray on September 18. This was to be named *Louisiana* and was laid down at the end of September at New Orleans. Lack of materials, particularly seasoned timber, caused delays in her construction, and much green wood was therefore used. When the ironclad was launched, water poured into her gundeck and she was nearly swamped. When *Louisiana* was later in action, she leaked badly; water swilled about knee-deep on the gundeck while the guns were being feverishly worked by her soldier crew from the "Crescent Artillery", no sailors being available.

The massive casemate sloped back from the sides of the hull at a 45-degree angle and was over 200 feet long. This was covered by two layers of railroad iron. Around the upper deck was a stout bulwark 5 feet high and iron plated inside to give protection from grapeshot to the sharpshooters stationed there. When joined by her second in command, John Wilkinson, later to become famous as the most successful blockade runner in the Confederacy, he found mechanics still working feverishly on the unfinished armor and machinery. Work continued ceaselessly when Commodore Whittle ordered her new captain, Commander C. F. McIntosh, to proceed down the river to the threatened forts now awaiting an attack by the gathering Union forces.

The paddle wheels were working but a great deal still had to be done to the screw machinery, and the crew were still mounting the battery.

On April 20, a bright Sunday morning, the ponderous vessel set off. Quickly the paddle wheels proved useless in stemming the rapid Mississippi current, and the vessel started to drift rapidly downstream, as water poured in through crevices in the bulkheads. She was aided on the seventy-mile trip by two transports sent along to escort her.

On the morning of the 21st, *Louisiana* was secured to the left bank near Fort St Philip, where the crew continued working on the engines and armament.

Rear Admiral David Porter's mortar boats, which formed part of the attacking force, poured down a continuous rain of mortar fire on the forts while remaining out of range of their targets. This incessant barrage slowed when the Union fleet began its run past the forts.

During the ensuing action nearly all the Confederate river defense force was destroyed, yet the *Louisiana* would still have posed a serious threat but for her lack of maneuverability. Also, the portholes allowed only a 5-degree elevation to the guns, thus limiting their effectiveness.

In spite of a fierce battering, *Louisiana* was little damaged, although many of the workers carried on the accompanying tenders were killed or wounded.

When the Confederate forts surrendered, the ironclad was fired and set adrift to explode down the river.

CSS *Manassas*

Displacement: 387 tons. **Dimensions:** 134ft x 33ft x 17ft. **Machinery:** Two-cylinder engines. **Armament:** One 9-inch, 64-pdr Dahlgren smoothbore, later replaced with a 32-pdr. **Crew:** 36.

Manassas started life as the icebreaker *Enoch Train*, built by J.O. Curtis at Medford, Massachusetts, in 1855. She was acquired by John A. Stevenson, who raised $100,000 by subscription to convert her into an ironclad for use as a privateer after her transfer to New Orleans as a tug boat in 1859.

Her conversion was carried out by J. Hughes at Algiers, and the 128-foot long, 385-ton vessel was quickly (and with some secrecy) cut down, losing the upper works. Upon the frame was built a convex deck of oak, 12 inches thick and sheathed with 1.5 inches of iron plate. the bow was filled in solid with timber so as to form a massive ram 20 feet long.

Manassas carried only one gun, firing through a small bow porthole which allowed no lateral training. The hatch automatically closed when the gun was run in. Two other hatches were the only other openings in her curved deck. Steam hoses were to be used to repel boarders.

On completion, the new *Manassas* was 15 feet lower and 5 feet wider, with a draft increased by 4.5 feet, and resembled a huge cigar floating on the water.

As soon as the first ironclad in the Confederate Navy was ready, Stevenson applied for a letter of marque which was granted on September 12.

On October 11 *Manassas* was clearly the most formidable vessel available riding at anchor between Forts Jackson and St Philip. Commodore Hollins, in command of Confederate forces afloat in the area, felt he could not allow her to act independently, so at the last moment she was seized by Lt. Warley from the gunboat *McRae*, and Stevenson went ashore,

quickly followed by the crew who were told that the prize money agreement with Stevenson no longer applied. Their places were quickly filled by volunteers from the fleet.

The next night *Manassas* led the surprise attack against Union forces, blockading the Head of the Passes on the Mississippi. In the pitch-black night the vessel glided noiselessly downstream, with Warley and the helmsman peering anxiously into the darkness, broken only by the slightly luminous spray that played over the conically-shaped bow.

As soon as the Union forces were sighted, tar, tallow and sulphur were hurled into the furnace to increase steam pressure. Rapidly, the low-lying and hard-to-see vessel shot forward to ram the USS *Richmond*. Although successful in this, she dislodged one of her own engines, thus greatly reducing the vessel's use. No shots had been fired by *Manassas*, although her presence was known, as she had only twelve shells aboard; it was decided to use the ram only. She was fired at as she retired but the shots simply glanced off. Two months later *Manassas* was directly purchased for Confederate Government ownership.

On April 24, 1862 *Manassas* was in action against Flag Officer Farragut's force as it pushed its way past the Confederate Forts St Philip and Jackson.

Manassas rammed USS *Brooklyn* but was fired on by the entire Union line in turn. She still doggedly pursued the Union fleet, but USS *Mississippi* turned on the luckless craft and forced her aground, where she was abandoned by her crew. *Mississippi* continued to pour in a heavy fire upon the stranded vessel, which later slipped off the bank and, in flames, drifted down the river casting an eerie light before exploding.

Louisiana *in April 1862.*

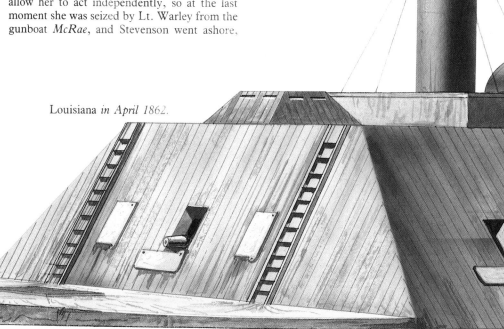

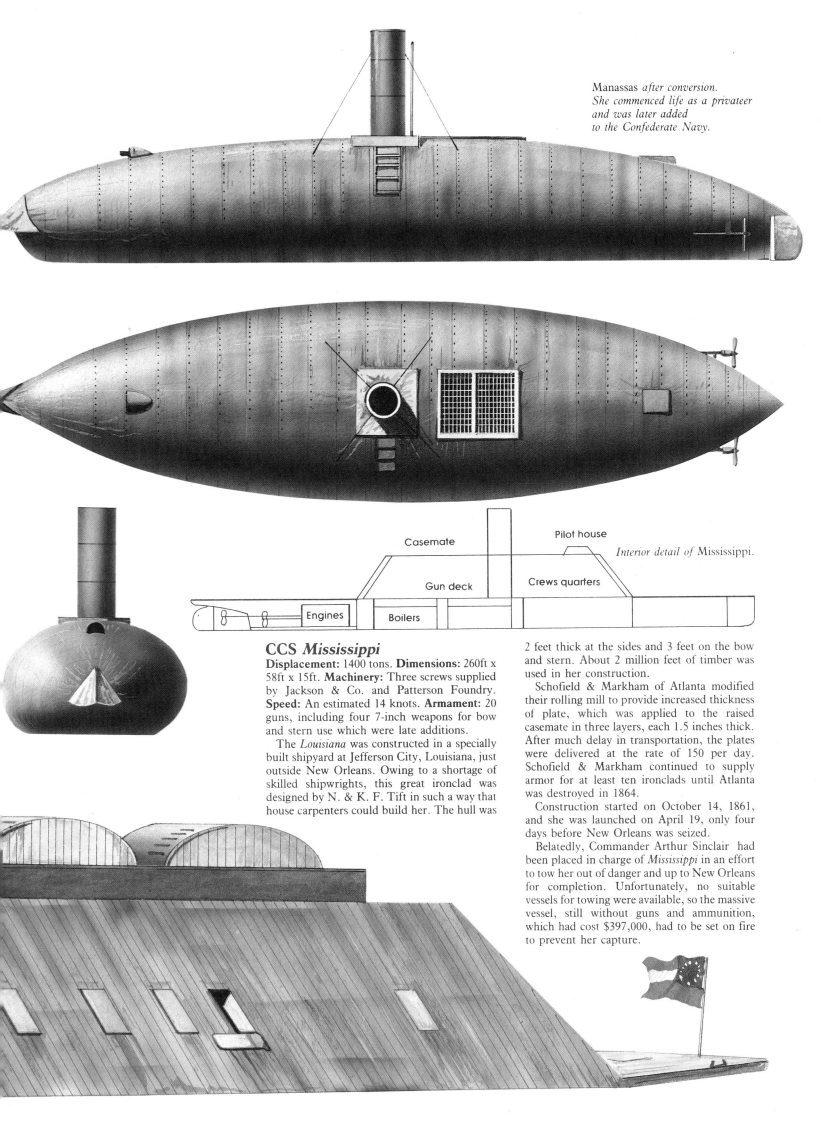

Manassas *after conversion.*
She commenced life as a privateer
and was later added
to the Confederate Navy.

Casemate

Pilot house

Interior detail of Mississippi.

Gun deck

Crews quarters

Engines

Boilers

CCS *Mississippi*

Displacement: 1400 tons. **Dimensions:** 260ft x 58ft x 15ft. **Machinery:** Three screws supplied by Jackson & Co. and Patterson Foundry. **Speed:** An estimated 14 knots. **Armament:** 20 guns, including four 7-inch weapons for bow and stern use which were late additions.

The *Louisiana* was constructed in a specially built shipyard at Jefferson City, Louisiana, just outside New Orleans. Owing to a shortage of skilled shipwrights, this great ironclad was designed by N. & K. F. Tift in such a way that house carpenters could build her. The hull was 2 feet thick at the sides and 3 feet on the bow and stern. About 2 million feet of timber was used in her construction.

Schofield & Markham of Atlanta modified their rolling mill to provide increased thickness of plate, which was applied to the raised casemate in three layers, each 1.5 inches thick. After much delay in transportation, the plates were delivered at the rate of 150 per day. Schofield & Markham continued to supply armor for at least ten ironclads until Atlanta was destroyed in 1864.

Construction started on October 14, 1861, and she was launched on April 19, only four days before New Orleans was seized.

Belatedly, Commander Arthur Sinclair had been placed in charge of *Mississippi* in an effort to tow her out of danger and up to New Orleans for completion. Unfortunately, no suitable vessels for towing were available, so the massive vessel, still without guns and ammunition, which had cost $397,000, had to be set on fire to prevent her capture.

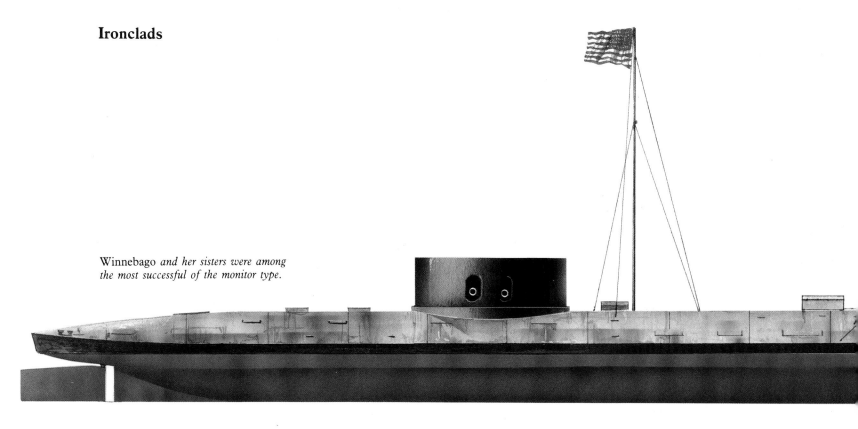

Winnebago and her sisters were among the most successful of the monitor type.

USS *Winnebago*

Displacement: 1300 tons (970 old tons).
Dimensions: 229ft x 56ft x 6ft. **Armor:** 8 inches on turrets, and 3 inches on sides.
Machinery: Four non-condensing horizontal engines, built by the Fulton Ironworks of St Louis; seven horizontal tube boilers; coal capacity 150 tons. This class had four screws and three rudders. **Speed:** 9 knots. **Armament:** Four 11-inch Dahlgren smoothbore guns in twin turrets. **Crew:** About 120.

In May 1862 the Navy Department awarded a contract to James Eads for four more shallow-draft monitors for river use. They were to be double-turreted and screw-driven, rather than using paddles.

Winnebago and *Milwaukee* were to be built by Eads, the *Kickapoo* by G. B. Allen & Co. of St Louis, and the *Chickasaw* by Thomas Gaylord of Cincinnati. Each vessel had one Ericsson turret aft, while the other one was an Eads design which made extensive use of steam power to elevate the guns, check the recoil, return the gun to battery, work the gunports and, by means of a piston, lower the guns into the hold for loading.

The Eads turret extended down into the hold and revolved on 6-inch iron spheres in a circular groove. The turrets were at each end of the vessel with the stack and pilot house protruding up through the turtleback deck. Side armor was a solid 3-inch plate, instead of the usual laminated type.

The contract price was $313,000, with the name ship finishing at $381,815, which was about average. When *Winnebago* was sold in 1874 she fetched $7350.

Winnebago and *Chickasaw* served with Admiral Farragut in the battle of Mobile Bay, and all served in the West Gulf Blockading Squadron.

Milwaukee was sunk by a mine in the Blakely River on March 28, 1865, as she was returning from an attack on a transport. The explosion occurred on the port side aft; the stern sank in three minutes, with the forward section remaining above water for another hour. No lives were lost.

All four boats had been laid down in 1862 and completed during the summer of 1864. They were considered by many to be the most successful of the monitor type.

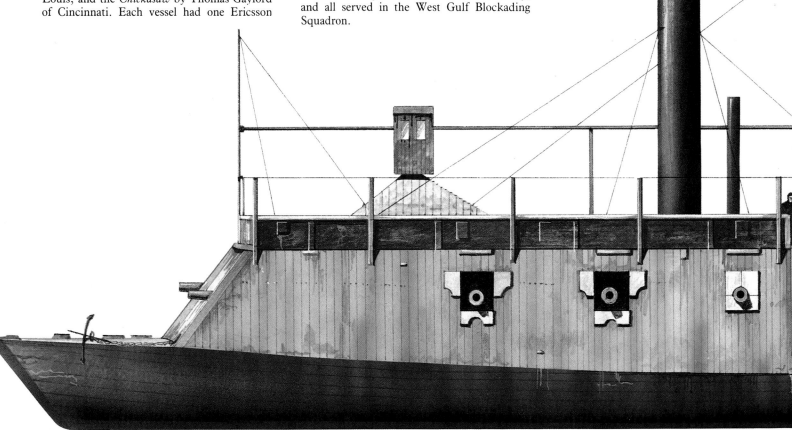

USS *Benton*

Displacement: 633 tons. **Dimensions:** 202ft x 72ft x 9ft. **Armor:** 2.5 inches over casemate and pilot house. **Machinery:** Inclined engines, single stern wheel. **Speed:** 5.5 knots. **Armament:** Varied, but on completion had seven 32-pdr, 43-cwt, two 11-inch, and seven 42-pdr army rifles.

Benton was originally the catamaran-hulled snag boat *Submarine No. 7*. She was rebuilt to James Eads' designs, who also converted her by planking over the 20-foot wide space between the twin hulls top and bottom. A new bow was added, plus a two-tier casemate plated over on the sides and front. Upon completion she was the most powerful unit in the Mississippi flotilla and was, for a time, the flagship. Started by the army, she was transferred to the Navy Department on October 1, 1862.

Commissioned on February 24, 1862, with Lt. J. Biship in command, she took part in the capture of Island No. 10, the attack on Fort Pillow, Tennessee, and the battle of Memphis.

During the Yazoo River expedition in December, her second commanding officer, Lt. Cdr. W. Gwin, was mortally wounded when struck by a rifle shot. He refused to enter the pilot house and still directed *Benton* in action which, owing to the narrow channel, was bearing the brunt of the Confederate fire.

Benton also took part in numerous actions before Vicksburg and participated in the Red River expeditions, capturing the Confederate ironclad CSS *Missouri*. In February 1863 a company of troops mutinied while on board.

Benton was sold at auction on November 29, 1865 at Mound City to D. Jacobs for $3000, the armor first being removed.

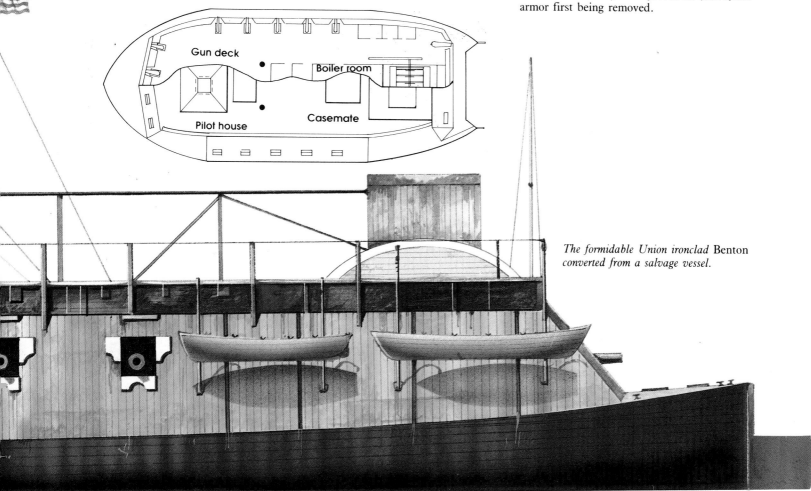

The formidable Union ironclad Benton *converted from a salvage vessel.*

USS *Eastport*

Displacement: 700 tons. **Dimensions:** 280ft x 6.5-ft draft. **Armament:** Various in Union service: in May 1862 had four 32-pdr, 33-cwt and one 12-pdr howitzer; in October 1862 had two 50-pdr Dahlgren rifles, four 32-pdr, 33-cwt, and two 12-pdr rifled howitzers; in January 1863 had two 100-pdr Parrott rifles and six 9-inch Dahlgren smoothbore shell guns; in July 1863 had two 100-pdr Parrott rifles, four 9-inch Dahlgren shell guns, and two 50-pdr Dahlgren rifles. **Crew:** 150.

Confederate General Leonardis Polk, commander of forces in western Tennessee, responded to the Union seizure of the mouths of the strategically important Tennessee and Cumberland rivers by forming a river defense fleet. On October 31, 1861 he paid $12,000 for the large, six-wheel steamer C. E. Hillman built at New Albany, Indiana, in 1852.

After purchase the vessel was towed upstream to Cerro Gordo, Tennessee, for conversion. On December 24 Lt. Isaac Newton Brown, who later became the commander of the famous CCS *Arkansas*, was appointed to oversee the work. Within a month this industrious and dedicated officer also managed to purchase at Nashville, Tennessee, more steamers for conversion into gunboats.

By the end of January 1862, *Eastport* had been cut down to main deck level, had boilers installed, and a slanting casemate frame with wooden backing added ready to receive the armor.

On February 6 Fort Henry was captured by Union forces. Quickly, a force of three wooden gunboats — *Lexington*, *Tyler*, and *Conestoga* — were sent up the river on a raiding expedition. As the Union force approached, the *Eastport* was scuttled by cutting the suction pipes and the Confederate forces fled,

burning six loaded steamers before they left. *Tyler* was left to guard the prize, and when the main force returned on the night of February 8, much of the armor intended for the ironclad was being loaded, plus 250,000 feet of timber also needed for the conversion. Before leaving, the timber mill was destroyed.

The newly raised ironclad was towed by USS *Lexington* to Cairo for completion, where $55,230 was expended before she entered Union service in August. Later, she grounded several times, causing the bottom to drag up 15 feet close to the underpart of the boilers. While out of service, she was used as a receiving ship.

Serving on the Red River in April 1864, she struck a mine, which was not discovered until water was found in her hold. Her captain failed to get canvas over the hole, and in a falling river the situation was serious; the vessel sank in five hours. Help arrived on the 17th when the *Champion* appeared with powerful pumps. More help came on the 19th when extra pumps were supplied by the *New Champion*.

By the 21st *Eastport's* boilers were in service, enabling the gunboat to start slowly down the river, but after grounding several times, and as

the river was steadily falling, it was decided to destroy the vessel. This, in spite of all the efforts of three streamers and the ceaseless toil of the crew for many days.

On the 26th the ironclad was set on fire and powder previously positioned about the vessel exploded, completely destroying her.

USS *Essex*

Displacement: 640 tons. **Dimensions:** 159ft x 47ft 6in x 5ft 10in. **Machinery:** Two single cylinder engines; four boilers. **Armament:** In January 1862 had one 32-pdr, 43-cwt, three 11-inch Dahlgren smoothbores, one 10-inch Dahlgren smoothbore, and one 12-pdr

Eastport, *although flying Confederate colors, is shown with the added Union conning tower placed on top of the existing protective structure forward of the superstructure.*

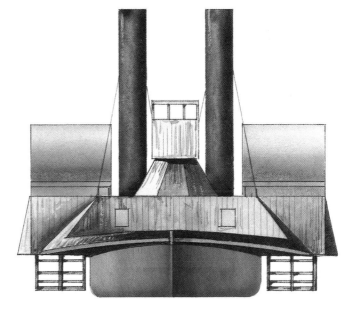

howitzer; armament then varied throughout career.

Originally named *New Era*, this large center-wheel steamer was built at St Louis by Page & Bacon (Bankers), who sold her to Wiggins Ferry Co. on October 14, 1856. *New Era* was then purchased on September 20, 1861 by the US government for $20,000.

Renamed *Essex*, progress in converting her into an ironclad — slow through lack of funds — finally totalled about $40,000. She had a high casemate housing two decks, the upper one forming apartments for officers. The pilot house was built into the vessel and only projected 3.5 feet above deck, while the arched upper deck was well protected. Armor was supplied by Theodore Adonis of St Louis. After the Fort Henry attack, the forward casemate was refaced with 1-inch iron over 1 inch of rubber.

Her conversion was carried out by James Eads at St Louis, and upon completion she joined the Western Flotilla, operated by the army but commanded by a naval officer.

Essex, commanded by W.D. Porter, took part in the Cumberland River expedition in November 1861. Serious damage to her boilers forced her out of action in February 1862 during the attack on Fort Henry. She rejoined the fray in July 1862 and took part in the numerous actions around Vicksburg, including an attack on the Confederate ironclad *Arkansas*.

Essex served on the Mississippi until May 1864, then moved to Memphis, Tennessee. She was sold at auction on November 29, 1865 at Mound City to W.L. Hambleton for $4000.

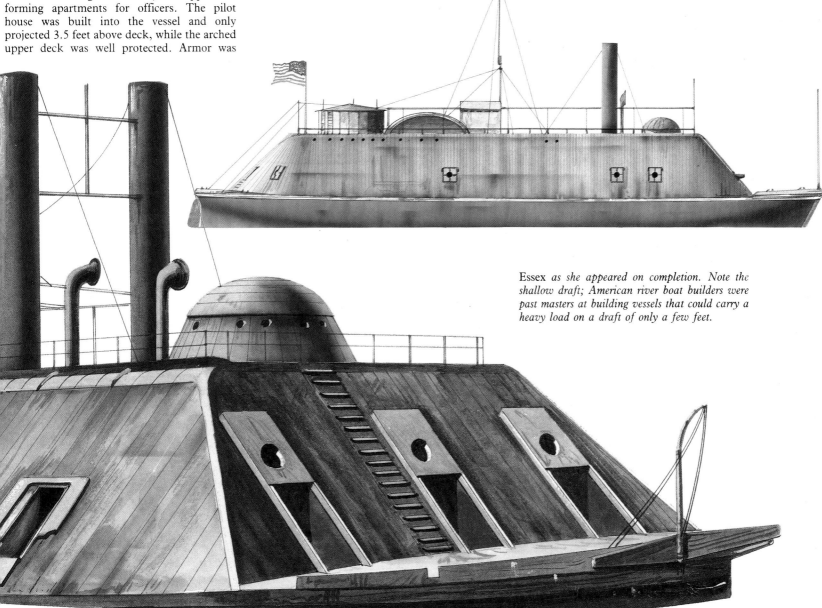

Essex *as she appeared on completion. Note the shallow draft; American river boat builders were past masters at building vessels that could carry a heavy load on a draft of only a few feet.*

USS *Cairo*

Displacement: 888 tons. **Dimensions:** 175ft x 51ft 2in x 6ft. **Armor:** 2½-inches on casemate, 1½-inches on pilot house. **Machinery:** Two non-condensing reciprocating engines driving single center 22-ft diameter paddle wheel. **Speed:** 8 knots. **Armament:** Three 7-inch 42-pdr army rifles, three 8-inch, 64-pdr, 63-cwt smoothbores, six 32-pdr, 42-cwt smoothbores and one 30-pdr Parrott rifle.

With the fall of Fort Sumter, the general-in-chief of the army, Winfield Scott, suggested that the citizen army enlisted for three months would not be able to seize back the South in such a short time, and that several years would be more likely for such a vast undertaking. In this he was correct, as later events showed. Some people in high places wanted the war over quickly by dashing into the Confederacy, but as many later land battles were to show, the South was fully equal to defending itself, in spite of having a smaller population and no major manufacturing resources to speak of.

The upper Mississippi and Ohio rivers were well served with shipyards and machine shops able to turn out the type of vessels needed in the protracted conflict. John Lenthall had already made a detailed study of armed screw steam vessels for the Mississippi and doubted that such vessels would be efficient as western rivers were generally too shallow to take them. Any warship would have to be sidewheel with a flat bottom. Lenthall's design was for a ship nearly 9 feet deep and 170 feet long, a mere 28 feet

wide and with a rudder at each end. Armed with four 8-inch guns, the vessel displaced 436 tons and drew 4 feet 7 inches.

Samuel Pook was called in to consult with Lenthall over the proposals and extensively revised them to produce a 175 x 50-foot boat drawing only 6 feet. There were three keels and a flat bottom, and mounted on the hull was an armored casemate running almost the entire length, its sides sloping 45 degrees at the front and 35 degrees on the sides. This structure was to be pierced for three guns in the bow and aft, with seven on each side. The engines were to be protected by iron plates.

Scott also wanted a naval blockade of Southern ports to keep out supplies from foreign countries. Another major plank in his plan was to send a column down the Mississippi. This would serve three purposes: it would split the Confederacy in two, stopping one half supplying the other with much needed produce at a time when it was busy fighting; the Mississippi would be open to the sea, thus enabling the farmers in the west to use it as an outlet for their crops; the thrust down the Mississippi would also complete the total blockade of the South.

The plan to regain control of the Mississippi called for between twelve and twenty gunboats. At first it was assumed that this project would be handled by the army. In early May, James Eads, a St Louis engineer, suggested the establishment of a protected base at Cairo, Illinois, so that such a scheme could be carried out.

Scott had also called for a detailed report to back up his plan for exploiting the Mississippi to bring about the downfall of the Confederacy. This revealed a huge potential transport fleet comprising about 400 steamers, many then out of work because of the unsettled times. The army could base its transport needs on this vast stock as the campaign unfolded.

Three proposals had also been prepared by the army. Two were for paddle-wheel engines and one for a screw-driven vessel, which would be impractical in shallow, timber-filled rivers where it would be bound to run aground. The army called for bids and when these were opened on August 5, 1861, Eads submitted a low quotation of $89,000 for four to sixteen craft. Two days later he signed a contract to build seven gunboats with stage payments, but with 25 percent held back until completion.

The class comprised *Cairo, Carondelet, Cincinnati, Louisville, Mound City, Pittsburgh,* and *St Louis.* The builders were Hambleton, Collier & Company of Mound City, who were to supply three hulls; the other four hulls were

to be built by the Carondelet Marine Railway & Dry Dock Company of Carondelet, Missouri. Two sets of engines and boilers were supplied by Hartupee & Company of Pittsburgh, Pennsylvania, while Eagle Foundry and Fulton Foundry, both of St Louis, supplied five sets each. The engines were designed by Thomas Merritt.

Armor plate was manufactured by Gaylord, Son & Company who had establishments in Portsmouth, Ohio, and Newport, Kentucky. The armor was rolled in lengths of 8 to 13 feet and 13 inches wide. The total of weight of armor was 75 tons but later, after the battle of Fort Pillow, the vessels were reinforced against ramming by putting more railroad iron around the stems and sterns; this added an extra 47 tons in weight. Protection was further increased by suspending logs along the sides.

The massive wheelhouse was built into the aft end of the long superstructure, extending 60 feet forward — almost the entire length of the vessel — and 18 feet across. It had a gentle curve from the waterline up to ease the flow of water onto the paddle wheel. The officers'

quarters were built into the aft section of the casemate, and the crew berthed on the gun deck.

Some 75 tons of protective iron plating were added around the boilers, which were squeezed into the lower part of the vessel. Engines were angled at 15 degrees and had a 6-foot stroke. Less than one ton of coal was consumed per hour.

All the vessels were laid down and launched in 1861, and completed during January 1862, several months later than planned, in spite of extra men being added to the workforce. Delays in payment to Eads forced him to use his own funds to settle wages and material costs, and his original quote of $89,600 was exceeded by about $101,808, mostly caused by changes.

The vessels led active lives and were the backbone of the River Squadron. They took part in every major action, initially serving with the army's Western Gunboat Fleet before transferring to the navy on October 1, 1862. Although at first part of an army command, their officers were supplied by the navy.

Cairo served at Fort Pillow and took part in action against Confederate rams at Memphis. She later served at Vicksburg, but while on the Yazoo expedition, she struck a mine during a clearing operation on December 12, 1862.

St Louis was also lost through striking a mine in the Yazoo River in July 1863. The remaining vessels continued to serve on the Mississippi until the end of the war, when four were sold in November 1865, and one in early 1866.

Plan showing the large area of the casemate housing the guns, which extended the full width of the vessel, leaving only the blunt bow and part of the stern uncovered.

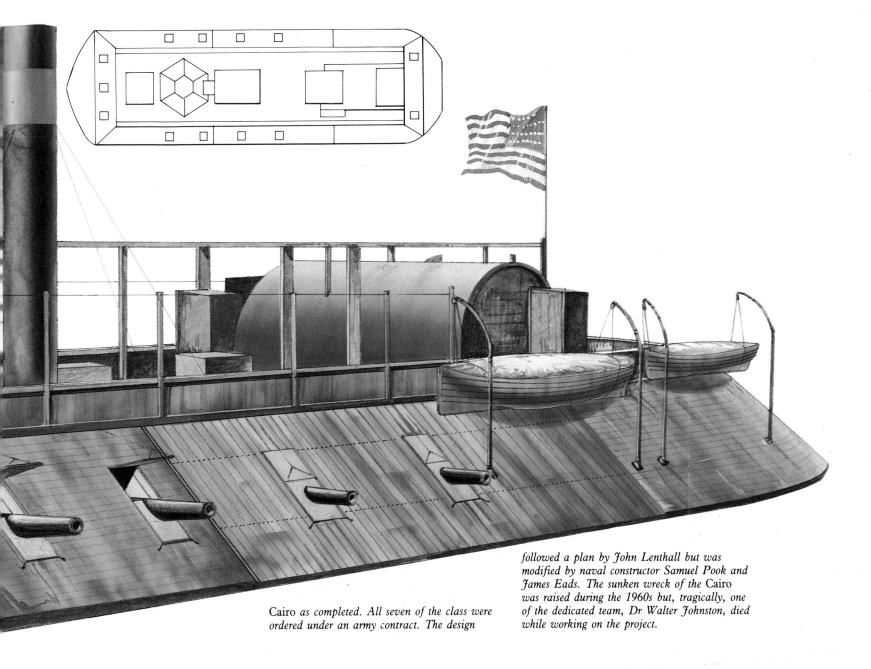

Cairo *as completed. All seven of the class were ordered under an army contract. The design* followed a plan by John Lenthall but was modified by naval constructor Samuel Pook and James Eads. The sunken wreck of the Cairo was raised during the 1960s but, tragically, one of the dedicated team, Dr Walter Johnston, died while working on the project.

FORT DONELSON, *Tennessee*

An early Union plan for attacking the Confederacy was to make a concerted drive into the South via Kansas, down the Mississippi River, on into Kentucky and then Tennessee, but with the main blow being aimed at Virginia.

The main line of Confederate defense in the West ran from Columbus on the Mississippi to Fort Donelson on the Cumberland River, via Bowling Green, Mill Spring, and Fort Henry on the Tennessee River. This line was intended to protect the two main rivers.

In January 1862 Union forces made demonstrations against Columbus and Fort Henry to prevent Confederate reinforcements being sent from Columbus against a Union Army under Buell which was beginning its own assault on the South.

Events now moved quickly, and Fort Henry fell to a combined Union Army and Navy assault in February. The capture of Fort Henry opened up the navigable waters of the Tennessee into Northern Alabama and severed the northernmost lateral railroad which crossed the river above the fort.

Fort Donelson fell soon after on a cold, snowy day. This fort had a 17,000-strong garrison defending a well-prepared position located on a bluff and having three levels. After several days' hard fighting, in which the ironclads suffered damage, the fort surrendered on February 16, 1862, thus removing the only real obstacle to navigation from the mouth of the Cumberland to Nashville. This was particularly useful as Nashville was the largest city after New Orleans in the Western Confederacy and supplied the Southern armies with a vast amount of supplies.

ISLAND No. 10, *Missouri*

Now seriously threatened by Union successes on the Cumberland and Tennessee rivers, the Confederates decided to evacuate Columbus before it too fell into Union hands. This gave the defenders an opportunity of removing all the guns and stores and sending them down to Island No. 10 which formed a natural barrier on the upper reaches of the Mississippi.

Union forces now moved down through Missouri to drive Confederate troops out of the state and came out at New Madrid, a heavily garrisoned town a few miles below the island, which lay near the Kentucky/Tennessee border in a tortuous double bend of the river. At this point more than fifty guns covered the river; they were split into ten batteries and occupied a three-mile stretch of island and riverbank.

A heavy mortar bombardment was directed at the Confederate defense with the gunboats joining in, but to no effect. Help simply could not be given to General Pope's Union troops who had occupied New Madrid and were now unable to cross the river through lack of transport.

Pope appealed for a few Union gunboats to run past Island No. 10 and help him, but the majority of gunboat commanders felt that such a move would end in disaster. However, Commander Walke of the *Carondelet* believed the run could be made, and at the height of a storm, on the night of April 4, he made the attempt, first adding logs to the roof of the casemate to keep out plunging fire, and placing bales of hay around the stern to protect the steering.

Lashed alongside was a barge loaded with coal to help shield the gunboat from heavy enemy fire. To muffle the unmistakable sound of the exhaust, the steam lines were diverted from the stack and piped into the paddle box to deaden the sound of escaping steam. Amid lightning flashes, which clearly lit up the gunboat he successfully passed the batteries and was fired at only when nearly past them.

More gunboats followed and Pope was able to land his troops, causing the Confederates on the mainland to surrender. Now completely cut off, Island No. 10 surrendered on April 6.

CSS *Merrimack (Virginia)*

Displacement: 4636 tons (as originally built).
Dimensions: 275ft x 38ft 6in x 22ft.
Machinery: Horizontal back-acting two-cylinder engines driving a single screw. **Speed:** Estimated at 9 knots but closer to 6. She also steered badly, needing about 40 minutes to turn 180 degrees. **Armament:** As *Virginia* — two 7-inch rifle pivots, two 6-inch rifle pivots, six 9-inch Dahlgrens in broadside, and two 12-pdr howitzers.

In April 1854 Congress authorized the construction of six first-class steam frigates all to be built in navy yards and to be named *Merrimack*, *Wabash*, *Minnesota*, *Roanoke*, *Colorado*, and *Niagara*. The first three were launched in 1855, with the rest following in early 1856.

All were near sisters, having *Merrimack* as the basic design, but *Wabash* and *Minnesota* had a few extra feet inserted amidships to give additional space to machinery and fuel, while *Roanoke* and *Colorado* were slightly broader.

They were ship-rigged, with the area of the principal ten sails being about thirty-two times the immersed midship section of the hull. This ratio was only slightly less than that used in the highly developed sailing frigates of the period. All were built of seasoned oak frames already in stock and initially intended for use in the old-style sailing ships. This material was adapted and the lines of the big frigates were, to a large extent, dictated by the need to work up the frames without waste. The resulting vessels were a great success and all were fast and handy under sail alone.

The entire group subsequently influenced designs in Europe, notably in England, who answered with the *Orlando* and *Mersey* classes.

Commissioned at Boston in December 1855. Late in 1860 *Merrimack* was sent to Gosport Navy Yard, Virginia, for badly needed repairs to her inadequate engines, but as Virginia now looked like breaking away from the Union it was planned to move her to the safer Philadelphia Navy Yard.

Merrimack could have been moved on April 18, 1861, the day after Virginia's order of secession from the Union, but owing to contradictory orders from Washington nothing was done. On April 20, 1861 the important yard was abandoned, but not before all that could not be moved was set alight, included seven major warships, one of which was the *Merrimack*.

However, the Union plan to destroy the abandoned yard failed as the Confederates entered in time to extinguish the flames. Without firing a single shot the South took one of the finest yards in the country, together with 1185 guns, and precious supplies the Confederate forces would have difficulties in obtaining elsewhere.

Secretary of the Confederate Navy, Stephen Mallory, realizing that the South desperately needed ironclads, immediately ordered the

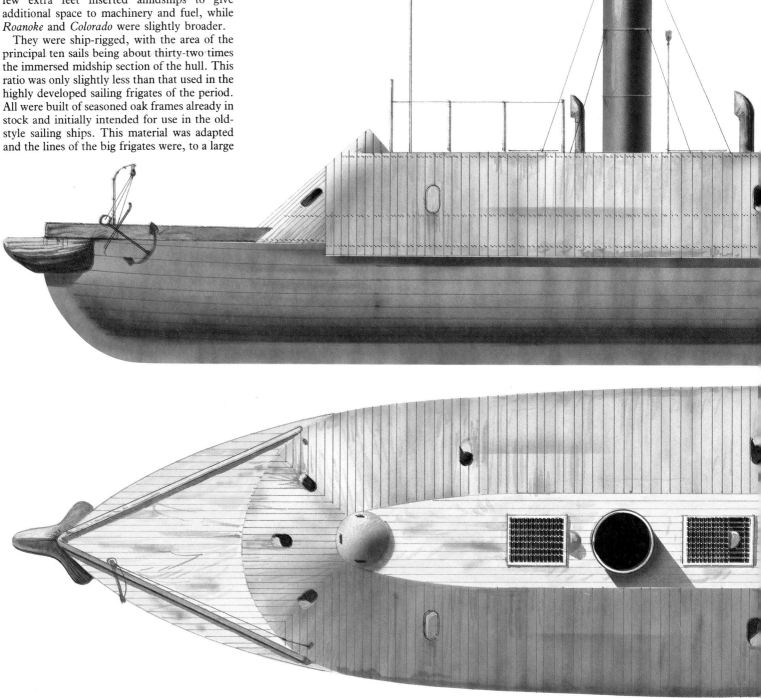

sunken *Merrimack* to be raised and converted at a cost of $172,000. Three officers were set to work on the epoch-making vessel — John Porter was in charge of construction, John Mercer Brooke, who had supplied initial plans for the conversion, was responsible for guns and armor, while William Williamson was made engineer-in-chief.

As no one officer was put in overall charge of the project, there was a certain amount of strain between Brooke and Porter. Realizing the error, Mallory would in future appoint one officer in overall control. In spite of these problems, both Brooke and Porter surmounted overwhelming odds.

By mid-July work was well under way on cutting out the burnt part of the ship. Soon a large center structure would be built on the mid-section of the hull. Armoring this structure, however, presented a problem; 1-inch thick armor proved inadequate, so 2-inch thick plates were called for instead. Starting in

October 1861, Tredegar Ironworks produced the armor in five months, but much time was lost in changing over to the thicker plates because they had to be drilled instead of punched.

When the plates were ready for shipment from Tredegar's works at Richmond, another problem arose. The overworked railroad could not keep up with deliveries because of the army's transportation needs, so in November 1861 Lt. Catesby ap R. Jones was appointed to speed things up and assemble a crew.

In spite of about 1500 men working on her virtually around the clock (without overtime pay), *Merrimack* was not ready to launch for some considerable time. Then it was found that the vessel rode too high in the water, leaving part of the unarmored hull exposed. Ballast in the form of coal and stores was added to correct this, but as these were consumed, the problem returned.

The transformed *Merrimack* had a 170-foot-long armored superstructure (casemate) amidships, with the sides sloping back at 36 degrees. Both ends of the structure were rounded, while its upper deck had iron gratings 2 inches thick. The armor, made from rolled railroad iron, was applied in two layers, the lower course running horizontally and the upper course running vertically. Fourteen elliptical gun ports were cut into the structure, three at each end and four unevenly spaced along each side.

Now under the command of Captain Franklin Buchanan, the vessel cast off on March 8 at 11 a.m. on what was thought to be a trial trip, but once under way Buchanan let it be known that he intended to attack the Union fleet. His first target was the sailing sloop *Cumberland;* after firing several broadsides he rammed and sank the luckless vessel, but lost the ram in the process.

The grounded *Congress* was the next to receive the ironclad's attention and was soon on fire, finally blowing up at midnight.

When the *Merrimack* returned to battle the following morning, she met the newly-arrived *Monitor* in an inconclusive action. The *Monitor* used reduced charges in her guns, so the full penetrating effect was not developed, while the *Merrimack*, now low on powder, had only shell rather than solid shot to use against her enemy.

When the Confederates were forced to evacuate Norfolk, the *Merrimack* had no safe base to operate from, so attempts were made to get her up the James River. However, her deep draft prevented this, so she was run aground near Craney Island on May 11 and set on fire.

Merrimack (Virginia) *after conversion into an ironclad, 1862.*

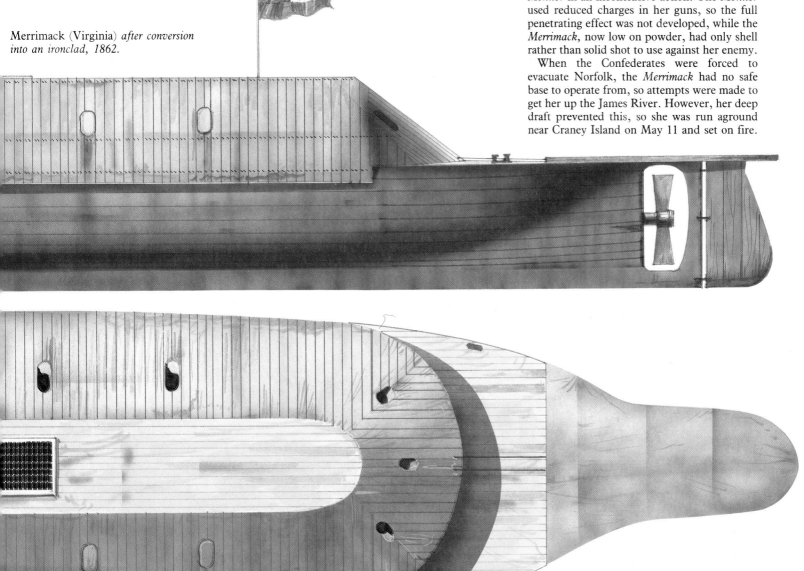

USS *Monitor*

Displacement: 987 tons. **Dimensions:** 172ft x 41ft 6 in x 8ft 4in. **Machinery:** Double-trunk cylinders with two-in-one casting, plus two large return box boilers. **Speed:** 6 knots.

Prior to the outbreak of the Civil War, America had shown little interest in the ironclad, being content to watch the rapid progress being made in Europe. By the spring of 1861, America had forty-two wooden vessels available, most of them in foreign stations. Only the incomplete Stevens battery, started in 1854, bore any resemblance to the French ocean-going *Gloire* and the 10,000-ton English *Warrior*-type already in service.

Meantime, an ominous development was taking place at the Norfolk Navy Yard captured by Confederate forces in April 1861; work had already begun on the conversion of the abandoned USS *Merrimack*, to be re-named *Virginia*.

In response to this development a bill was passed by the US Congress on August 3 instructing the Navy Department to appoint a board of three officers to examine proposals for ironclads. Known as the Ironclad Board, $1.5 million was set aside for the construction of any vessels it selected.

The original proposals called for vessels with a draft of 10–16 feet, so they could operate in the shallow rivers and coastal areas of the Confederacy.

Sixteen proposals were received, including one for a rubber-clad vessel. Three were accepted — one for C. Bushnell's *Galena*, one from Merrick & Sons of Philadelphia for the *New Ironsides* (both ships being conventional ironclads then in favor in Europe), and one, which nearly missed submission, for a less conventional vessel designed by John Ericsson.

One can appreciate the board's hesitation in recommending such a novel design; it was thought that no one had sufficient experience to construct a totally new type of ironclad — especially someone outside the Navy Department.

Speed was now all important, as it was realized that Ericsson's vessel, the *Monitor*, was the only one that had any chance of being completed in time to meet the Confederate threat now taking shape. The contract was signed on October 4, 1861, even as the first plates for the *Monitor* were rolling through the mill. Completion was stipulated within 100 days, and the agreed price was $275,000, payable in five regular instalments of $50,000, with the balance due on completion. Owing to the experimental nature of the craft, however, 25 percent of each instalment was withheld in case the vessel did not live up to expectations.

As Ericsson had no capital of his own to finance construction, he entered into an agreement with Bushnell, now building the *Galena*, John F. Winslow and John A. Griswold. Winslow held a partnership in both the Rennselaer Ironworks in Troy, New York, and the Albany Ironworks, while Griswold was a partner in Rennselaer only. The partners agreed to divide any profit or loss evenly. As a team, they made a well organized group, while their individual connections would later prove an asset when Ericsson's work was overshadowed by designs put forward by the Navy Department for double-turreted monitors using turrets designed by the leading English inventor Captain Cowper Coles. Through some inside political activity, the use of the Coles turreted vessels, although in many ways superior to Ericsson's, was shelved. Later, another possible threat was deflected when an engineer named Timby, who had designed a turret similar to Ericsson's, was paid a $10,000 royalty in order to avoid a time-consuming legal battle in the courts.

Ericsson's design called for a low freeboard vessel made up of two hulls, with the lower hull containing the machinery, furnaces, crew's quarters, coal, stores, and so forth which in turn was surmounted by a larger armored raft fastened to the top of the lower hull.

The upper hull, or raft, stood only 18 inches out of the water, thereby presenting a small

target area. This upper structure was the full 172 feet in length and overlapped the lower hull by 14 feet in the bow and 32 feet at the stern. The sides were plated with five layers of 1-inch iron armor on a thick wooden backing. This massive amount of armor was made possible by the small area to be covered, as the greater part of the raft and the hull proper would be under water and therefore safe from enemy attack. The deck had only 1 inch of armor as it was expected to cope with shot fired at a shallow angle.

In order to save construction time the frames and plates were not curved. The sides were straight for about 80 feet of the middle section, and each end followed the same simple curve using a radii arc of 75 feet. More time was saved by subcontracting much of the work, so when launched on January 30, 1862, the *Monitor* was almost complete — a feat not possible with a conventional vessel.

As an answer to the numerous 7- and 8-inch weapons likely to be faced, it was thought that two 11-inch Dahlgren smoothbores would be adequate. This heavy armament was possible because the low freeboard allowed great savings to be made in armor. The single turret, giving an all-round field of fire, was covered with eight 1-inch plates — believed to be more than a match for hostile fire — and were twice as thick as the armor on the *Merrimack*.

The *Monitor's* draft was 10 feet, but by allowing for a 5-foot hollow space in the raft, a 9-foot-diameter screw was carried, but this was not always effective as the hull partly blocked the flow and caused turbulence. The anchor was also housed in a well and controlled from inside the vessel.

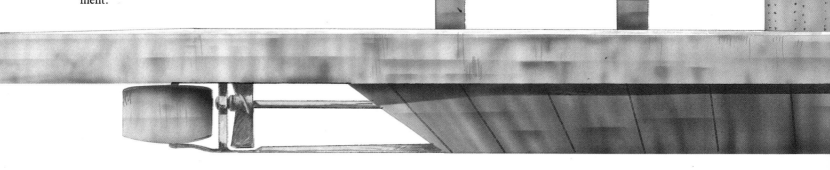

The unusual shape of the Monitor's *hull, with its flat floor, can be clearly seen. The shelf formed by the overlapping raft was intended to keep the vessel steady, making her a good gun platform. This, combined with the low freeboard, enabled the sea to wash freely over* the deck, thus reducing roll. Unfortunately, the constant pounding of the sea would later open the area between the two hulls with fatal results. During the action of 9 March reduced charges were used in the guns; had full charges been used it is possible that Merrimack's armor might have been pierced.

Turret traversing gear

Rudder

Shaft

Engine room

Engine

Boilers

Boiler

The guns which were taken from the *Dacotah*, were lowered into the turret through its open roof. This was then plated with railroad iron laid several inches apart to form a large grating through which fresh air was sucked below, as the turret acted as a giant ventilating shaft.

Even with such careful thought, ventilation would always be a problem in such a vessel. Later, on the journey to Hampton Roads, the engine-room was flooded when water found its way in via the 4-foot high shafts on the deck.

Trouble was experienced with the main engines on trial as the improperly set cut-off valves stopped steam from reaching the engine. Steering also caused problems, but when the rudder was balanced, all worked well. The *Monitor* now left for Hampton Roads, arriving at 2 o'clock on the morning of Sunday, March 9.

Dawn that day came bright and clear with a calm sea. At 8 o'clock the *Merrimack* came into view belching thick black clouds of smoke from her damaged funnel. Across the river at Newport News gleamed the white tents of the Federal camp, and small sailing craft and tugs scurried across to the far shore upon sighting the strange-looking craft now bearing down on them.

The *Monitor* moved out to place herself between the *Merrimack* and the vulnerable frigates. *Monitor* proved to be more agile, and as *Merrimack* tried to ram the smaller vessel, *Monitor* simply moved aside. During one lunge *Merrimack* ran aground but quickly floated off. The action continued to be fought at close range with neither one able to pierce the armorplating of the other. The *Merrimack* was struck twenty times and many of the shots cracked and splintered the wood backing of the inner structure. Each blow caused concussion within

the citadel.

Monitor was struck twenty-four times, and anyone near the turret wall when it was struck was knocked down by the concussion. She fired fifty-five rounds, loading and firing every six or eight minutes in the three and a half-hour battle.

Monitor briefly served on the James River but as the delivery dates of the *Passaic* class monitors slipped back, *Monitor* was detained on station, although now ready for a refit.

At the end of December 1862, she was ordered to Charleston. After a refit she was towed by *Rhode Island*. At 8 o'clock on the

night of December 31, a violent storm broke over them and the sea rapidly rose, causing the *Monitor* to wallow as waves up to 30 feet high broke over her, forcing seawater down the turret and ventilators and leaving several inches of water in the engine-room. At first the pumps coped, but then a sudden upsurge doomed the long-suffering vessel as water forced its way between the two hulls weakened by the incessant pounding of the waves. By 11 o'clock the fight with the sea was lost and the crew were taken off, except for a few who defiantly remained on the turret roof and went down with the ship.

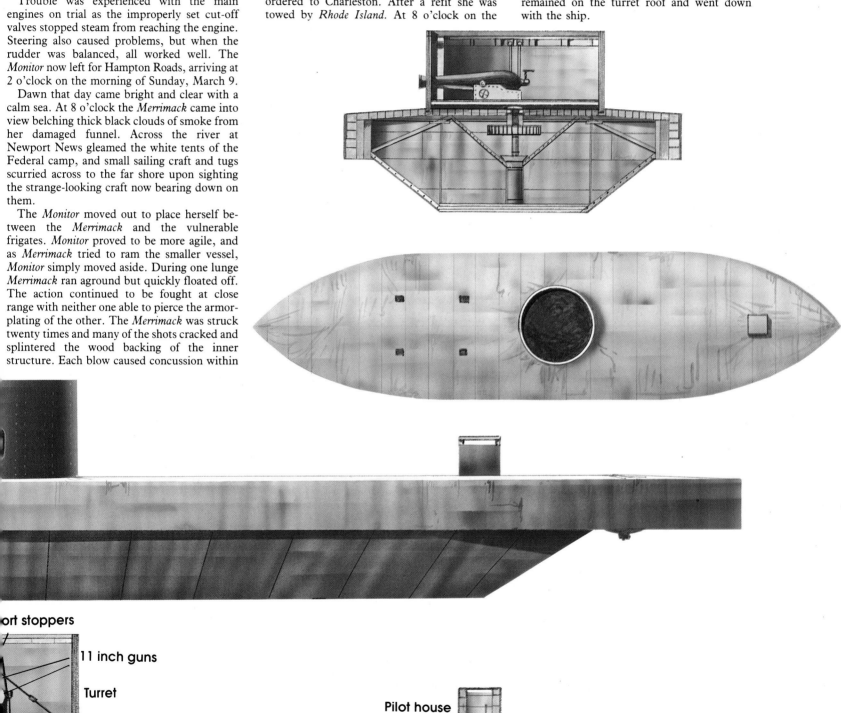

ort stoppers

11 inch guns

Turret

t traversing gear

Quarters

Pilot house

Anchor well

USS *Passaic*

Displacement: 1875 tons. **Dimensions:** 200ft x 46ft x 10ft 6in (some up to 12ft). **Armor:** 11 inches on turret, 5 inches on hull side, 1 inch on deck and 8 inches on pilot house. **Machinery:** Two trunk engines developing 340 hp, driving a single screw. **Speed:** 7 knots. **Armament:** Varied; most had one 11-inch Dahlgren smoothbore and one 15-inch Dahlgren smoothbore. *Camanche* had two 15-inch Dahlgrens. Later armament varied as smaller weapons were added. **Crew:** 67 to 88.

With the rapidly growing threat of the ironclads then being built in Southern yards, and at a time before the *Monitor* was completed, Ericsson offered to build a group of warships that would better it. Two were to be ready by the end of April 1862, with a further four completed by the end of May. This was in answer to the Navy Department's original recommendation for twenty armored gunboats.

Although the *Monitor* was now well advanced, Ericsson and his partners were to experience great anxiety over the Navy Department plans prepared by Isherwood and Lenthall at the impatient behest of Gustavus Fox, Assistant Secretary of the Navy. They feared that this alternative design, so similar to the *Monitor*, would be a serious threat to their own scheme.

The department's plan, submitted in early December 1861, called for a low freeboard, twin-turreted, armored gunboat 217 feet long, 48 feet wide and drawing less than 12 feet of water. The average cost would vary between $500,000 and $580,000 and the vessel would be able to withstand most of the Confederate harbor defenses likely to be encountered.

The Navy Department plan incorporated several improvements over Ericsson's *Monitor*, such as the use of Coles' turrets. These were superior in many ways, having an armored protective ring or "glacis" around the base of the turret where it emerged through the upper deck. It also turned on rollers situated on its outer wall at its base. These rollers rested in a circular groove set in the lower deck so that the entire weight of the turret was evenly supported

and could better withstand the shock of heavy blows. The turret, in effect, became an armored cylinder standing upright, with the guns housed in the top section, while the extra armor carried on its sides gave even more protection to its working machinery.

Ericsson's turret turned on a central spindle and had to be jacked up when going into action. The turret could easily be jammed by shell fragments finding their way between the exposed gap at the base of the turret and the deck. This is what happened before Charleston in April 1863. Furthermore, the entire weight of the turret was supported on the massive center spindle.

The supply of iron for the 4½-inch thick sides and the turret was undoubtedly a considerable problem at the time as armor manufacturers in America were already fully occupied with war work. Doubts were also expressed over the contractors' ability to manufacture plates of sufficient size. The supply of machinery was less likely to be a problem as a number of firms offered to build several sets, provided the department would guarantee a large enough order and supply advance payments. Even companies of doubtful financial stability were seriously considered.

Secretary of the Navy, Gideon Wells, realizing the limitations of home suppliers, decided that engineer Daniel Martin, then supervising the construction of the ironclad *Galena*, should go to England, France, and Belgium in order to obtain further suitable suppliers. However, he was unsuccessful as all the European manufacturers had sufficient orders on hand from their own governments.

The situation seems bizarre, for while Martin was touring Europe on his fruitless task, Webb of New York had already laid down two massive ironclads in August 1861 for the Italian government.

Although the threatened department proposal never materialized in its present form, Ericsson wisely took no chances and started a campaign to point out all the advantages of his system over that of his rivals. His arguments were lucid but not entirely correct, as Coles'

turret possessed many advantages and eventually inspired the turret design on the still-active *Iowa* class battleships serving in the US Navy today.

Not content to rely on his own persuasive powers, Ericsson enlisted the aid of Congressman Corning, who was also a partner of Winslow in the Albany Ironworks. Corning and Winslow traveled to Washington together and, judging by later events, their activity in the capital produced a successful outcome.

There was now a long delay in the passage of the ironclad program as it was handed by the Senate to a naval committee who cut the number of vessels from twenty to twelve. Further, the committee recommended that the President, and not the Secretary of the Navy, allocate the funds involved. This caused a bitter wrangle, as Secretary Wells had appointed his brother-in-law, George Morgan, as purchasing agent of shipping for the government. In this role Morgan had made $70,000 commission in five months!

Wells pressed Senator Hall, chairman of the naval committee, to speed matters through. Hall now came back with specific points he wanted answers to, including a demand to know what plan the department proposed adopting. Wells replied (on February 7, 1862) that they did not wish to confine themselves to any one design but would prefer to await the results of those now under construction, one of which — Ericsson's *Monitor* — was almost ready.

This guarded pledge by Wells, so much desired by Ericsson and his backers, had the desired effect. The bill was promptly passed and received President Lincoln's signature six days later.

All three vessels, *New Ironsides*, *Galena*, and *Monitor*, recommended by the Ironclad Board in September 1861, entered service during 1862, but the diminutive *Monitor* had the shortest career. At the time of her tragic loss in

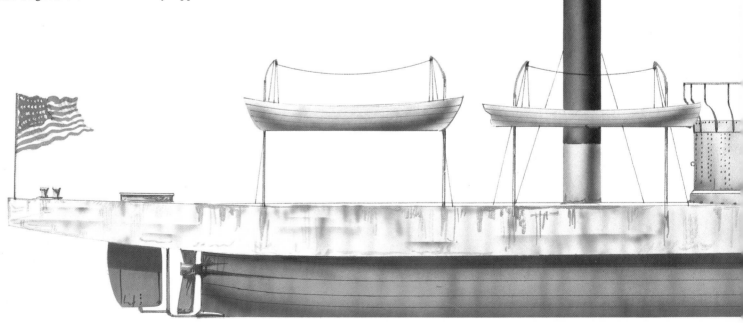

December 1862, there were four units of the improved *Passaic* class in commission, with a further six ready to follow.

This class, spread among private contractors, were *Camanche*, *Catskill*, *Conestoga*, *Lehigh*, *Montauk*, *Nahant*, *Nantucket*, *Passaic*, *Patapsco*, and *Weehawken*. All had been laid down and launched in 1862, with the last, *Camanche*, entering service in May 1865 at San Francisco.

The vessels were designed as enlarged versions of the *Monitor*, carrying only one turret with an almost all-round range of fire. The hull was again made up of two separate structures, one above the other, with the top hull overlapping the lower as in the *Monitor*. The lower hull also had an almost flat floor and was shorter than the one above by 16 feet at the bow and 25 feet at the stern. Freeboard, when correctly trimmed, was 2 feet 6 inches forward and 1 foot 6 inches aft.

The increased displacement allowed significant improvements. One 15-inch weapon was substituted for one of the 11-inch ones. (It had been intended to carry two 15-inch Dahlgren weapons in the larger turret but the foundries were unable to deliver sufficient numbers of the larger weapon.)

Another improvement was the mounting of the pilot house on top of the turret and its fixing to a stationary, 12-inch diameter, vertical shaft. The turret rotated freely and the field of fire forward was now greatly improved. Armor used on the sides was still laminated, being made up of single 1-inch plates.

Although other more powerful monitors would join the fleet, these vessels were the real workhorses.

During the attack on Charleston, South Carolina, in April 1863, all were heavily damaged. The Navy Department had had high hopes of the fleet penetrating the harbor and forcing the city to surrender. Later the same day, after the failed attack, Stimers pointed out that Ericsson had never intended these vessels to take on forts — a great surprise to all the officers present who had spent the day under the most terrific fire from the fortifications.

Contracts were awarded at the end of March 1862 and Stimers was the construction supervisor. The majority of the class had long careers, the last not being sold until 1904, forty-two years after completion.

Camanche's hull was built by Donahue, Ryan & Secor, and machinery was supplied by Colwell. Launched in November 1864, she was commissioned in May 1865.

Catskill's hull was built by Continental Ironworks and the machinery was built by Delamater Ironworks. Launched in early December 1862, she was in service by the end of February 1863.

Conestoga's hull was built by Reaney, with machinery supplied by Morris, Towne, who also built the engine for *Lehigh*. Launched in October 1862, she was in service by February 1863.

Lehigh was launched from Reaney's yard in mid-January 1863 and completed four months later.

Montauk was built by Continental, and Delamater supplied the engines. She too was completed quickly after launching, being ready in mid-December 1862 after a launch date of October 9.

Nahant's hull was built by Loring, with machinery constructed at City Point. She was launched on October 7 and ready by December 29, 1862.

Nantucket was built by Atlantic, who also supplied the engines. She was launched in December and ready by February 1863.

Passaic was built at Continental Ironworks with engines supplied by Delamater. Launched in August 1862, she was ready in November 1862.

Patapsco was built and engined by Harlan & Hollingsworth. She was launched in September 1862 and completed by January 2, 1863.

Weehawken was built by Secor, with Colwell supplying the engines. Launched in early November 1862, she was ready by January 18, 1863.

In 1871 the badly decayed wooden deck beams of these vessels were replaced with iron, and during 1872 each was given a major overhaul. Quotes for repairs went as high as $225,000, but one contractor, John Roach, offered to do the job at $180,000 per vessel and this was the price paid to all contractors.

During 1873 a war between Spain and America seemed likely. The cause was the execution of American citizens who were captured running supplies to insurgents on Cuba, then going through a violent upheaval. Consequently work was speeded up on the monitors, as America needed every vessel available to face Spain's respectable navy.

In 1890 the question of more repairs arose but at an estimated price of $400,000 per unit, equal to the original cost some thirty years earlier, it was not deemed worthwhile to carry out the work. Consequently, the vessels were turned over to various naval militias as training ships.

Many changes had been made to the outward appearance of these vessels. A light flying bridge ran from the turret to near the stern, and several deck houses were added.

During construction *Camanche* had parts of her machinery taken to finish up other units more quickly because she had been earmarked for the Pacific coast which was not felt to be under any threat.

While taking on supplies at Charleston in December 1863, *Weehawken* sank at her moorings through water entering an open hatch. Next to be lost was *Patapsco*, which was mined off Charleston in January 1865. *Camanche*, *Passaic*, and *Nantucket* were sold in 1899, *Passaic* fetching about $12,000, having originally cost $256,142. *Catskill* was sold in 1901, and *Conestoga*, *Lehigh*, *Montauk* and *Nahant* were sold in 1904. Several served as coastal defense vessels in the Spanish–American war of 1898, but saw no action.

Camanche as she appeared in the all-white scheme at San Francisco in 1865. Parts of her machinery had been used to repair the broken-down Weehawken. She was finally shipped out in sections to the Pacific by a ship which sank when it arrived, so causing more delays as the parts were salvaged.

CHARLESTON, *South Carolina*

Originally, the US Navy Department had planned that the navy would take Charleston, South Carolina, alone and had hoped to do this by using the newly introduced ironclads. Admiral Du Pont's instructions were that once the outer ring of defenses had been overcome, the warships should proceed up to the city and force its surrender. However, the defenders of Charleston had not been idle and the fortifications were greatly strengthened. In fact, by the summer of 1862 no other city in the South was so well defended against a seaward attack.

The Union fleet's attack on April 7, 1863, failed, and although the navy would renew the attacks during the following months, it would eventually take a combined operation with the army to force Charleston's surrender. When the city did eventually fall, it was brought about by attacks from the army launched from inland.

Charleston, like other major seaports in the South, was vital as a place from which blockade runners could operate, but even their activity could not cope with the needs of the Confederacy; the general tightening of the blockade was forcing the Southern economy into decline.

As the blockade runners insisted on payment in gold for the goods brought in, the Confederacy's slim gold reserve was quickly drained, so cotton had to be taken in exchange for goods.

Although over one million bales of cotton were run out through the blockade to Europe between 1862 and 1864, it was a mere one-tenth of pre-war exports. The situation was made worse when cotton production was reduced in favor of food, thus decreasing the South's main income even further. Ordinary necessities of life became scarce and prices rose to horrendous levels, with tea fetching $500 per pound.

When the Civil War was in its early stages and the blockade at its weakest, no effort was made to bring in railroad equipment and other materials from Europe as no one thought the war would last long. Consequently, the Southern railroad system fell into rapid disrepair once the crippling demands of the war effort were made on it. By the end of the war, when General Lee's army was starving in Virginia, food intended for that force was rotting in Carolina and Georgia depots for want of an effective railroad system.

USS *Canonicus*

Displacement: 2100 tons. **Dimensions:** 225ft x 43ft x 13ft 6in, with minor variations between units as completed. **Armor:** 10 inches on turret, 5 inches on sides, and 10 inches on the pilot house. **Machinery:** Two double-trunk horizontal engines driving a single screw. **Speed:** 8 knots. **Armament:** Two 15-inch Dahlgren smoothbore guns. **Crew:** 85.

Many shortcomings of the original *Monitor* and *Passaic* classes were successfully overcome in this group, which comprised *Canonicus*, *Catawba*, *Mahopac*, *Manayunk*, *Manhattan*, *Oneota*, *Saugus*, *Tecumseh*, and *Tippecanoe*.

It was found possible to incorporate the lessons learnt in the *Monitor/Merrimack* conflict and the attacks upon Charlseston, as well as the day-to-day operations of this unique type of warship.

The designer, John Ericsson, preferred to retain the single turret layout, so the vessels bear a close relationship to the *Passaic* class. But here the similarity ended, as a number of major design improvements made the *Canonicus* class a superior monitor. Although only able to operate in sheltered waters, this was still the major area of Union operations when the contracts were placed in 1862.

Displacement was slightly greater than on the *Passaics*, and they were also slightly longer, but they had a narrower beam. Mean planned draft was 11 feet 6 inches, but it rose on completion to between 13 feet and 13 feet 8 inches. These vessels had a double hull made up of an armored raft resting on top of a lower hull, which contained the machinery, quarters, and so forth. However, the hull was given finer lines and had the deadwood aft cut away, which greatly improved their performance.

Superior protection was provided by the addition of 6½-inch wide armored stringers at the bow and stern, reducing to a 4-inch thickness along the side. This, combined with the existing 5-inch armor, made them extremely strong along the waterline.

One vulnerable area was the gap between the turret base and the deck. Here, an armored sloping glacis plate 15 inches high and 5 inches thick was added. Armor on the turret was 1 inch less than that on the *Passaic*. The armored pilot house stood on top of the turret and had a fine field of view.

As gun manufacturers overcame their problems which forced unwelcome mixed armament on the *Passaic* class, it became possible to equip the new monitors with two 15-inch Dahlgren smoothbores. These weapons were 16 inches longer and the cumbersome smoke boxes fitted to the *Passaics* were dispensed with.

Ventilation was greatly improved by the installation of more powerful blowers and a permanent ventilator. Only in speed did they fall down, making a mere 8 or 9 knots instead of the expected 13.

The contract price was $460,000 per unit, but each vessel eventually cost about $640,000. Much of this extra cost was caused by improvements carried out during building.

All the vessels were laid down in private yards in 1862, four were launched in 1863 and the remainder the following year. Five were completed during 1864, the rest following later.

Tecumseh was lost in Mobile Bay in August 1864. During the early stage of the battle, the Confederate ironclad *Tennessee* made straight for the Union Fleet but Captain Craven, commander of *Tecumseh*, saw this and headed his monitor directly at her. Unfortunately, this course took her over a minefield marked by buoys. *Tecumseh* struck a mine and sank within two minutes, losing ninety-three of her crew, including Craven, who had bravely stood aside to let the pilot escape from the conning tower first.

Canonicus was built by Loring, who also supplied machinery. She was the last to be disposed of.

Catawba was built by Swift, Evans, with machinery supplied by Niles. She was never commissioned.

Mahopac was built by Secor with engines by Colwell. She was launched in May and completed in September 1864.

Manayunk, built and engined by Sowden, was launched in December 1864, then laid up until commissioned in 1871.

Manhattan was built by Secor with engines by Colwell. She was launched in October 1836 and commissioned in June 1864.

Oneota's hull was built by Swift, Evans, and engines were supplied by Niles. Launched in May and laid up, she was sold back to Alex Swift in 1868.

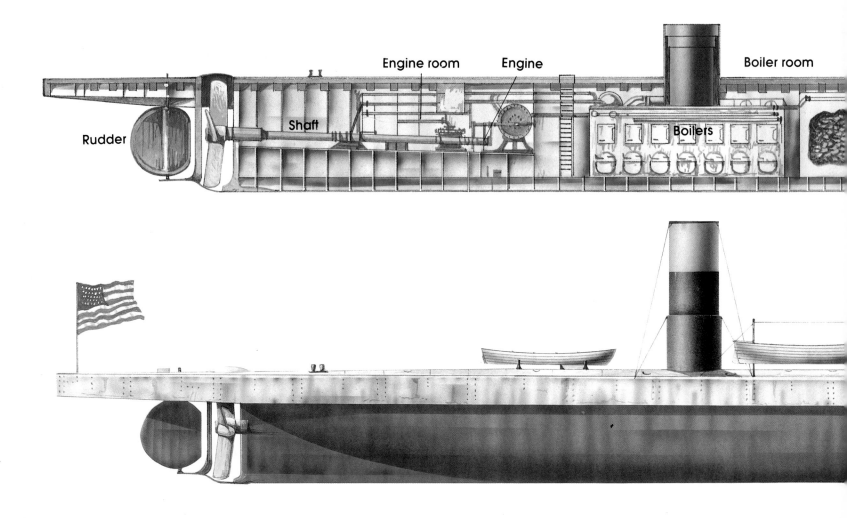

Saugus was built and engined by Harlan & Hollingsworth. She was launched in December 1863 and commissioned in April 1864.

Tecumseh, built by Secor with machinery supplied by Colwell, was launched in September and ready by April 1864.

Tippecanoe's hull and machinery were supplied by Greenwood. She was launched in December 1864 and completed in 1866.

Several of the vessels were overhauled in 1872 – 73 at an estimated cost of $180,000 each. A further $16,000 was spent toward the end of their lives, but not all received this last overhaul.

Catawba was completed too late to see service in the war and she was sold to Peru, having been bought back by her builder. For the long journey to Peru a light, steadying rig was added and the sides built up. *Oneota* was also sold to Peru in 1868 and renamed *Manco Capac*. She joined *Catawba* (renamed *Atahualpa*) on the journey down. Both saw extensive service in the 1879 – 81 war between Chile and Peru. *Atahualpa* was sunk at Callao at the end of the war, while *Manco Capac* was sunk on June 7, 1880, at Arica which she was helping to defend.

Many of the vessels ended their days as training ships, and during the Spanish – American War of 1898 were used as port guard ships. The last, *Canonicus*, was not sold until 1908.

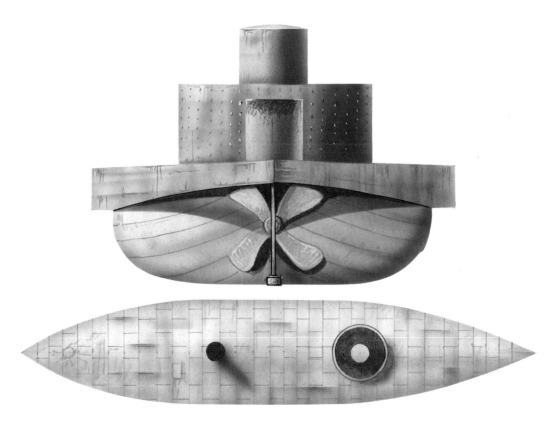

The finer lines of the Canonicus class monitor can be seen in this stern view. While the smoother hull shape greatly improved performance, none made the anticipated speed of 13 knots

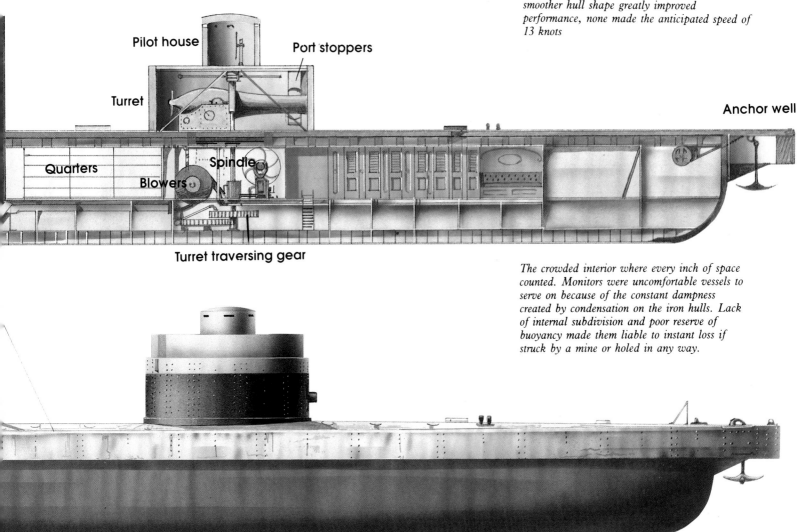

Pilot house

Port stoppers

Turret

Anchor well

Quarters

Spindle

Blowers

Turret traversing gear

The crowded interior where every inch of space counted. Monitors were uncomfortable vessels to serve on because of the constant dampness created by condensation on the iron hulls. Lack of internal subdivision and poor reserve of buoyancy made them liable to instant loss if struck by a mine or holed in any way.

USS *New Ironsides*

Displacement: 4210 tons. **Dimensions:** 232ft x 57ft 6in x 15ft 8in. **Armor:** 4 inches on sides, 1 inch on deck and 10 inches on the conning tower. **Machinery:** Two horizontal direct-acting engines of 700 hp. **Armament:** Two 150-pdr Parrott rifles, two 50-pdr Dahlgren rifles, and fourteen 11-inch Dahlgren smoothbores, which had a range of about 1.25 miles. **Crew:** 460.

New Ironsides was the third ironclad recommended by Commodore Smith's Ironclad Board. She was a formidable vessel, similar to HMS *Warrior* and the French *Gloire*. Being a conventional broadside ironclad type, she carried the belt and battery system on a wooden hull with a tumble home of about 17 degrees.

The contract was given to Merrick & Sons, who subcontracted the hull and fittings to Cramp's Shipyard. Charles Cramp and B.H. Bartol, who was the superintendent of Merrick & Sons, designed the vessel, while Merrick supplied the armor and I. Vaughan Merrick designed the machinery, which was a duplicate set already supplied to a single-screw sloop. The original contract price was $780,000 with a forfeit of $5000 per day for delay, and a

complete refund if the vessel did not live up to expectations. Although the contract speed of 9.4 knots was never reached, *New Ironsides* was considered a success and no penalties were incurred by the builders. The final cost was $865,514, with a further $54,818 being spent on her during her short career.

Originally it was planned to carry sixteen 8-inch smoothbore guns, which were considered the heaviest caliber that could successfully be worked in a broadside vessel, but three months into construction, when the frames were up and beams in, the Navy Department decided to arm the ship with fourteen 11-inch Dahlgrens and two 8-inch, 200-pdr Parrots.

Fortunately, Cramp had the foresight to allow for an extra margin of 1 foot in displacement, so when the heavier armament was

installed the original draft of 15 feet remained.

The gunports were 7 feet above water but had a limited arc of fire. Slight changes were later made to the smaller guns carried, but the main armament remained the same.

The sides were plated with 4-inch armor, which also covered the battery for 170 feet amidships. Below this was a continuous belt covering an area from 3 feet above to 4 feet below the waterline.

Athwartship bulkheads protected the ends of the battery from the gun deck to the spar deck, with a 1-inch thick iron layer under the spar deck completing the armor.

The 4-inch thick side armor was hammered out of scrap iron at Pittsburgh and Bristol,

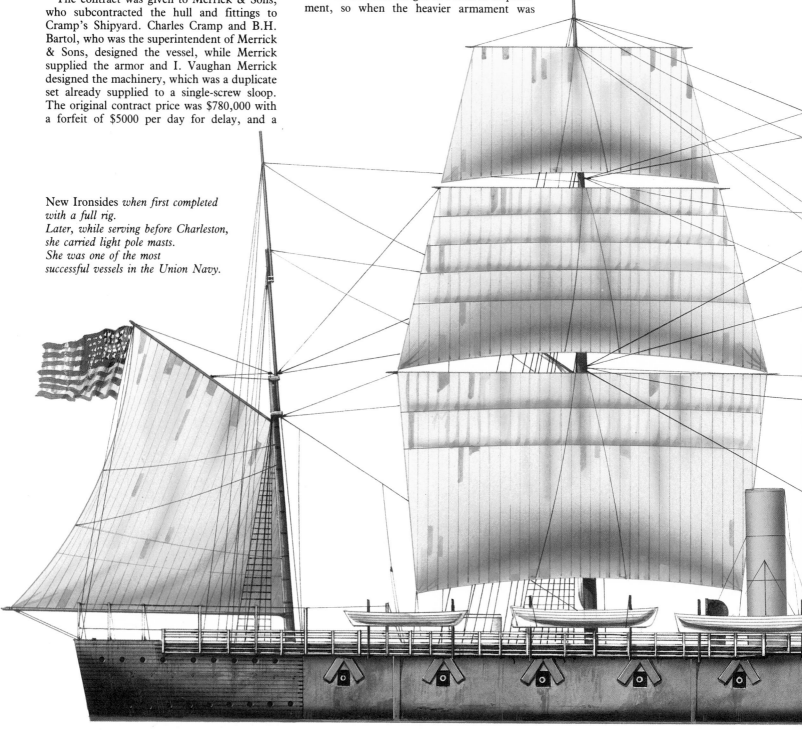

New Ironsides *when first completed with a full rig.*
Later, while serving before Charleston, she carried light pole masts.
She was one of the most successful vessels in the Union Navy.

Pennsylvania, in strips 15 feet long and 28 inches wide. It was not possible at that date for American manufacturers to roll armor of sufficient thickness, and it was to be many years before they could catch up with their European rivals. This sorry state of affairs was because inadequate funds were spent on the US Navy and prevented armor plate manufacturers from investing sufficient money to develop the techniques.

During the numerous actions with the Charleston forts, sandbags were placed on the spar deck for extra protection. These stopped the bolts securing the deck to the beams from being loosened by concussion and raining down like bullets on the crew below whenever a shell struck.

All the woodwork fore and aft was barricaded by more sandbags to a depth of 8 or 9 feet, and to the height of the beams. Before going into action, these were thoroughly soaked.

The massive oak hull was 12 inches thick at the waterline, tapering to 5 inches at the bilge; trees 45 feet high were needed to give sufficient lengths of timber for strength. This caused immense problems as such trees were scarce in Pennsylvania and the surrounding countryside was denuded of suitable timber. Later, when the light-draft monitors of the *Casco* class were being built, their construction was delayed as insufficient timber was available because of the first run on suitable trees. More problems followed when the skilled workmen left to work in the Navy Yard and were replaced by workers from Baltimore and Maine who had left their homes to avoid conscription or secure higher rates of pay. When the contract was made, shipwrights earned $1.75 per day but in two months this nearly doubled, as did the price of many materials needed to complete the ship. In spite of all the problems, *New Ironsides* was ready for launching a mere six months from the layout of the keel when the timber for her hull was still standing in the forests.

New Ironsides proved to be a steady sea boat, but her underpowered engines could only drive her at 6.5 knots, even when all sail was set. Furthermore, this was coupled with a heavy coal consumption of 40 tons per day instead of the planned 25 tons, which allowed for only sixteen days' steaming, and thus greatly reduced her radius of action.

On January 7, 1863 she joined the South Atlantic Blockading Squadron off Charleston as Admiral Du Pont's flagship and to guard the wooden blockading fleet from attacks by Confederate ironclads.

By early April a large force of Union monitors had assembled, and at noon on April 7, an attack was launched on the defenses of Charleston. This attack was beaten off after a fierce action in which *New Ironsides* was struck fifty times in two hours. She had to anchor twice to avoid running aground in the tricky currents of the narrow channel, but in spite of these precautions the ironclad collided twice with the monitors. At one stage *New Ironsides* had anchored over an observation mine containing over a ton of powder, but luckily the cable had been broken ashore when a Confederate wagon ran over it, thus preventing the mine from being detonated by the observer ashore.

Almost constantly in action with the forts, *New Ironsides* was attacked on the night of October 5 by a Confederate torpedo boat, which successfully exploded its charge against the ironclad's hull but without causing much damage.

She came out of commission in May 1864, and in August was back in service, this time with the North Atlantic Blockading Squadron. In December she formed part of the force attacking Fort Fisher which defended Wilmington, the last port left open to the Confederacy. During the prolonged attack, the ironclad fired nearly 1000 shells.

The ironclad then joined the James River division supporting General Grant's final drive against a doomed Richmond. She was decommissioned at League Island on April 6, 1865, where she remained until destroyed by fire later that year on December 16.

In spite of her low speed and crowded battery, *New Ironsides* was considered an overall success, having been in action on more occasions than any other warship in the Civil War. Although struck hundreds of times, her armor had not once been pierced. She remained the only example of her type in the US Navy, although Cramp had suggested building two improved versions with twin screws. Instead, the monitor type was developed for inshore and ocean-going purposes.

Two large, 5700-ton broadside ironclads of similar type, *Re di Portogallo* and *Re d'Italia*, were laid down by Webb of New York for the Italian Navy in 1861. At the time of their commencement, the war was only reckoned to last three months, but as the conflict dragged on there must have been some people who wondered why so much effort was put into building powerful vessels from precious resources for a foreign navy.

CCS *Texas*

Dimensions: 217ft x 50ft 4in x 13ft.
Machinery: Two pairs horizontal direct-acting
engines driving two propellers. **Armament:**
Four pivot and two broadside guns. **Crew:** 50
plus.

Texas was a casemate ironclad of the
Columbia type laid down at Rocketts just
outside Richmond. She was a well constructed
vessel, possibly one of the best ironclads the
South produced. She was launched in mid-

January, then moved to the outfitting berth to
await completion.

When Richmond fell on April 3, 1865, the
river force defending the capital was destroyed
but the Confederates failed to blow up the
unfinished ironclad.

After being seized by Union forces, *Texas*
was moved to Norfolk Navy Yard and sold
there on October 15, having originally cost
$218,068.

CSS *Huntsville*

Dimensions: 150ft x 34ft x 10ft 6in. **Speed:** 3
knots. **Armament:** One 6.4-inch Brooke rifle
and three 32-pdr. **Crew:** 120.

Huntsville and her sister ship *Tuscaloosa* were
ordered on May 1, 1862, from Henry D.
Bassett by the Confederate Navy Department
for $100,000 each. They were laid down at a

newly prepared yard at Selma, Alabama, part of
a quartet of ironclads built on this site. The
yard, however, proved unhealthy, causing
much sickness among the shipbuilders and
adding to the delays in construction. One other
large ironclad was never completed, while the
fourth was the famous *Tennessee.*

The vessels were launched on February 7,
1863, before completion, to take every advan-

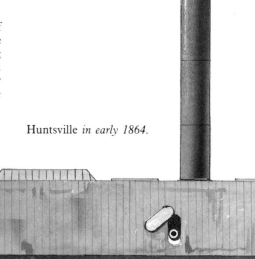

Huntsville *in early 1864.*

CCS *Neuse*

Dimensions: 152ft x 34ft x 9ft. **Armament:**
Two 6.4-inch Brooke rifles or 8-inch rifles.

Neuse was an *Albermarle*-type ironclad laid
down at Whitehall for the Confederate Navy by
Elliot Smith & Co. in 1863. The design of the
hull differed from some of the earlier vessels,
such as *Merrimack (Virginia)*, and were intended to operate on rivers. They were given flat
floors and could operate in only 6 feet of water.

The armor was rolled railroad iron but there
were problems in getting it to the vessel as the
army virtually monopolized the railroad for
shifting their supplies.

Later the *Neuse* was shelled and damaged by
an attacking Union force in December 1862.
The hull was repaired, handed over to the navy
and towed to Kingston, North Carolina, for
completion.

By April 1864 *Neuse* was completed, but
during an attempted attack upon New Bern,
the vessel ran aground in a falling river, which
continued to fall in spite of heavy rains since
early March. She remained stranded and help-
less on the Neuse River, unable to get any help
from the army because of lack of troops.

CSS *Richmond*

Dimensions: 172ft 6in x 34ft x 12ft. **Armor:** 4
inches on the sides running down to 3ft 6in
below the load line. **Machinery:** Twin engines.
Speed: 5–6 knots. **Armament:** Four rifles
guns, two on each side, and one shell gun on
each side. **Crew:** 150.

Richmond was the first of a new-style hull
designed by John Porter, and first conceived in
1846 as a design for an ocean-going ironclad 150
feet long, 40 feet wide and with a 19-foot draft.
With modifications it was approved of as a
harbor defense ship.

Laid down at the Norfolk Navy Yard in 1862
and launched on May 6, the incomplete hull
was towed up the James River to Rocketts, a
small suburb of Richmond, where she was
completed six months later. She had been
financed by collections made in Virginia and
was the first ironclad to be completed at
Richmond.

She supported the wooden gunboats in their
constant skirmishes with Union forces until
joined by other ironclads, then under construction at Richmond, that would form a powerful
trio with her.

During 1864 the fleet was frequently in
action, not only with troops ashore but with
Union ironclads that could sometimes be seen
across the land between stretches of the
winding river.

Richmond *on completion.*

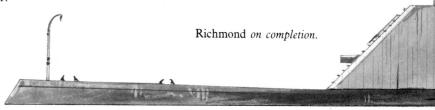

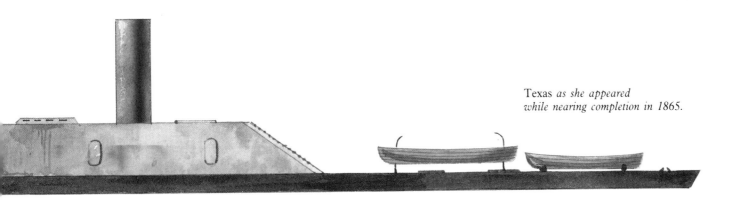

Texas *as she appeared*
while nearing completion in 1865.

tage of the high state of the river at the time. *Tuscaloosa* had already received her machinery in January, so she was able to steam down to Mobile for completion. *Huntsville*, along with the larger *Tennessee*, were towed down the twisting river with its numerous shoals by the magnificent steamer *Southern Republic*. The trip took a week and each night the group would tie up along the high riverbanks, exciting much local curiosity.

Once at Mobile the two ironclads received their armament, armor supplied by Shelby Iron Co. of Mobile and Schofield, and Markham of Atlanta, and completed the crew. *Tuscaloosa* took her trials in early April and *Huntsville* followed two weeks later. Both were disappointing as they made only 3 knots.

By the summer both vessels were operational but because of their slow speed it was decided not to use them in the bay. In common with all

Confederate ironclads, living conditions were unbearable in hot weather as none were fitted with blowers.

Both took part in the defense of Mobile, shelling Union forces as they closed in upon the city. When Mobile fell in April 1865, the two ironclads headed up the Tombigbee River, transferred their crews and most of their supplies to the *Nashville*, then were scuttled on April 12.

It had been hoped to get the *Neuse*, now the only remaining ironclad in the area, to co-operate in covering the army's retreat but this was impossible and the vessel was sunk in shallow water on March 9, 1865.

Neuse *in 1864 showing the new*
hull design suitable for shallow water.

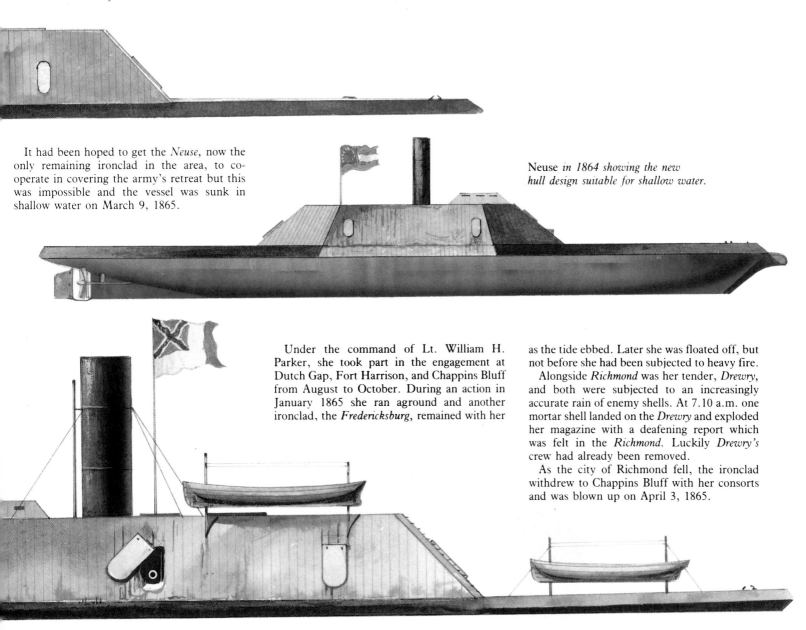

Under the command of Lt. William H. Parker, she took part in the engagement at Dutch Gap, Fort Harrison, and Chappins Bluff from August to October. During an action in January 1865 she ran aground and another ironclad, the *Fredericksburg*, remained with her

as the tide ebbed. Later she was floated off, but not before she had been subjected to heavy fire.

Alongside *Richmond* was her tender, *Drewry*, and both were subjected to an increasingly accurate rain of enemy shells. At 7.10 a.m. one mortar shell landed on the *Drewry* and exploded her magazine with a deafening report which was felt in the *Richmond*. Luckily *Drewry's* crew had already been removed.

As the city of Richmond fell, the ironclad withdrew to Chappins Bluff with her consorts and was blown up on April 3, 1865.

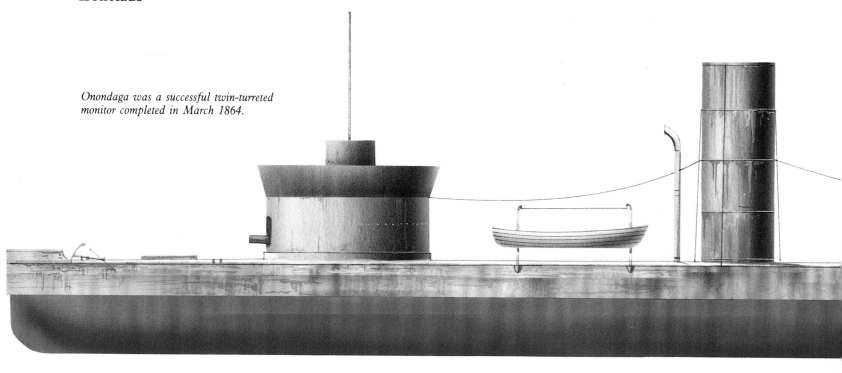

Onondaga was a successful twin-turreted monitor completed in March 1864.

USS *Onondaga*

Displacement: 2592 tons. **Dimensions:** Designed as 226ft 6in x 49ft 3in x 13ft, but completed as 228ft x 51ft x 13ft. Contracted vessels, when completed, often differed in size from that specified in the original design. **Armor:** 11 inches on turret, 5.5 inches on hull sides, and 1 inch on deck. **Machinery:** Four horizontal back-acting engines driving twin screws, developing 642 hp; coal capacity 268 tons, but only sufficient buoyancy for 160 tons. **Speed:** Designed for 9 knots, but only 6–7 knots realized. **Armament:** Two 15-inch Dahlgren smoothbores and two 150-pdr Parrott rifles.

The *Onondaga* was built under contract of May 26, 1862 with George Quintard. The hull was subcontracted to Continental Ironworks of Greenpoint, New York, while Quintard built the machinery at his Morgan Ironworks in New York. The original contract price was $625,000 but the final cost was $760,521.

Launched in July 1863 and commissioned the following March, *Onondaga* was the first double-turreted monitor completed for the US Navy, and although only a few feet longer then the *Passaic* class then being built, she was a more powerful vessel.

She served on the James River where she had one skirmish with Confederate ironclads. During her career, bullet-proof shields were fitted to the tops of the turrets. Quintard purchased the ship back from the navy in July 1867 for $759,673. He, in turn, sold her to the French Navy, where she served until 1905.

USS *Roanoke*

Displacement: 6300 tons. **Dimensions:** 265ft x 52ft 6in x 23ft 6in. **Armor:** 11 inches on turret, 4.5 inches on sides, 1.5 inches on deck, and 9 inches on the pilot house. **Machinery:** Two horizontal direct-acting trunk engines develop-

ing 997 hp and driving a single screw; coal capacity, 550 tons. **Speed:** 6 knots. **Armament:** The forward and aft turrets each contained one 15-inch Dahlgren smoothbore and one 150-pdr Parrott rifle, while the center turret housed one 15-inch Dahlgren and one 11-inch Dahlgren, both smoothbores. **Crew:** 350.

Originally launched in 1855 at the Norfolk Navy Yard, *Roanoke* was completed as a three-masted screw frigate in May 1861. She was armed with two 10-inch Dahlgren smoothbore guns, twenty-eight 11-inch Dahlgren smoothbores, and fourteen 8-inch, 63-cwt guns.

Roanoke lay at Hampton Roads in early March 1862 unable to move owing to the breaking of her shaft, but steam was blown off occasionally to give the impression that the vessel was still mobile. Although she should have been sent off for repairs, the blockading squadron could not afford to lose the tremendous fire power she developed.

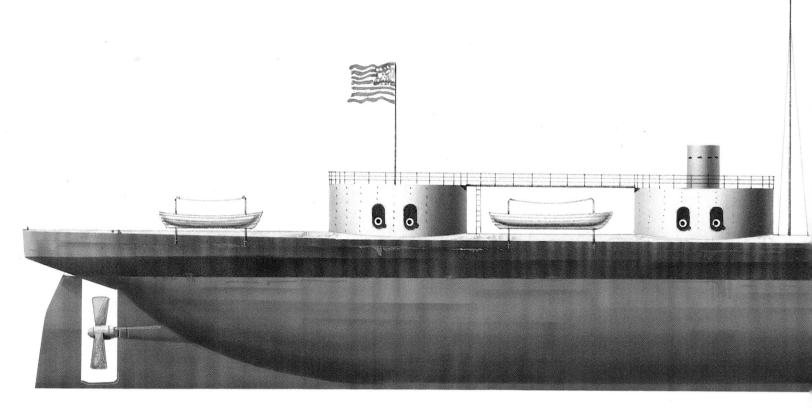

On March 8, when the CSS *Merrimack* came out to attack the squadron, the *Roanoke* ran aground while struggling to the aid of the wooden vessels *Congress* and *Cumberland.* She was only saved from certain destruction because the Confederate ram drew too much water to get within effective range.

It was obvious that such large vessels were useless in confined shallow waters and could certainly not withstand an attack from the powerful Confederate ironclads then under construction. *Roanoke* was taken out of service, only seventeen days after her narrow escape, for conversion into a turret ship.

The job of conversion was given to Lenthall and Isherwood who, realizing that their ambitious program of turret ships using the Coles turrets must be shelved, quickly prepared plans for cutting *Roanoke* down to the gun deck. Armor 4.5 inches thick was to be added to the

sides, thinning down to 3 inches on the ends, with 2.25 inches on the deck. They planned to carry eight 12- or 15-inch guns in four Coles turrets arranged along the center line. Total estimated cost was just under half a million dollars, and three and a half months was the estimated time needed for this dramatic transformation.

There were delays in construction because of the Navy Department's insistence on using 4.5-inch plates instead of laminated armor made up of thinner single plates. No navy yard could produce such heavy plates, so the department had to go to private yards, and the Novelty Ironworks of New York provided the armor and turrets. Isherwood and Lenthall now realized that the vessel could not support four turrets, so three were carried instead, and those were of the Ericsson design. Even this reduction was not enough, as the final weight carried

on the wooden hull was still too much and the vessel drew too much water. It was also a poor seaboat, rolling heavily in a seaway. Continuous firing of the heavy guns proved too much and this, coupled with the heavy turrets, caused the hull to sag.

Recommissioned in June 1863, she served as a harbor defense ship at Hampton Roads, Virginia, where she remained throughout the war. Placed in reserve two years later and struck from the navy list in August 1882, she was sold the following September at Chester, Pennsylvania, to E. Standard & Co. for $45,070.

Although not a success, *Roanoke,* with its three center-line turrets housing heavy guns, was the forerunner of World War I and World War II battleships. She was the only multi-turreted monitor built for the US Navy, and the most powerful.

Roanoke *after conversion from a frigate.*

Casco as originally designed.

USS *Casco*

Displacement: 1175 tons; *Squando*, 1618 tons; *Nausett*, 1487 tons. **Dimensions:** 225ft x 45ft 6in x 9ft. **Armor:** As designed, was to have been 8 inches on the turret, 3 inches on deck, and 10 inches on the pilot house. **Machinery:** Two inclined direct-acting engines driving two screws. **Speed:** Estimated at 9 knots. **Armament:** Varied as the twenty vessels were completed: *Casco*, *Napa*, and *Naubuc* each had one 11-inch Dahlgren smoothbore and one spar torpedo; *Cohoes*, *Shawnee*, *Squando*, and *Wassuc* each had two 11-inch Dahlgren smoothbores; *Chimo* had one 150-pdr Parrott rifle and one spar torpedo; *Modoc*, one spar torpedo; *Tuxis*, one 150-pdr Parrott rifle and one 11-inch Dahlgren smoothbore; *Etlah*, *Klamath*, *Koka*, *Nausett*, *Shiloh*, *Suncook*, *Umpqua*, *Waxsaw*, *Yazoo*, and *Yuma* all had 11-inch Dahlgren smoothbores.

During the summer of 1862 it became obvious to the Navy Department that it required something more capable of dealing with the powerful and well organized Confederate defenses along the Mississippi and its tributaries. The existing gunboats were finding it increasingly difficult to cope with the worsening situation, and further powerful vessels like CSS *Albemarle* were likely to pose a serious threat to the Union's light, conventional warships operating in the bays, rivers and sounds that made up so much of the Confederacy. It was not possible to use the existing

monitors because of their comparatively deep draft.

Specifications were therefore prepared for a twin-screw vessel with an exceptionally shallow draft of 4 feet, and carrying the lightest armor of any monitor built for the US Navy on a length of 221 feet and a beam of 41 feet. All were to have a single turret housing two guns. Ericsson was approached for designs but he was already heavily engaged in work on the *Passaic* and the *Canonicus* classes, as well as the huge *Dictator* and *Puritan*. He was, however, able to prepare preliminary sketches in about two days and he submitted them to Assistant Secretary of the Navy, Gustavus Fox, who had initiated the project. Ericsson felt that it was not possible to achieve the type of craft required with adequate protection on a draft of only 4 feet; he therefore increased it to 6 feet. Although still busy, Ericsson was persuaded by Fox to work these sketches up into more detailed drawings, and these were ready by October. Ericsson was to receive $10,000 for every unit built.

Now under heavy pressure himself, Fox turned over the plans to chief engineer Alban B. Stimers for substantial revision. Ericsson knew nothing of this — indeed, he only learned of the revision in February 1863 when bids were being invited — and was appalled at the many changes made to his plans without any prior consultation.

Among the numerous changes, Stimers had reverted to the earlier 4-foot draft. The

overhanging raft upper hull was also done away with, and large, 2-foot wide ballast tanks were fitted internally along each side of the hull so that the vessel could be immersed further when going into action, thus presenting an even smaller target. This was basically sound, but no one questioned the extra weight of the ballast tanks, piping and pumping engines on a craft of only 1000 tons displacement, and with a planned freeboard of only 15 inches on a 4-foot draft.

Further changes were now forced upon Stimers, as the experience gained in action against the Charleston defenses had shown the need to protect the turret bases. This was done by adding a heavy base-ring to the turret, which added an extra 18 tons.

Not content with this, it was decided to strengthen the pilot house, which not only meant even more weight, but greatly added to the cost, as most of the vessels were now under contract.

The Navy Department made it clear that it did not expect to be troubled with details and Stimers was instructed to set up headquarters

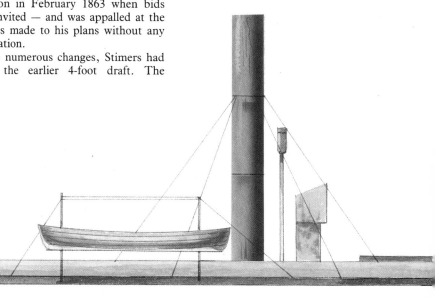

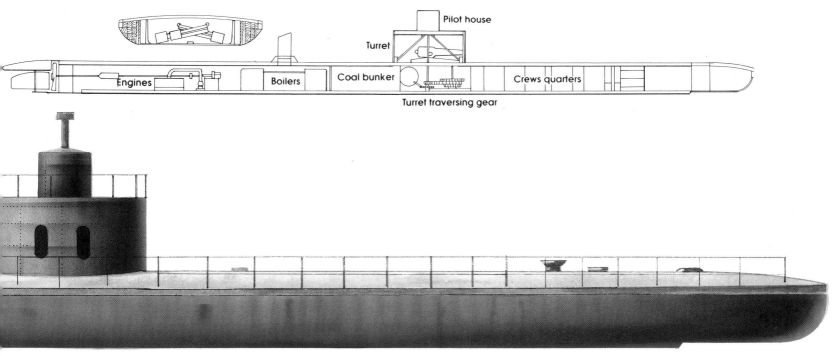

in New York so that he could be near Ericsson and therefore more easily consult with him on matters of detail. Unfortunately the two men rarely got together, and then only briefly to discuss minor points.

To complicate matters, Ericsson was not pleased at the way Stimers had carried out tests on the recoil system of the *Canonicus* class of monitor. From this point on, the relationship between the two men deteriorated rapidly and Ericsson preferred to leave his former friend to his own devices.

Stimers was now left in sole charge of one of the most ambitious building programs ever initiated. Worth about $14 million, it was spread between Boston, New York, St Louis, Cincinnati, Philadelphia, Pittsburgh, and Baltimore.

Stimers was also experiencing problems with other naval departments as he tended to bypass them and deal direct with the contractors in order to save time. This attitude does not seem unreasonable when viewed against the fact that Union forces were then suffering serious setbacks in the Mississippi campaign.

Meantime, Ericsson informed Fox that the new design was unsound and offered to redesign the vessel, but nothing came of the offer and Stimers was still left to run this huge project from a department now almost as big as the Navy Department. While this complex scheme was getting under way, Stimers was ordered to inspect the *Passaic* class monitors

now before Charleston. This later led to charges being made against Stimers by Admiral Du Pont, flag officer at Charleston, who strongly opposed Stimers' favorable report on the monitors.

Stimers now had to defend himself at a critical stage of the entire monitor program, although later the charges were dropped. However, he was still under immense pressure, being forced to spend much time away from New York supervising various stages of the program.

More changes were made to the *Casco*-type vessels when Stimers altered the design of the engines, making them heavier. Consequently, when *Chimo*, the first of the class, was launched, she had only 3 inches of freeboard — and this without turret, stores or crew on board — instead of the planned 15 inches when equipped for service.

An even worse error was now discovered. When the weight of the large amount of white oak required in the construction was calculated, no allowance was made for using unseasoned timber, although it was already known that all the seasoned timber had been used up. Despite the fact that this serious error had been made by one of his draftsmen, Stimers himself could not escape blame. He was immediately removed from control and the entire affair was handed over to Admiral Gregory, in charge of the Bureau of Construction, who promptly called in Ericsson to help out.

It was decided that the only solution was to build up the sides by 22 inches, thus adding an

extra 130 tons to the displacement and greatly reducing the vessels' usefulness even more. Fifteen were converted in this manner and some weight was saved by also removing the ballast tanks.

At this time requests were made for torpedo boats, so it was decided to quickly convert the five vessels nearest completion. These had the sides built up an extra 15 inches and carried an exposed 9-inch pivot gun instead of a turret. A spar torpedo was fitted to the bows. The cost of these alterations again added considerably to the total, initially calculated at $395,000 for thirteen vessels built in six months, and $10,000 less for units built in eight months.

The vessels selected for conversion to torpedo boats were *Casco*, *Chimo*, *Napa*, *Naubuc*, and *Modoc*, but their low speed of 5 knots made them useless in this role.

The cost of conversion varied according to the stage reached during construction; it ranged from $55,275 for *Wassuc* to $90,000 for *Waxsaw*, with many coming near to the latter figure.

Only eight were completed in time to see service in the Civil War, and these were employed on guard duties. All were disposed of between 1874 and 1876.

Stimers, after being removed from overall control of the light-draft monitor program, later found himself serving aboard one of them! No further action was taken against him and at the end of the war he resigned from the service and started up a successful design consultancy. He died from smallpox soon after in New York.

At a time when men in positions of authority just could not see the immense strides being made in warship design, Stimers was one of the few who saw the tremendous advantages of the ironclad, and the monitor type in particular.

Tuxis as completed
with exposed main armament.

USS *Keokuk*

Displacement: 677 tons. **Dimensions:** 159ft 6in x 36ft x 8ft 6in. **Armor:** 4 inches thick; partly covered the hull. **Machinery:** Four condensing engines driving two small screws. There were additional engines for driving the blowers, supplying feed water, and pumping ballast. **Speed:** 9 knots. **Armament:** Two 11-inch Dahlgren smoothbores.

Keokuk, formerly named *Moodna,* was an unusual ironclad with high sloping sides surmounted by two stationary, lightly-armored gun towers each housing one gun that could fire through one of three gunports at a 90-degree angle.

The armor was 4-inch flat iron clamped on edgeways and an inch apart, with the intervening space filled with wood. This arrangement was to prove extremely vulnerable to Confederate shells.

Keokuk was designed by C.W. Whitney, one of Ericsson's partners, and built at the Underhill Ironworks, New York, who also supplied the machinery. Whitney, together with his partner Thomas Rowland, had first submitted plans for an armored gunboat to the Navy Department in April 1861. This was for a 750-ton vessel 150 feet long and 30 feet wide, with an 8-foot draft. Side armor was 5.5 inches thick and made up of three even layers with wood laid between each strip. This belt extended along the center section for 110 feet and also protected the sides of the two fixed gun houses which had sloping sides. An 11-inch gun fired through ports which had 4.5-inch armored shutters and were automatically operated.

An armored pilot house stood between the towers to provide protection to the navigating officers.

Grating covered the top of the gun towers through which two fan blowers drew in fresh air. All the machinery was placed below the waterline and a speed of 10 knots was guaranteed. The vessel also had ballast tanks.

The partners offered to built this possible rival to the original *Monitor* in five months at a cost of $200,000. By July the plans were changed. The stationary towers were to be replaced by two revolving Coles turrets each having four gun ports, so that the guns could still be used if the training mechanism should be put out of action.

If breechloaders were available, the turrets would be only 15 feet in diameter, but 20 feet if muzzle loaders were mounted. The weight of armor and turrets was an estimated 230 tons. Whitney and Rowland offered to build the vessel in four months at a cost of $110,000.

Doubts were expressed by the Ironclad Board about the likely cost of this vessel, plus its ability to carry the amount of armor specified on its reduced length of 140 feet.

Rowland now withdrew from the partnership and undertook to build the hull of the *Monitor* for Ericsson. Whitney decided to carry on and revise the plans once more to overcome the objections. In September he demonstrated a 40-ton turret to the Ironclad Board but again left the meeting a disappointed man. He was, however, promised another chance should more ironclads be needed. Not until March 1862, after the battle of Hampton Roads, was Whitney's persistence rewarded. By this time the Navy Department had received six suggestions for the turret ships, including Whitney's and Ericsson's *Monitor.* With the success of the latter vessel in combat, the department was now eager to construct further ironclads. Even an earlier plan by Lenthall and Isherwood featuring Coles turrets was accepted, although Ericsson turrets were used instead. This became the *Miantonomoh* class.

Whitney submitted yet another design on March 17, which did away with the Coles turrets and reverted to the stationary towers. He was promptly awarded a contract and this unique warship was laid down on April 19,

1862, launched on December 6 of the same year, and commissioned the following February.

The *Keokuk,* captained by Commander A.D. Rhind, joined the fleet before Charleston and took a disastrous part in that abortive attack. While running ahead of the crippled *Nahant,* and to avoid fouling her in the narrow channel and strong tide, *Keokuk* came within 600 yards of Fort Sumter's guns. She remained there for thirty minutes, receiving ninety hits which completely riddled the vessel and wounded sixteen crew, including Rhind. Nineteen of the hits were below the waterline, so Rhind, finding it impossible to keep her afloat much longer under this extraordinary fire, withdrew the battered vessel from action at 4.40 p.m. She anchored out of range and was kept afloat that night as, fortunately, the water was smooth. However, the next morning a rising sea made it obvious that the vessel was doomed in spite of help from the tug *Dandelion.* Rhind removed the wounded and abandoned ship at 7.40 a.m. when she sank, leaving only the riddled funnel sticking up above the waves.

Attempts were made to destroy the hulk but without success. When it was found that she was rapidly filling with sand, making it impossible to set explosive charges, she was simply left.

The Confederates were able to salvage the guns when a gang of men, led by James La Costa, worked on the slippery roofs of the turrets, with water washing over them, for about two hours a night when the tide was right. After two weeks of strenuous effort an old lightship hulk was used to hoist out and transport the guns to Charleston in early May. During the last stages, the Confederate ironclads *Chicora* and *Palmetto State* stood by in case of need, but the Union forces were unaware of what was happening.

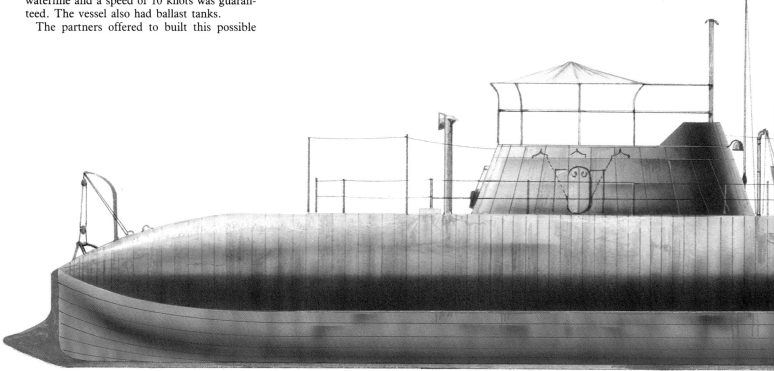

USS *Galena*

Displacement: 950 tons, later reduced to 738 tons after removal of armor in late 1863.
Dimensions: 181ft x 37ft x 13ft. **Armor:** 3.75 to 4 inches made up of interlocking bars.
Machinery: Two vibrating lever engines driving a single screw. The engines were Ericsson's successful designs used on many vessels. **Speed:** 8 knots. **Armament:** In 1862 had four 9-inch Dahlgren and two 200-pdr Parrott rifles; by 1865 she mounted eight 9-inch Dahlgren, one 60-pdr Parrott rifle, plus two lighter weapons. **Crew:** 150.

The bark-rigged *Galena* was the third ship recommended by the Ironclad Board. She was designed by Samuel Pook and built by C.S. Bushnell, who subcontracted the hull to Maxon & Fish, while Delamater Ironworks supplied the engines. She was laid down in 1861 at Mystic, Connecticut, launched on February 14, 1862, and commissioned in April 1862. The finished vessel, which had a pronounced 45-degree tumble home to the hull sides, cost $247,284.

Galena served at Hampton Roads and then up the James River under Commander John Rodgers. On the morning of May 15, she came up to Drury's Bluff, eight miles below the Confederate capital, Richmond, where the river was obstructed with sunken vessels and defended a heavy battery mounted 200 feet above the water. At a range of about 600 yards *Galena* opened fire but was subjected to a fierce plunging fire which pierced her sides thirteen times, once setting the ship on fire. Although horribly exposed, Rodgers kept her in action for three hours, before finally withdrawing when the ammunition started to run low and thirteen men had been killed and eleven wounded.

Later, *Galena* served at Mobile Bay. In 1871 she was broken up, but under the guise of repairing her, a new 1900-ton sloop was built, as Congress would not fully fund new construction.

Galena. She was one of the original three designs submitted as an answer to the growing threat of the Confederate ironclads.

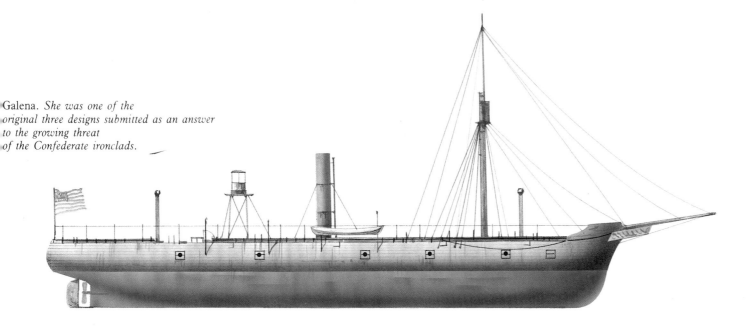

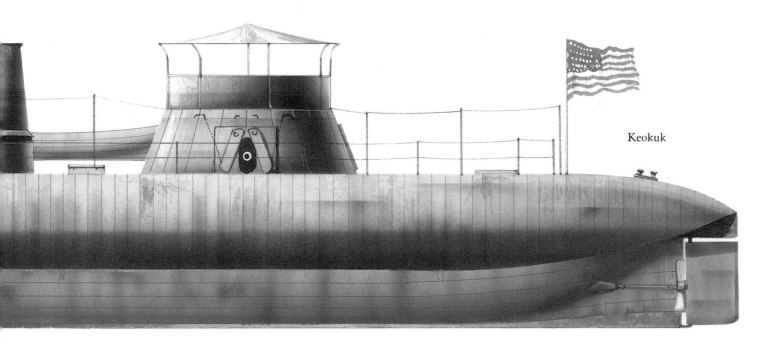

Keokuk

CSS *Baltic*

Displacement: 642 tons. **Dimensions:** 186ft x 38ft x 6ft 5in. **Armor:** 2.5 inches. **Armament:** One 42-pdr, two 32-pdr, and two 12-pdr howitzers. **Crew:** 86.

Baltic was a wooden sidewheel steamer built as a tow boat for the Southern Steamship Company in 1860 and purchased by the State of Alabama for conversion into an ironclad. When ready, after many delays, she was turned over to the Confederate Navy for service in Mobile Bay. When completed she was the only ironclad available for defense.

At one time seven ironclads or differing sizes were under construction in Alabama waters; if only these could have been completed quickly and sent to confront the Union force of nine wooden gunboats then blockading Mobile in 1864, the blockade stood every chance of being broken. As usual, however, the delays over machinery and materials generally put a stop to any such movements.

The accommodation aboard *Baltic* was very basic. Her commanding officer had a small room on deck, while a larger room below in the upper structure of the vessel was used by the officers as a mess and berth area. Bunks were provided below for the petty officers and the rest of the crew slept on deck.

The engines were in good repair but the boilers leaked. Also the state of the hull above water was not good, although the lower part, which had been strengthened during conversion, was in good condition. The inclined engines, which had a 7-foot stroke, drove two independent wheels 26 feet in diameter and 8 feet wide.

Like many of the vessels serving at that time, living conditions were not good and over a short period her crew reported sick an average of three times each.

Throughout the conflict *Baltic* operated in Mobile Bay and the Alabama, Tombigbee, and Mobile Rivers, at one time helping to tow the ironclad *Tennessee*.

Reported in February 1863 as unfit for service, she was unable to take part in the defense of Mobile Bay. Her armor, made up of railroad iron, was removed in July 1864 and used to plate the *Nashville*.

Prior to this she laid 180 floating torpedoes (mines) in Mobile Bay, leaving a gap for the blockade runners to slip through. Later the monitor *Tecumseh* would sink by striking one of these mines.

Baltic was captured at Nanna Hubba Bluff on the Tombigbee River on May 10, 1865, and sold to the US government.

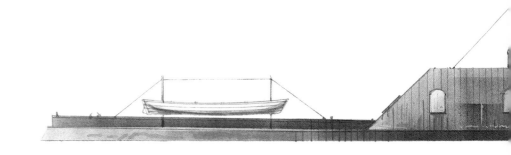

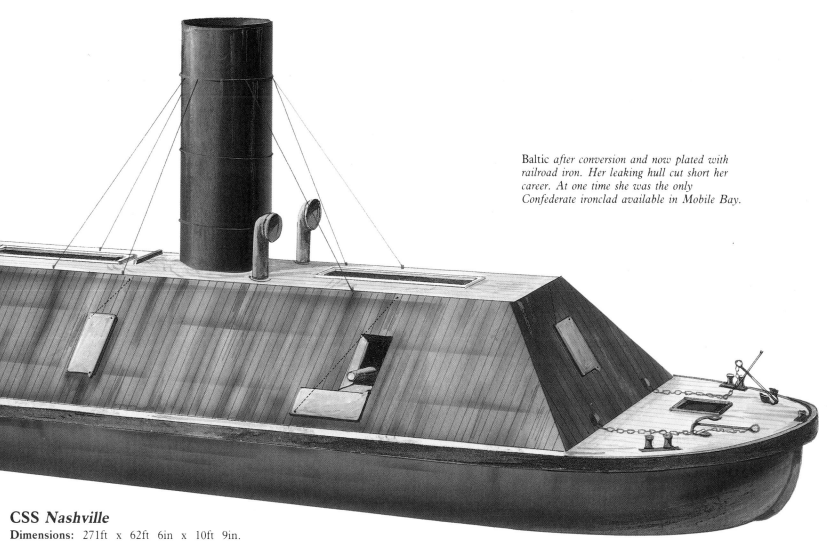

Baltic after conversion and now plated with railroad iron. Her leaking hull cut short her career. At one time she was the only Confederate ironclad available in Mobile Bay.

CSS *Nashville*

Dimensions: 271ft x 62ft 6in x 10ft 9in. **Armament:** In November 1863 had six guns; in May 1865 had three 7-inch Brooke rifles and one 24-pdr howitzer. **Armor:** Three layers of 2-inch plate on front of casemate and pilot house; one layer of 2-inch plate laid vertically on rear of casemate. **Machinery:** Twin engines with a 9-ft stroke obtained from abandoned river steamers.

Nashville was a large sidewheel steamer built in 1864 at Montgomery, Alabama, and completed at Mobile. She was not fully armored, the sides being left unprotected. Even without the extra weight of side armor, the hull still hogged, possibly through a miscalculation of the weights she was expected to carry.

Completed early in 1865 and placed under the command of Lt. John Bennett, she carried out much valuable work in the defense of Mobile when she assisted over many days at Spanish Fort, one of the Confederates' main defense positions on the Blakely River. Here she held back numerous attacks between March 27, 1865 and the time of her surrender in May. Although her deep draft precluded her

operating in the most favorable places, Bennett still managed to squeeze the vessel out of some tight spots, on several occasions being almost out of ammunition.

During this period the ironclad returned to Mobile for damage repairs but was soon back in action.

When Mobile surrendered, *Nashville* headed up to Tombigbee River to make a last stand. Here she ran aground and surrendered with the rest of the squadron on May 10.

The imposing profile of Nashville. *The massive paddle boxes, 95 feet 6 inches across, were unarmored and created a great impression of power. She was built at Montgomery, Alabama, and completed at the Mobile Navy Yard after many delays caused by lack of materials.*

CSS *Tennessee*

Displacement: 1273 tons. **Dimensions:** 209ft x 48ft x 14ft. **Armor:** 5 inches on sides, 6 inches on the forward end, and 2 inches on the deck. **Machinery:** Two geared non-condensing engines with 24-inch cylinders and a 7-ft stroke. Engines were geared to an idle shaft by spur gearing with wooden teeth, then from the idle shaft by iron bevel gear. **Armament:** Two 7⅛-inch Brooke rifles on pivots and four 6-inch rifles on broadside. **Crew:** 133.

Mobile was a major port used by blockade runners, and its importance as such was not lost on its defenders. When New Orleans fell, the Confederates fully expected Mobile to be next, and feverish efforts were made to strengthen its defenses. As no Union troops were available, the Confederates had time to build up the city's strength, which made it eventually harder to take.

After the loss of New Orleans, Rear Admiral Franklin Buchanan was ordered to assume command of the naval defenses, which he began to strengthen with obstruction in the shape of piling between the two forts, Gaines and Morgan, which guarded the entrance. Mines were planted in deeper water, leaving a narrow channel 500 yards wide so that blockade runners could slip in.

Meanwhile, at Selma on the Alabama River, the Confederates built one of their largest naval stations; during 1863 five warships were under construction there at the Naval Ordnance Works. One of these, the *Tennessee*, was among the most important and was probably the most powerful ironclad built in the Confederacy. She had a rather broad beam in comparison to her length but she was well armed and well protected. However, shortage of labor and delays in delivering material caused difficulties in casting the guns. The Selma works could produce only one gun per week, so the 6-inch rifles were obtained from Atlanta.

Heavy iron shutters were fixed over the ports which were meant to close automatically when the gun was run back in, but these were liable to jamming if struck by enemy shot.

A more serious design fault was the placing of tiller ropes in open channels on the deck. Although *Tennessee's* commanding officer, James Taylor, was aware of the problem, time did not allow the necessary changes to be made before her forthcoming battle.

She had been laid down in October 1862 and built by Henry D. Bassett. Launched in February 1863, the massive wooden hull was towed by the *Baltic* to Mobile for completion. Her engines came from the *Alonzo Child* left stranded up the Yazoo River by advancing Union forces. These engines were woefully inadequate and their complicated gearing presented further problems.

Once ready, the difficult task of getting the vessel down to the lower bay had to be faced. This entailed maneuvering the deep draft vessel over the Dog River bar which was only 9 feet deep at high tide. It would have been useless to remove the guns and other ballast to lighten the vessel, as the draft would decrease by only 4 inches and there were no facilities for getting the heavy guns back on again.

In the end, wooden pontoons called "camels" were built to float her over the bar. These were filled with water, lashed to her side and then emptied. As they rose, so did the ironclad, but by a mere 2 feet. As extra efforts were made to move the now vulnerable vessel, *Huntsville*, *Tuscaloosa*, and *Baltic* were sent down to strengthen the guard at the lower passes. This added to the problems of the Confederate admiral as these vessels, being unable to stem the tide, were placed in a position from which it would be difficult to recover them. New and larger camels were built which proved successful, but not before one set was destroyed in a fire at the naval yard. *Tennessee* finally slipped

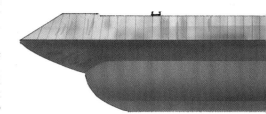

into the lower bay on the night of May 17.

Buchanan planned to run through the blockade the same night and capture Fort Pickens and Pensacola, but *Tennessee* ran aground. Although she was quickly floated off, the plan was abandoned.

Farragut was now ready to attack Mobile, so on August 5, 1864, the main column, made up of seven large ships each with a gunboat lashed on the port side, commenced their run in.

The line of monitors ran into trouble when one of them, the *Tecumseh*, struck a mine and sank. As the Union fleet passed, the *Tennessee* fired into them. Soon the lone ironclad was surrounded by enemy ships all pouring hot fire into her, but without success, as the shots bounced off harmlessly into the air.

Tennessee as completed. She was the largest ironclad built in the Confederacy and progress on her construction was reasonably fast. When towed to Mobile for completion, her armor had already been delivered from Atlanta. She took only four months to finish from the time of launching.

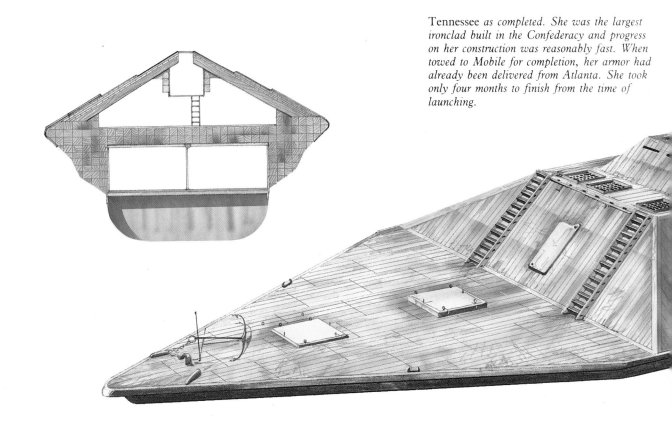

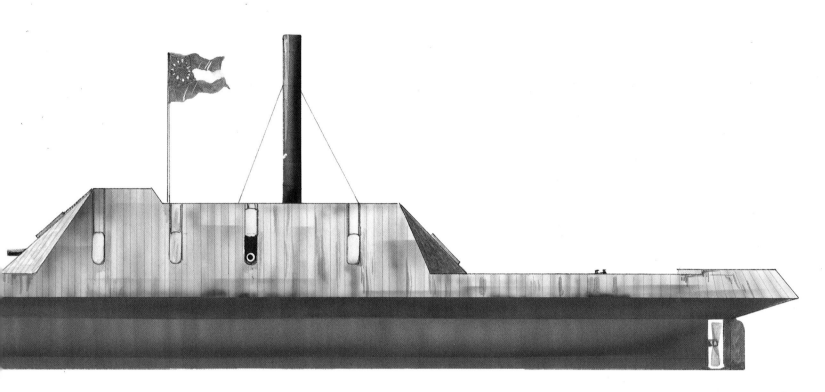

CSS *Atlanta*

Eventually, the monitors shot away the exposed chains on the after deck, as well as the relieving tackles. Thus rendered unable to steer, the *Tennessee* surrendered after a three-hour battle.

She was taken into the Union Navy during August and $7258 was spent on repairs. She went out of service in August 1865, and was sold in November 1867 to J.F. Armstrong for $7100, having originally been valued at $595,000.

Displacement: 1006 tons. **Dimensions:** 204ft x 41ft x 15ft 9in. **Armor:** 4 inches. **Speed:** 7 knots. **Armament:** Two 6.4-inch rifles on broadside and two 7-inch pivot rifles at each end. **Crew:** 145.

The blockade-runner *Fingal* arrived at Savannah in November 1861 with a large cargo of war materials. Unable to get out again, she was purchased in January 1862 by the Navy Department for conversion into an ironclad to be named *Atlanta*. She was cut down to the water's edge and an armored deck projecting 6 feet beyond the original hull was fitted. The wooden main deck was 3 feet thick.

A casemate was built up on the center section of the vessel and armored with railroad iron that had formed part of her original cargo. John A. Tift supervised the conversion.

Atlanta served around Savannah, but was captured at Wassaw Sound by the monitors *Weehawken* and *Nahant* at dawn on June 17, 1863, having run aground after a short fight.

Far left: *Cross section of* Atlanta *showing the massive build-up of timber on top of the original hull.*

Above: *The slab-sided* Atlanta *after conversion.*

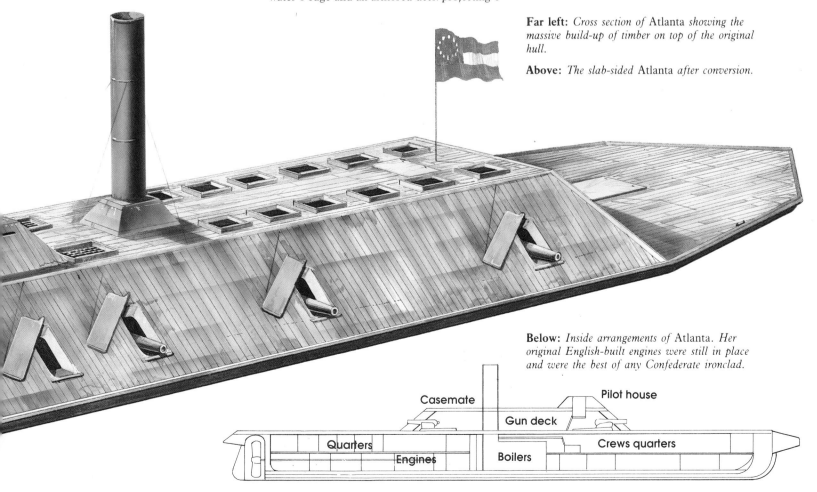

Below: *Inside arrangements of* Atlanta. *Her original English-built engines were still in place and were the best of any Confederate ironclad.*

Casemate   Pilot house   Gun deck   Quarters   Crews quarters   Engines   Boilers

Ironclads

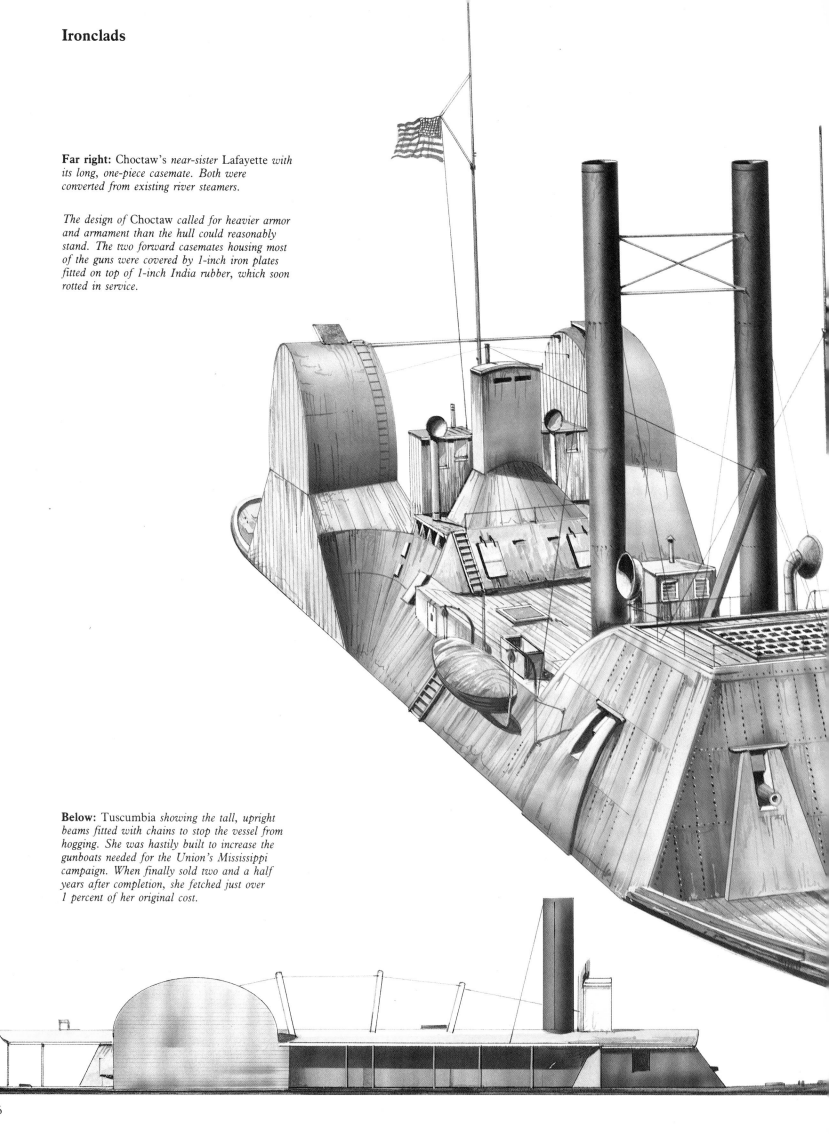

Far right: Choctaw's *near-sister* Lafayette *with its long, one-piece casemate. Both were converted from existing river steamers.*

The design of Choctaw *called for heavier armor and armament than the hull could reasonably stand. The two forward casemates housing most of the guns were covered by 1-inch iron plates fitted on top of 1-inch India rubber, which soon rotted in service.*

Below: Tuscumbia *showing the tall, upright beams fitted with chains to stop the vessel from hogging. She was hastily built to increase the gunboats needed for the Union's Mississippi campaign. When finally sold two and a half years after completion, she fetched just over 1 percent of her original cost.*

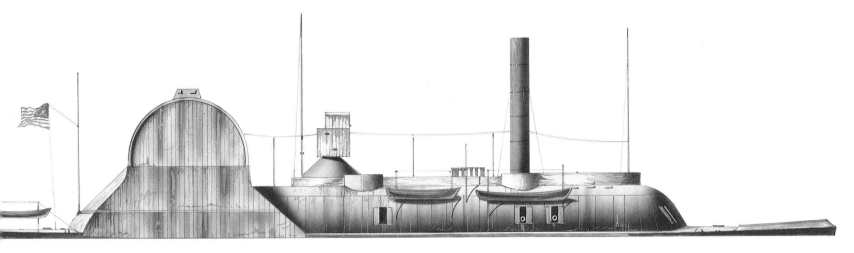

USS *Choctaw*

Displacement: 1004 tons. **Dimensions:** 260ft x 45ft x 8ft. **Armor:** 1-inch iron, plus 1-inch rubber on casemate. **Machinery:** Two engines with 8-ft strokes, each driving a wheel. **Speed:** 2 knots against stream. **Armament:** In December 1863 had one 100-pdr Parrott rifle, three 9-inch Dahlgren smoothbores, two 30-pdr Parrott rifles, and two 24-pdr smoothbores. **Crew:** 106.

The first nine gunboats, including the *Cairo* class, of the 1861 Eads program, were a success. They participated in the successful capture of Forts Henry and Donelson, plus the brilliant exploits of Walke in the *Carondelet* at Island No. 10 when, during a violent storm at night, he successfully passed one of the Confederates' strongest positions on the Mississippi. More was expected from the type in forth-

coming actions, and as more gunboats were going to be needed, a second group of four units was started. Ordered by the army, they eventually transferred to the navy.

Choctaw and her near sister *Lafayette* were the most powerful of the second generation gunboats and were designed by Commander William Porter, older brother of Admiral David Porter.

Choctaw was converted from the merchant ship of the same name which was built in 1855 at New Albany, Indiana. She was a sidewheel steamer of the type that had independent wheels which provided better steering and subtle control in the waters of the Mississippi.

Choctaw was given a massive casemate forward which housed three 9-inch guns and the one 100-pdr rifle. Just forward of the large paddle boxes was a second casemate holding two 24-pdr howitzers pointing ahead and intended to sweep the forward structure in case of boarding. The third casemate aft, with the 30-pdr rifles, was not armored.

The rubber on the casemate soon rotted, and the hull could not safely bear the weight of armor. Alterations were carried out by Eads in 1862 and *Choctaw* was commissioned during March 1863. She saw extensive service on the Mississippi in operations around Vicksburg, and was sold in March 1866 for $9270.

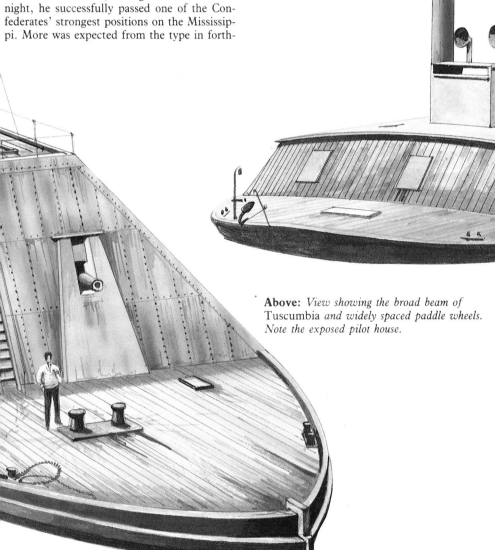

Above: *View showing the broad beam of* Tuscumbia *and widely spaced paddle wheels. Note the exposed pilot house.*

USS *Lafayette*

Displacement: 1000 tons. **Dimensions:** 280ft x 45ft x 8ft. **Armor:** 1-inch plate over 1-inch India rubber. **Machinery:** Two engines with an 8-ft stroke driving two side wheels. **Speed:** 4 knots against river. **Armament:** In early 1863 had two 11-inch and four 9-inch Dahlgren smoothbores, and two 100-pdr Parrott rifles; later, four 24-pdr howitzers were added. Armament then varied slightly. **Crew:** 106.

Lafayette was a near-sister to *Choctaw* and had also been converted from a river steamer built at New Albany, Indiana, in 1858. First named *Alick Scott*, she was renamed *Fort Henry* for a short time while serving as a quartermaster's steamer, then renamed *Lafayette*. She was converted by Eads at St Louis during 1862 and commissioned in February 1863.

She was very similar to *Choctaw*, except that the casemate was continued back to the wheels, and two 11-inch guns faced forward through the rounded front section which resembled half a dome. The 9-inch guns were in broadside, with the 100-pdr rifles pointing aft. As in *Choctaw*, the rubber under the iron plating soon rotted.

Lafayette participated in action against the Vicksburg defenses and at Grand Gulf, and was used in patrolling the Mississippi.

Decommissioned in July 1865, she was laid up at New Orleans until sold in March 1866 for $10,770.

USS *Tuscumbia*

Displacement: 915 tons. **Dimensions:** 178ft x 75ft x 7ft. **Armor:** 6 inches on the casemate. **Machinery:** Four engines driving two side wheels and two screws. **Speed:** 10 knots. **Armament:** In March 1863 had three 11-inch and two 9-inch Dahlgren smoothbores; in June three more 11-inch Dahlgren smoothbores were added.

Laid down in the spring of 1862, launched in December 1982 and commissioned on March 12, 1863, *Tuscumbia* followed the same general plan as *Choctaw* but was slightly smaller. She had 11-inch guns in the forward casemate and 9-inch guns in the aft one.

Designed by Joseph Brown, who subcontracted the hull to a shipbuilder at New Albany, she was intended only as a stopgap to swell the numbers of gunboats needed on the Mississippi. Hastily and poorly built, the hull was never strong enough to carry the weight of armor fitted, so it soon sagged and became distinctly warped.

The deck had settled down over the boilers by 7 inches and much of it rested upon the safety valves and steam drum. To rectify this, two bridgetrees were rigged which supported the deck from above. The arched deck had been laid athwartships, with the ends of the planks resting on the gunwhales. It was supported by five 6 x 8-inch beams running the length of the ship, but had no other support, not even over the boilers.

Among her many other faults, the wheels were very exposed, and during the action at Grand Gulf, six shells entered the engine-room. In addition, the armor had not been properly secured, the plates being held onto the thin wood backing by drift bolts 4 inches long. (In action, one plate fell overboard when struck.)

The badly protected shell room and magazines were exposed to any shot entering large ports nearby. One such shot at Grand Gulf nearly set the magazines on fire.

The hogging of the hull was partly cured by erecting 20-foot high posts with chains that could take up the tension and ran from one end of the vessel to the other. However, these were often shot away in action.

In spite of these drawbacks, *Tuscumbia* performed well in the Mississippi campaign, serving at Fort Heiman, Hayne's Bluff, and Grand Gulf. She was taken out of service in early 1865 and sold in November 1865 to W.K. Adams for $3300, having originally cost $227,669, including $81,669 for extra work.

USS *Indianola*

Displacement: 511 tons. **Dimensions:** 175ft x 52ft x 5ft. **Armor:** 3 inches on casemate and 1 inch on deck. **Machinery:** Four engines; two with a 6-ft stroke drove the paddle wheels, and two drove the twin screws. **Speed:** 6 knots. **Armament:** Two 11-inch and two 9-inch Dahlgren smoothbores. **Crew:** 114.

Indianola was designed by Joseph Brown under contract with the War Department and built by his company at Cincinnati in 1862. Machinery was supplied by McCord & Junger. She was a powerful vessel and incorporated improvements over the *Cairo* class by having a casemate forward containing 11-inch guns on pivots so they could fire through ports over a good range. *Indianola* had the twin screws between the paddles but the center engines took up too much space, leaving no space for quarters for the crew.

When a Confederate force threatened Cincinnati, Brigadier General Lew Wallace took the unfinished ironclad from the contractor to use it in defending the city. Delayed by low water, *Indianola* eventually joined the Mississippi Squadron in early 1863, but her life was a short one. She was retiring before a superior Confederate force of two rams and two steamers filled with troops for boarding, but was finally caught and repeatedly rammed. Not having all her crew on board, she was forced to surrender. The Confederate ram *Queen of the West* stood by the wreck as a salvage party tried to raise her, but when a false alarm about an attack was given they blew up the gunboat.

USS *Chillicothe*

Displacement: 395 tons. **Dimensions:** 162ft x 50ft x 4ft. **Armor:** 2 inches on sides, 1 inch on deck, and 3 inches on pilot house. **Machinery:** Two engines with an 8-ft stroke driving side wheels. **Speed:** 7 knots. **Armament:** Two 11-inch Dahlgren smoothbores; one heavy 12-pdr smoothbore was added in October 1863.

Chillicothe was a smaller version of *Tuscumbia* and suffered from the same hasty construction. Her bulwarks were not strong enough to support the armor, although she and *Tuscumbia* were faster than many vessels then in service on the river. The pilot house was located so far

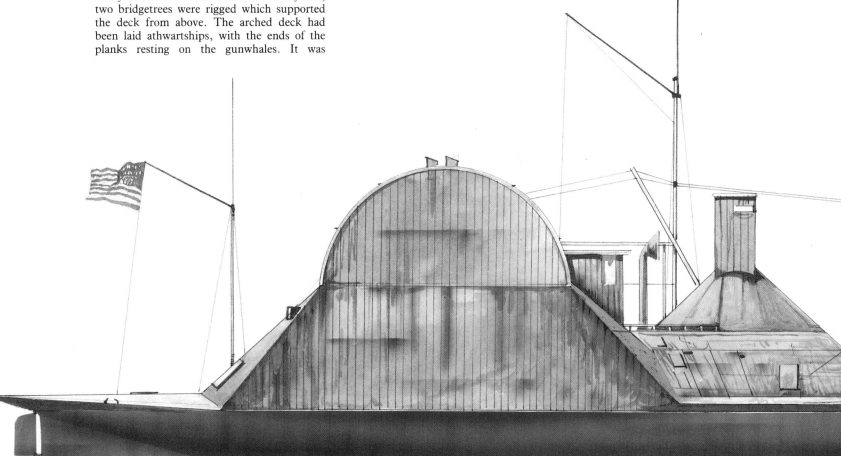

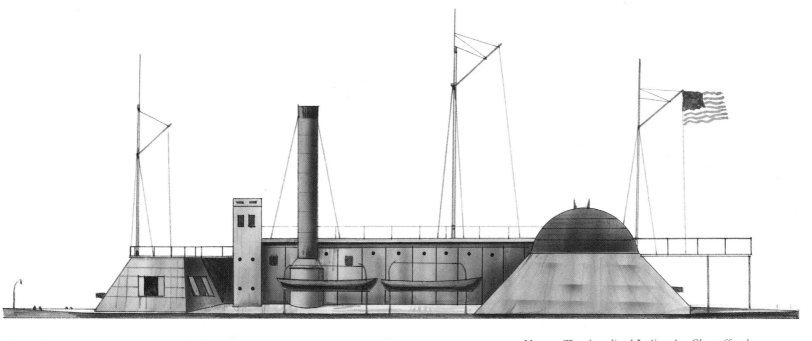

forward that she could not be steered when the guns were firing.

Designed by Samuel Hartt, the hull was built by Joseph Brown at Cincinnati, and engines were supplied by McCord & Junger. *Chillicothe* was laid down, launched and commissioned in 1862, having taken less then nine months to build. She was sold in November 1865 to Cutting & Ellis for $3000, having originally cost $92,690.

Above: *The short lived* Indianola. *She suffered through lack of small guns and was of poor quality through hasty construction.*

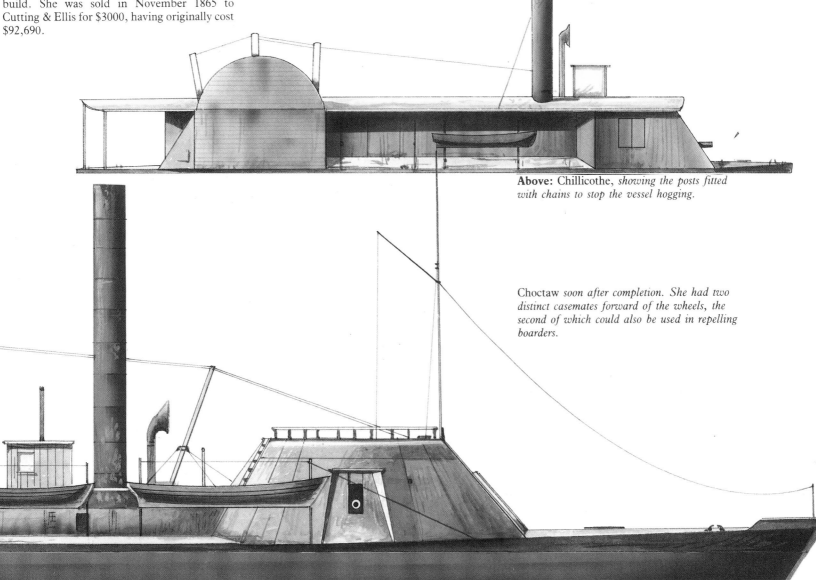

Above: Chillicothe, *showing the posts fitted with chains to stop the vessel hogging.*

Choctaw *soon after completion. She had two distinct casemates forward of the wheels, the second of which could also be used in repelling boarders.*

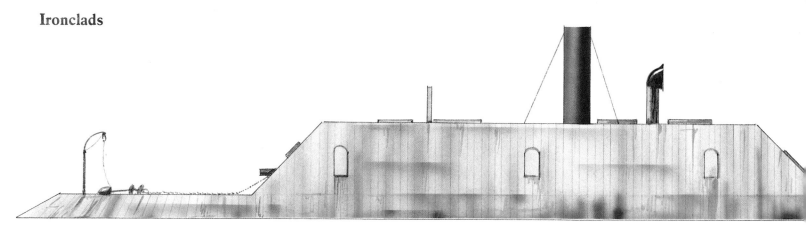

CSS *Chicora*

Dimensions: 150ft x 35ft x 14ft. **Armor:** 4 inches thick on sides, with 22 inches of oakwood backing and 2 inches at each end of the battery. **Speed:** 5 knots. **Armament:** Two 9-inch smoothbore shell guns and two 7-inch Brooke rifles. **Crew:** 150.

Chicora and her sister *Palmetto State* were designed by John Porter and followed the usual raised, armored casemate on a low freeboard hull. Both were to play a leading role in the defense of Charleston.

Chicora was built by James M. Eason in 1862 and cost $263,892, nearly exhausting the entire $300,000 budget set aside for the construction

of warships. Eason also received a bonus for prompt delivery.

Palmetto State was built by Cameron & Co., also of Charleston, and completed by September 1862.

The two vessels' engines had been taken from small steamers, so were not strong enough to make good speed. Although designed for 8 knots, they could make barely 5 in calm water. At one time, *Chicora* had to anchor while out on picket duty, as the vessel could not stem the 2-knot ebb tide. In spite of engines being kept at full power, she still dragged her anchors.

Manning had presented a problem as it took time for full crews to be mustered, in spite of Charleston being well supplied with seamen. As they became available, trained sailors, including three "free" negroes, were added to the crews, thus building up a well-disciplined force.

Both vessels sallied forth from the harbor in the pre-dawn haze of January 31, 1863, to attack the wooden Union gunboats blockading the entrance. USS *Mecedita* was forced to surrender to *Palmetto State*, who also disabled USS *Keystone State*, forcing the vessel to be towed out of action. *Chicora*, meantime, carried out a long-range duel, helping to drive off the enemy.

Both were actively employed around Charleston aiding Fort Sumter during the attack by Union ironclads in April 1863.

Their slowness and general unseaworthy condition made the two ironclads useless for any offensive action against the greatly enlarged Union force now blockading Charleston. Even

so, they discouraged any attacks against the harbor defenses, and every night one or both of them could be found waiting in the darkness for any attack.

On February 17, as Charleston was about to fall, the Confederates destroyed the shipyard, including an ironclad on the stocks and one just launched. The next morning both vessels were blown up, sending a shower of debris down on the wharfs and setting several on fire.

CSS *Charleston*

Dimensions: 180ft x 34ft x 14ft. **Speed:** 6 knots. **Armament:** Six guns. **Crew:** 150.

The success of the *Merrimack* in keeping at bay a strong Union force excited a great deal of enthusiasm for ironclad construction in the South. As a result of newspaper coverage, it was not long before the public started to raise funds for the building of such a vessel. This ironclad was named *Charleston* and was financed mainly by women's organizations whose members raised funds by selling their jewelry.

Laid down in Charleston in December 1862 and ready for service nine months later, *Charleston* still needed time to gather sufficient crew. She was finally fully manned in early 1864, becoming the flagship of the squadron with Commander I.N. Brown in command.

She aided in the defense of Charleston harbor, taking it in turns with the *Chicora* and *Palmetto State* to do night duty to forestall any sudden attack upon the harbor itself.

Widely known as the "Ladies Gunboat", she was blown up in Charleston harbor on the morning of February 18 to avoid capture when Charleston fell to Union forces.

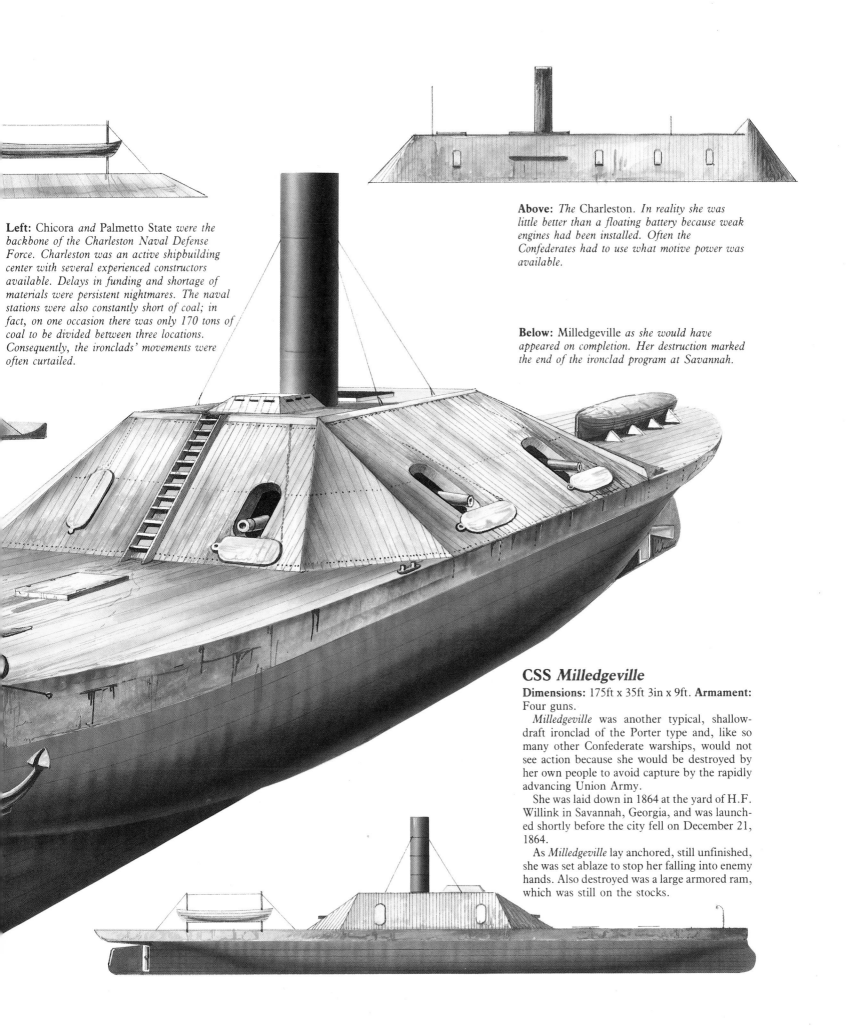

Left: Chicora *and* Palmetto State *were the backbone of the Charleston Naval Defense Force. Charleston was an active shipbuilding center with several experienced constructors available. Delays in funding and shortage of materials were persistent nightmares. The naval stations were also constantly short of coal; in fact, on one occasion there was only 170 tons of coal to be divided between three locations. Consequently, the ironclads' movements were often curtailed.*

Above: *The* Charleston. *In reality she was little better than a floating battery because weak engines had been installed. Often the Confederates had to use what motive power was available.*

Below: Milledgeville *as she would have appeared on completion. Her destruction marked the end of the ironclad program at Savannah.*

CSS *Milledgeville*

Dimensions: 175ft x 35ft 3in x 9ft. **Armament:** Four guns.

Milledgeville was another typical, shallow-draft ironclad of the Porter type and, like so many other Confederate warships, would not see action because she would be destroyed by her own people to avoid capture by the rapidly advancing Union Army.

She was laid down in 1864 at the yard of H.F. Willink in Savannah, Georgia, and was launched shortly before the city fell on December 21, 1864.

As *Milledgeville* lay anchored, still unfinished, she was set ablaze to stop her falling into enemy hands. Also destroyed was a large armored ram, which was still on the stocks.

CSS *Columbia*

Dimensions: 216ft x 51ft 4in x 13ft 6in. **Armor:** 6 inches on sides. **Armament:** Six guns.

Columbia was an exceptionally strong vessel designed by John Porter, and built of the usual yellow pine and white oak at Charleston, North Carolina, in 1864. The hull was built by F.M. Jones, and machinery was supplied by James M. Eason. Porter reduced the length of the heavily-armored casement to make greater savings of iron, now in short supply.

Columbia was launched on January 12, 1865, but had run onto a wreck and partly broke her back when the tide fell. Efforts were made to float her off by removing the guns and some of the armor, but she was still firmly aground when Union forces captured the city on February 18, 1865. After much effort, the ironclad was floated off on April 26, and after being patched up she was towed to Hampton Roads, Virginia, by USS *Vanderbilt*, arriving there on May 25.

She was one of Porter's latest designs and the total cost, including repairs, was $193,480. The hull was strengthened with iron fastenings. These gave additional strength to the massively thick wooden sides which were surrounded by thicker armor than that usually applied.

The machinery was a single pair of non-condensing engines with a 2-ft stroke driving three 10ft 8in-diameter propellers. Confederate ironclads were usually single- or twin-screwed; the triple-screw idea was a distinct advance, having been used previously on the unsuccessful *Mississippi* built at New Orleans two years earlier.

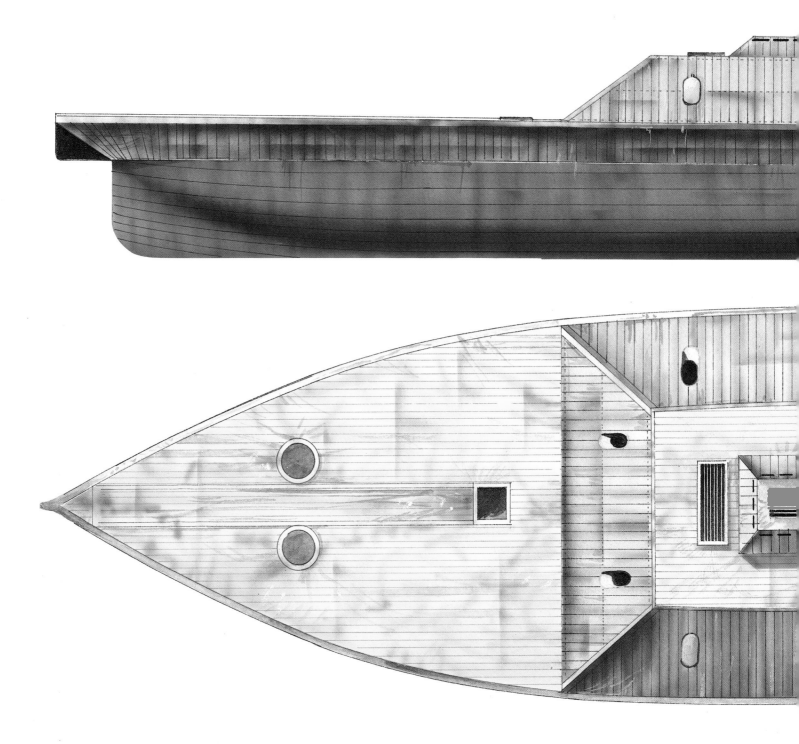

Confederate shipbuilding policy at Charleston, as elsewhere, was plagued with problems. Funds were slow in reaching the suppliers, and when they arrived were usually too late or too little. Some suppliers refused to supply goods, and people working on the ironclads suffered a great deal because of the irregular payments.

The supply of labor was another problem. Bitter rivalry developed between the navy yard and suppliers over the procurement of skilled workers. Complaints were lodged that interservice rivalry was often made worse when foundry mechanics, for example, were lured away to work in the yards, as both establishments were working for the navy.

Wages were another cause of trouble. The rapidly depreciating value of Confederate money meant that wages were continually rising and companies were forced to match each other's increases in order to attract and retain staff.

To help speed work along, the navy yards followed other methods applied by local industry. Shift work and Sunday work became the norm, and skilled workers were moved between one naval facility and another to help expedite construction.

Negro labor was used extensively by the navy for both skilled and unskilled work. At the beginning of the war, slaves were hired from local planters to perform unskilled work, cut timber and work in the mines. As the war ground on, however, skilled Negro workers were increasingly being employed. For example, many of the skilled carpenters at Charleston were Negro. By the beginning of 1885, the number of Whites and Negroes employed in the ordnance factories were roughly equal.

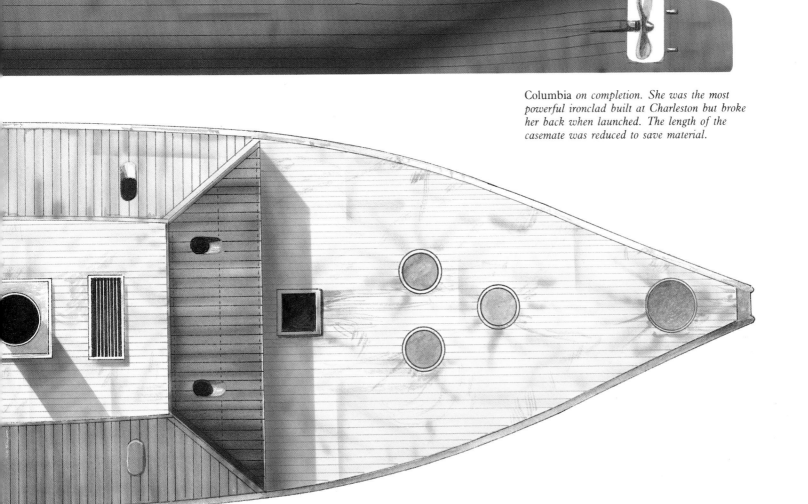

Columbia *on completion. She was the most powerful ironclad built at Charleston but broke her back when launched. The length of the casemate was reduced to save material.*

CSS *Arkansas*

Dimensions: 165ft x 35ft x 11ft 6in.
Armament: In July 1862 had two 8-inch, 64-pdr, two rifled 32-pdr, two 100-pdr columbaids, and a single 6-inch naval gun on each side.
Crew: 232.

Arkansas was a twin-screw ironclad ram laid down by J.T. Shirley in October 1861 at Fort Pickering, a landing below Memphis. She was one of a pair, and the contract called for them to be completed by December 24, or sooner if possible. The usual problems of obtaining material and transporting it to the site, plus shortage of skilled workmen, greatly delayed construction, so the builder decided to complete the vessels one at a time. However, delays continued to dog the craft, which was only slowly taking shape, prompting one officer to complain of poor workmanship.

General Beauregard, who had taken command of the Army of the Mississippi, and who realized the value of such vessels, offered to free any number of skilled workers from the army to help Shirley finish her, but the offer was not taken up. Perhaps Shirley felt that he now had enough people to complete the job, despite the increased sense of urgency caused by the rapid advance of Union forces.

When New Orleans fell it was decided to move *Arkansas* to a safer place for completion. While her sister was destroyed on the stocks, she was towed up the Yazoo River to Greenswood where, for one month, she lay moored to a pier in the rain-swollen stream with machinery, guns, and stores cluttering her decks. As it turned out, a month was to pass before Memphis was in danger — a period in which *Arkansas* could have been finished and gone to the city's defense. Her wood was all in place, except for minor details, and the main deck was armored to about 1 foot below the waterline. However, the casemate armor still needed fitting and the two engines and boilers were on board but not working.

On May 26, 1862, Lt. Isaac Newton Brown took command and soon had things moving. He obtained slaves and 200 men from the army as his workforce. Construction then went on twenty-four hours a day under pressure of the Union advance. Yazoo City was still an important building center with facilities for repairing the river steamers, and also had the largest timber mill in the area.

A steamer was anchored alongside the *Arkansas* for the workers to live on and several were arrested and imprisoned for insubordination. Work continued throughout the hottest weather, and as men fell ill with heatstroke or malaria, so others took their place. At night work continued relentlessly by lantern-light.

The steamer *Capitol* was anchored alongside so that her hoisting engine could be used to drive the drills needed for fitting the railroad iron to the shield. Without waiting for the forge to bend the railroad iron so that it could be fitted to the sweep of the quarters and stern, Brown had boiler plate tacked over these areas. The iron was laid on at an angle of 35 degrees and backed by thicker timber walls. The large funnel came up through the top of the battery, and in front of this stood a small pilot house with an iron speaking tube for passing on orders below.

Six of the heavy guns came from Memphis, while four more were obtained from two stranded gunboats. Gun carriages were made of railroad iron and dragged to the ship by ox-teams.

After spending an active five weeks at Yazoo City, *Arkansas* left Liverpool Landing on June 20 and started downstream. The vessel was still not finished but the rapidly falling river made it imperative to get the craft into deeper water.

Eventually, by July 14, when the crew numbers were finally made up, the vessel was to make a run to Memphis, stopping only at Vicksburg for supplies. On her way down the twisting Yazoo River, *Arkansas* encountered the Union ironclad *Carondelet* accompanied by the gunboat *Tyler* and the army ram, *Queen of the West*, coming up the river on a reconnaissance mission. The ensuing fierce action ended with *Carondelet* being disabled and forced ashore. *Arkansas* pursued the other two vessels into the Mississippi.

The lone ironclad now ran past the Union fleet, having been badly damaged in the action and losing many men.

While anchored off Vicksburg, she was attacked by *Queen of the West* and the ironclad *Essex* on July 22, but managed to beat off the assault. In action again with *Essex* on August 6 about five miles above Baton Rouge, but now with engine trouble, she was unable to maneuver or escape. The long-suffering vessel

drifted ashore where she was set on fire to avoid capture. She had originally cost $76,920, and her loss was a disaster to Confederate efforts in the west, one of many such sad losses to the cause. Her performance against superior Union forces, combined with the success of the *Merrimack (Virginia)*, proved the value of the ironclad to the Confederate cause and bore out Mallory's faith in the type. From then on even more effort would be put into their construction.

CSS *Raleigh*

Dimensions: 150ft x 32ft x 12ft. **Armament:** Four 6-inch rifles. **Crew:** 188.

Raleigh and her sister ship *North Carolina* were built in 1862 from the plans of John Porter at Wilmington, North Carolina. *Raleigh* was launched at Church Street and completed at J.L. Cassidy & Sons' shipyard.

Limited resources and materials contributed to the delays in completing these vessels. The situation was made worse when the shipwrights went on strike because the Navy Department

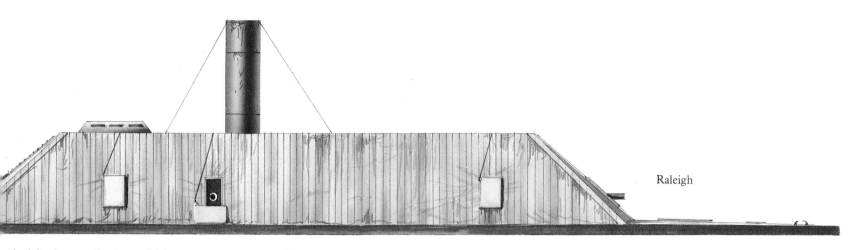

Raleigh

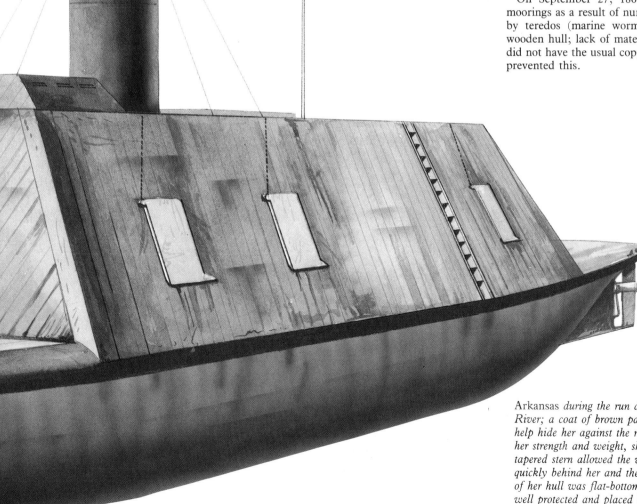

had inadequate funds available to pay them. More delays occurred in late 1862 and again in 1863 when three serious outbreaks of yellow fever forced the workers to flee the city. Finally, when nearly ready, one of the shipyards was partly destroyed by fire, occasioning even more delays.

On May 6, 1863, six days before entering service, *Raleigh*, accompanied by the wooden gunboats *Yadkin* and *Equator*, slipped across the bar at New Inlet during high tide at 8 p.m. and engaged a group of Union blockaders, forcing them to retire in the gathering gloom. *Raleigh* continued to give chase, but failed to find any enemy vessels in the night, until 11.45, when she exchanged shots with the wooden sidewheel steamer *Nansemond* before that vessel also disappeared into the darkness.

Dawn found *Raleigh* several miles away from the bar and her two consorts. The Union blockaders were now scattered; only two were visible from the ironclad, so she promptly closed with the nearest. Soon, reinforcements came up to support the hard-pressed Union gunboat, and after a brief cannonade in which no hits were scored, *Raleigh* broke off the action at 7 a.m. She retired toward the bar, which she safely passed over, only to run aground on her way back to Smithville, a small hamlet three miles up New Inlet. All efforts to refloat the vessel failed, and as her back was broken, the guns and armor were removed.

North Carolina was built by Berry & Bros. and entered into service late in 1863. Having unreliable engines taken from an old tugboat, she was used as a floating battery to protect the blockade runners' anchorage off Smithville.

On September 27, 1864, she sank at her moorings as a result of numerous leaks caused by teredos (marine worms) boring into her wooden hull; lack of materials meant that she did not have the usual copper-sheathing which prevented this.

Arkansas during the run down the Yazoo River; a coat of brown paint was applied to help hide her against the riverbanks. In spite of her strength and weight, she was quite fast. The tapered stern allowed the water to close up quickly behind her and the middle 8-foot section of her hull was flat-bottomed. The engines were well protected and placed below the waterline, but the engine-room reached temperatures of over 120 degrees.

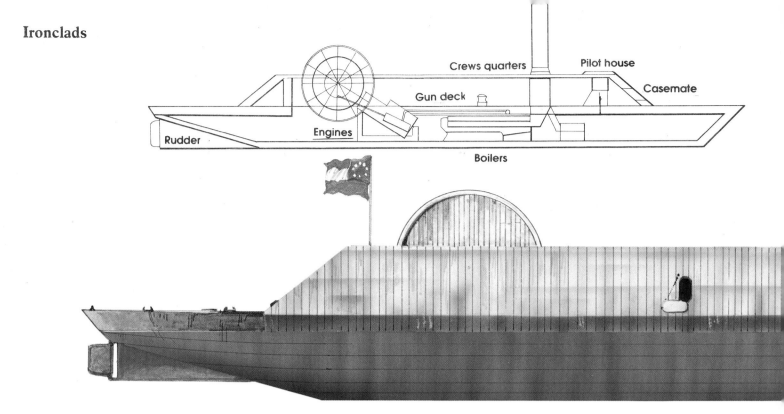

CSS *Missouri*

Dimensions: 183ft x 53ft 8in x 8ft 6in. **Armor:** 4.5 inches on the sides. **Machinery:** Two poppet-valve engines with a 7ft 6-in stroke connected to the shaft at right angles. **Speed:** 6 knots, although she was supposed to make 10. **Armament:** In June 1863 had one 11-inch Dahlgren, one old 32-pdr siege gun, and one 9-inch Dahlgren.

Missouri was probably the last ironclad to serve the Confederate Navy. On October 3, 1862, the Navy Department ordered Lt. Jonathan Carter to place an order for two ironclads at one of the new interior sites being used to construct warships. These sites were: Edward's Ferry and Whitehall in North Carolina; Columbus, Georgia; Yazoo City, Mississippi; Selma, Montgomery, and Oven Bluff in Alabama; Shreveport on the Red River, Louisiana. The latter place was chosen for *Missouri* and the second ironclad, but none of the sites was ideal and many were not served by railroads, which caused further problems over delivery of materials.

Many of these yards were also very basic, comprising a small clear area on a riverbank or inlet where the water at the end of the slipway was deep enough for a successful launching. The facilities available usually consisted of a small mill, forges, and a blacksmith shop. Although such places would never have been used for constructing ocean-going vessels, they served as well as could be expected when it

came to turning out the small ironclads Mallory desperately needed.

Mallory also favored building several sidewheel ironclads similar to the large *Nashville* because the standard type of steamboat machinery was more readily available and could be easily adapted. However, only two others were laid down and these were never finished for service in the Confederate Navy. Only the converted *Baltic* would share with *Missouri* and *Nashville* the distinction of being the only sidewheel ironclad steamers to join the navy.

Carter issued the contract on November 1, 1862, the vessel was laid down during December, launched on April 14, 1863, and ready by August. She entered service on September 12.

She had been designed for river service and was powered by a wheel 22 feet in diameter and 8 feet wide in a recess at the aft end of the superstructure. Nearly 8 feet of the wheel was exposed at the top of the casemate, which was 130 feet long — longer than those usually seen on Confederate ironclads —and sloped back at an angle of 30 degrees. This structure housed the armament. Although originally designed for six guns — one at each corner firing through two ports each, plus two broadside guns amidships — only three were carried and these were mounted on carriages made of railroad iron. The 11-inch gun fired ahead and to

starboard, the 32-pdr fired ahead and to port, while the 9-inch weapon fired from either of the aft broadside ports.

This mix of weaponry came from the captured *Harriet Lane*. The steering wheel was located under the pilot house which rose 19 feet above the top deck and was made up of iron gratings to help ventilation. The three balanced rudders were located beneath the fantail.

Armor was laid in two interlocking layers and extended to 6 feet below the waterline. The exposed portions of the main deck also carried armor. The backing was 23 inches of yellow pine.

The vessel had a number of defects: it failed to make more than 6 knots, in spite of alterations to the hull and machinery; the single stern wheel made her difficult to steer; and she could hardly stem the current. Built out of unseason-

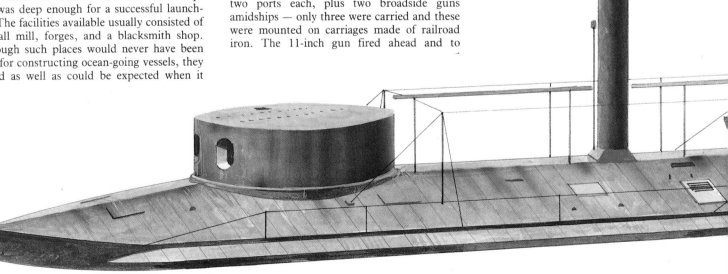

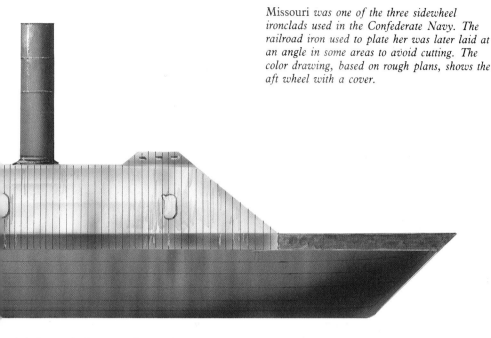

ed timber and of poor workmanship, she leaked badly, having been caulked with cotton.

Missouri was to have cooperated with Confederate Army units trying to stem the tide of the Union advance in the area, but her destination, Alexandria, fell while the vessel was waiting for the river to rise sufficiently to enable her to get down there. Union gunboats now passed through the rapids above Alexandria with difficulty and started toward Shreveport where the *Missouri* still lay, having been only briefly used as a troop transport and to lay mines. She surrendered on June 3, 1865, and was later sold at Mound City, Illinois, in November 1865.

USS *Osage*

Displacement: 523 tons. **Dimensions:** 180ft x 45ft x 4ft 6in. **Armor:** 2.5 inches on sides, 6 inches on turret. **Machinery:** Two non-condensing horizontal engines driving a stern wheel; coal capacity 50 tons. **Speed:** 7.5 knots. **Armament:** Two 11-inch Dahlgren smoothbores.

In April 1862 the Navy Department was anxious to increase the number of light-draft armored gunboats of the *Cairo* type to help clear the river of enemy forces. James B. Eads

was approached and responded with a design similar to the *Cairo's*, having a long casemate and a 5½-foot draft. While these plans were being examined, the *Monitor's* successful performance at Hampton Roads was noted, so the department requested a vessel with turrets and even less draft.

The revised design was impressive. It had a single turret with 8-inch armor, a fully enclosed armored stern wheel, and a 4 foot 6-inch draft. However, the department wanted even less draft, so Eads produced another design which drew only 3 feet 6 inches and featured a turtle-back deck which became an Eads trademark.

Contracts were awarded in mid-1862 for two vessels — *Osage* and *Neosho* — to be launched within a month of each other in early 1863. They were laid down soon after the contract was signed on May 18. *Osage* was launched on

January 13, and *Neosho* followed on February 18.

Both were built by Eads at his Union Iron-works in Carondelet, Missouri. Machinery was supplied by the Fulton Ironworks of St Louis. When launched they drew only 3 feet, so an extra half-inch of iron plating was added to the deck.

The turret, mounted right forward, was a modified Ericsson type which had a 300-degree field of fire. Slight modifications in service were needed to the recoil system which initially jammed the turret. At first only a single wooden structure was carried just before the large paddle wheelhouse, but as time went on, more structures were added. The vessels, which proved unsuitable for rough weather or heavy duty, were used for supporting troops ashore in field operations.

Osage patrolled the Red River and took part in expeditions up the Black and Washita rivers in early March 1864. She also took part in the Red River expedition to Alexandria, Louisiana, from March 12 to the end of May. Earlier, during a trip off Memphis, *Osage* had been badly damaged by a large tree drifting in the rapid current, which swept away part of the deck structure and pilot house aft. She was almost out of control at the time, unable to maintain steerage way.

Osage transferred to the West Gulf Squadron on February 1, 1865, and took part in the attack on Spanish Fort. While stationed in a previously swept channel, Osage was struck by a mine on March 29. The vessel filled and settled rapidly, killing two of the crew and leaving some wounded. The wreck was raised and sold at public auctions, together with the ex-Confederates *Nashville, Calhoun,* and *Tennessee,* for $20,467.

Neosho served off Vicksburg and patrolled along the river on the lookout for raiding cavalry. On December 8, 1863, she and the gunboat *Signal* drove off a raiding party armed with artillery who were attacking the disabled transport *Henry Von Phul.*

She later took part in the Red River expedition which narrowly escaped disaster while trying to establish an army base in Texas. *Neosho* went out of commission in July 1865 and was sold to David Campbell in 1873 for $13,600.

Osage as first completed, clearly showing the turtleback deck and large armored wheelhouse aft. These vessels had an extremely shallow draft but could sometimes be difficult to control in a swift current.*

Ironclads

CSS *Albemarle*

Dimensions: 152ft x 34ft x 9ft. **Machinery:** Two horizontal non-condensing, engines geared to the propeller by four gear wheels. **Armament:** Two 8-inch rifles.

After the end of McCellan's peninsula campaign in Virginia, when Union forces seized Norfolk and Yorktown, a relative calm settled over the Virginian and Carolina waters. Although Union gunboats still actively patrolled the river and tidewaters and escorted the troop movements, the tidewater areas tended to belong to neither side.

A similar situation existed at Albemarle Sound in North Carolina. Union garrisons were at Beaufort, which was the base used by the Wilmington blockading force and vessels supporting New Bern, Washington, and Plymouth. Only a small force of gunboats was available to patrol and support the Union troops, but 1863 was a relatively quiet period in the area, with most of the effort being devoted to sealing off Wilmington from the ever-active blockade runners.

This fairly quiet situation started to change in 1864, and fresh efforts by Confederate forces, such as their attack on New Bern in February, were nearly successful.

Confederate shipbuilding was also under way at several of the newly created inland sites, which, in spite of limited resources, poor transportation, and shortage of skilled workers, were to produce a number of desperately needed warships. Eighteen ironclads were laid down in these yards by the end of 1862 but not all were completed.

In North Carolina contracts were awarded to Gilbert Elliott and William P. Martin to build two ironclads and a wooden gunboat, but only one — the ironclad *Albemarle*, built at Edwards

Ferry — was finished. Elliott was an engineer who conceived the idea, and he also acted as agent for Martin who was based in Elizabeth City.

When New Bern, Plymouth, and much of the surrounding waters fell to Union forces, the local ironclad program had to be changed. A new contract dated April 16, 1862 was agreed on, which gave the contractors a free hand in selecting a suitable site for an ironclad. As the local military situation settled down, revised contracts were put out in September. These identified specific sites for building two vessels with a completion date in March 1863.

In spite of careful planning, it was to be a slow process, as all manner of unforeseen delays occurred. Construction was not even started until January 1863, so to speed things up John L. Porter was appointed to supervise the work. He arrived at the yard near Halifax on the Edwards Ferry River, and found a cornfield with none of the usual shipbuilding facilities available. Despite this, work was started but progress was slow. One reason for this was that Porter allowed Elliott to hire men by the day. After a year, Porter was replaced by Commander James W. Cooke, who brought extra men and equipment to hurry things along.

Cooke overcame the shortage of iron by collecting every scrap available from local farms, and he kept in close touch with the ordnance suppliers at Richmond and the Charendon Foundry at Wilmington to ease things along.

When completed *Albemarle* would have a modified hull form (produced by Porter) that allowed the vessel to float in only 6 feet of water. This was achieved by giving the vessel a

flat bottom and a flared side in place of the knuckle — a design usually associated with Confederate ironclads built for service on shallow waters.

She had an octagonal shield 60 feet long which was covered with two layers of 2-inch iron plating. The prow, strengthened for ramming, was plated with 2-inch iron tapered to a point.

Service aboard was not comfortable, as water constantly trickled down the inside walls. In fact, the crew usually slept ashore, leaving only a few on board to stand watch. *Albemarle's* men lived in a shed, but other Confederate ironclads chose alternative accommodation. *Tennessee's* men, for instance, lived on a barge moored alongside.

News of the ironclads' progress was supplied to Union forces by Michael Cohen, who had fled likely service in the Confederate Army. As the iron plating was being attached to the vessel in June and July, the local US Navy commanding officer, Lt. Cdr. C.W. Flusser, requested additional help but without success; Union ironclads drew too much water to enter the sound.

By the end of 1863 extra vessels were sent to Plymouth which was being threatened with attack by combined Confederate forces, and mines were laid at the mouth of the Roanoke River.

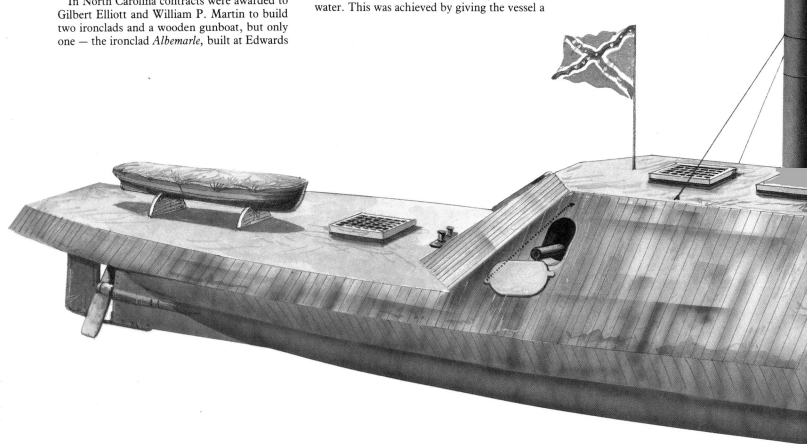

Toward the end of March the water level in the river began to fall, and although *Albemarle* was not quite finished, it was thought safer to send her downriver to Hamilton where the work could be completed. On the 17th, with men still working on her, she cast off. *Albemarle* towed a flat boat carrying a portable forge. This was soon needed to repair her machinery — a job that took six hours.

Next, the rudder head broke. Once repaired, Cooke turned the vessel around and ran stern first down the river to slow up the vessel. He also dragged chains from the bows which made it easier to steer.

Albemarle was able to get over the obstructions at Thoroughfare Gap, placed there by Union forces, and as she passed Warren's Neck, a Federal fort opened fire but caused no damage. In the gloom she now came upon two Union gunboats steaming up the river. These were *Miami* and *Southfield* (a converted ferryboat) and were lashed together. Flusser's plan was to ram the *Albemarle* and fight at close quarters.

Cooke realized what was intended, so ran up to the south shore, turned into the middle of the stream and steamed full speed at his entangled enemies, striking *Miami* a passing blow and plunging his beak deep into *Southfield*'s hull. *Albemarle*'s engines were immediately reversed but the chain plates of the ram's forward deck became lodged in the frame of the sinking gunboat and she was dragged down with her victim until torrents of water started to pour through her gunports.

As *Southfield* came to rest on the bottom, *Albemarle* pulled free and bobbed back on an even keel. Meantime, *Miami* was pouring in a furious fire, but without effect, as the shells harmlessly bounced off the ironclad. In fact,

one shell landed back on *Miami*'s deck and killed Flusser. The Union vessel then broke off the action and retired, pursued by *Albemarle* who was unable to keep up with the speeding gunboat.

Now that the Union vessels were cleared from the sound, *Albemarle* set about helping the Confederate troops to recapture any Union strongholds. On the 18th Plymouth fell.

The Confederates planned to recapture New Bern sixty miles away at the mouth of the Neuse River. As the ironclad in the Neuse was aground and could not be refloated, it was decided to use *Albemarle*, although it meant that she would have to take a tortuous route past Union defenses.

On May 5 she started out on her hazardous journey accompanied by a former army transport CSS *Bombshell*. During the afternoon they were confronted by a force of Union warships — *Miami*, *Mattabesett*, and *Sassacus*. In the ensuing fierce action, *Albemarle* received some damage to a gun and funnel, and was rammed by the *Sassacus*. But in the mêlée the Confederate put the gunboat boilers out of action and *Sassacus* drifted away.

Albemarle now retired up the Roanoke River for repairs to her funnel, as the damage had seriously reduced her speed. While under repair, and surrounded by a log boom, she was attacked and sunk on the night of October 27/28, 1864 by Lt. W.B. Cushing using a picket boat fitted with a spar torpedo. She was later raised and towed to Norfolk Navy Yard by the *Ceres*, arriving on April 27, 1865. *Albemarle* was sold in October 1867 to J.N. Leonard & Co. for $3200, having originally cost $79,944.

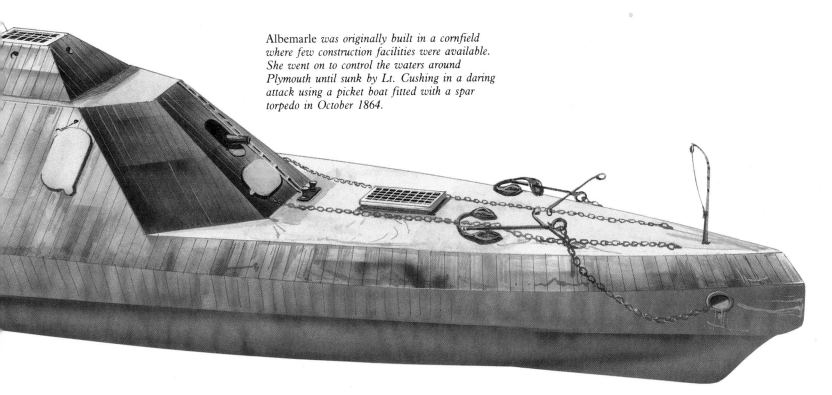

Albemarle *was originally built in a cornfield where few construction facilities were available. She went on to control the waters around Plymouth until sunk by Lt. Cushing in a daring attack using a picket boat fitted with a spar torpedo in October 1864.*

CSS *Jackson (Muscogee)*

Dimensions: 175ft x 35ft.

During 1863, increased activity in the Confederate ironclad program caused new sites to be established. Not all of these were good locations because some had no rail links and all were hindered by the constant lack of materials and skilled workmen.

Jackson was built at a Columbus yard during 1863 – 64. Great delay was experienced with the armor, which was only delivered just before her destruction. Problems arose at launching and she remained incomplete up to the end of the war, when she was sunk.

CSS *Savannah*

Dimensions: 150ft x 34ft x 14ft (12ft 6in). **Machinery:** Low pressure developing only 15 pounds. **Speed:** 6.5 knots. **Armament:** Two 7-inch Brooke single-banded rifles and two 6.4-inch Brooke double-banded rifles. **Crew:** 171.

By the fall of 1862, eighteen ironclads had been laid down in the increasing number of small yards which had been opened, often up winding rivers of shallow depth accessible only to riverboats of shallow draft. Although this was taken into account when ordering the new ironclads (often built with flat bottoms), they were still greatly handicapped by having a draft of anything from 8 to 12 feet, which restricted their use in rivers that were often low. To help move craft over very shallow bars, large, empty, wooden drums called "camels" were sometimes lashed alongside to create buoyancy. However, these were not available when the *Neuse* and *Missouri* needed shifting, so they were destroyed near their bases.

As the ironclad building program expanded in 1863, construction of *Savannah* began in her namesake city by H.F. Willink of Galveston. Ready in June, she was transferred to the Confederate Navy on the 30th under Flag Officer W.W. Hunter. She remained with the squadron and was burnt to avoid capture on

December 21, 1864, when General Sherman's army entered Savannah. Union forces had entered the city earlier and had reached the river bluff at 11 a.m., opening fire on the *Savannah* which was anchored off Screven's Ferry. Soon their fire began to take effect, nearly every shot striking the stationary vessel; one even plunged down the funnel, but it failed to explode. As night fell, the crew left the vessel and set her on fire. She blew up at 11.30 p.m. with a terrific explosion that could be heard for miles and lit up the countryside. *Savannah*'s deep draft had prevented her from going above the city to help in its defense at a critical time. She was the last vessel in the squadron to be destroyed.

Jackson

The Savannah squadron had included the floating battery *Georgia*, which could not move under her own power and had to be moored to a log crib so that, by warping the vessel, she could train a broadside down either channel of the Savannah River. Three gunboats and two tenders completed the squadron and much reliance had been placed upon the *Savannah*, completed after the *Atlanta* was captured. *Georgia* was sunk and the gunboats set alight when the city fell.

Savannah was lost, not to sea power, but to an army coming in from the rear. Many Union ironclads, that would have been useful elsewhere, were tied down in tiresome blockade duty off the cities of Charleston and Savannah.

CSS *Wilmington*

Dimensions: 224ft x 42ft 6in x 9ft 6in.
Armament: Two guns.

Designed by John Porter, *Wilmington* was a fast, light-draft, double-casemate vessel laid down at Wilmington, North Carolina, and built during 1863–64.

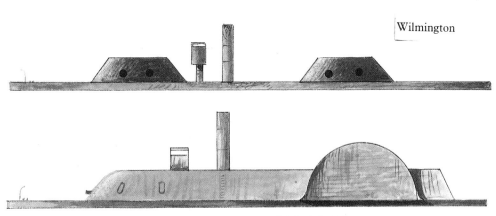

Wilmington

Savannah

She had twin engines, each driving an 8-foot diameter screw. Four boilers supplied the steam, and a single funnel rose above the deck between the two fixed rounded casemates near each end of the vessel. These each contained a single gun which fired through one of three ports of the casemate wall.

Wilmington was greatly delayed through lack of materials, and serious outbreaks of yellow fever in the city which forced the workers to flee the area until the scare was over.

The vessel was destroyed on the stocks when the city fell to Union forces.

CSS *Mobile*

The loss of the *Arkansas* in the west had been a serious blow to the Confederates, made worse by the capture of New Orleans and the destruction of naval forces, including the unfinished *Eastport*. The rivers were now open to invasion and every effort was made to replace the lost vessels.

The *Mobile*, a wooden sidewheel gunboat armed with four guns, had been ordered to Yazoo City for conversion into an ironclad. A budget of $300,000 had already been set aside so that a large sidewheel ironclad could also be built there. Through a mix-up her armor was delayed and unsuccessful efforts were made to get it from Columbiana. As the Union forces were advancing up the Yazoo River, the unfinished vessel was destroyed.

USS *Ozark*

Displacement: 578 tons. **Dimensions:** 180ft x 50ft x 5ft. **Armor:** 6 inches on turret, 2.5 inches on sides and 1.25 inches on deck. **Machinery:** Four engines driving two screws; coal capacity 100 tons. **Speed:** 2.5 knots. **Armament:** Two 11-inch Dahlgren smoothbores in the forward turret; by summer 1864, three 9-inch and one 10-inch Dahlgren smoothbores were mounted in the open in exposed positions. **Crew:** 120.

Ozark, like the never completed *Sandusky* class, was a single-turreted vessel designed for river service. She had a large turret, with an inside diameter of 20 feet, forward surmounted by an armored pilot house and a substantial deck house aft to provide extra quarters for officers and crew. The additional heavy guns mounted outside the turret were all on pivots and very exposed to Confederate fire from the heavily-wooded river banks.

The contract was awarded on May 14, 1862, to George C. Bestor of Peoria, Illinois, who subcontracted the hull to Hambleton, Collier & Co. of Mound City. Machinery was supplied by Charles W. McCord from his Franklin Foundry at St Louis, Missouri. Extra work increased the original price of $215,676 by a little over $9000.

The designed speed was for 9 knots in still water, but 2.5 or 3 was the best the vessel could manage. However, her low draft enabled her to penetrate extremely shallow parts of the river.

She was launched on February 18, 1863, and commissioned the following February, ready to take part in the Red River expedition. This was part of the unconventional war on the western rivers and far removed from the normal actions played out on the high seas and along the coasts.

Union warships operating along the rivers were kept under constant pressure from Confederate forces who would suddenly turn up along the banks, often with artillery, and open accurate fire on any unsuspecting vessel. The small ironclad gunboats, like their unarmored wooden counterparts, shared the dangers, sometimes with heavy losses. They also had to contend with the rapidly increasing trade in cotton from the South, which would change hands for much-needed manufactured goods from the North. Cotton purchased for a few cents in the South went for much more in the North and returned a huge profit. In fact, more cotton reached the North this way than reached England through the exploits of the blockade runners.

During the summer of 1863, Lincoln's government became concerned over the exploits of Napoleon III in Mexico, where he was about to establish an empire with his brother-in-law Maximilian on the throne. It was decided to organize a show of force in Texas, so troops were ordered there, but the plan changed when it was decided to move against the Texas coast. The outcome of this was the ill-fated attack at Sabine Pass.

When the plan to invade Texas was later revised in 1864, it was decided to attack via the Red River. The Union Army under Banks was to move against Shreveport with the aid of a large force of gunboats, including *Ozark*. By March, all was ready, but heavy rains delayed the departure. Meantime, Porter had assembled a force of fifteen ironclads and gunboats. Now joined by more troops from Sherman's command, the army moved and captured the first obstacle, Fort de Russy, a few miles below Alexandria. Hastening on in an attempt to head off the retreating Confederate forces, they arrived in time to see the last of the enemy transports heading up the river.

Banks pressed on with the gunboats, moving with great difficulty up the river and through the rapids on April 7. In a few days the warships and the army met up at Springfield. However, Banks was defeated at Pleasant Hill and forced to retire. The gunboats followed.

The river, which should normally have risen at that time of year, had fallen instead, stranding twelve gunboats above the rapids. Plans to destroy the boats to stop them falling into enemy hands were shelved when the army came to the rescue. They built a massive dam, which was the inspiration of Lt. Col. Joseph Bailey, an engineering officer. Porter was not impressed, but luckily reason prevailed and construction started. Trees were felled and sunk in the stream facing upriver, while mills and

houses were torn down to add to the rapidly growing structure that now fully occupied 3000 troops.

When the dam broke at one point, Porter ordered the nearest boats to go through quickly. By May 12, when the dam had been strengthened to hold enough water, a passage was made and the rest of the boats succeeded in getting away.

Ozark continued on patrol in the area until taken out of service in July 1865. She was sold on November 29, 1865.

USS *Sandusky*

Displacement: 479 tons. **Dimensions:** 170ft x 50ft x 5ft. **Armor:** 6 inches on turret, 1.25 inches on sides. **Machinery:** Two engines of the standard Western type, driving four 6ft 6-in diameter screws; coal capacity 150 tons. **Speed:** As designed, 9 knots in still water. **Armament:** Two 11-inch Dahlgren smoothbores. **Crew:** 100.

The contract for *Sandusky* and her sister *Marietta* was signed on May 16, 1862. Andrew

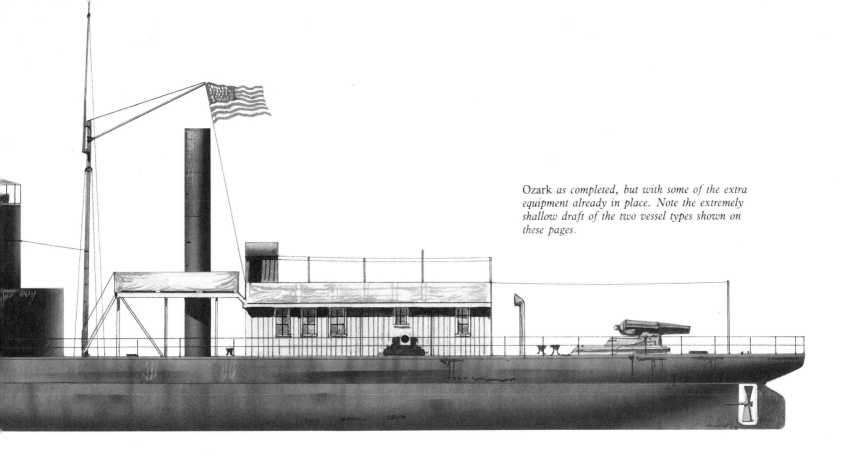

Ozark as completed, but with some of the extra equipment already in place. Note the extremely shallow draft of the two vessel types shown on these pages.

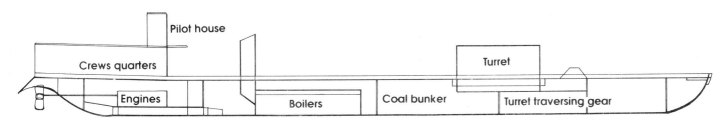

Pilot house

Crews quarters

Engines

Boilers

Coal bunker

Turret

Turret traversing gear

Tomlinson, Andrew Hartupee, and Samuel Morrow were responsible for the hull and machinery. Both vessels were launched in early 1865 and completed in December 1865, finally being accepted in April 1866.

The vessels were designed by the contractors, but during construction numerous changes were made by the navy which added to the delay. They were planned with a deck house aft surmounted by the bridge and carried the cylindrical turret forward. A small pilot house stood just forward of the bridge, and two tall smokestacks, common to Mississippi riverboats, completed the outfit. Reports during construction frequently mentioned the need for more workers.

The original contract price for *Sandusky* was $188,000 but the final cost was $235,039, which included two allowances for extra work, one in April 1865 for $10,000, and the second in January 1867 for $37,039. She was sold in 1873 to David Campbell at Mound City for $18,000. *Marietta* was sold to the same buyer for $16,000.

Sandusky as originally designed.

Later the pilot house may have been moved to the top of the turret. She had a flat base, three fore-and-aft bulkheads, two in the stern, and seven athwartship. Sandusky and her sister Marietta were driven by quad screws 7 feet in diameter operating directly under the fantail.

USS *Dictator*

Displacement: 4438 tons. **Dimensions:** 312ft x 50ft x 20ft 6in. **Armor:** 15 inches on turret, 6 inches on hull sides, and 12 inches on the pilot house. **Machinery:** Two vibrating lever engines driving a single 21ft 6in-screw, developing about 1000 hp. **Speed:** 9 knots, but usually 6. **Armament:** Two 15-inch Dahlgren smoothbores. **Crew:** 174.

The huge monitors *Dictator* and *Puritan* were near-sisters, and in this type of vessel the Navy Department was looking for a true ocean-going craft. As designed, they were to have had the extremely high speed of 16 knots, combined with a large radius made possible by a coal capacity of 1000 tons, but experience showed she could carry only half this amount.

When contracted for in the summer of 1862, *Dictator* and *Puritan* were among the largest warships built during the Civil War and were only equalled by the later *Dunderberg* and *Kalamazoo* classes.

With the initial success of the *Monitor* in March 1862, contracts were awarded by the Navy Department for a great many vessels of that type during the summer, and work was spread throughout the North.

Of all the plans considered during that summer, the *Dictator* and *Puritan* were the most favored by Ericsson. His partners, however, were alarmed at his interest in this project, as they feared his efforts would directly oppose their own.

The Navy Department originally wanted these two units to carry two turrets, but eventually Ericsson won his argument for fitting only one. The massive single turret weighed 500 tons and had an inside diameter of 25 feet. The armoring of this structure was unique, being made up of an inner cylinder of four layers of 1-inch plate separated by a 5-inch gap from the other cylinder, which was made up of six layers of 1-inch plate. Curved segments of iron were fitted into the space between.

The original overhang of the first *Monitor* was considerably reduced, as experience showed that the wave action along the joint between the upper and lower hulls would create a dangerous weakness; later that year the *Monitor* would sink through just this reason. Overhang was cut down to 4 feet but Ericsson still felt that this overhang reduced the effect of rolling. The hull section here was also given finer lines.

Freeboard was 2 feet and the armor, made up of six 1-inch plates, was 6 feet deep and mounted on 42 inches of wooden backing. The weight of armor was estimated at 500 tons. It was once considered plating the turret with 24 inches of iron, but it was found that 15 inches would give adequate protection.

Three immense blowers were installed, two for ventilating the ship and one for the engine-room. Air was drawn in through the top of the turret and an air trunk aft.

Ericsson excelled himself with the machinery, which was planned to develop 5000 horsepower! The cylinders were 8 feet 4 inches in diameter and supplied with steam from six large Martin boilers which, when filled with water, weighed 700 tons.

In 1871 the idea of installing compound engines to save fuel and space was rejected. Coal consumption at full power was about 140 tons per day.

Some likely problems became apparent during *Dictator*'s construction. One was the strength of the bearings used to support the massive 19-inch diameter main shaft. This was later found worn down 3/8-inch after a twenty-mile voyage, thus forcing the monitor to return to port when she was due to join the fleet before Fort Fisher.

Another weakness which could have ended in disaster was the narrow space between the deck and the boilers through which the tiller ropes ran. Once, during a severe storm, these ropes parted and it became necessary to draw the fires so that a repair party could go in. (It was not possible for the men to work in such a confined space with steam up.) During the time it took to make the repairs, heavy seas swept continuously over the *Dictator*, submerging her decks and leaving only the turret, funnel, and light bridge above the swirling water.

The tugs sent along as escort proved useless, one of them almost running into the wallowing giant. Fortunately, there was sufficient steam left in the monitor's boilers to move her ahead, thus narrowly avoiding disaster.

Dictator was laid down on August 16, 1862, launched on December 26, 1863, and commissioned in November 1864. Ericsson subcontracted the hull and machinery to the Delamater Ironworks, New York. The vessel was sold in 1883 for $40,250, after spending thirteen years laying idle, and having originally cost $1,393,566.

The *Dictator* could not be viewed as a total success, being less buoyant than intended.

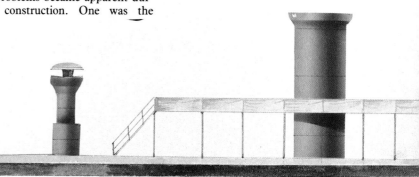

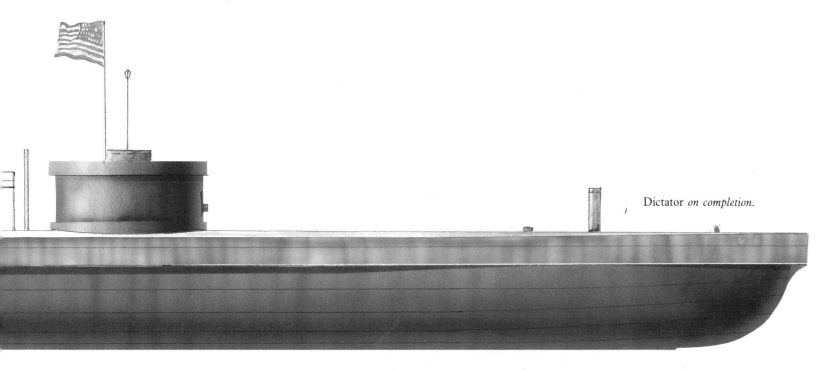

Dictator *on completion.*

However, she was a good sea boat. Many felt that she would be no match for a typical battleship of the period, so she reverted to a coastal defense role where her deep draft seriously hampered her effectiveness. Even so, she would still have been a formidable craft to tackle.

USS *Puritan*

Displacement: 4912 tons. **Dimensions:** 340ft x 50ft x 21ft. **Armor:** 15 inches on turret, 6 inches on sides, and 12 inches on the pilot house. **Machinery:** Same as *Dictator*, but driving twin screws.

Puritan was laid down in 1863 and launched on July 2, 1864, but never completed, being broken up in 1874.

Ericsson wanted to install two 20-inch smoothbores in the huge single turret but problems in the manufacture of these massive weapons greatly added to the delay in completing this vessel. Work eventually ceased in 1865. The hull was built at the Continental Ironworks, and the machinery was supplied by Allaire Works of New York.

Later, under the guise of "repairs" to the original *Puritan*, a second large monitor was started in the 1870s. This subterfuge was carried out by the Navy Department because Congress would not vote funds for new construction and it was the only way of building up a respectable navy in spite of the politicians.

Bow view of Dictator *showing the clean hull lines.*

Puritan *as she would have appeared on completion.*

CSS *Stonewall*

Displacement: 1560 tons. **Dimensions:** 194ft x 31ft 6in x 15ft 8in. **Armor:** 4.5 inches thick on sides and 3.5 inches at ends; 4 inches on aft turret and 5.5 inches over bow gun; 24 inches of wood backing behind side armor. **Machinery:** Horizontal direct-acting Mazeline engines driving twin screws. Coal capacity 280 tons max. **Speed:** 10.8 knots. **Armament:** One 9-inch 300-pdr and two 70-pdr guns. **Crew:** 135.

In 1863 the Confederate Navy accepted an offer from Arman of Bordeaux to construct four sloops and two armored rams suitable for operations in the shallow waters of the Confederacy.

The rams were composite hulled with a complete armor belt. The 9-inch gun was housed forward firing directly ahead, with the two 70-pounders carried aft in a fixed turret. Twin rudders and screws made these vessels very maneuverable. Delivery was planned for the summer of 1864 when they could safely weather an Atlantic crossing.

Before completion, however, the French government stopped their sale to the Confederates. The vessels, now named *Sphinx (Stonewall)* and *Cheops*, were to be sold to Prussia and Denmark who were then at war with each other and desperate to increase their naval forces. Prussia purchased *Cheops*, which differed slightly from her sister, and named her *Prinz Adalbert*. She served in the German Navy until broken up in 1878.

Sphinx was sold to Denmark and renamed *Staerkodder*, but as the war had now ended, she was no longer needed so she was sold back to Arman who, by careful concealment, managed to sell her to the South.

Now named *Stonewall*, she sailed under Captain Page for the Confederates. Although shadowed in Spanish waters by the wooden frigates *Niagara* and *Sacramento*, the formidable *Stonewall* remained unchallenged by these wooden unarmored vessels.

By May, having weathered severe storms, Page successfully got the vessel as far as Cuba. Here he learned that the Civil War had ended, so he sold her to the Spanish Captain General to pay off the crew.

The vessel was handed over to the US authorities who later sold her to the Shogun of Japan, but when the vessel arrived at Yokohama in April 1868 she was seized by the Emperor's forces. Renamed *Koketsu*, she led the attack on the Shogun's stronghold at Hakodate in July 1869. Renamed *Adzuma* in 1881, she was removed from the effect list in 1888 but was used for many years as an accommodation ship.

CSS *North Carolina*

Displacement: 2750 tons. **Dimensions:** 224ft 6in x 42ft 6in x 16ft 3in. **Armor:** 4.5 inches on sides, 10 inches on turret face. **Machinery:** Lairds' horizontal direct-acting engines driving a single screw. **Speed:** 10.5 knots. **Armament:** Four 9-inch muzzle-loading rifle guns. **Crew:** 153.

In July 1861 Bullock contracted with Laird Brothers of Birkenhead to build two small turret ships of long range and shallow draft to enable them to operate up the Mississippi River, as well as at its mouth.

The two vessels, the second named *Mississippi*, were to be delivered early in 1863 but they were seized by Britain and added to the Royal Navy under the names of *Scorpion* and *Wivern*. They were well protected vessels but rolled heavily and steered badly because of small rudders and flat hull bottoms.

Below: Stonewall, *during her brief career with the Confederate Navy. Her captain was not happy with her performance but she led a varied life which lasted until the turn of the century.*

Right: *The massive broadside ironclad that North hoped to command upon completion.*

Bottom Right: HMS Wivern, *showing the raised bulwarks for better sea-keeping in the down position to enable the turrets to fire. She also had Coles' tripod masts which reduced the amount of rigging needed.*

Danmark (*Santa Maria*)

Displacement: 4747 tons. **Dimensions:** 270ft x 50ft x 19ft 6in. **Armor:** 4.5 inches amidships, 3.5 inches at ends. **Speed:** 8.5 knots. **Armament:** Twelve 8-inch and twelve 6-inch muzzle-loading rifles. **Crew:** 520.

Lieutenant North was sent to Europe to purchase ironclads early in the war. He contracted with Thompson of Glasgow to build a completely armored broadside frigate able to stow 700 tons of coal. This would enable the vessel to remain at sea for twenty days' continuous steaming, rivalling the USS *New Ironsides*.

Had this vessel entered Confederate service, she would have been their most powerful vessel, although it is likely that great problems would have been experienced in raising such a large crew. In addition, her deep draft would have prevented her from entering many of the southern harbors.

As the Confederate funds were low and they were $700,000 short on purchases, it was decided to sell her to Denmark who needed more ships for her war with Prussia. Renamed *Danmark*, she served until 1893.

CSS *Fredericksburg*

Displacement: About 700 tons. **Dimensions:** 188ft x 40ft 3in x 9ft 6in. **Armor:** 4 inches. **Armament:** One 8-inch rifle forward, one 11-inch smoothbore aft, and two 6.4-inch rifles on broadside.

Fredericksburg was an enlarged *Albemarle*-type built in 1862/63 at the navy yard set up at Rocketts, a suburb of Richmond, from designs of the Brooke/Porter type. She had the usual raised, sloping-sided casemate rising above the hull, but this time the roof was built of wood and not made up of the usual iron gratings. Later, iron bars replaced the wood, so that the vessel would be better protected against plunging fire. By November 1863, *Fredericksburg* was only awaiting her armament, although many delays had been experienced with procuring adequate supplies of iron for the armor, manufactured by the Tredegar Ironworks of Richmond, who also supplied the engines. Tredegar, in fact, were the most important suppliers to the Confederacy.

Ready in March 1864, this ironclad, under Commander T.R. Rootes, joined *Virginia II* and *Richmond*, which now formed the most powerful force the Confederate Navy ever assembled, and set into action. Unfortunately, they had only twenty miles of the James River to operate in above City Point, as General Butler's Union force had completely blocked the river by sinking hulks and laying mines.

Even so, this Confederate force was frequently in action against Federal forces and successfully tied down a powerful force of Union ironclads that would have been better employed at Charleston or Mobile.

Fredericksburg was in action at Trents Reach on June 21, 1864 and again in August when shore-based Union working parties constructing a canal were driven off. On the 16th an assault by Union forces was carried out against the outlying Confederate position at Chaffins Bluff in order to tie down Confederate troops badly needed in the Shenandoah Valley. After a bombardment that went on throughout the night and lasted eighteen hours, the ironclads drove off the Union forces, but not before the *Fredericksburg* crew experienced severe heat fatigue caused by the need to close down the vessel while in action. Later, sixty-one crew

reported sick, forty-seven being sent ashore to the hospital, thus worsening the lack of trained men needed to work the vessel.

By January 1865 heavy rains raised the level of the river and washed away part of the obstructions. It was decided to attack the reduced Union naval force, but owing to several days' delay, the attack was not made until the 23rd, by which time the Federal forces had been alerted.

In total darkness, *Fredericksburg*, the lightest ironclad of the trio, led the way, but *Virginia II* and *Richmond* both ran aground and *Fredericksburg* was forced to return to provide cover for the stranded ironclads. They eventually got free after being heavily bombarded.

With the evacuation of *Richmond* on April 3, 1865, *Fredericksburg* was set on fire and blown up the next day.

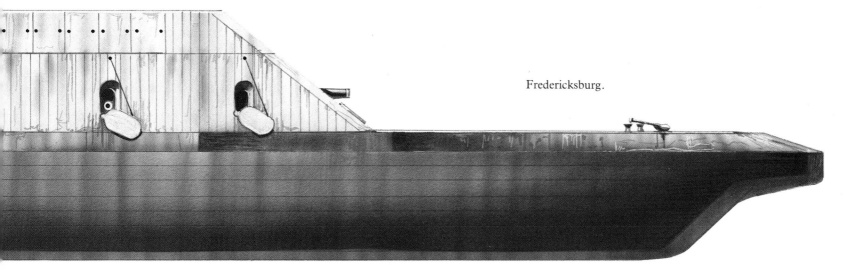

Fredericksburg.

USS *Miantonomoh*

Displacement: 3400 tons. **Dimensions:** 258ft 6in x 52ft 9in x 12ft 8in. **Armor:** 10 inches on turrets and 5 inches on sides. **Machinery:** Two back-acting horizontal engines in name ship and *Tonawanda;* two vibrating lever engines of Ericsson design in *Monadnock* and *Agamenticus.* All had twin screws. Coal capacity, 300 tons. **Speed:** 9 knots, except *Tonawanda*, which only achieved 6.5. **Armament:** Four 15-inch Dahlgren smoothbores.

In 1862 four more double-turreted monitors, larger than the *Onodaga*, were ordered from the designs of Lenthall. Like the preceding monitors, these had wooden hulls, which in this class, rapidly deteriorated.

Freeboard was increased to 2 feet and the overhang was done away with. Like the

Dictator, these were the only monitors fitted with a flying bridge. All four were built in Navy Yards, the first monitors so constructed.

Weight of broadside was 1800 pounds, but the rate of fire was slow — about one round every seven minutes. Turrets were 9 feet high and had an inside diameter of 23 feet, only 2 feet more than the *Monitor.*

The early plans called for Coles turrets, but in the 1862 version Ericsson turrets were stipulated.

Armor protection was worked into the funnel and ventilator. The former had a 10-inch thick band 9 feet tall and 10 feet in diameter, weighing 40 tons, built into the base. The pilot house had 10 inches of protection, stood 6 feet 4 inches high and was nearly 8 feet in diameter. This structure weighed 53 tons. Deck armor was 2 inches thick and weighed 350 tons. All in all they were well protected vessels.

The cost was to compare favorably with the single-turreted monitors of the later *Casco* class, although the *Miantonomoh*s were not subject to the expensive alterations carried out on the smaller vessels. *Miantonomoh* was the cheapest, costing $606,009. *Monadnock* cost $737,343, with *Tonawanda* reaching $806,502.

These vessels needed a crew of only 150, which clearly demonstrates the economy of personnel possible when compared to the smaller *Cairo* class river gunboats and the

relatively large sloops which needed 335 men. Two of the class made lengthy ocean cruises, the first monitors to do so: *Miantonomoh* to Europe, where she created a favorable impression and sparked a number of smaller copies for various navies, while *Monadnock* journeyed from the east coast to San Francisco. During this trip, made mostly under her own steam, the *Monadnock* encountered several severe storms. During one of exceptional violence, the tiller ropes were twice parted but the monitor was able to lay under control by using her twin screws until the rudder was back in use. A small set of canvas was carried briefly on a mast stepped on the forecastle.

The vessels were steady, rolling, at most, 7 degrees in a heavy sea. It was claimed that the guns could still have been worked with a 4-foot sea streaming across the deck. (Even in a normal sea, water constantly washed across the deck.)

Monadnock was the only vessel of this class to be completed in time to see service in the Civil War, and then only for the last nine months. Three were laid down in 1862, *Tonawanda* in 1863, and all were launched between March 1863 and May 1864.

Miantonomoh was built at New York with engines supplied by the Novelty Ironworks. *Tonawanda* was built at Philadelphia and engined by Merrick & Sons. *Agamenticus* was built at Portsmouth, and *Monadnock* was constructed at Boston; both were engined by Morris. All were broken up in 1874/75.

Miantonomoh *on completion.*
This class was a successful type
produced from the designs
of John Lenthall and Benjamin Isherwood.

USS *Kalamazoo*

Displacement: 5600 tons. **Dimensions:** 345ft 5in x 56ft 8in x 17ft 6in. **Armor:** 10 inches on turrets, 6 inches on sides, plus 3 inches on the deck. **Machinery:** Four horizontal direct-acting engines driving twin screws; coal consumption was an expected 80 tons per day at full power. **Armament:** Four 15-inch Dahlgren smoothbores.

Toward the end of 1863 it was decided to build four powerful double-turreted monitors capable of fighting their guns in a seaway. These craft were the largest warships, except for the solitary *Dunderberg*, to be ordered for the United States Navy during the Civil War, and this group would be the closest thing the US Navy would get to possessing true ocean-going battleships for the next thirty years. Not until the early 1890s and just prior to the war with Spain in 1898, would America have such vessels of extended ocean-cruising capabilities and armament in the shape of the *Oregon* class, *Maine*, and *Texas*.

The *Kalamazoo* class, consisting of *Shackamaxon*, *Passaconaway*, and *Quinsigamond*, had composite hulls designed by Benjamin F.

Dalano, and machinery of John Baird's design. Only in proposed speed — 10 knots — would they fall short, as many European ironclads of the period could reach 14 knots.

The hulls were plated with 6 inches of iron made up of two 3-inch plates backed by 30 inches of wood. The weight of this armor and supports was 800 tons. Three-inch thick armor was unusual in the United States, as American manufacturers were still experiencing problems in rolling plates thicker than 1 inch. The depth of side armor was 6 feet 9 inches.

Deck armor weighed 810 tons, almost the total displacement of the original monitor. This

plating was 3 inches thick laid over a 6-inch wooden deck. A further 3 inches of wood was laid on top of the plating, forming a deck. With the usual low freeboard and a 12-inch thick deck, these vessels were virtually solid from side to side. The smoke pipes were also heavily armored.

All four were constructed in navy yards. New York built the name ship, Philadelphia constructed *Shackamaxon*, *Passaconaway* came from the Portsmouth yard, while Boston built *Quinsigamond*.

Machinery was supplied by outside contractors, Delamater providing two sets, with Pusey

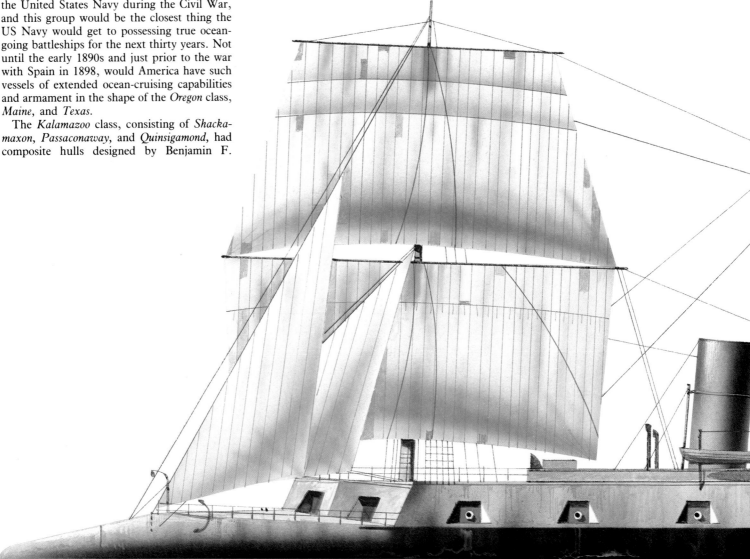

& Jones and Atlantic Ironworks building a set each. M.K. Moorhead of Pittsburgh supplied some of the armor.

Three were laid down in 1863 and one in 1864 but work progressed slowly. By the time it was decided not to complete these vessels, most of the parts contracted were almost ready. Costs were enormous. The machinery alone for *Kalamazoo* amounted to $590,000, and all cost just over $1 million, with *Shackamaxon* reaching $1,300,417.

While under construction, these craft gave the impression of great strength as their hulls were made up of a maze of cross trees and girders of great thickness. Construction was suspended in November 1865. After this their wooden hulls, made up of improperly seasoned timber and exposed to the elements, gradually rotted away until one, *Shackamaxon*, was broken up on the stocks in 1874, with the other three following in 1884.

USS *Dunderberg*

Displacement: 7060 tons. **Dimensions:** 377ft 4in x 72ft 10in x 21ft. **Armor:** 3.5 inches on sides and 4.5 inches on the casemate. **Machinery:** Two horizontal back-acting engines of 4500 hp driving a single screw; coal capacity 1000 tons. **Armament:** Two 15-inch and eight 11-inch Dahlgren smoothbores; later,

one 15-inch and one 11-inch were added to each broadside, and one 11-inch to each end. Four of the 11-inch weapons could traverse at the end ports. **Crew:** 590.

Dunderberg was designed by John Lenthall as a brigantine-rigged casemate ironclad with two turrets and a speed of 15 knots. However, the turrets were dropped and the final vessel had a low freeboard hull surmounted by a casemate. The sides sloped back at 35 degrees with six ports along each side only 4 feet 8 inches above water — two on each corner, two pointing ahead and two aft.

The hull was built up of heavy timbers with a massive 7 foot 6-inch thickness at the knuckle. Much unseasoned timber was used, which led to rapid deterioration. Her engines were designed by E. Smith and T. Main and constructed by Etna Ironworks.

Laid down in October 1862 and launched in July 1865, *Dunderberg* had a double bottom, a collision bulkhead, transverse and longitudinal watertight bulkheads, and a 50-foot solid oak ram. The 13-foot diameter funnel had armored gratings fitted to keep out debris. Armor weighed 1000 tons.

Shortage of materials meant that construction was slow and she was no longer needed. She was taken back by her builder, W.H. Webb of New York, who refunded $1,041,660 of the $1,250,000 spent on the vessel, and he sold her to France, where she served in the French Navy as *Rochambeau* until stricken in 1872 after serving in the Franco Prussian war of 1870.

Right Dunderberg *was one of the few major Civil War ironclad warships of the Union Navy that differed from the usual monitor principle; it bore a close resemblance to the numerous Confederate vessels, having a tall center casemate and low ends. The machinery of this huge vessel was built by John Roach who later fell foul of the authorities over his dealings in warships for the emerging US Navy of the 1870s and 1880s.*

USS *Lexington*

Displacement: 448 tons. **Dimensions:** 177ft 7in x 36ft 10in x 6ft maximum. **Armament:** In 1862 had two 32-pdr, 43-cwt, four 8-inch Dahlgren smoothbores; armament then varied during career.

Lexington was built at Pittsburgh in 1860 as a sidewheel freight and passenger steamer. She made only two trips between Pittsburgh and New Orleans before being laid up at Cincinnati, Ohio, and sold to the government in 1861. She formed part of a trio of converted steamers that eventually grew into a large fleet of vessels fighting along the Mississippi and its tributaries.

Commander John Rodgers had been loaned to the army to help them assemble a small fleet of gunboats they were anxious to acquire. Without authority Rodgers purchased three suitable vessels at Pittsburgh and Cincinnati. The three-year-old *Conestoga*, costing $16,000, was the smallest and fastest of the trio, having a speed of 12–14 knots against the current.

Lexington was relatively slow, able to make only 7 knots, while the four-year-old *A.O. Tyler* could make 8–10 knots. Rodgers agreed to pay $25,000 for *Lexington*, the newest boat, and $21,000 for *Tyler*, the oldest. He then contracted with Daniel Morton of Cincinnati to convert them into gunboats for $41,000. Rodgers reckoned that their true cost to the builders was $97,000.

The alterations were few in comparison with the changes made to vessels converted at a later date, but Rodgers had no guide to follow. Nonetheless, the results, despite shortcomings, were to his credit. The boilers and steam pipes were lowered into the hold, the superstructures were removed and high, 5-inch thick oak bulwarks were built all around the vessels to protect the crew from rifle fire, the sides were pierced to take the guns, and the decks were strengthened to take the additional weight of these heavy weapons.

As Rodgers had purchased the vessels and supervised their conversion without written orders — the army did not even know of their acquisition — there were considerable delays in payment for all the work, and many consequent headaches for Rodgers and the contractors.

When Rodgers made a progress report and request for funds to the Navy Department on June 8, he was informed that the department was responsible only for crews and guns. All requisitions had to go through the army, who responded quickly once the initial mix-up was sorted out. However, Rodgers received a severe rebuke for his actions from the Navy Department. Although this was correct naval procedure, it should be remembered that Rodger's unorthodox approach got these vessels into action more quickly than would otherwise have been possible.

The guns came from the Erie Ordnance Depot, but as no carriages were available, Rodgers had them made up at Cincinnati.

The Ohio waters now began to fall and there was a distinct danger that the vessel might be stranded at Cincinnati. Losing no time, Rodgers hired a local crew, purchased stores, and sent the still unfinished craft downriver to Cairo in the charge of civilian boatmen. In spite of these precautions, the flotilla was delayed until mid-July by low water at Louisville, and until August at New Albany, Indiana.

Rodgers used the time to obtain permanent crews for the gunboats but this proved difficult as the pay being offered by the navy was far lower than the river men could earn on steamboats. Many who did apply were not fit enough. Finding suitable pilots also caused problems, as they too could earn more piloting merchant vessels in the ever-changing rivers. Two were needed per boat, so to obtain them, Rodgers eventually agreed to pay $150 a month — three-fifths of what they would usually earn.

Work continued on the gunboats as they journeyed downriver, and they were as near ready as possible by August 9. By then the waters had risen enough to allow the vessels to leave New Albany, and they steamed up to the Cairo level on the 12th. All the officers were present but they still had only half the required number of ratings.

The boats suffered from poor workmanship, but there were other problems too. There was

insufficient paint available to finish painting *Lexington*, but even worse, *Tyler* had no protective iron bars over the boilers, and the lack of a fore and aft gangway meant walking over the top of them.

Lexington and *Tyler* quickly got into action engaging Confederate shore batteries, and later helped to take the important towns of Paducah and Smithland, Kentucky. In September, at the mouth of the Tennessee and Cumberland rivers, they helped stop a Confederate drive, thus saving Kentucky for the Union.

At Belmont they gave covering fire to Union troops silencing enemy batteries. Later, as the Union forces withdrew to their transports, a large force of Confederate troops was driven back by the gunboats at a critical time.

In February gunboats then attacked Fort Henry which guarded the South's heartland. Troops should have been present but heavy rain delayed them and the gunboats forced the fort to surrender.

Later, at Shilo, the gunboats saved the Union Army from defeat when threatened with a Confederate attack in large numbers. As the Southern troops got to within 150 yards of Union lines, the gunboats fired over the heads of their own troops and held off the attack. *Lexington* continued to serve on the Tennessee River and the Mississippi before Vicksburg. She took part in the Red River campaign in April 1864. She was sold in August 1865 to Thomas Scott & Woodburn at Mound City, Illinois, for $6000.

Tyler led a full and active career, first serving with the army, then transferring to the navy. She fought a running battle on the narrow confines of the Yazoo River with the powerful Confederate ironclad Arkansas.

USS *Tyler*

Displacement: 575 tons. **Dimensions:** 180ft x 45ft x 6ft. **Armament:** In 1862 had one 32-pdr, 43-cwt, and six 8-inch, 63-cwt guns; armament then varied.

Tyler was built in 1857 at Cincinnati and purchased by the army in June 1861 to form part of the Western Flotilla. She transferred to the navy in October 1862 and was subsequently in action at Belmont covering the withdrawal of Union forces. She later fought at Forts Henry and Donelson and Pittsburgh Landing, where she helped drive back superior Confederate forces. When the ironclad *Carondolet* was damaged, and the ram *Queen of the West* returned,

Tyler alone faced the Confederate ironclad *Arkansas*. After a running fight down the Yazoo River, *Tyler* was able to reach the safety of the Union fleet before Vicksburg.

She later took part in several expeditions up the Yazoo, as well as serving on the Mississippi. She was sold in August 1865 to David White at Mound City for £6000.

The 572-ton *Conestoga* was part of the Union Army's Western Gunboat Flotilla before being transferred to the Navy Department in October 1862. Armed with four 32-pdr, 43-cwt guns, she helped capture the half-finished, powerful Confederate ironclad *Eastport*. On the night of March 8, 1864, she collided with the *General Price* off Bondurant Point and sank immediately.

Lexington was one of the trio of converted river steamers which formed the basis of the army's Western Flotilla and performed much valuable service. Although at first under army control, they were officered by the navy.

73

Left: *The Confederate warship* Patrick Henry. *Later she became a school ship for midshipmen who were needed in the rapidly expanding Confederate Navy.*

Right: *The ex-merchant ship* Varuna *as she appeared after being taken over by the Navy. She was sunk at New Orleans.*

CSS *Patrick Henry*

Displacement: 1300 tons. **Dimensions:** 250ft x 34ft x 13ft. **Armament:** Varied. In March 1861 had ten guns; in July 1861 had two 10-inch pivot in broadside; in March 1862 had six guns; from November 1863 had four guns. She carried a mixture, with six 8-inch and one 64-pdr, as well as two 32-pdr. **Crew:** 150.

Patrick Henry was a sidewheel merchant steamer which ran between New York and Richmond, Virginia. Formerly known as the *Yorktown*, this brigantine-rigged steamer was built in New York in 1859 for the Old Dominion Steamship Line. She was seized by the state authorities when Virginia seceded on April 17, 1861, and turned over to the Confederate Navy. At the time of her seizure she was anchored in the James River. The lightly protected warship was immediately taken into the James River Squadron and served near Mulberry Island to help protect the right flank of the Confederate position on the peninsula.

In September and December she made brief forays down the James River and fired at long range at the Union gunboats. Later, during the battle between the *Merrimack* and the wooden Union vessels on March 8, *Patrick Henry* approached the stranded *Congress*, assuming that the Union vessel had surrendered. As she neared it, she came under accurate fire from supporting Union vessels and was driven off after receiving a shell in her steam chest which killed four men.

With the surrender of Norfolk on May 10, 1862, the Confederate force retired up the James River, repulsing pursuing Union vessels on the way. As the Confederate Government needed young officers for its growing navy, the *Patrick Henry* was chosen as a school ship, taking on its first class of fifty midshipmen in October 1863. Numbers later increased to sixty, with thirteen teachers in attendance.

Sometimes she took part in action with the midshipmen on board.

On April 2 her career ended when she was set on fire after Richmond was evacuated. Her cadets guarded the public treasure of $500,000 which was destined for the new government seat of Danville. After this they were each given $40 in gold to help them reach their homes.

USS *Signal*

Displacement: 190 tons. **Dimensions:** 150ft x 30ft x 1ft 10in. **Armament:** Two 30-pdr Parrott rifles, four 24-pdr howitzers and two 12-pdr Dahlgren rifle howitzers.

Signal was a wooden sternwheel steamer built in 1862 and purchased in September 1862 from Thomas and Andrew Sweeney for $18,000 at St Louis, Missouri. She was in action during October heading down to Vicksburg. First used as a dispatch vessel which was sniped at from the shore, an answering salvo from her own guns usually cleared the riverbanks. She served in numerous expeditions that eventually forced Vicksburg to surrender, and then continued her patrolling duties.

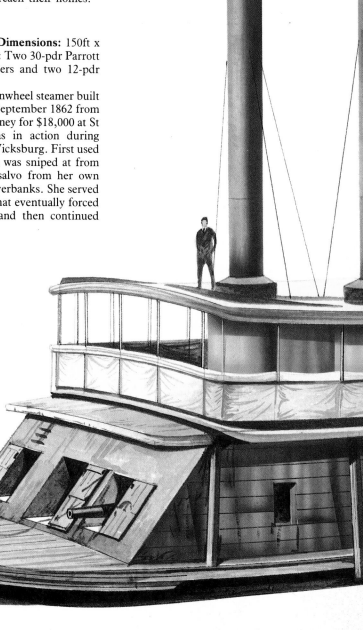

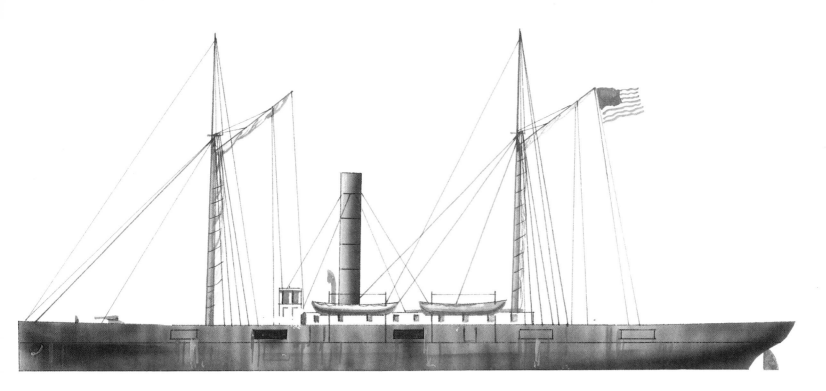

Early in May 1864 she became involved in an action with Confederate forces while escorting two transports. During the mêlée one of the transports ran aground and blocked the channel. Soon *Signal* was disabled and also ran aground, where she was set on fire to avoid capture.

USS *Varuna*

Displacement: 1300 tons. **Dimensions:** 218ft x 34ft 8in x 18ft 3in. **Armament:** Six 8-inch, 63-cwt guns, and two 8-inch, 5-cwt guns, plus two 30-pdr Parrott rifles.

Varuna was a large-screw steamer intended for merchant service between New York and New Orleans. She was laid down in early 1861 and purchased for the navy from C. Mallory and C.S. Bushnell for $127,000. An extra $34,947 was spent to fit her out for naval service.

She was to have escorted the ironclad *Monitor*, but was then quickly transferred to the newly formed West Gulf Blockading Squadron which was about to attack New Orleans.

She took part in the run past the forts on a gloomy April 24, and a fierce battle ensued. The Confederates put up a determined resistance, sending down flaming fire rafts that were pushed away by the crews of the Union vessels as soon as they came into contact.

The ram *Governor Moore* of the Louisiana State Navy was heavily shelled at the start of the battle, but dashed upstream in pursuit of the *Varuna* which was the fastest of the Union warships.

Varuna was rammed twice by the *Governor Moore* and the cottonclad *Stonewall Jackson*. During this fierce action the Confederates were unable to depress their guns sufficiently to fire at the Union vessel, so they blew a hole in their own bow and used it as a gun port.

Varuna continued the unequal struggle but rapidly filled with water, so she was run aground and abandoned. She was the only major loss to the fleet during the run past the forts.

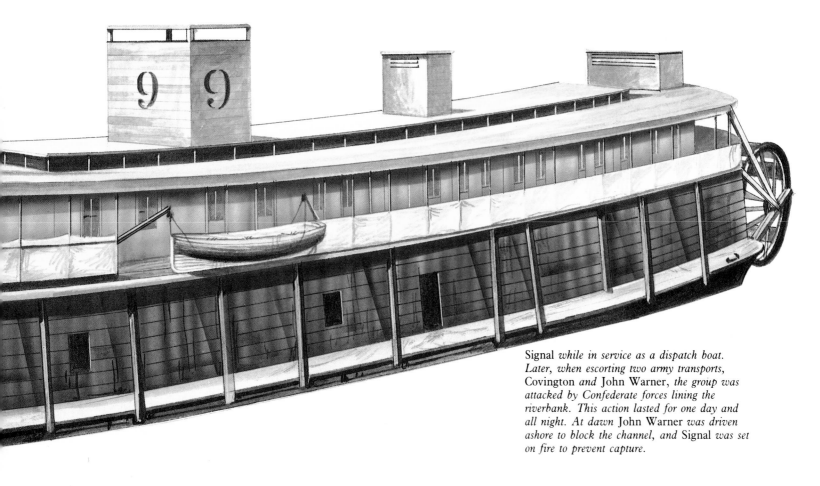

Signal while in service as a dispatch boat. Later, when escorting two army transports, Covington *and* John Warner, *the group was attacked by Confederate forces lining the riverbank. This action lasted for one day and all night. At dawn* John Warner *was driven ashore to block the channel, and* Signal *was set on fire to prevent capture.*

75

USS *Fuchsia*

Displacement: 240 tons. **Dimensions:** 98ft 3in x 21ft 9in x 8ft. **Armament:** One 20-pdr Parrott rifle and two 24-pdr howitzers. In March 1864 one 12-pdr rifle and two more 24-pdr rifles were added.

Fuchsia was a wooden-screw steam tug built in 1863 by Fincourt at New York. She was sold to the Navy Department by Henry Ward for $30,000 in June 1863, and commissioned in August. *Fuchsia* was sent to the Washington Navy Yard to join in patrol duty being carried out by the Potomac Flotilla. She served on the Potomac, Rappahannock, Piankatank, Tappahannock, Curitoman, and St Mary rivers, attempting to stop any illegal contraband. On one occasion she sent ashore a landing party to seize two men who were well-known blockade-runners.

She ascended the Piankatank River in early March 1864 in search of the army tug *Titan* previously captured by the Confederates. Upon finding the burnt out hulk of the tug, members of *Fuchsia*'s crew completed her destruction by destroying the boilers. *Fuchsia* remained in the same waters for the entire war but was frequently in action against Confederate forces ashore. She was sold in September 1865 to N.L. & G. Griswold for $11,000.

USS *Sibyl*

Displacement: 176 tons. **Armament:** In June 1864 had two 30-pdr Parrott rifles and two 24-pdr; in July two more 24-pdr rifles were added. Later the number of smaller weapons was increased.

Sibyl, originally named *Hartford*, was built in 1863 at Cincinnati, Ohio, and sold to the Navy Department in April 1864 for $30,000. She was a wooden sidewheel steamer typical of many seen on the river at the time. Heavy baulks of timber were added to the lower hull for protection. She was used primarily as a dispatch boat and for gathering information along the river.

She was sold at Mound City, Illinois, to R.J. Trunstall and A. Silver for $10,000. Renamed *Comet* in September, she continued to serve along the river until abandoned in 1876.

USS *Bibb*

Bibb was a wooden sidewheel steamer belonging to the US Coast Survey Department but employed by the Union Navy off Charleston where she served from November 1861 to June 1862. She was operating out of Port Royal Harbor in early 1863 when she was called to the aid of army transport, *Pilot Boy*, that had burst its boilers and was drifting. *Bibb* went in search, finding her about midnight, and eventually towed her the thirty miles or so back to base. Such accidents were all too common on the early steamers.

On March 17, 1865, while returning to Charleston after carrying out surveys on the bar, she struck a mine under the port bow. Although the mines were anchored low and a naval inshore steamer would not have struck one, *Bibb* was drawing her usual 10 feet. Fortunately, the heavy, rolling sponsons absorbed most of the impact, but the vessel was still damaged. Later she was beached for repairs.

USS *America*

Displacement: 100 tons. **Dimensions:** 111ft x 25ft x 12ft. **Armament:** One 12-pdr rifle and two 24-pdr smoothbores.

The racing schooner *America* is probably one of the most famous vessels in the world. The hotly contested America's Cup is named after her. She was also one of the finest sailing vessels ever created and a true credit to her designer and builders who helped keep the US in the forefront of sailing ship design.

Some years before 1850 it had been thought desirable by the Stevens brothers that an international yacht race between Britain and America should be held. It was not until the Great Industrial Exhibition of 1851 that the idea became a reality in London. An American merchant who was in London at the time suggested that an American schooner should compete against a British vessel of the same type.

The Stevens brothers quickly interested their friends in the idea and the resulting vessel was the graceful craft designed by George Steers, one of the world's leading designers, whose company, Hathorne & Steers, unfortunately went into liquidation in 1849. Steers was also to supervise the construction by William Brown.

The vessel had a sharp entry and was wider abaft the middle section, a feature common in Virginian pilot boats. The claims that she was the fastest American yacht of her period cannot be borne out as, through lack of time before her first contest with the British challenge, it was not possible to race her against fellow American yachts, but this in no way detracts from her performance.

She won the first British/American cup race in 1851. Just after Fort Sumter surrendered, she was brought back to America and sold to the Confederate Government for a reputed $60,000 — possibly for getting the Confederate agents Slidell and Mason over to Europe.

In June 1861 she took Lt. James North and Colonel E.C. Anderson to London to buy ships and weapons. She then became a blockade runner. In 1861 her name had been changed to *Memphis*.

She was discovered sunk by a boat expedition from USS *Ottawa* in Dunn's Lake, St Johns River, Florida, 147 miles from its mouth. She was purchased by a US prize court for $700 after being raised by the Federal Navy. She was then used as an armed schooner after being fitted out at Port Royal, South Carolina.

Memphis captured one prize in May 1863 while serving with the South Atlantic Blockading Squadron. Later she was transferred to the Naval Academy as a school ship where she continued until sold in June 1873. In 1921 the yacht was presented to the Navy Department by the Eastern Yacht Club of Marblehead, Maine, to be preserved as a relic.

The solidly built craft remained at Annapolis until 1942, when the hull collapsed under a heavy fall of snow. The hulk was broken up in 1945.

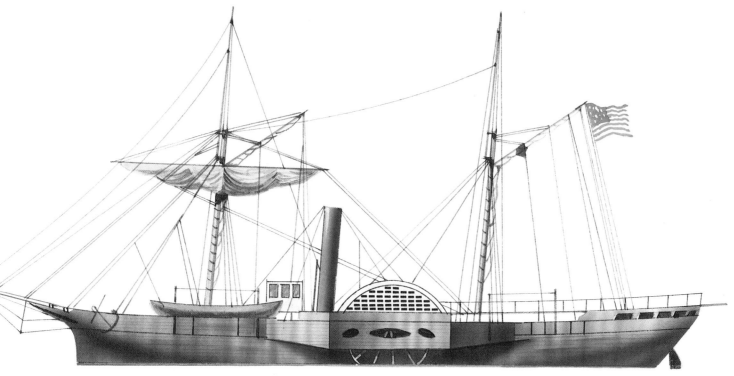

Top: Sibyl *was a typical sidewheel steamer commonly found trading on the western rivers and pressed into service by the navy.*

Above: *The coast survey vessel Bibb served the blockade off Charleston harbor. Hundreds of such craft were pressed into service by the Union to block up the escape routes from the South.*

Left: *One of the world's most famous and distinguished craft — the graceful racing schooner America, designed by George Steers.*

Far left: *The former tug Fuchsia served out a fairly uneventful career. Service on such craft was often long and tedious with no chance of seeing any action. Due to the shortage of officers, many of the small craft had specially appointed acting masters as their commanding officers.*

Gunboats

CSS *Governor Moore*

Displacement: 1215 tons. **Armament:** Two 32-pdr rifled guns. **Crew:** 93.

This vessel was formerly named *Charles Morgan*, after the founder of the Southern SS Company who owned her. The wooden side-wheel steamer was built at New York in 1854 as a schooner-rigged vessel fitted with a low-pressure, walking-beam engine.

In mid-January 1862 she was seized at New Orleans by Confederate Brigadier General Mansfield Lovell. Renamed after the Louisiana state governor, she was given a reinforced bow for ramming by adding two strips of rail-road iron along her length. Pine timber and a large number of cotton bales were added to protect the boilers, which stood well above the waterline.

She was the larger of two cottonclads owned by the state of Louisiana, who also operated them. She was captained by Lt. Beverly Kennon, who was serving without pay as a commander in the Louisiana Navy.

Governor Moore was part of the force that fought against the Union fleet attacking New Orleans. As she approached the oncoming enemy fleet, the cottonclad first had to free the disabled tug *Belle Alterine* before she could move on. However, she was hampered by lack of room in which to build up headway for ramming, so was forced to move along the east bank to the bend above the forts and then turn downstream. As she turned, the telegraph

steamer *Star* and the *Quitma* were set on fire at their berths by the passing Union vessels.

Once clear of the crossfire of the forts *Governor Moore* encountered the USS *Oneida* and *Cayuga*, who fired at the Confederate vessel from only a few feet away. A large frigate then loomed out of the haze of battle and fired a hail of shells from the howitzers in her tops, killing many men at the guns. Next came the *Pinola* on the port quarter, delivering a deadly broadside that killed five more of the crew.

Governor Moore had broken away from her antagonists and now sighted a large steamer — *Varuna* — pulling ahead of the Union fleet. Taking advantage of the dark background behind the vessels, *Governor Moore* bore down on the speeding craft. Eventually at close quarters, the two vessels poured deadly fire into each other and *Governor Moore* was able to ram *Varuna* twice near the gangway amidships, forcing the vessel aground. At that moment *Varuna* was rammed by the *Stonewall Jackson*.

As *Governor Moore* turned round to head back downstream, her decks were swept with gunfire from *Oneida*, forcing the Confederates to run their vessels aground just before the beached *Varuna*.

USS *Westfield*

Displacement: 822 tons. **Dimensions:** 215ft x 35ft x 13ft 6in. **Armament:** One 100-pdr Parrott rifle, one 9-inch Dahlgren smoothbore and four 8-inch, 63-cwt guns.

Westfield was a sidewheel steam ferry boat purchased for $90,000 from Cornelius Vanderbilt in November 1861. She was fitted out for $27,500 by J.A. Westervelt at New York, and was ready in January 1862.

She arrived at the passes of the Mississippi on March 18 and spent the next three weeks assisting *Mississippi* and *Pensacola* in their efforts to get over the bar so they could ascend the river.

Westfield covered a coastal party employed in preparing more accurate maps of the area prior to an assault on the Confederate forts defending New Orleans. She was briefly in action against two Confederate gunboats who retired upon a group of six more gunboats. The well armed *Westfield* continued the action, and in the second brief encounter the shaft of CSS *Defiance* was broken and she had to be sunk by her crew. The gunboat remained with Porter's mortar boats, acting as a supporting force supplying ammunition.

Early summer saw *Westfield* moving up the Mississippi in support of the mortar boats, prior to their first attack on a strongly defended Vicksburg. She was transferred to the Gulf Blockading Squadron in the summer and took part in the successful attack and seizure of Galveston, Texas, on October 4, 1863.

During the bright moonlit night of January 1, 1864, the Confederates launched a fierce attack on the Union forces defending Galveston and succeeded in recapturing the place. During the action, *Westfield* saw suspicious craft moving down the river, so she set out to head them off, but ran aground in Bolivar Channel. As she could not be saved, it was decided to blow her up, but unfortunately there was a premature explosion and nearly twenty men died, including Commander W.B. Renshaw who was in charge of Union naval forces in the area.

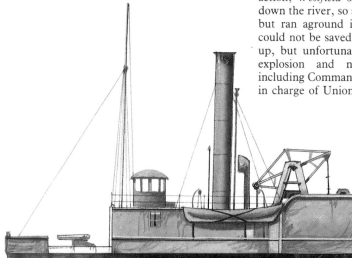

USS *De Soto*

Displacement: 1675 tons. **Dimensions:** 253ft x 38ft x 16ft. **Speed:** 8 knots. **Armament:** In 1861 had eight 32-pdr, 42-cwt, and one 30-pdr Parrott rifle; armament then varied slightly. **Crew:** 130.

De Soto was a wooden sidewheel steamer completed in October 1859. Purchased at New York for $161,250 in August 1861 from Livingston, Crocheron & Co., she served with the West Gulf Blockading Squadron, capturing

six blockade runners before leaving for repairs in October 1862.

During her next cruise, from February 1863 to June 1864, she made seventeen more captures. *De Soto* received new boilers in 1865 at Baltimore, Maryland, and was in service again by August 1865. On November 18, 1867, she was badly damaged during an earthquake at St Thomas in the West Indies, when she was driven onto some iron poles. After repairs she cruised in the Caribbean until August 1868. She was sold in September 1868 at New York for $47,600.

Left: Westfield *served on the James River at a critical time for the Union in that area.*

Below: *The* Tallapoosa *painted a light gray color similar to that used by blockade runners.*

USS *Tallapoosa*

Displacement: 974 tons. **Dimensions:** 205ft x 35ft x 6ft 6in. **Armament:** In 1864 had two 100-pdr Parrott rifles, four 9-inch Dahlgren smoothbores, two 20-pdr Parrott rifles, and two 24-pdr howitzers; armament later varied.

Tallapoosa was a wooden, double-ended steamer built at the New York Navy Yard. Engines were supplied by Neptune Ironworks of New York, and the total cost of the vessel was $174,577. Launched in early 1863 and rebuilt by C.W. Booz of Baltimore for $213,338, she was completed in August 1864.

During November 1864 she encountered a severe two-day storm in the Atlantic, which badly damaged the vessel, forcing her to put into Boston. After the war she served in the Gulf Squadron and in 1869 became a dispatch vessel. In 1872 she became a training ship at Annapolis, Maryland.

Just before midnight on August 24, 1884, *Tallapoosa* collided with the schooner *J.S. Lowell* and sank near Vineyard Haven, Rhode Island. She was raised and repaired by Merritt's Wrecking Organization for $30,000 and subsequently served along the South American coast. She was sold at Montevideo, Uruguay, in 1892.

USS *Queen City*

Displacement: 212 tons. **Armor:** Tinclad, with 1.5 inches of iron. **Armament:** On April 1 had two 30-pdr Parrott rifles, two 32-pdr, 42-cwt, and four 24-pdr howitzers; in October one 12-pdr was added. **Crew:** 65.

Queen City was a wooden sidewheel steamer purchased on February 13, 1863 at Cincinnati, Ohio, by the Navy Department for $16,000 from Samuel Wiggins of Cairo, Illinois.

The diminutive gunboat No. 26 was a typical tinclad. She initially operated up the Tennessee River before transferring to the Mississippi in the summer, where she patrolled the lines of communication and supply always open to disruption by the active Confederate forces along the riverbanks.

On October 13, with 100 troops, she steamed to Friars Point, Mississippi, where the force landed to surround the town. The following day they seized a large quantity of cotton.

She continued to operate along the rivers of Arkansas when, while anchored off Clarendon, Arkansas, at 4 a.m. on Friday, June 26, 1863, the solitary gunboat was completely surprised by Brigadier-General Shelby's force of 2600 cavalry with four guns. Within minutes, the starboard engine was disabled and the port steampipe was out. After fifteen or twenty minutes, the boat was completely riddled by shell and rifle fire and Captain Hickey decided, in order to save life, to surrender the doomed vessel. Soon the Confederates were aboard and started to remove ammunition and one of the guns, while the Union crew swam ashore to avoid capture.

At 9 o'clock a Union force, headed by the gunboat *Tyler*, came into view after hearing of the *Queen City*'s loss. This forced the Confederates to abandon the vessel, but before doing so, two charges were set and the gunboat blew up, sinking in two fathoms and becoming a total wreck as the upper works had collapsed into the hull. Later, Union forces were able to salvage three guns.

Queen City was typical of the smaller type of river steamer normally used for commercial purposes, and which provided the only means of transport in many areas. They were able to operate in extremely shallow waters, so when hostilities commenced, both the Union and Confederate forces pressed them into service in increasing numbers.

During the winter of 1862, approximately twenty vessels of this type were pressed into service with the Union forces (both Navy and Army). They were purchased in cities along the rivers and armored with thin iron plates; extra protection was given to the boilers exposed above the waterline. The sides were pierced to house four to six guns. Rifled guns of good range were usually placed in the bow, and 24-pdr brass howitzers were mounted in broadside.

With a draft of only 3 feet — sometimes as little as 18 inches — these boats were able to cruise up and down the tributaries fighting Confederate regular forces and guerrillas who constantly harassed the Union supply lines along the rivers. By the end of the war more than sixty had seen service.

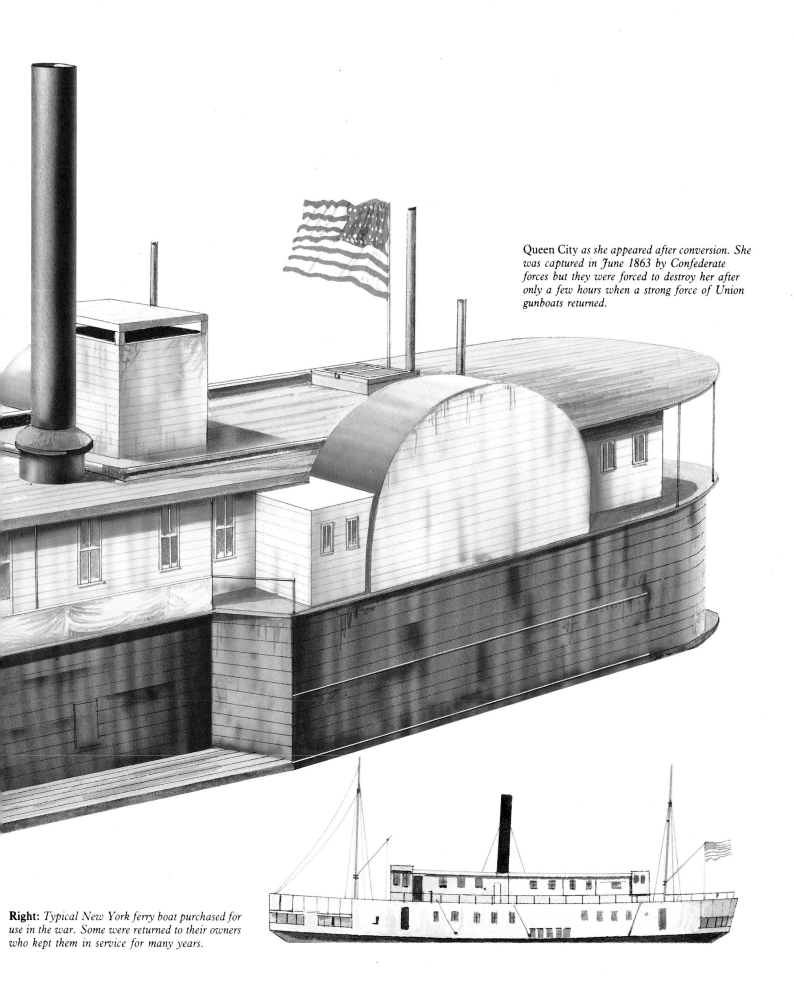

Queen City *as she appeared after conversion. She was captured in June 1863 by Confederate forces but they were forced to destroy her after only a few hours when a strong force of Union gunboats returned.*

Right: *Typical New York ferry boat purchased for use in the war. Some were returned to their owners who kept them in service for many years.*

USS *Jacob Bell*

Displacement: 229 tons. **Dimensions:** 141ft 3in x 21ft x 8ft. **Armament:** In 1861 had one 8-inch Dahlgren smoothbore and one 32-pdr, 32-cwt; armament later varied.

Jacob Bell was built in New York in 1842, and purchased for $12,000 from O.T. Glover and F.R. Anthony in 1861. She served on the Potomac and James rivers where, in July 1862, with other gunboats, she supported the Army of the Potomac after its unsuccessful campaign against Confederate forces under General Lee. She was lost on November 6, 1865, while being towed to New York by *Banshee*.

USS *Housatonic*

Displacement: 1934 tons. **Dimensions:** 205ft x 38ft x 16ft 6in. **Machinery:** Two horizontal direct-acting engines. **Speed:** 10 knots. **Armament:** In 1862 had one 100-pdr Parrott rifle, three 30-pdr rifles, one 11-inch Dahlgren smoothbore, plus smaller. **Crew:** 214.

Housatonic and her three sisters *Adirondack*, *Juniata*, and *Ossipee* were bark-rigged sloops and formed the second part of a large increase in US Navy sloops, which had been authorized in 1861 and followed a proven design. All were built in navy yards, being laid down in 1861; two were launched that same year, with two following in early 1863. All were completed during 1862. The original cost of the *Housatonic* was $231,526.

Adirondack was wrecked on the Little Bahama Bank on August 23, 1862. *Housatonic* briefly engaged the Confederate ironclad *Chicora* at Charleston. Later, while off the bar, she was sunk at about 9 p.m. on the night of February 17, 1864, by the Confederate submarine *R.L. Hunley* — the first successful torpedo attack carried out by a submarine. *Juniata* and *Ossipee* served at the Battle of Mobile Bay and were sold in 1891.

USS *Harriet Lane*

Displacement: 600 tons. **Armament:** In September 1861 had one 8-inch rifle; during August 1861 at Hatteras Inlet she had to throw four 32-pdr rifles overboard to lighten the vessel, having gone aground; in 1862 had three 9-inch guns, one 30-pdr rifle, and one bronze 12-pdr rifle.

Named for President Buchanan's niece and official hostess, *Harriet Lane* was a wooden sidewheel steamer built at a cost of $150,000 by William H. Webb for the Treasury Department at New York. She was launched in November

1857 and at the outbreak of the war was the only steam vessel in service with the Revenue Department.

In 1858 she was dispatched to Paraguay after an attack on a US vessel by forces belonging to the dictator Lopez. Two years later she was used by the Prince of Wales as a tender.

Harriet Lane was taken over again by the navy in March 1861 to serve on the Charleston expedition intended to supply the beleaguered garrison at Fort Sumter.

In August 1861 she took part in the attack on Forts Clark and Hatteras on the outer banks of North Carolina. On the 29th she ran aground when attempting to enter Pamlico Sound through Hatteras Inlet, suffering severe damage while stranded. She was refloated, but only after most of her guns, rigging, and stores had been thrown overboard.

After five months in dock for repairs she joined Admiral Porter's mortar flotilla at Key West prior to attacking Confederate forts at New Orleans. *Harriet Lane* was damaged in an action with a Confederate battery at Shipping Point, Virginia. She took part in the attack on the forts defending New Orleans and operated up the Mississippi until Farragut retired down the river because many of his ships needed overhauling and most of his men were ill. Indeed, service on the Mississippi was extremely harsh. At one time Porter reported that he needed 600 men to replace those ill on his flotilla.

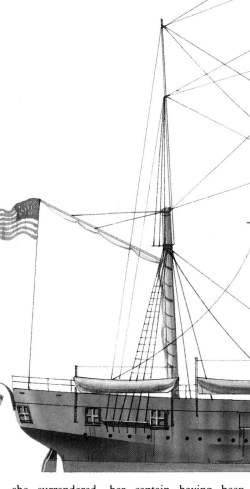

Harriet Lane took part in the successful attack on Galveston, Texas, and was anchored in the harbor several months later when, on January 1, 1863, Confederate forces attacked a wharf where Federal troops were quartered. At 4 a.m., when the moon went down, two Confederate steamers, *Bayou City* and *Neptune*, moved in to attack the weak Union force. Both vessels, packed with troops, had cotton bales protecting their decks and were accompanied by two small vessels loaded with wood for fuel.

Bayou City attacked the *Harriet Lane* at dawn but the strong tide separated them and in scraping free the Confederate vessel lost the port wheelhouse. She was then rammed by *Neptune* and began to sink. *Bayou City* rammed her again and the two became locked together. Confederate troops stormed on board and soon

she surrendered, her captain having been killed. The rest of the Union fleet retired and the small Union land force of 250 troops soon surrendered.

Harriet Lane subsequently served in the Confederate Army's Marine Department of Texas. She was purchased by T.W. House, who converted her into a blockade runner named *Lavinia*. In April 1864 she escaped from Galveston and sailed to Havana, where she was laid up. After that she was handed back to the US in 1867 and sold to E. Richie of Boston, who had her converted to a bark rig and renamed *Elliot Richie*. She was later abandoned on May 13, 1884, off Pernambuco, Brazil.

Jacob Bell in 1862. She formed part of a squadron on the James River that gave valuable help to the army in its seven-day campaign against General Lee's forces.

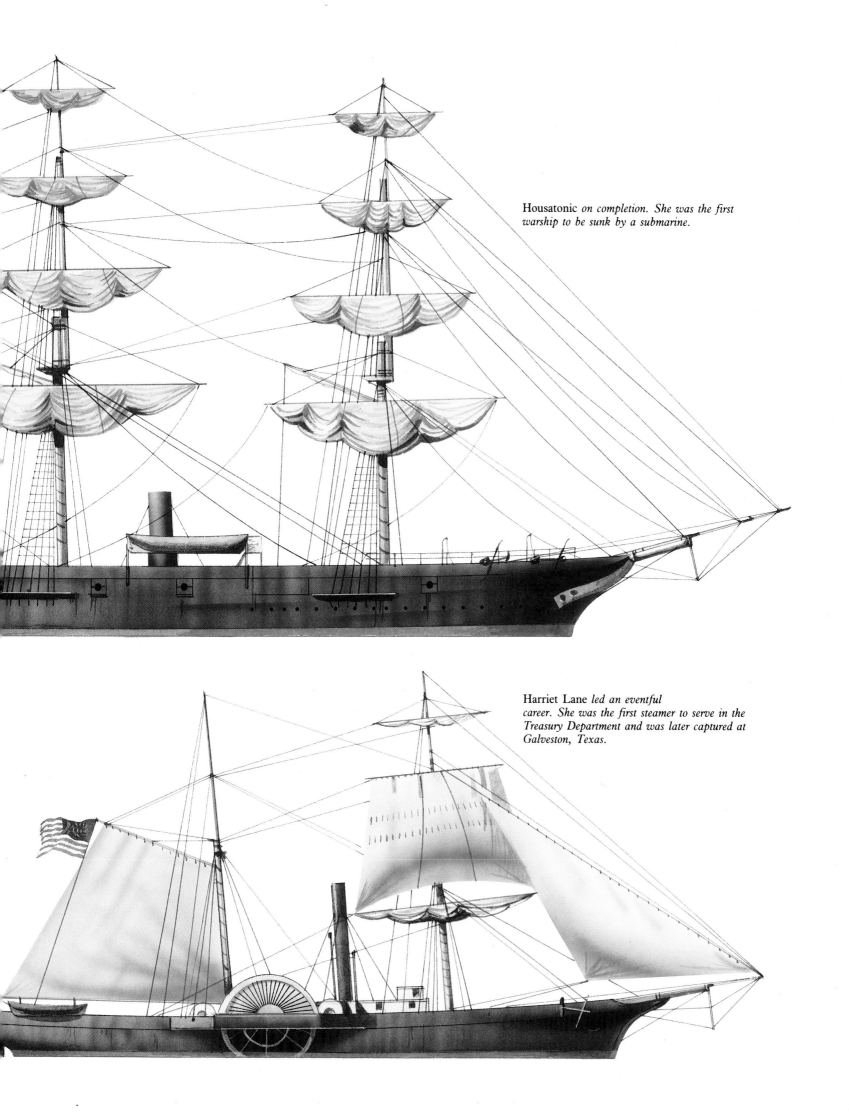

Housatonic *on completion. She was the first warship to be sunk by a submarine.*

Harriet Lane *led an eventful career. She was the first steamer to serve in the Treasury Department and was later captured at Galveston, Texas.*

USS *Sciota*

Displacement: 507 tons. **Dimensions:** 158ft x 28ft x 9ft 6in (11ft maximum). **Machinery:** Two horizontal back-acting engines driving a single screw. **Speed:** 10 – 11 knots. **Armament:** In 1862 had one 20-pdr Parrott rifle and two 24-pdr howitzers; at the end of 1863 an 11-inch Dahlgren smoothbore was added, plus a heavy 12-pdr smoothbore. **Crew:** 62 – 114, according to role.

Sciota was a schooner-rigged, wooden-hulled gunboat, one of a class that eventually totalled twenty-three units. They were ordered as an emergency measure by the Navy Department (without Congressional approval), and even before some of the earlier sloops of the *Oneida* group had been started. Their rapid construction led them to become known as the "ninety-day gunboats."

The contracts were given out to private yards during the first two weeks in July 1861, and all were laid down and launched in 1861. Eleven were completed by the end of 1861, with the rest following in 1862; all were in service by July of that year. Although they were hastily built of poorly seasoned wood, they were well constructed and good sailers, but were liable to roll badly.

The machinery of four — *Sciota*, *Huron*, *Sagamore*, and *Itasca* — were constructed by the Novelty Ironworks of New York, who duplicated for them the engine already supplied for two Russian gunboats. The remaining nineteen vessels had machinery designed by engineer-in-chief Isherwood. These were similar to the first four, but had about 60 percent more boiler power.

Work on this group was pushed to such an extent that four of them served at Port Royal in November 1861, and seventeen were in active service by the end of the year.

Aroostook's hull was built by Thompson and engines were supplied by Novelty Ironworks. She was sold in October 1869, having served with the North Atlantic Blockading Squadron at Hampton Roads, and then with the Gulf Squadron. She captured six vessels during the war and was active along the Texan coast.

Cayuga's hull was supplied by Gildersleeve & Woodruff, while Morgan built the engines. She was ready in February 1862 and served along the lower Mississippi and the Gulf of Mexico, only once leaving the area for repairs. She served at the capture of New Orleans and was sold in October 1865.

Chippewa was built by Webb & Bell, with the engines coming from the Morgan Works. She was ready in October 1861, having been fitted out at the New York Navy Yard. After serving at Hatteras Inlet, she cruised to southern Europe in search of CSS *Florida*, returning via the West Indies. Subsequently, she took part in the capture of Fort Fisher and was sold in November 1865.

Chocura was built by Curtis & Tilden, with Loring supplying the engines. After being damaged in a storm and kept out of service until April, she then blockaded Yorktown.

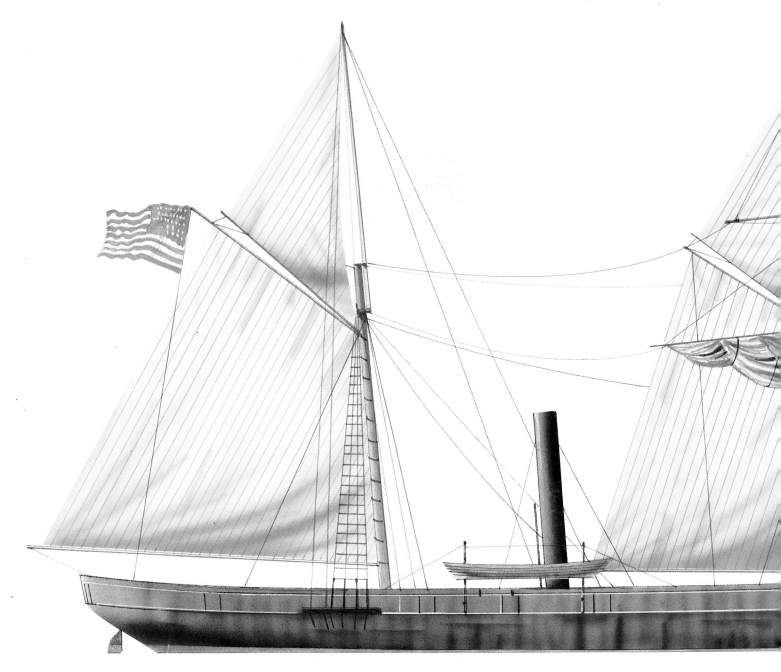

Later she served off Wilmington, and after the war she cruised in the Gulf of Mexico. She was sold in July 1869.

Huron was built by Curtis and engined by Loring. Ready in January 1862, she served off the coast of Georgia and Florida, taking part in numerous shore expeditions. Later, she served off Charleston, taking several prizes during the conflict. She was sold in June 1869.

Itasca, built by Hillman & Streaker and engined by Morris, was ready in November 1861. She captured several blockade runners and was then present at the capture of New Orleans. *Itasca* helped to refloat the *Hartford* when she went aground near Vicksburg, a task that lasted three days. She was sold in November 1865.

Kanawha was built by Goodspeed and engined by Pacific. Completed in January 1862, she served off Mobile and caught a number of blockade runners during the war. She was sold in June 1865.

Katahdin, built by Larrabee & Allen, with engines by Morgan, was ready in early 1862 and fought at New Orleans and Vicksburg. She chased the escaping *Harriet Lane* as she escaped from Galveston, but without success. She was sold in November 1865.

Kennebec, built by Lawrence and engined by Novelty Ironworks was completed in February 1862. She served on the Mississippi, then transferred to the Gulf, taking part in the attack on Mobile. She remained off the Texas coast when the war ended, and was sold in November 1865.

Kineo, built by Dyer and engined by Morgan, was ready in February 1862 and saw action at New Orleans. Later she patrolled the Mississippi and ran aground under fire while lashed to the cruiser *Monongahela*, but *Kineo* managed to drag the disabled vessel to safety. She was sold in October 1866.

Marblehead was built by Jackson with engines by Highland. In service by March 1862, she saw action on Virginian rivers and other inland water. In 1864 she briefly served as a practice ship for midshipmen. She was sold in September 1868.

Ottawa, built by Westevelt and engined by Novelty Ironworks, was ready in October 1861. She served in the waters of the Carolinas, Georgia and Florida, later serving off Charleston, and fought in nearly twenty actions with enemy forces. She was sold in October 1865.

Pembina was built by Stack with engines by Novelty Ironworks. She was completed in October 1861 and fought at Port Royal Sound. She subsequently escorted transports and carried out patrol duties, being sold in November 1865.

Penobscot, built by Carter, was engined by Allain and ready in July 1862. During her career she destroyed ten blockade runners. She was sold in October 1869.

Pinola's hull was built by Abrahams and engines were supplied by Reeder. When completed in January 1862, she served on the Mississippi and, with *Itasca*, broke the chain which obstructed progress before New Orleans while under fire from the powerful Confederate forts. After serving off Vicksburg and Mobile, she was sold in November 1865.

Sagamore, built by Sampson with engines by Atlantic, was ready by the end of 1861 and saw service along the Florida coast. She helped to capture several towns, and during the war destroyed a number of blockade runners. She was sold in June 1865,

Sciota's hull was built by Birely, and the engines were constructed by Morris. In service by the end of 1861, she was present at the capture of New Orleans. Later, while helping to clear a harbor along the Texas coast, she struck a mine on April 14, 1885. Early in July she was raised and sold for $16,000. She had cost $15,735 in repairs while in service.

Seneca's hull was built by Simonson, and engines were supplied by Novelty Ironworks. Completed in October 1861, she took part in the capture of Port Royal and operated between Wilmington and Florida. Later she was present at the attack on Fort Fisher, and was sold in September 1868.

Tahoma, built by Thatcher with engines by Reaney, was completed by the end of 1861. She served her entire career with the East Coast Blockading Squadron, and was sold in October 1867.

Unadilla's hull was built by Englis, and engines were supplied by Novelty Ironworks. Ready in September 1861, she served on the Savannah River and helped capture Fort Pulaski in April 1862. Later she served on blockade duty and saw service before Wilmington. She was sold in November 1869.

Wimona was built by Poillon with engines by Allain. Ready at the end of 1861, she served on the Mississippi and before Vicksburg, and was briefly in action with the Confederate ironclad *Arkansas* when that vessel steamed through the startled Union fleet. She was sold in November 1865.

Wissahickon, built by Lynn with engines by Merrick & Sons, was completed in November 1861. In action against the New Orleans forts and at Grand Gulf, she also served before Vicksburg. In January 1863 she helped destroy the Confederate raider *Rattlesnake*. Placed on routine patrol duty for nearly the rest of the war, she was sold in October 1865.

Sciota *in early 1862. She and her sisters were speedily completed to help swell the Union Navy during its massive task of helping to overcome the Confederacy. All twenty-three units were ordered without Congressional approval as part of an emergency program.*

Gunboats

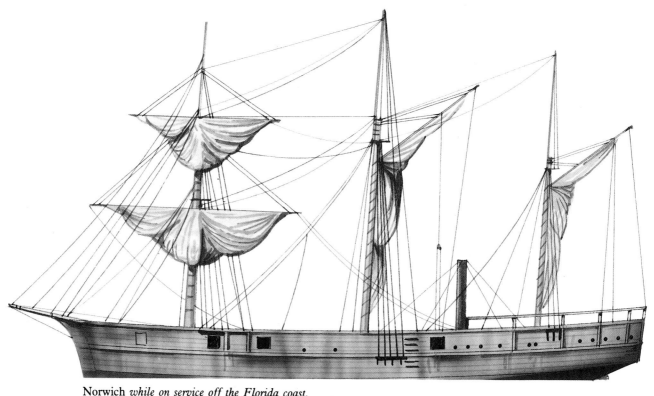

Norwich *while on service off the Florida coast.*

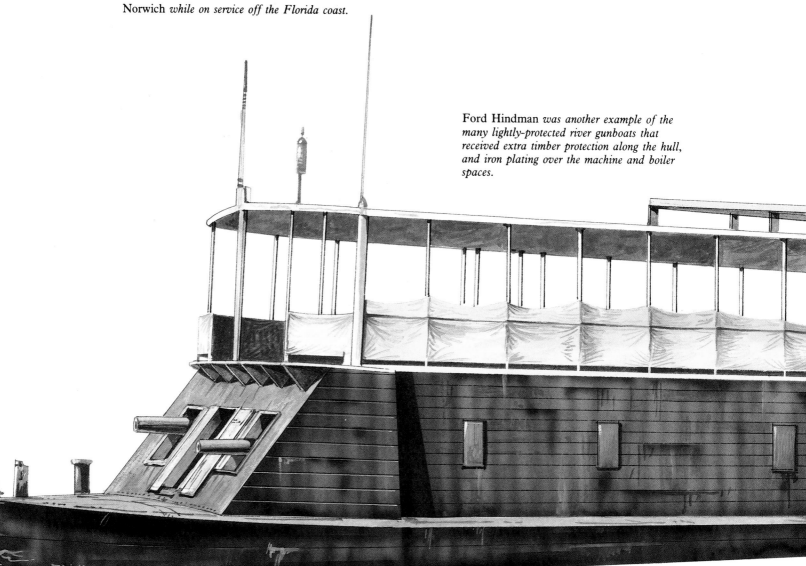

Ford Hindman *was another example of the many lightly-protected river gunboats that received extra timber protection along the hull, and iron plating over the machine and boiler spaces.*

USS *Norwich*

Displacement: 450 tons. **Dimensions:** 132ft 5in x 24ft 6in x 10ft. **Speed:** 9.5 knots, but averaged 5. **Armament:** In 1862 had one 30-pdr Parrott rifle and four 8-inch, 55-cwt.

Norwich was a wooden-screw steamer built in 1861 at Norwich, Connecticut, and purchased from J.M. Huntington & Co. by the Navy Department for $43,137.

During the early part of her career she blockaded Savannah for several months. In March 1863 she and the *Uncas* acted as escorts to troop transports moving up St Johns River, shelling Confederate positions as they went. In action at Jacksonville, Florida, *Norwich* shelled enemy positions, and in mid-August sent a boat party, which included members of *Hale*'s crew, to destroy a Confederate signal station near Jacksonville.

It was then decided to land a force in Florida on the west bank of St Johns River. *Norwich*, together with *Ottawa*, escorted troop transports once more to Jacksonville which had previously been evacuated by Union troops after destroying the town.

More gunboats were assigned to the attack and eventually, guns, plus a large quantity of cotton, were captured. *Norwich* trapped the merchant ship *St Mary's* in McGirt's Creek above Jacksonville on February 7, 1864, forcing her captain to scuttle the vessel and her cargo of cotton.

Later the Confederates launched a strong attack, driving the Union troops back to Jacksonville where the gunboats were able to provide covering fire. They also landed their howitzers which were manned by seamen.

For the rest of the war *Norwich* performed blockade duty along the coasts and up the rivers of Georgia and Florida. She was decommissioned at Philadelphia at the end of June 1865, and sold at public auction in August for $12,300. She remained in the merchant service until she was lost in February 1873.

USS *Fort Hindman*

Displacement: 286 tons. **Dimensions:** 150ft x 37ft x 1ft 8in. **Machinery:** Two direct-acting engines. **Armament:** In 1863 had two 8-inch, 55-cwt smoothbores, and four 8-inch, 63-cwt; in December 1864 one 100-pdr Parrott rifle was added; armament then varied slightly.

Fort Hindman was a wooden sidewheel river steamer purchased by the Navy Department at Jeffersonville, Indiana, in April 1863 for $35,000. In June she was renamed *Manitou*, but her name was changed back to *Fort Hindman* in November 1863. In July she led an expedition up the Little Red River and captured large amounts of ordnance and supplies, as well as the 743-ton Confederate gunboat *Louisville*.

Frequently in action, the tinclad gunboat also captured a merchant vessel in the Red River in March. Later she engaged a Confederate battery ashore, as well as groups of sharpshooters who could command her exposed upper deck from heights along the river. She continued to transport troops, and successfully got down the rapids at the end of the abortive campaign in May.

Fort Hindman next moved to Louisiana, where she operated along the rivers and bayous using Natchez as her main base.

She became involved in the chase of the Confederate ram *Webb* in April 1865 when the latter passed her while burning normal navigation lights so as not to arouse suspicion. The Union vessel was not convinced and set off in pursuit, but by now the *Webb* was making 18 knots in the swift current and soon left the gunboat behind.

Fort Hindman next went to Mound City, Illinois, in August 1865 where she was decommissioned. Later the same month she was sold at public auction to S.A. Silver for $12,500.

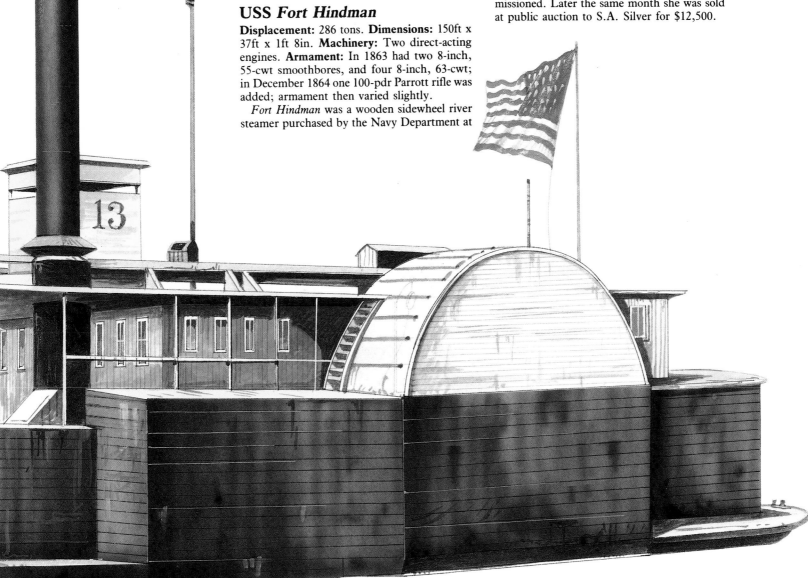

VICKSBURG, Mississippi

Vicksburg was the last important center on the Mississippi to surrender to Union forces after a lengthy and costly siege. The Confederate forces, led by General Pemberton, put up a splendid defence while enduring terrible hardship — a hardship shared by the population who had taken to living in caves to avoid the non-stop bombardment of the city. Matters came to a head in 1863 when Confederate troops were on the point of mutiny over lack of food.

When Vicksburg fell, Union control of the Mississippi was almost complete. They were able to cut off Confederate food supplies to the east where most of the campaigns were still being bitterly fought.

Another development was that for the 30 months during which trade was unable to use the river, the railroad system had expanded to cope with the heavy demand of shifting the bumper grain crop out to seaports for shipment to Europe where there had been several poor harvests.

Gunboats

USS *Vindicator*

Displacement: 750 tons. **Dimensions:** 6-ft draft. **Speed:** 12 knots. **Armament:** In 1864 had one 110-pdr Parrott rifle and two 24-pdr howitzers, plus smaller; armament then varied.

Vindicator was originally built for use by the army in 1863 at New Albany, Indiana. She was transferred to the navy in 1864 and partly rebuilt at Mound City, Illinois, for use as a ram. She joined the Mississippi Squadron in early July 1864 and patrolled the river. She took part in the Yazoo River expedition in November, transported cavalry, and provided covering fire when they were landed. Later she took part in the Black River expedition, when thirty miles of railroad and an important bridge were destroyed. She remained on the Mississippi and took part in the chase of the Confederate ram *Webb*.

Vindicator was withdrawn from service and laid up at Mound City, where she was partly dismantled in July. In November she was sold to S.A. Silver and W.L. Hambleton for $5000.

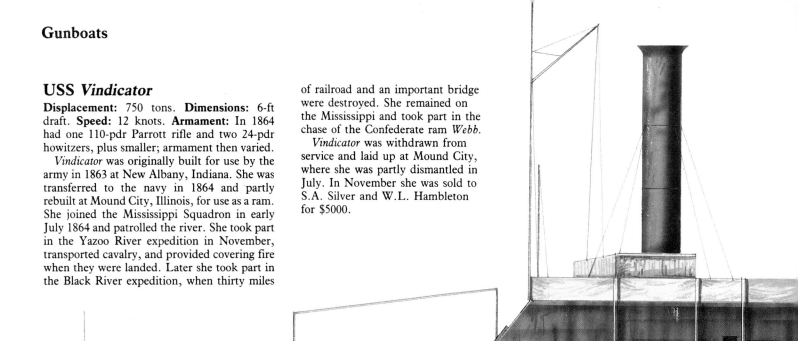

USS *Pawnee*

Displacement: 1533 tons. **Dimensions:** 221ft 6in x 47ft x 10ft. **Machinery:** Two horizontal direct-acting engines. **Speed:** 10 knots maximum, 5 average. **Armament:** In 1861 had eight 9-inch and two 12-pdr; in 1863 one 100-pdr Parrott rifle was added; in 1864 four 9-inch Dahlgren smoothbores were added, plus some smaller. **Crew:** 181.

Laid down in October 1858 at the Philadelphia Navy Yard, *Pawnee* was launched a year later and completed in September 1860. She was a wooden, twin-screw sloop and one of a group of three similar vessels.

Pawnee differed greatly from the other two in the form of her hull and in having twin screws. She was built from the designs of John W. Griffiths of New York, who held a temporary appointment as a naval constructor while directing this work.

It had been decided to arm *Pawnee* with four 11-inch Dahlgren guns, and it was demonstrated that this could be done without exceeding the specified draft of 10 feet. Griffiths' design for *Pawnee* made her considerably longer and broader than other vessels in her class, but still maintained a draft of less than 10 feet when armed and equipped for service, which made her invaluable in the shallow waters of the Southern coast during the war. Besides having to carry a heavy battery, the engines for driving the twin, 9-foot

The Pawnee *with its unusual hull, which incorporated a concave base. She was able to carry a heavy armament on a shallow draft.*

diameter screws were considerably heavier than those used in other vessels of this class. Griffiths solved this problem by building a hull with a concave bottom. Instead of supporting the blades on struts beneath the fantail, the shafts were extended to the stern post where they were held by a crossbar. Reaney Neafie & Co. built the machinery.

Pawnee was sent to Charleston, North Carolina, to relieve Major Anderson's beleaguered garrison at Fort Sumter. Delayed by severe storms, however, she arrived too late and found the fort in Confederate hands. Next she went to Norfolk to save the ships and stores at the Gosport Navy Yard, but arrived after all

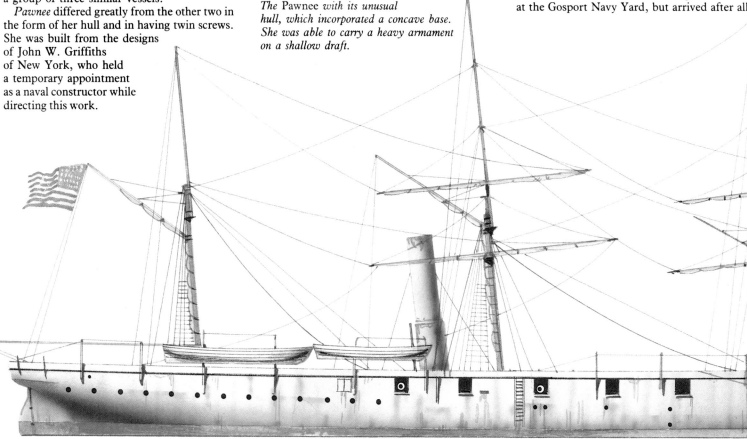

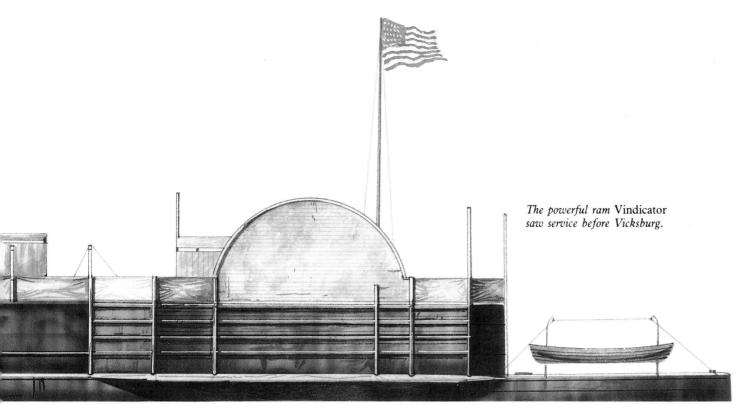

The powerful ram Vindicator *saw service before Vicksburg.*

Below: *Another example of the ram, this time the Confederate* Stonewall Jackson *with its armored bow.*

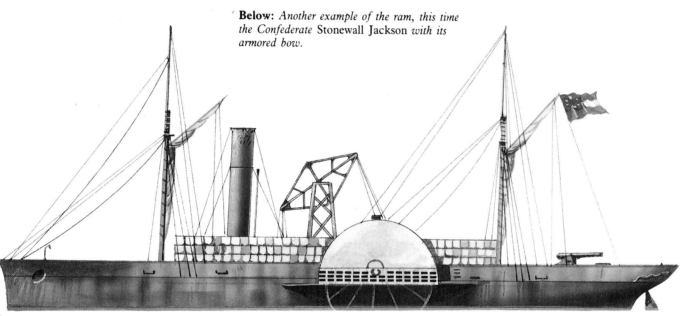

the ships, except *Cumberland*, had been scuttled. She saved *Cumberland* by taking her in tow.

Subsequently, *Pawnee* served at Port Royal, and later, in 1863, at Charleston when Union troops carried out a successful attack on James Island up the Stono River. During this attack *Pawnee* was hit many times and was barely able to get down the river out of danger.

After the war *Pawnee* served off the coast of Brazil looking after US interests during the war between Brazil and Paraguay. In 1869 her worn-out machinery was removed and she was

fitted out as a sailing ship. During the next twelve years or so she served as a hospital or store ship, until finally sold in 1884 to M.H. Gregory for $6011.

CSS *Stonewall Jackson*

Stonewall Jackson was a sidewheel tug with a crew of thirty, and armed with two 32-pdr smoothbore pivot guns. She formed part of the River Defense Fleet at New Orleans in early 1862. On January 25 work started on her conversion into a cottonclad ram by fitting a 4-inch oak covering, with 1-inch iron skin on her bow. Double pine bulkheads were also fitted, with compressed cotton bales between. She was ready on March 16, just in time to take part in the action against Farragut's fleet as it fought its way past the forts defending New Orleans.

In the mêlée, *Stonewall Jackson* rammed the crippled *Varuna*. As *Varuna*'s shot bounced off her bow, *Stonewall Jackson* backed off for another blow which crushed *Varuna*'s hull. The Confederate vessel turned, exposing her unarmored side as a result of the shock of ramming and was struck by five 8-inch shells from *Varuna*. *Stonewall Jackson* was then driven ashore by the *Oneida* and burnt.

CSS Gaines, *lost at Mobile in 1864.*

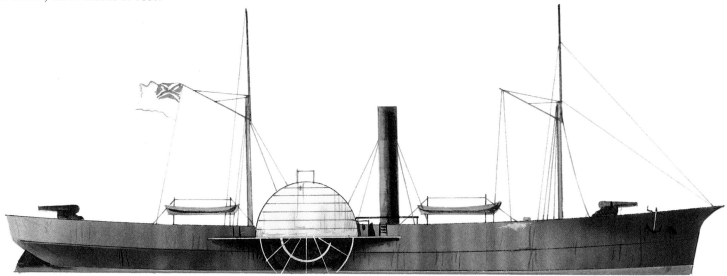

CSS *Gaines*

Displacement: 863 tons. **Dimensions:** 202ft x 38ft x 6ft. **Speed:** 10 knots. **Armament:** In 1863 had six 8-inch in broadside and two 6-inch rifles on pivot; by August 1864 armament was reduced to six guns. **Crew:** 120.

Gaines was hastily built at Mobile, Alabama, in 1861–62 to strengthen the river defenses. The hull, made of unseasoned timber, was partly plated with 2 inches of iron. Crewing, as often happened on Confederate vessels, presented a problem. At one time not one person on *Gaines,* apart from the officers, was American.

Together with two other gunboats, *Gaines* fought alongside *Tennessee* in the combat against Farragut's fleet at Mobile on August 5, 1864, but was finally driven ashore by her crew and set on fire.

USS *Peosta*

Displacement: 233 tons. **Dimensions:** 151ft 2in x 34ft 3in x 6ft (when fully loaded). **Speed:** 5 knots. **Armament:** In 1863 had three 30-pdr Parrott rifles, three 32-pdr, 42-cwt, six 24-pdr howitzers, and two heavy 12-pdr smoothbores.

Peosta was a wooden sidewheel steamer purchased for $22,000 at Dubuque, Iowa, in June 1863, and ready for service on October 2, 1863. She served on the Tennessee River and was in action against a strong Confederate land and river offensive designed to capture Paducah and roll back the Union line along the river.

She was sold at Mound City, Illinois in August 1865 to John Waggener for $8350.

Colonel Lovell

During 1862, the Confederate War Department purchased fourteen river steamers and con-verted them into lightly-armed rams. These were intended to assist the Confederate Navy in defending the Mississippi against the combined Union forces which were growing stronger by the day.

The Confederate rams had been converted by the addition of heavy timbers and iron to the bows. Double bulwarks, with compressed cotton bales between them, were added around the machinery and extra protection was provided by adding light armor made from railroad iron.

As these vessels could develop a reasonable speed, they would charge down upon the enemy, often aided by the current, and deal a swift, frequently fatal blow to their opponent who might only have had enough time to get off one broadside.

Eight of the fourteen operated around Memphis: *Colonel Lovell, General Beauregard, General Bragg, General Earl Van Dorn, General M. Jeff Thompson, General Sterling Price, General Sumter,* and *Little Rebel.* The other six units were stationed on the lower Mississippi and were all converted tug boats: *Defiance, General Breckinridge, General Lovell, Resolute, Stonewall Jackson,* and *Warrior.* Six were lost on April 24, 1862, during the battle with Farragut's fleet before the forts. *Defiance,* although damaged, managed to escape and was sunk by her own crew on the 28th.

The group, stationed at Memphis and crewed by army personnel led by Captain James E. Montgomery, had two major actions with Union forces. The first was at Plum Point where, since mid-April, Union mortar boats were towed four miles downstream from their base and moored under Craigshead Point. These vessels, guarded by a gunboat, then fired

A typical Confederate ram used on the Mississippi in 1862.

their shells across the point toward Fort Pillow.

On May 10, during a hazy dawn, Mortar Boat No. 16 got into position with its attendant guard, the *Cairo* class ironclad *Cincinnati*, moored to a tree slightly above the mortar boat. Just as it fired its fifth shell, eight Confederate rams came charging around the point with funnels belching and headed straight for the lone ironclad. Slowly the heavy vessel swung downstream, and as she gathered steerage way, she fired off a salvo from the forward guns which tore into the *General Bragg*, sending the cotton bales tumbling into the river. *Bragg* continued on course and struck the ironclad on the starboard quarter just aft of the armor plate. The two vessels remained locked together for several seconds. As they broke free, *Cincinnati*

fired a full broadside from only 10 feet away, causing the ram to drift downriver.

General Price then struck the ironclad a blow near the stern which turned the Union vessel toward the advancing *Sumter*, who rammed her at full speed. The ironclad began to sink, but the crew maneuvered her away from deep water and brought her to rest in 12 feet.

Help for the stricken Union vessel now began to arrive. *Van Dorn* singled out the newcomer *Mound City* and struck her a glancing blow, which tore away part of the Union vessel's bow. She started to sink but the crew succeeded in getting her into shallow water, where she came to rest. The Confederate forces wisely decided not to wait for the rest of the more powerful Union ironclads to arrive, and returned to Memphis.

Later, during an expedition up the White River, Arkansas, *Mound City* was struck by artillery fire from a battery on the high bank of the river and her boiler exploded. Over 100 crew were reported killed or missing, with

thirty-eight wounded; only twenty-six escaped injury. These losses were among the heaviest suffered by a single vessel during the war.

The next action was not a success for the Confederates, as the Union vessels were now reinforced by a fleet of rams (nine converted steamers), under the command of Charles Ellet. They arrived just after Fort Pillow had fallen, and joined the ironclads anchored above Memphis. No sooner had they arrived than the Confederate rams were seen coming toward them. In full view of the watching crowds of Memphis, battle commenced. *Queen of the West*, leading the Union squadron, rammed the *General Lovell*, almost cutting the vessel in two and causing her to sink immediately. Another Ellet ram, the *Monarch*, smashed into the *General Price*, knocking away the starboard paddle wheel and leaving the vessel immobilized. *Queen of the West* then became involved in a fierce action with *Beauregard* and *Sumter*, who rammed her from opposite sides and forced her ashore. *Monarch* smashed into *Beauregard*, forcing her to surrender, then sank the *Little Rebel*, which was already disabled by a shot in its steam chest.

Union fire had left *Sumter* and *Bragg* immobilized in the water. *Bragg* was captured and added to the Union fleet, while the burning *Thompson* blew up. Ellet later died of the wound he received at this battle.

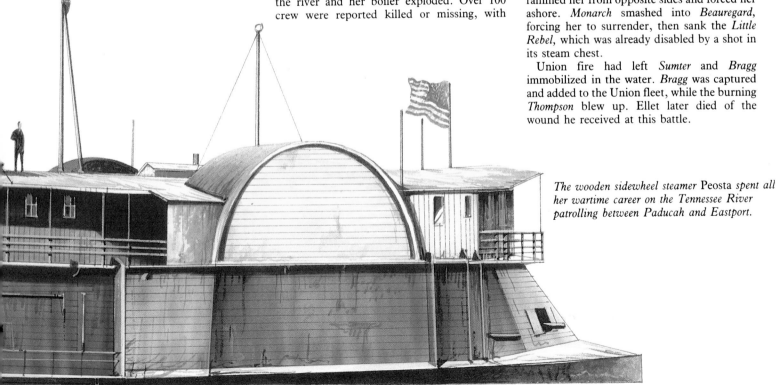

The wooden sidewheel steamer Peosta *spent all her wartime career on the Tennessee River patrolling between Paducah and Eastport.*

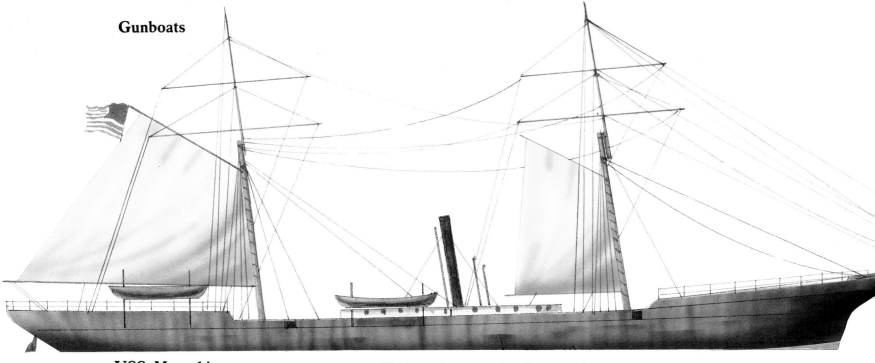

Gunboats

USS *Memphis*

Displacement: 791 tons. **Dimensions:** 227ft x 30ft x 15ft 6in. **Machinery:** Two English-built vertical, direct-acting engines. **Speed:** 14 knots maximum, 6 average. **Armament:** Four 24-pdr, two 12-pdr rifles, and one 30-pdr Parrott rifle. By 1865 *Memphis* had one 30-pdr Parrott rifle, four 20-pdr Dahlgren rifles, two 2-pdr rifles, and four 24-pdr.

Originally a blockade runner, *Memphis* was built in 1861 by William Denny & Bros of Dumbarton, Scotland. She was captured by the sidewheel gunboat *Magnolia* in July 1862 while running the blockade from Charleston, South Carolina, with a cargo of cotton. She was sold to the navy for $103,000 by the prize court, and commissioned in October 1862 for service before Charleston. In eighteen months she captured two blockade runners. After *Mercedita* was rammed and disabled by the Confederate ironclad *Palmetto State*, *Memphis* towed her out of action.

Memphis herself was unsuccessfully attacked by a Confederate "David" while on patrol in the North Edisto River on March 6, 1864. She served until 1869 and was sold in May 1869 to V. Brown & Co. for $54,470.

CSS *McRae*

Displacement: 830 tons. **Armament:** In April 1862 had six light 32-pdr smoothbore broadside guns, and one 9-inch shell gun on pivot amidships.

McRae was originally the bark-rigged pirate ship *Marques de la Habana*, captured in March 1860 by the *Saratoga*.

On March 17, 1861, she was purchased by the Confederate States at New Orleans and fitted out as the *McRae* under the command of Lt. T.B. Huger. Arming the gunboats at New Orleans caused concern to the Confederates as no more weapons could be supplied; the naval authorities hoped to get some of the 125 weapons allocated to the army from the guns taken at Norfolk.

McRae gave repeated help to blockade runners as they slipped in and out of New Orleans, and when Union warships established a close blockade of the Head of the Passes in September 1861, she and several other Confederate gunboats drove the Union vessels off in a night action on October 12.

Her last action came when Farragut's fleet pushed past the defense outside New Orleans on the night of April 24. During the fierce fight, *McRae* was in action against several Union vessels at once and was badly damaged. She extricated herself from danger and limped upstream to New Orleans, where she was sunk alongside a wharf.

USS *Genesee*

Displacement: 803 tons. **Dimensions:** 209ft x 35ft x 10ft 6in. **Speed:** 8.5 knots. **Armament:** In 1862 had one 11-inch Dahlgren smoothbore, one 100-pdr Parrott rifle, and six 24-pdr howitzers; armament then varied.

Genesee was launched at the Boston Navy Yard in April 1862. She was a wooden, double-ended sidewheel steamer, and originally cost $128,593.

She served on the James River, helping to blockade Wilmington and Beaufort, before serving on the Mississippi. Later she took part in the campaign against Vicksburg, and was badly damaged below when a 6-inch shot pierced her hull and detonated an 11-inch shell.

Genesee served at Mobile as a store ship and assisted in clearing the many mines in the harbor. Several vessels were lost in this dangerous work. She was sold in 1867 to Purvis & Son for $14,400.

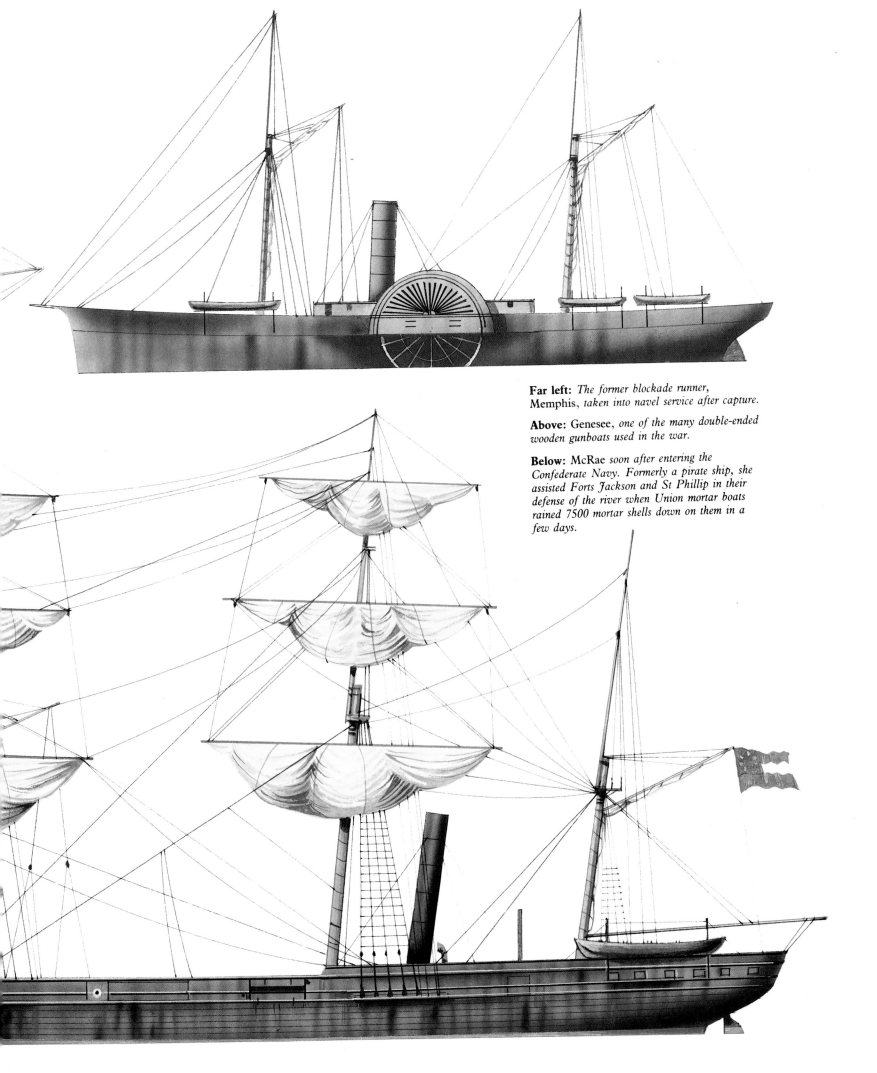

Far left: *The former blockade runner,* Memphis, *taken into navel service after capture.*

Above: Genesee, *one of the many double-ended wooden gunboats used in the war.*

Below: McRae *soon after entering the Confederate Navy. Formerly a pirate ship, she assisted Forts Jackson and St Phillip in their defense of the river when Union mortar boats rained 7500 mortar shells down on them in a few days.*

Gunboats

Below: Nymph, *also known as Gunboat No. 54.*

Far right: Paul Jones *one of the hardworking double-ended gunboats.*

Lower right: Port Royal *was another of the hardworking, well-armed gunboats designed by Lenthall which had machinery designed by Isherwood. They were unusual vessels, built specially to travel equally well in both directions, thus avoiding the necessity of making difficult turns in narrow, twisting rivers.*

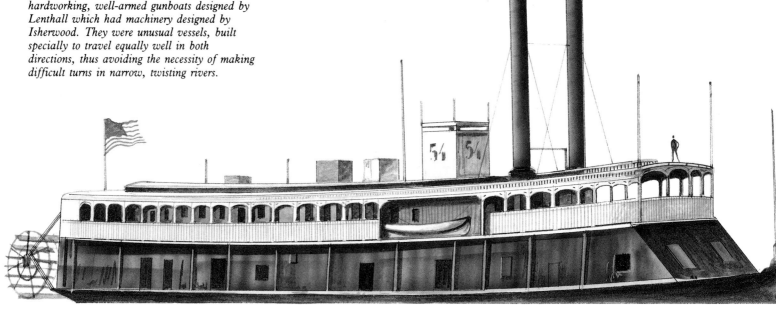

USS *Nymph*

Displacement: 171 tons. **Dimensions:** 161ft 2in x 30ft 4in x 5ft. **Speed:** 4 knots. **Armament:** Eight 24-pdr smoothbores and four 24-pdr.

Nymph was a wooden sternwheel steamer originally named *Cricket No. 3*. She was built at Cincinnati in 1863 and purchased by the Navy Department in March 1864 for $32,000. She was fitted out as a tinclad at Mound City and ready by April 11, 1864, when she began patrolling the Mississippi. This duty lasted until the end of the war, when she was sold to A.M. Hutchinson in August 1865 for $9000.

USS *Port Royal*

Displacement: 974 tons. **Dimensions:** 209ft x 35ft x 7ft 8in. **Machinery:** Inclined direct-acting engines driving side wheels. **Speed:** 9.5 knots. **Armament:** In 1862 had one 100-pdr Parrott rifle, one 10-inch Dahlgren smoothbore, and six 24-pdr howitzers; in 1863 two 9-inch Dahlgren smoothbores were added, the 10-inch weapon being removed; armament then varied slightly. **Crew:** 131.

Port Royal, built by Thomas Stack of New York at a cost of $100,000, was a double-ended gunboat. Her hull was designed by Lenthall, while her engines were designed by Isherwood and built by the Novelty Ironworks. She was laid down in 1861, launched on January 17, 1862, and commissioned in April 1862 at the New York Navy Yard. When delivered from the builder, the vessel was complete apart from the guns.

Early in May she left New York to join the North Atlantic Blockading Squadron, where she served on the James River. Almost immediately she found herself in action against Confederate shore batteries, first at Sewells Point, Virginia, then at Fort Darling, Drury's Bluff.

When the Union Army withdrew from the peninsula as a result of Lee's brilliant campaign against General McClellan, the naval forces in the area were changed. *Port Royal* was transferred to the North Carolina Sounds and she took part in the attack upon Kingston in mid-December 1862.

She transferred to the Florida coast in the spring of 1863. In April she landed an armed boat party at night at Apalachicola and seized a quantity of cotton and ordnance stores. However, she was unable to proceed further because of chains stretched across the river which were protected by a battery.

In May *Port Royal* carried out another raid up the Chattahoochee River. Using the ship's launch, she captured a small sloop and later seized more small craft.

At the end of May, forty-five miles above the town of Apalachicola, she captured a sloop named *Fashion* which was loaded with cotton and ready to run the blockade. Later she destroyed a ship repair yard at Devil's Elbow, and seized a barge for use as a tender.

Port Royal patrolled the Confederate coast, sometimes exchanging shots with enemy batteries. She took part in the operations at Mobile in August 1864 when she was lashed alongside *Richmond* in the run past the forts. She was sold at Boston in October 1866 for $4500. During her varied career, $15,939 had been spent on repairs.

USS *Paul Jones*

Displacement: 1210 tons. **Dimensions:** 216ft 10in x 35ft 4in x 8ft. **Machinery:** Inclined direct-acting engine driving side wheels. **Speed:** 9.5 knots. **Armament:** In 1862 had one 100-pdr Parrott rifle, two 9-inch Dahlgren smoothbores, one 11-inch Dahlgren smoothbore, two 50-pdr Dahlgren rifles, and two 24-pdr howitzers. **Crew:** 131.

Paul Jones was a wooden, schooner-rigged double-ender designed, like her near sisters, for service in the rivers of the southeast, and had a rudder at each end. She was also the largest of

the group. Her hull was designed by John Lenthall and built by J.J. Abrahams of Baltimore, Maryland, while her engines were designed by Benjamin Isherwood and built by Reaney, Son & Archbold of Chester, Pennsylvania. Laid down in 1861, she was launched in January 1862 and commissioned on July 9.

As part of the South Atlantic Blockading Squadron, *Paul Jones* was in action within a few days of being commissioned, when she engaged the fort at Jones Point Ogeechee River at the end of July. In September she was in action against the fort on St Johns Bluff, St Johns River, Florida.

Paul Jones formed part of a covering squadron in the destruction of a railroad bridge near Pocotaligo, South Carolina, in October. While on general blockade duty in April 1863, she helped capture the schooner *Major E. Willis*, later catching the sloop *Mary*, loaded with cotton, on July 8, 1863, off St Simons Sound. She took part in attacks on the defenses of

Charleston, South Carolina, between July 18 and 24, concentrating upon Battery Wagner. During one attack, the 100-pdr Parrott rifle gave way at the seventy-eighth round.

After the abortive attacks on Charleston in the summer of 1863, it was realized that the navy alone would not force the city to surrender. Many more troops would be needed to subdue the place, thus proving Du Pont correct in his doubts about the navy taking Charleston with the ships he had available in April.

After repairs at New York, *Paul Jones* carried out coastal duties until the end of the war, finishing up at Mobile, Alabama. She was sold in July at New York for $10,000.

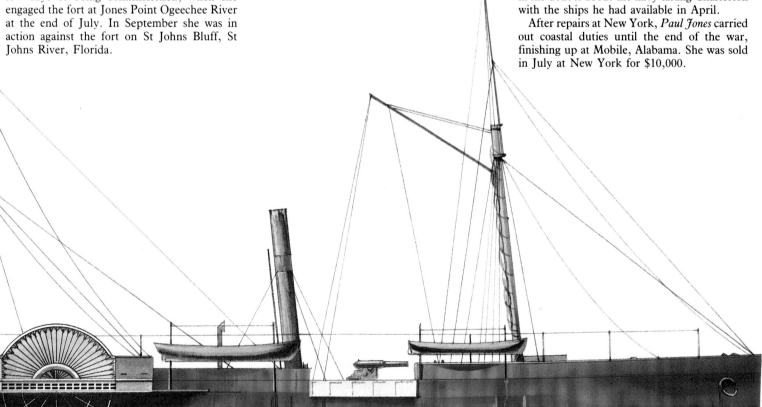

USS *Silver Lake*

Displacement: 236 tons. **Dimensions:** 155ft 1in x 32ft 2in x 6ft. **Speed:** 6 knots. **Armament:** In 1863 had six 24-pdr Dahlgren howitzers; in early 1865 had two 20-pdr Parrott rifles, three 24-pdr howitzers, and three heavy 12-pdr smoothbores; in July 1865 had two 25-pdr Parrott rifles, two heavy 12-pdr smoothbores, and four 24-pdr howitzers.

Silver Lake was a wooden sternwheel steamer built at California, Pennsylvania, in 1862. She was purchased in Cincinnati in November for $21,000, and added to the fleet on December 24.

She joined a squadron of gunboats on the Cumberland River in order to stop Confederate supplies and forces from crossing over. *Silver Lake* then pushed on up the river to Fort Donaldson, where Union forces were surrounded by Confederate troops. She arrived after dark and took the exposed Confederate positions by surprise, forcing them to evacuate the area and leave behind their captured material.

During February 1863 a serious outbreak of smallpox occurred on the *Silver Lake*. The sick were removed to Paducah, the nearest center that could take them. Many cases were reported in the area — another example of the problems facing both sides during the war.

By April *Silver Lake* was in need of repairs to her badly damaged gun platforms, which had been unable to withstand constant use. Prior to this, in March, she, *Leamington* and *Robb* had shelled Confederate troops, forcing them to abandon Florence, Tennessee. On April 3 the small town of Palmyra was destroyed in retaliation for attacks on gunboats by guerrilla forces. In fact, it was common Union practice to destroy towns and hamlets close to areas of guerrilla or Confederate troop attacks, which brought great suffering to many innocent inhabitants of such places.

In December 1864 *Silver Lake* was in action against Confederate batteries near Bells Mills, Tennessee, and a few days later recaptured three transports taken earlier by Southern troops.

She was sold at Mound City in August 1865 to J.H. Kenniston for $9500.

CSS *General Stirling Price*

Displacement: 633 tons. **Dimensions:** 182ft x 30ft x 13ft. **Speed:** 12 knots.

Formerly known as *Laurent Millaudon L. Millandon* (or *Milledon*), *General Stirling Price* was built at Cincinnati, Ohio, in 1856. She was taken into Confederate service in 1862 at New Orleans for conversion into a cottonclad ram for service with the Mississippi River Defense Fleet. Work started on January 25. A 4-inch covering of oak topped by 1 inch of iron was placed over the bow, while double pine bulkheads filled with compressed cotton were installed to protect machinery.

General Stirling Price left New Orleans for Memphis on March 25 to have the ironwork completed. Once ready, she steamed to Fort Pillow and on May 10, 1862, was in action against the Union ironclad *Cincinnati* who was covering a mortar boat firing at the fort. *General Price* was able to ram the ironclad in the stern, knocking off the rudder and dislodging the stern post, as well as a large piece of the hull, causing the vessel to settle slowly.

Cincinnati was able to get off a salvo that damaged the ram and made her leak. She was quickly repaired at Memphis and in action again in time to cover Confederate troops as they evacuated Fort Pillow.

Union forces now pressed on toward their next goal, Memphis. On June 6, unable to retire through lack of fuel, Confederate rams made one last desperate attack upon the advancing Union vessels. In this one-sided combat the Confederates were completely beaten and *General Price* was left slowly sinking on a sandbank. Her crew managed to scramble ashore before she was taken over by the Union squadron.

General Price was raised by the army, who took her to Cairo for repairs before handing her over to the navy. Repairs were finished by March 11, and after serving along the Mississippi, she took part in the capture of Grand Gulf.

Subsequently, she served on the Red River and was present at the capture of Alexandria, Louisiana. She then served before Vicksburg, and after it fell was sent to Cairo for much needed repairs.

After four months in dockyard hands, she was back in service ready for the Red River campaign due to start in March. However, before this she accidentally rammed the gunboat *Conestoga*, causing her to sink and become a total loss. In March 1863 she was armed with

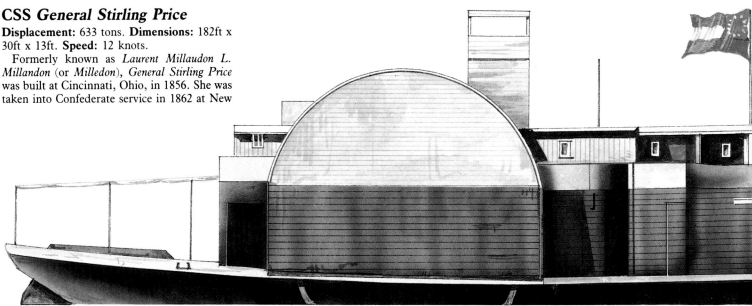

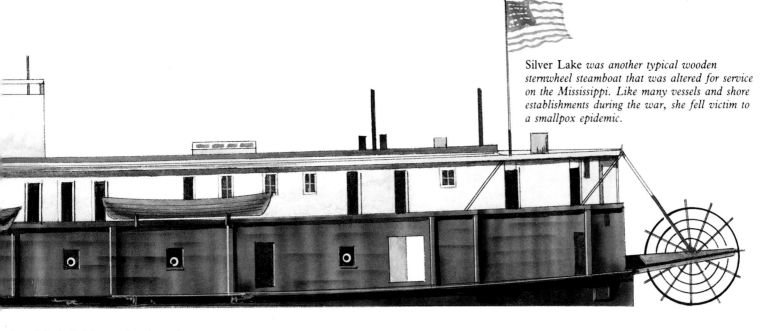

Silver Lake was another typical wooden sternwheel steamboat that was altered for service on the Mississippi. Like many vessels and shore establishments during the war, she fell victim to a smallpox epidemic.

four 9-inch Dahlgrens, but later the armament varied. She was sold to J.W. Livingston at Mound City, Illinois, in October 1865 for $14,000

USS *Maratanza*

Displacement: 786 tons. **Dimensions:** 209ft x 32ft x 9ft 6in. **Speed:** 10 knots. **Armament:** In 1862 had one 100-pdr Parrott rifle, one 9-inch pivot smoothbore, and four 24-pdr; armament then varied.

Maratanza was one of the numerous double-ended gunboats. Built at the Boston Navy Yard in 1861, machinery was supplied by Harrison Loring. She was launched in November 1861 and commissioned in April 1862.

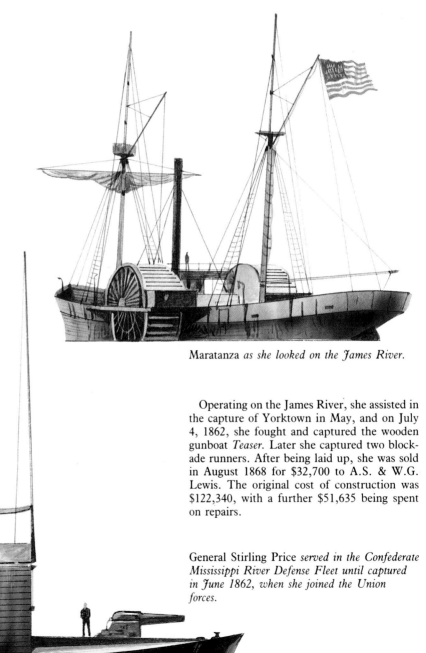

Maratanza as she looked on the James River.

Operating on the James River, she assisted in the capture of Yorktown in May, and on July 4, 1862, she fought and captured the wooden gunboat *Teaser*. Later she captured two blockade runners. After being laid up, she was sold in August 1868 for $32,700 to A.S. & W.G. Lewis. The original cost of construction was $122,340, with a further $51,635 being spent on repairs.

General Stirling Price served in the Confederate Mississippi River Defense Fleet until captured in June 1862, when she joined the Union forces.

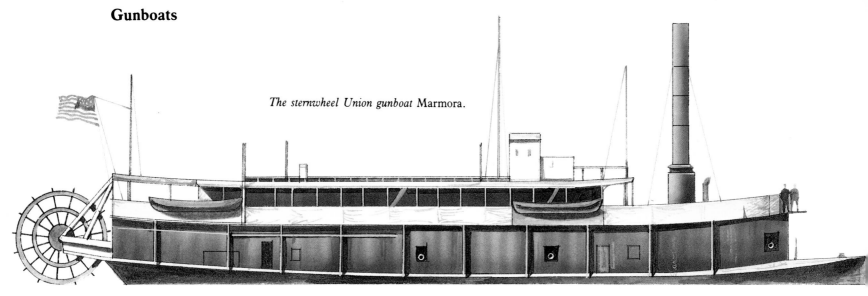

The sternwheel Union gunboat Marmora.

USS *Marmora*

Displacement: 207 tons. **Dimensions:** 155ft 33ft 5in x 4ft 6in maximum. **Speed:** Almost 7 knots. **Armament:** In 1862 had two 24-pdr and two 12-pdr rifles; in June 1864 four more 24-pdr were added; in December 1864 had eight 24-pdr, which were changed in March 1865 to two 24-pdr and six 14-pdr.

Marmora was a typical sternwheel river steamer. Built at Monongahela in 1862, she was sold to the navy for $21,000 by C.L. Brennan, W. Nelson and James McDonnell at St Louis, Missouri, in September 1862. In October she was commissioned and joined the Mississippi Squadron. In early December she helped re-float the *Queen of the West* who had gone aground on Paw Paw Island.

While patrolling up the Yazoo River, *Marmora* came across several mines, one of which exploded and severely shook the vessel, although it was 50 feet away.

On December 12 she led *Signal*, *Cairo*, and *Pittsburgh* up the river, stopping only when she came under hot musket fire from the riverbank as she attempted to round a tight bend. As she backed ready to turn, *Marmora* was joined by *Cairo*. Boats were eventually lowered after discovering parts of a torpedo or mine. *Marmora's* cutter discovered a line in the water and upon being cut, up bobbed another mine. When another line was found, the mine attached to it was towed to the shore.

While attention was focused on the activities of the boats' crews in their quest for mines, no one noticed that *Cairo* had drifted into the shore and had to be backed into the stream. Both *Marmora* and *Cairo* now proceeded slowly ahead, but a mine detonated with terrific force beneath *Cairo's* hull, sinking her instantly. The

mine was a pair of five-gallon, wicker-covered jars in wooden boxes connected by 20 feet of wire and suspended below the surface. As the vessel struck the wire, the two containers were drawn to the sides of the warship so detonating the friction primer fuses.

Marmora helped rescue the crew of *Cairo*, then pulled down the funnels of the sunken vessel to stop the Confederates from finding the wreck. Meantime, the banks were bombarded to keep away enemy sharpshooters.

At the end of December *Marmora* was in action against Drumgould's Bluff in a probing expedition to find a weak spot in Vicksburg's defenses. She later aided Union troops in their withdrawal from Chickasaw Bluffs after heavy rain prevented any movement and because of the arrival of large Confederate reinforcements.

Marmora fought at Fort Hindman, Arkansas, in January, and in February went back up the Yazoo River on another expedition. She subsequently helped in the defense of Yazoo City when the tenuous Union hold was almost lost during a determined Confederate attack.

She was sold in August 1865 to D.D. Barr at Mound City, Illinois, for $8650.

General Bragg *formed part of the Confederate River Defense Fleet.*

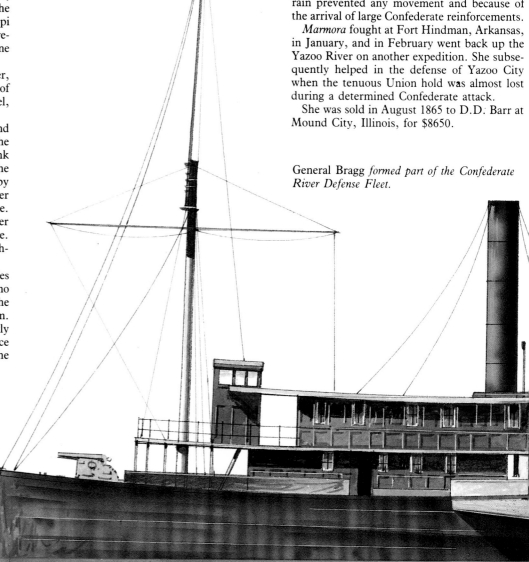

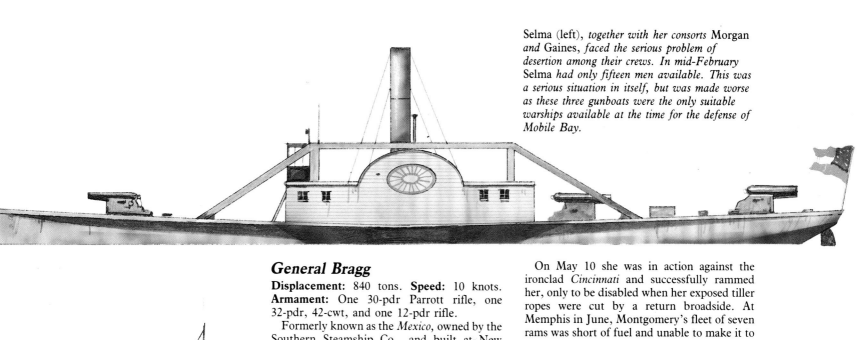

Selma (left), together with her consorts Morgan and Gaines, faced the serious problem of desertion among their crews. In mid-February Selma had only fifteen men available. This was a serious situation in itself, but was made worse as these three gunboats were the only suitable warships available at the time for the defense of Mobile Bay.

General Bragg

Displacement: 840 tons. **Speed:** 10 knots. **Armament:** One 30-pdr Parrott rifle, one 32-pdr, 42-cwt, and one 12-pdr rifle.

Formerly known as the *Mexico*, owned by the Southern Steamship Co., and built at New York in 1851, *General Bragg* was taken over by the Confederate War Department at New Orleans in January 1862. She was selected to form part of the River Defense Fleet being formed by Captain J.E. Montgomery, a former river captain, and work on her conversion started on January 25. A 4-inch oak sheath with a 1-inch covering of iron was added to the bows, and double pine bulkheads filled with compressed cotton were also added. She was ready by the end of March.

On May 10 she was in action against the ironclad *Cincinnati* and successfully rammed her, only to be disabled when her exposed tiller ropes were cut by a return broadside. At Memphis in June, Montgomery's fleet of seven rams was short of fuel and unable to make it to Vicksburg. On June 6 it was decided to put up a last-ditch fight against the approaching Union warships. In the brief but hectic action, *General Bragg* was set alight and beached on a sandbar. She was captured and added to the Union Navy. Total cost of repairs was $2481, and she was later sold to D. White in September 1865 for $52,100.

CSS *Selma*

Dimensions: 252ft x 30ft x 6ft. **Speed:** 9 knots. **Armament:** In 1864 had two 9-inch, one 8-inch and one 6-inch pivot guns. **Crew:** 65.

Formerly the *Florida*, built for the coast trade in 1856 at Mobile and owned by the Mobile Mail Line, *Selma* was taken into the Confederate Navy in April 1861. Work started on her conversion in June, when she was cut down and strengthened with extra framing. Iron plating ⅜ inch thick was added to the upper deck and angled back on the sides to give some protection to the boilers and machinery. She was ready in November 1861.

In October 1862 she went aground for thirty-six hours. Later she was in action against *Massachusetts*, setting her on fire. On December 4, while escorting *Pamlico* who was carrying troops, she was in action against *Montgomery*. On February 5, 1863, *Selma* was damaged while crossing Dog River bar and sank in 8 feet of water. She was hastily pumped out and back in service by the 13th.

In action against Farragut's fleet on August 5, *Selma* surrendered to the gunboat *Metacomet* after an hour-long fight. Seven of her crew were killed, and eight wounded. She was added to the Union fleet and cost $4475 in repairs. She was sold in July 1865 at New Orleans for $4325.

USS *Rhode Island*

Displacement: 1517 tons. **Dimensions:** 236ft 7in x 36ft 9in x 15ft loaded (12ft when light). **Machinery:** Single-beam engine with a 12-ft stroke. **Speed:** 16 knots maximum, 9 average. **Armament:** In 1861 had four 32-pdr, 42-cwt; later in the year had one 30-pdr Parrott rifle and two 8-inch, 55-cwt. Armament then varied; by 1863 had one 9-inch, two 30-pdr and eight 32-pdr, plus smaller.

Originally to be named *John P. King*, *Rhode Island* was built by Lupton & McDermut in 1860 at New York, but was burnt and rebuilt as the *Eagle* in 1861. She was purchased by the Navy Department in June 1861 for $185,000 from Spofford, Tileston & Co. During the Civil War she was used mainly as a supply ship, but during her service succeeded in capturing or driving ashore four blockade runners.

She was used on several occasions for towing monitors, including the original *Monitor* who, on her final journey in December 1861, sprang several leaks as a result of the constant pounding of the sea. *Rhode Island* remained as near as possible to the position where *Monitor* sank in an effort to pick up survivors, but without success.

Rhode Island subsequently cruised along the Atlantic coast searching for the Confederate raiders *Oreto* and *Alabama*, and taking part in the attack on Fort Fisher in late 1864 and early 1865. In May *Rhode Island* cruised with the large, ocean-going monitor *Dictator*. She remained in service after the war and escorted the Confederate ram *Stonewall* back to the United States from Cuba in November 1865. The large sidewheel steamer continued to serve until October 1867.

She was sold at New York in October 1867 to G.W. Quintard for $70,000. The total cost of repairs while in US service was $106,674.

USS *Rattler*

Displacement: 165 tons. **Armament:** In 1863 had two 30-pdr Parrott rifles and four 24-pdr; armament then varied.

Rattler was formerly the wooden river steamer *Florence Miller*, built in 1862 at Cincinnati, Ohio. She was purchased by the navy for $24,000 in November 1862 and commissioned the following month, she took part in the attack on Fort Hindman in January 1863 and went on to serve on the Mississippi. Here she acted as flagship to a flotilla of tinclads and transports conveying General Sherman's command of 6000 men in the Yazoo Pass expedition. The plan was to isolate Vicksburg by seizing the bayous, but it ended in failure.

Rattler subsequently took part in the attack on Fort Pemberton, the Red River campaign, and raids up the Black, Tensa, and Ovachita rivers. In September 1863 her commanding officer and sixteen crew were captured while ashore attending church. On December 30, 1864, after dragging her cable in a severe storm, she was driven onto an obstruction and sank. Later she was set on fire by Confederate troops.

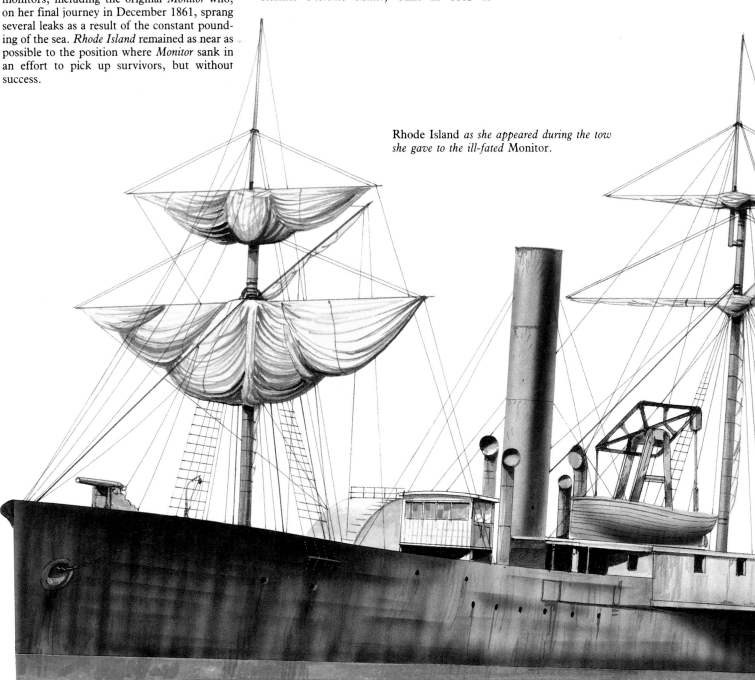

Rhode Island *as she appeared during the tow she gave to the ill-fated* Monitor.

Rattler, *a small tinclad gunboat, led an active career on the Mississippi.*

USS *Malvern*

Displacement: 627 tons. **Dimensions:** 240ft x 23ft 2in x 8ft 5in. **Machinery:** Direct-acting, single-beam engines with an 11-ft stroke. **Armament:** In 1864 had four 20-pdr Dahlgren rifles and eight heavy 12-pdr smoothbores.

Malvern was built in 1860 by Harlan & Hollingsworth Co. of Wilmington, Delaware, for Charles Morgan's Southern Steamship Co. She entered service in January 1861 as the *William G. Hewes*, travelling between New York and New Orleans.

Seized by the governor of Louisiana at the end of April 1862, she was pressed into service as a blockade runner. Her high speed and great cargo capacity — up to 1440 bales of cotton — made her extremely valuable in this role, and she made her first run to Havana, Cuba, in April 1862. After the fall of New Orleans, she transferred to Charleston, was renamed *Ella and Annie*, and was operated by the Importing and Exporting Co. of South Carolina, running to Bermuda.

She was damaged in a storm in September and needed repairs at Bermuda. On her way again, with Frank Bonneau, one of the leading blockade-running captains in command, she was delayed by another storm and fell in with USS *Niphon* off New Inlet, North Carolina. Bonneau rammed the Union vessel but was forced to surrender when *Ella and Annie* was damaged by gunfire.

She was taken into the navy after hasty repairs at the Boston Navy Yard in early 1864, renamed *Malvern* and became part of the North Atlantic Blockading Fleet. Here, she served briefly as Admiral Porter's flagship during the attacks on Fort Fisher, North Carolina, in December 1864 and January 1865. Later that month she captured two blockade runners.

Malvern was sold in October 1865 to S.G. Bogart for $113,000. He then sold the vessel to her original owners, who rebuilt her in early 1866 at Wilmington, Delaware, and operated her between New Orleans and the Texas ports. She served for many years in the West Indies' fruit trade until wrecked in a storm on Colorado Reef off the Cuban coast in February 1895.

Right: *Former blockade runner* Ella and Annie *named* Malvern *in Union service.*

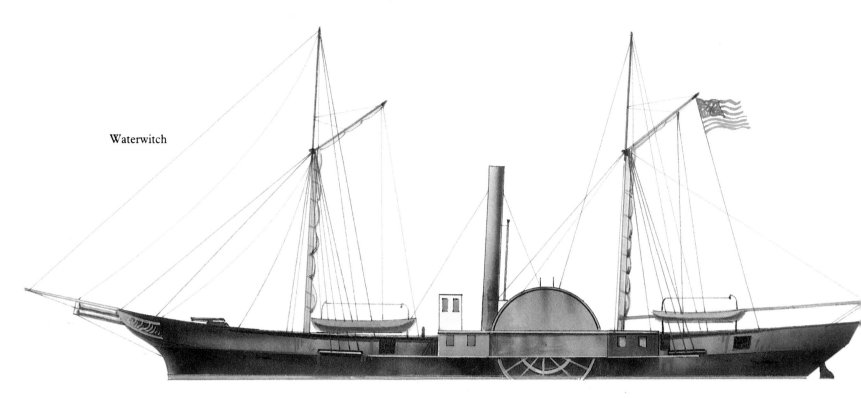

Waterwitch

USS *Waterwitch*

Displacement: 378 tons. **Dimensions:** 150ft x 2ft x 9ft. **Armament:** In 1863 had one 30-pdr Parrott rifle, one 12-pdr rifle, and two heavy 12-pdr smoothbores.

Waterwitch was a wooden sidewheel steamer built in 1851 at a cost of $232,563 in the Washington Navy Yard. Commissioned around late 1852 or early 1853, she spent the next few years on survey work along the South American coast and rivers. While surveying the La Plata River in Paraguay on February 5, 1855, she was fired on by a Paraguayan fort and one man was killed.

At the start of the Civil War her shallow draft made her ideal for carrying out surveys of the Mississippi. At the beginning of 1862 she was briefly in action against Confederate forces. Later she acted as a dispatch boat, as well as patrolling coast lanes and rivers of the Confederacy.

On the night of June 3, 1864, while at anchor in Ossabaw Sound, she was captured by a Confederate force who had succeeded in approaching unseen in small boats. She was taken into the Confederate Navy, but was burnt on December 19, 1864, to avoid capture at White Bluff.

USS *Iosco*

Displacement: 1173 tons. **Dimensions:** 205ft x 35ft x 9ft 6in. **Machinery:** Direct-acting inclined engines. **Speed:** 13 knots. **Armament:** In 1864 had two 100-pdr Parrott rifles, four 9-inch Dahlgren smoothbores, two 24-pdr howitzers, and smaller; in 1865 one 11-inch Dahlgren was added. **Crew:** 200.

Iosco was one of a class of twenty-eight double-ended gunboats designed by Lenthall and Isherwood. The others were *Agawam*, *Algonquin*, *Ascutney*, *Chenango*, *Chilopee*, *Eutaw*, *Iosco*, *Lenapee*, *Machinaw*, *Massasoit*, *Mattabesett*, *Mendota*, *Metacomet*, *Mingoe*, *Osceola*, *Otsego*, *Pawtuxet*, *Peoria*, *Pontiac*, *Pontoosuc*, *Sassacus*, *Shamrock*, *Tacony*, *Tallahoma*, *Tallapoosa*, *Wateree*, *Winooski*, and *Wyalusing*. All but three were laid down in 1862; the rest were started in early 1863 and launched the same year, except for *Sassacus*, which was launched in late December 1862. Three — *Eutaw*, *Mendota*, and *Sassacus* — entered service in 1863; the rest, apart from three which were never completed, followed in 1864. Only one of the vessels had an iron hull; the remainder were built of wood.

These warships were of a very unusual type that had been created especially to cope with operations against Confederate forces stationed along tortuous inland waterways. The hazards of turning vessels in these situations created the need for shallow-draft, speedy craft that could travel equally well in each direction. For this reason the Navy Department decided on a large group of sidewheel steamers called "double-enders" which had a rudder at each end.

These vessels had the usual direct-acting engine designed by Isherwood, plus the added innovation of forced draft from mechanical blowers.

It had been hoped to get these vessels into service quickly, but as the war continued it became increasingly hard to obtain machinery. In 1863/64, when thirty engines were put out to tender for the *Iosco* group, only four proposals were received. Isherwood was forced to use widely scattered engine builders to get anything started, and because of the fixed price and short construction time, he could not include a penalty clause in the contract.

Another cause for concern was the scarcity of skilled labor, which was exacerbated by competition between the private yards and navy yards. The former could retain workers more easily because they could more readily adjust their rates; the navy yards however, were less flexible and often had to resort to private companies for their own repair work.

To rectify this situation government workers were to be offered 50 percent more. This would ensure an adequate force would be available to make full use of the costly navy yard facilities which were often left idle through lack of workers. It was also felt that machinery built in a navy establishment was sturdier and more reliable as it was built without regard to profit.

As the speed of Confederate blockade runners increased, it became necessary to improve the performance of any Union warship likely to come into contact with them, including any double-ender doing inshore patrol duty. A number of experiments were made, including the introduction of forced draft in the boilers. The speed of the early double-enders was about 10 knots but later examples were capable of over 13 knots.

Only one vessel in the *Iosco* group (*Wateree*) had an iron hull; the remainder were built of wood. However, all the vessels suffered from various defects. For example, *Algonquin's*

Hetzel

machinery, designed by Edward Dickeson, was a complete failure. *Eutaw*, *Massasoit*, and *Mattabesett* were reported to have been poorly built, while *Osceola* and *Shamrock* were converted into rams in 1864. They were all reported to be poor sea boats that steered badly.

Two of the group were sold in 1866, twelve in 1867, and eight more in 1868. One was sold in 1889 and the last unit was sold in 1892. *Otsego* was wrecked off Jamesville, North Carolina, in December 1864, while *Wateree* was wrecked by a tidal wave at Arica, Peru, in August 1868, having been driven 500 yards inland. Later the hulk was converted to living space ashore and she acted as an inn for several years.

USS *Hetzel*

Displacement: 200 tons. **Armament:** In 1862 had one 9-inch Dahlgren smoothbore and one 80-pdr rifle.

Hetzel was built in 1861 at Baltimore for the US Treasury Department and handed over to the navy in August 1861. She served mostly on the Carolina coast, taking part in many actions, including one on February 10, 1862, in which five Confederate gunboats were captured or destroyed. She was present at the capture of New Bern in March 1862, later helping to defend it against Confederate counter-attacks. She returned to survey work in October 1865.

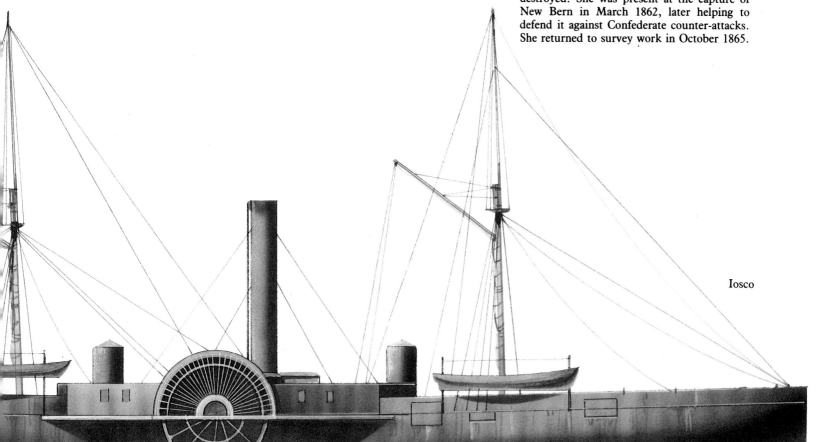

Iosco

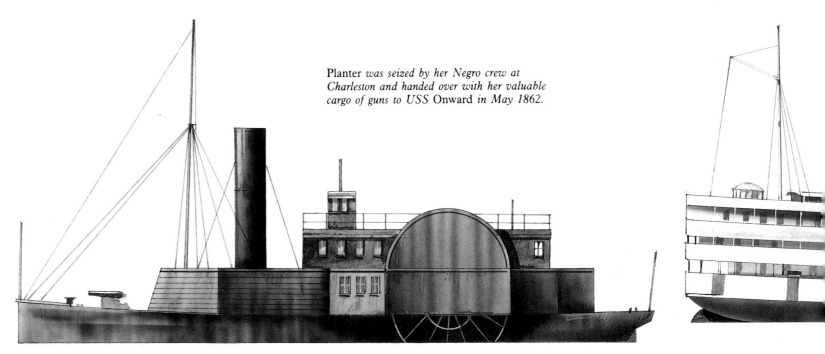

Planter was seized by her Negro crew at Charleston and handed over with her valuable cargo of guns to USS Onward in May 1862.

CSS *Planter*

Displacement: 300 tons. **Dimensions:** 147ft x 30ft x 3ft 9in. **Machinery:** Two non-condensing engines with a 6-ft stroke **Armament:** In 1862 had one long 32-pdr, and one 24-pdr howitzer.

Planter was a wooden, wood-burning, side-wheel steamer built in 1860 at Charleston for cargo use. She served as an armed dispatch boat and transport with the Engineer Department at Charleston, where she was used to carry armament and supplies to the local forts and batteries. She had White officers and a Negro crew of eight.

In early May 1862 the Negro crew plotted to seize the steamer and escape. At 3 a.m., when they and their families were safely aboard and the officers asleep ashore, the *Planter* left the wharf and headed off into the harbor, still flying the Confederate flag. The tiny band was led by pilot Robert Smalls, and as they passed each fort, they gave the usual signal on the steam whistle, so the unsuspecting sentinels let the vessel pass.

Now well away from danger, *Planter* ran up a white flag and headed for the nearest Union vessel. When handed over, *Planter*'s cargo consisted of one 7-inch rifle plus four smaller weapons that were to have been installed in a battery ashore. Smalls and the crew received half the estimated value of the ship and cargo — some $4500 — as a result of a special act of Congress.

Planter was not retained by the navy as she was not a coal-burner.

USS *Miami*

Displacement: 730 tons. **Dimensions:** 208ft 2in x 33ft 2in x 8ft 6in. **Machinery:** One inclined direct-acting engine with a 7-ft stroke. **Speed:** 8 knots. **Armament:** In 1862 had one 80-pdr Parrott rifle, one 9-inch Dahlgren smoothbore, and four 24-pdr; in April 1863 five more 9-inch Dahlgren guns were added. **Crew:** 134.

Miami was a strongly built double-ender designed by Lenthall and Isherwood. Laid down in 1861 at the Philadelphia Navy Yard,

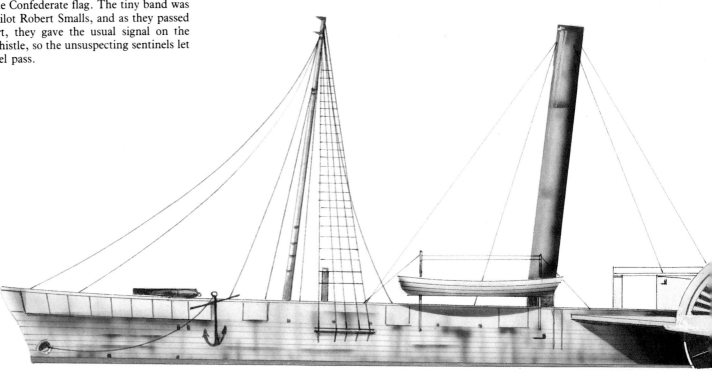

Admiral Porter's well appointed flagship Black Hawk. *He kept two horses aboard ready for a canter ashore when the opportunity presented itself.*

she was launched in November 1861 and completed January 1862 at a cost of $179,051.

In April 1862 she served with the Mortar Fleet before Forts St Philip and Jackson, towing three mortar boats at a time. After providing covering fire as needed, she helped transport troops to the forts prior to their surrender. She then spent several days at New Orleans before towing mortar boats upriver ready to attack Vicksburg in June.

Miami was employed to move the mortar vessels into suitable firing positions and she also took part in firing at the cliffside Confederate defenses.

She served next on the James River, then was refitted at Norfolk prior to moving on to the North Carolina Sounds in November for blockade duty.

It was well known that the Confederates had several ironclads under construction in the rivers of North Carolina, but Union efforts to destroy them failed. The first of these powerful vessels ready for service was the *Albemarle* which was stationed in the Roanoke River and was to assist Confederate troops in their attack on Plymouth on April 17

Miami, with Lt. Cdr. C.W. Flusser as senior officer, was backed up by three Union gunboats in its defense of Plymouth. Flusser planned to lash his gunboat to the *Southfield*, and together they would ram *Albemarle*.

On April 19 at about 3.30 a.m. the gunboat on picket duty above the defenses ran down to report that the ironclad was on its way. *Miami* and *Southfield* were already lashed together, so they steamed at her as soon as she came into view. As the vessels collided, *Albemarle* scraped across the bow of the *Miami* and rammed *Southfield*, cutting a fatal hole in her starboard side which caused her to sink immediately.

Miami poured in a hot fire but the shots simply bounced off the casemate of the ironclad. Flusser was killed by a shell which landed back on his own vessel. *Miami* then retired down the river.

She later returned to the James River in support of General Grant's final drive on Richmond. She was sold at Philadelphia in August 1865 for $19,000.

USS *Black Hawk*

Displacement: 902 tons. **Dimensions:** 260ft x 45ft x 6ft. **Armament:** In 1863 had two 32-pdr, 57-cwt, two 32-pdr, 33-cwt, two 30-pdr army Parrott rifles, plus two 12-pdr, one Parmenter & Bromwell's gun, plus two Union repeating guns; armament later varied.

Black Hawk was built in 1848 at New Albany and named *Uncle Sam*. She was purchased by the navy in November 1862 at Cairo, Illinois, for $36,000 and converted into a lightly protected gunboat, but still retained her luxurious cabin fittings. She was commissioned in December 1862 for service on the Mississippi and became Admiral Porter's flagship. She was one of the fifty-four vessels Porter added to the rapidly expanding Mississippi Squadron before the fall of Vicksburg.

Black Hawk served before Vicksburg, Fort Hindman, Arkansas, in January 1863, Hains Bluff, Mississippi, in April and May, and the Red River expedition from March to May 1864. She continued to patrol the Mississippi and its tributaries until she accidentally caught fire on April 22, 1865 three miles above Cairo. The flames swept rapidly through the vessel as she started to drag, owing to the action of the current on the wheels which had now fallen into the water.

Fortunately, the *Tempest*, who was nearby, had steam up and was able to draw alongside and take off the crew. *Tempest* pulled away from the flaming wreck just in time, as showers of sparks threatened to set her on fire too.

Black Hawk sank, but the wreck was eventually raised, fetching $389, of which one quarter went to the government.

Miami *at the time of her action in April 1864 with the Confederate ironclad* Albemarle. *She had been in action all day helping the Plymouth garrison to resist a determined Confederate attack, when the ironclad struck her consort,* Southfield.

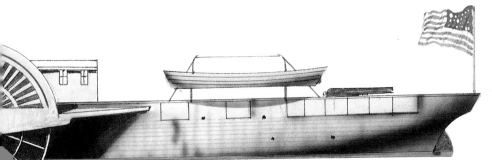

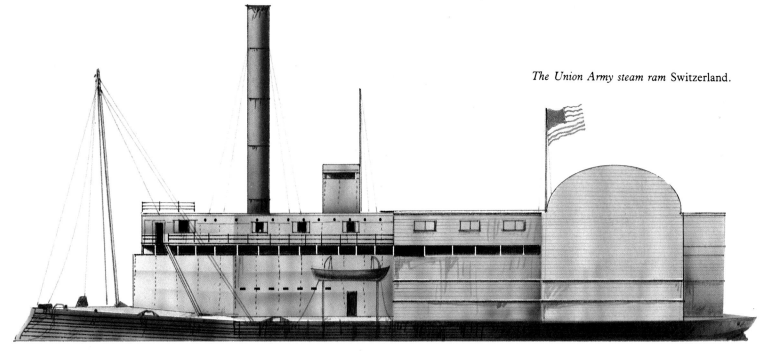

The Union Army steam ram Switzerland.

Switzerland

Switzerland was a 500-ton steam ram purchased by the War Department for service with the Mississippi Marine Brigade, which was commanded by naval personnel. Although many of the vessels taken over by the army were transferred to the navy in late 1863, the Marine Brigade remained essentially an army unit.

Switzerland took part in blockading the Red River, but was sunk on March 25, 1863, by gunfire while trying to pass the Vicksburg batteries.

USS *Santiago de Cuba*

Displacement: 1567 tons. **Dimensions:** 229ft x 38ft x 6ft 2in. **Machinery:** Single-beam engine with an 11-ft stroke. **Speed:** 14 knots maximum, but averaged 8 knots. **Armament:** In 1861 had two 20-pdr Parrott rifles and eight 32-pdr, 57-cwt guns; armament then varied. **Crew:** 114.

Santiago de Cuba was a large, wooden-hulled, brigantine-rigged sidewheel steamer built at Brooklyn, New York, in 1861, and purchased the same year for $200,000. The total cost of repairs while in the navy was $104,088.

She first served off Cuban waters, then moved on to the Bahamas. During this ten-month period, ending in August 1862, she captured six blockade runners.

In September she joined a flying squadron created to hunt down the elusive Confederate raiders *Alabama* and *Florida*. Although the squadron never caught up with them, it did capture several blockade runners.

In June 1863 *Santiago de Cuba's* high speed enabled her to capture the fast runner *Victory* after a long chase. She eventually went out of service in December 1863 for much needed repair work.

Fort Jackson

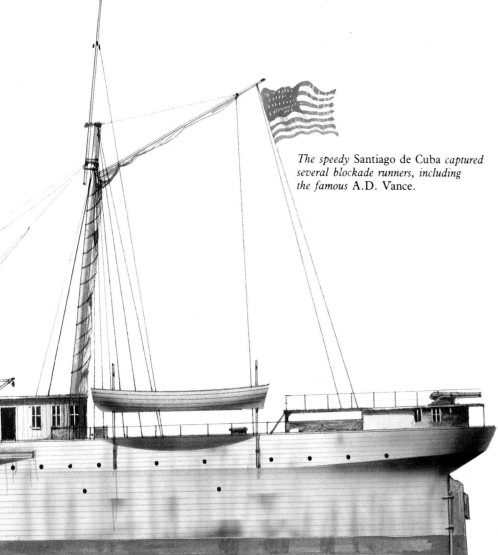

The speedy Santiago de Cuba *captured several blockade runners, including the famous* A.D. Vance.

After a three-month refit she was back in service, and in September 1864 captured the famous blockade runner *A.D. Vance*, with a cargo of cotton, off Wilmington, North Carolina. At the end of 1864 she took part in the attack on Fort Fisher which lasted for three days.

With her high speed, which she could maintain as long as needed when chasing the swift blockade runners, she was a valuable addition to the Union force. She was usually stationed on the third outer ring of a blockade line where she could chase after any boat that broke through the first two cordons.

Santiago de Cuba was sold in September 1865 for £108,000, and served for over twenty years in the mercantile marine. In December 1886 her engines were removed and she was rigged as a schooner.

USS *Fort Jackson*

Displacement: 1850 tons. **Dimensions:** 250ft x 38ft 6in x 18ft. **Speed:** 14 knots. **Armament:** In 1864 had one 100-pdr Parrott rifle, two 30-pdr rifles and eight 9-inch Dahlgren smoothbores; armament then varied.

Fort Jackson was a large, fast, wooden side-wheel steamer, formerly named *Kentucky*, and then *Union*. She was purchased in July 1863 for $350,000 from C.W. Vanderbilt.

While on her first cruise in September 1863 on the lookout for blockade runners, she burnt out a boiler, forcing her to New York for repairs. She subsequently served on the North Atlantic squadron, where she captured four blockade runners. She was sold at public auction in New York in September 1865 for $108,000.

Gunboats

USS *Commodore Perry*

Displacement: 512 tons. **Dimensions:** 143ft x 33ft x 10ft. **Armament:** In 1863 had one 12-pdr smoothbore howitzer, two 9-inch Dahlgren smoothbores, and two 32-pdr, 47-cwt; in 1864 had one 100-pdr Parrott rifle, four 9-inch Dahlgren smoothbores, and one heavy 12-pdr.

Commodore Perry was built by Stack & Joyce of Williamsburg, New York, in 1859. She was purchased by the navy in October 1861 for $38,000. Commissioned at the end of October, she sailed for Hampton Roads in January 1862 to join the North Atlantic Blockading Squadron. Here she took part in the capture of Roanoke Island, going on to help secure parts of the North Carolina coast as the blockade started to become effective. In March she was present at the capture of New Bern, and in April helped to capture five vessels in the Pasquotank River and Newtogen Creek.

The gunboat was subsequently in action against Franklin, Virginia, and Plymouth, North Carolina, where she supported army units during the end of 1862. By early 1863 she was patrolling Pamlico and Albemarle Sounds, constantly making trips up the numerous streams that led into those waters, and frequently exchanging fire with small groups of the enemy ashore.

During late 1863 she underwent repairs at Norfolk and Baltimore, returning to duty in March 1864. She patrolled the rivers and inland waterways of Virginia, taking part in further ambitious expeditions.

She sailed for New York in June 1865 and was sold there by public auction in July to the New York and Brooklyn Ferry Co. for $16,200. During her service she had cost the navy $56,431 in repairs.

USS *Commodore McDonough*

Displacement: 532 tons. **Dimensions:** 8ft draft. **Armament:** In 1862 had one 9-inch Dahlgren smoothbore, one 20-pdr Parrott rifle, and four 24-pdr smoothbores. **Crew:** 75.

Commodore McDonough was a wooden side-wheel ferry boat purchased from the Union Ferry Co., New York, for $42,409 in August 1862. She was fitted out at the New York Navy Yard and ready in November, when she joined the South Atlantic Blockading Squadron at Port Royal. She operated mainly off Charleston, South Carolina, but also took part in many minor actions up the shallow rivers,

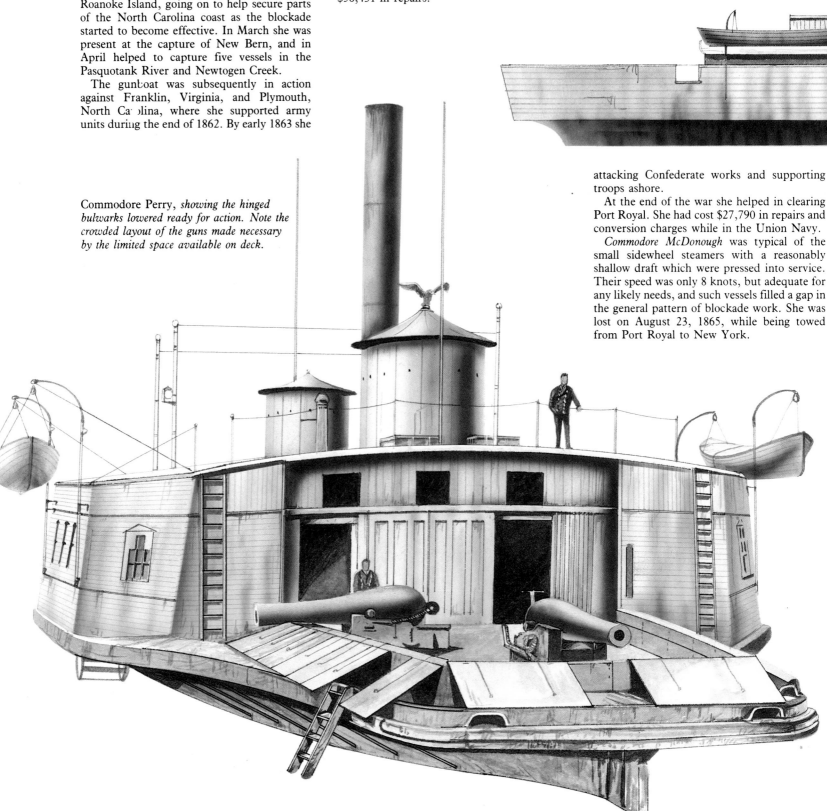

Commodore Perry, *showing the hinged bulwarks lowered ready for action. Note the crowded layout of the guns made necessary by the limited space available on deck.*

attacking Confederate works and supporting troops ashore.

At the end of the war she helped in clearing Port Royal. She had cost $27,790 in repairs and conversion charges while in the Union Navy.

Commodore McDonough was typical of the small sidewheel steamers with a reasonably shallow draft which were pressed into service. Their speed was only 8 knots, but adequate for any likely needs, and such vessels filled a gap in the general pattern of blockade work. She was lost on August 23, 1865, while being towed from Port Royal to New York.

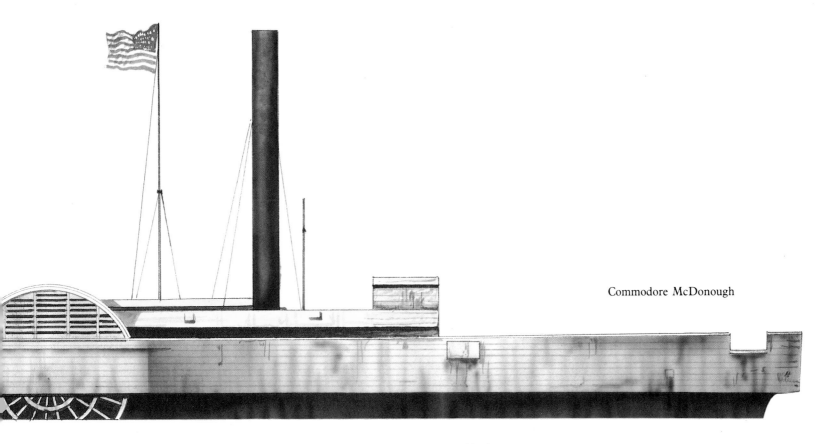

Commodore McDonough

USS *Queen of the West*

Displacement: 406 tons. **Dimensions:** 180ft x 37ft 6in x 8ft. **Armament:** In 1863, while in Confederate service, had one 30-pdr Parrott rifle, one 20-pdr Parrott rifle, and three 12-pdr howitzers. **Crew:** 120.

Queen of the West was a wooden riverboat built in 1854 in Cincinnati and purchased by the US Army in 1862. They converted her into a ram, forming part of Colonel Ellet's ram fleet that operated with gunboats of the US Navy.

She ran past the Vicksburg defenses in early February 1863, and on into the Red River, but then ran aground near a shore battery which fired at her. This cut her steam pipe and disabled the vessel, so the crew abandoned ship and escaped downriver in a steamer they had seized earlier.

Queen of the West then served briefly with the Confederate Army who placed iron around the machinery for protection. With CSS *Webb*, she forced the Union ironclad *Indianola* to surrender on February 24, 1863, but was herself attacked on April 14 by *Calhoun*, *Estrella*, and *Arizona*. A shell from *Calhoun* set her cotton protection alight, so the vessel was abandoned and drifted down the river in flames before exploding.

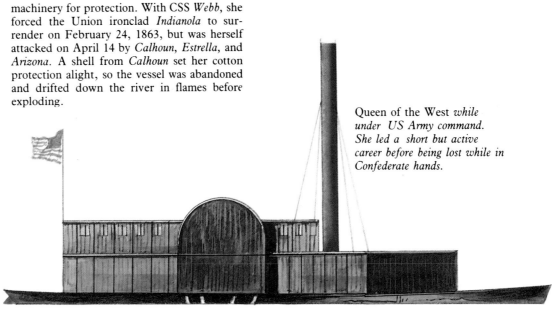

Queen of the West *while under US Army command. She led a short but active career before being lost while in Confederate hands.*

CSS *Lady Davis*

Displacement: 250 tons. **Armament:** One 24-pdr and one 12-pdr rifled gun.

Lady Davis was purchased at Charleston in March 1861 by Governor Pickens of South Carolina, who armed her. Formerly named *James Gray*, she was built in 1858 at Philadelphia as a steam tug. In May 1861 she was purchased by the Confederate Navy for $32,000 and employed along the Georgia and South Carolina coasts.

On May 19, while searching for the US brig *Perry*, she captured the 980-ton sailing ship *A.B. Thompson*. She subsequently took part in the battle of Port Royal in November 1861. Her engines were transferred to the ironclad *Palmetto State* toward the end of 1862, but as the displacement of the ironclad far outweighed that of the iron tug, they were not really effective.

Lady Davis continued in service because of the shortage of good iron hulls, and became a privately-owned blockade runner. She was captured in 1865 at Charleston after it fell.

Lady Davis *was an iron-hulled tug built in 1858. Later her sturdy engines were used in one of the Confederate ironclads at Charleston.*

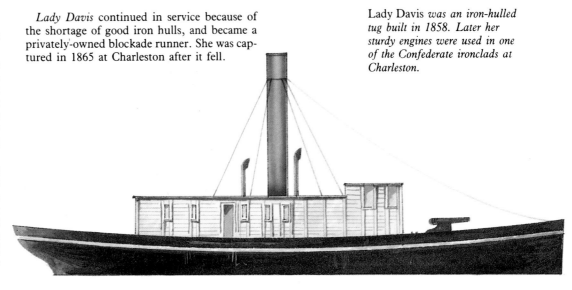

CSS *Sumter*

Displacement: 449 tons. **Dimensions:** 184ft x 30ft x 12ft 6in. **Speed:** 10 knots. **Armament:** One 8-inch shell gun and four 32-pdr.

Sumter was originally the bark-rigged screw steamer *Havana* built in 1859 by Vaughn & Lynn of Philadelphia for McConnell's New Orleans and Havana Line. She was capable of maintaining 9 or 10 knots for lengthy periods, and made the run between New Orleans and Havana, Cuba, in fifty-five hours.

She was purchased in April 1861 at New Orleans for conversion into a commerce raider. Her decks were strengthened to take the additional weight of guns amounting to over 11,000 pounds. Extra quarters were built into the vessel for the additional crew needed. Magazines and shell-rooms were also added,

The exposed machinery caused concern as, like all merchant ships, the *Havana*'s engines were partly above the waterline, which would leave them very exposed in action. It was not possible to carry out any modifications to the machinery, so iron bars were placed in position to protect the upper parts of the engines.

Captain Raphael Semmes, who had been appointed her commander and overseen the lengthy conversion, was now ready to sail. He received $10,000 from the Confederate Navy Department to pay for the initial costs of the cruise and it was hoped that any extra expense would be covered by the sale of prizes. This hope was not realized; the entire cruise cost about $18,000 more than the original $10,000. The difficulty of selling prizes abroad to raise funds was to prove a constant headache for the captains of the raiders.

Sumter put to sea on June 30, narrowly escaping from the pursuing US *Brooklyn*. The two main outlets of the Mississippi were guarded by the two fast and powerful cruisers *Brooklyn* and *Powhattan*. Semmes closely watched the entrances for any sign that the Union blockaders might relax their grip, but it was not until June

30 that the way seemed clear. The blockaders came in so close that their mastheads could be seen from the *Sumter*.

Brooklyn left her station to chase a distant vessel, so Semmes took his chance and slipped out to sea. He turned back, however, when he sighted the telltale trail of smoke coming from a steamer trying to escape. *Brooklyn* swiftly turned and headed back. Meanwhile, *Sumter* had to squeeze past a stranded vessel on the bar, which lost her valuable time. *Brooklyn* was now only seven miles away from the *Sumter*, doing 11.5 knots against the raider's 9.

As the *Sumter* sped along, the gap between the two vessels closed and was soon down to

four miles. At this point the *Sumter*'s boilers started to foam as a result of suddenly heating the salt water in them. Steam pressure was built up from 18 to 25 pounds, a dangerously high figure on the raider. In order to lighten the ship, a gun and 1500 gallons of water were dumped.

With *Sumter*'s rig of large fore-and-aft sail, she could sail close to the wind, yet still take advantage of her engine. *Brooklyn* could not match this ability, only being able to move under steam alone. At that moment a rain

Sumter during conversion into a raider. Sections 12ft wide were cut into the bulwarks and could be hinged back, allowing the deck guns a wide arc of fire.

squall hid the two opponents from each other, but when *Brooklyn* reappeared she still seemed too close for comfort.

At that point the *Sumter's* engineer reported that the boilers had stopped foaming, which removed the danger, at least. Coincidentally, a fresh breeze sprang up of which *Sumter* took advantage. As *Brooklyn* trailed in the raider's wake, she was compelled to take in more sail.

Sumter, in those conditions, could still hold on to her canvas, so was soon drawing away.

After a three and a half-hour race, the *Brooklyn* turned back toward her blockading station.

Sumter commenced operations in the West Indies, before moving on to Brazil. She captured her first prize, the *Golden Rocket*. After removing the crew, coal, provisions, sailing gear, chronometers and any available food, the vessel was set on fire. This procedure was usually followed with each capture as it was not possible to send the prize into port because of manning problems. Occasionally, a boat would be spared and used to take away the prisoners. Semmes, like so many other raider commanders, did not like the idea of destroying fine

sailing vessels. Many were owned by their captains and much hardship was caused by their loss.

Sumter was caught coaling at St Pierre on Martinique, by USS *Iroquois*, who waited nine days for her to come out. However, the raider eventually escaped at night by successfully tricking her enemy and made straight for Spain, putting into Cadiz on January 4, 1862, for necessary repairs.

Forced to move on to Gibraltar, where she was eventually sold at auction to the Fraser–Trenholm interests in December 1862, *Sumter* was renamed *Gibraltar* and continued as a blockade runner.

During her illustrious career, *Sumter* captured a total of eighteen enemy ships, destroying seven of them. Although the damage inflicted on the Union cause may not seem great, there were indirect effects: insurance rates rose and great losses were incurred through the forced sale of American merchant vessels to foreign buyers.

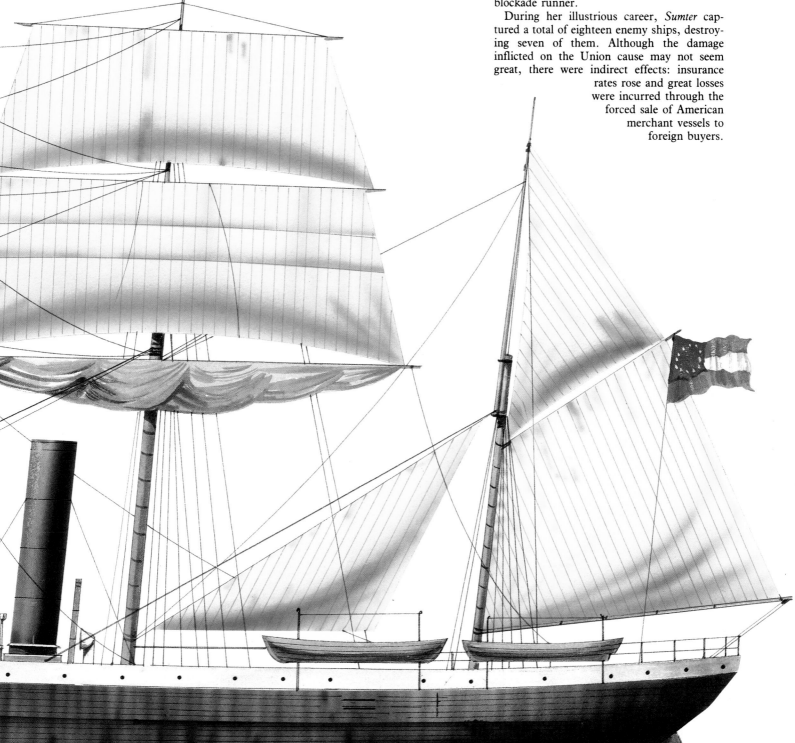

CSS *Alabama*

Displacement: 1050 tons. **Dimensions:** 220ft x 31ft 8in x 14ft. **Armament:** Six 32-pdr, one 110-pdr and one 68-pdr. **Crew:** 144.

The *Alabama* was probably one of the most famous vessels of the Civil War period, and the diplomatic rumpus caused by her activities rumbled on for many years after her demise. In fact, England eventually had to pay out vast sums in compensation for *Alabama* and her consorts' depreciations, as the raiders had been built in English yards.

Bullock, soon after arriving in Europe, set to work purchasing suitable vessels for the Confederacy. He also placed orders with several yards for suitable raiding vessels, the plan being to cause as much damage as possible to the United States mercantile marine, and simultaneously force the US Navy to remove cruisers from blockade duty in order to search for the elusive raiders.

Laid down in 1862 at the yard of Laird Brothers in Birkenhead, England, *Alabama* was a fast screw sloop-of-war with a good spread of canvas.

Bullock was anxious to get her completed quickly to back up the *Florida*, so he put pressure on Lairds to hurry things along. Although he had been assured by his legal advisers that he was operating within the law in having the war vessel built in an English yard, he knew that pressure was being put on the British government by the US authorities, and that it would not be long before the vessel was detained.

Construction work continued with irritating slowness, partly because the builders insisted on quality workmanship and materials. Workmen had to fit four different stern posts before Lairds' officials would approve the work. More delays were caused by Bullock's frequent absences on business at times when critical decisions were needed.

As the vessel took shape, it was evident that she was no ordinary craft, being a splendid example of the shipbuilders' art. She had tall lower masts which enabled her to carry large fore and aft sails. Her scantlings were light in comparison to vessels of her class, but her lines allowed her to steam and sail well.

Alabama was fitted with a lifting screw, which could be raised in fifteen minutes. This reduced the drag of an idling propeller through the water when the vessel was under sail alone.

On trials she made 11.5 knots, but in service her usual best was 10. However, on one occasion in favorable conditions, *Alabama* managed just over 13 knots. Her final cost when complete was $250,000.

Now ready for sea, Bullock hoped to be given the command of *Alabama*, but Semmes was appointed instead. His cruise in the *Sumter* had ended in Gibraltar in April when his ship, with its well worn engines, had been blockaded there by Union warships. Bullock remained in Europe to try and obtain more ironclads for the South. Understandably, he was bitterly disappointed not to get the sea-going command, but the South desperately needed someone of his outstanding ability to look after their needs ashore.

At the end of July Bullock was privately informed that *Alabama* was about to be seized

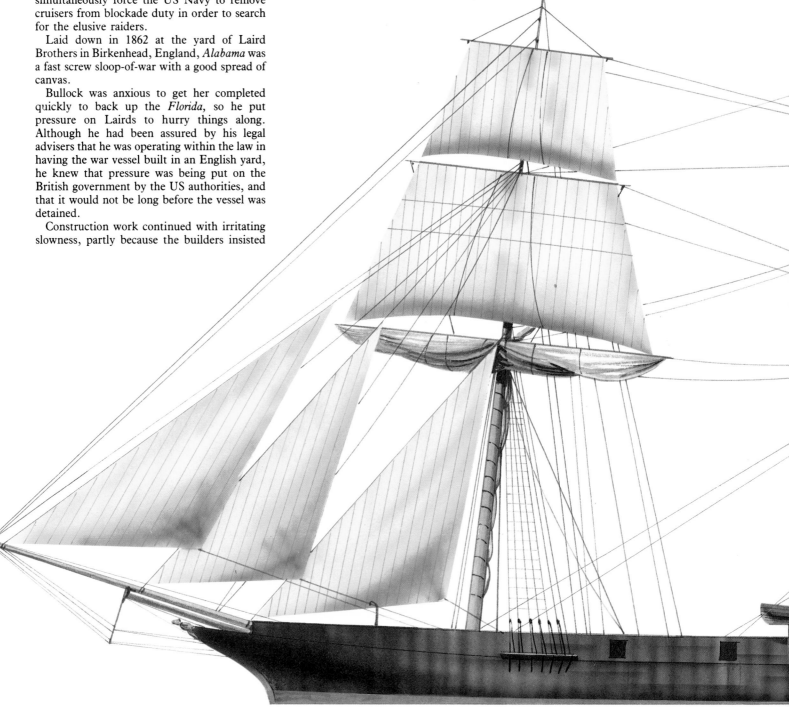

by the British government and that he had less than forty-eight hours to get her away. He told Lairds that he wanted to have another trial run, but once at sea, after landing passengers taken aboard as part of the cover up, he headed out to sea. Bullock left the vessel on August 1 and returned to Liverpool to resume his duties.

Meantime, *Alabama* met up with her tender *Agrippina* off Terceira in the Azores to transfer guns, ammunition, and stores. By August 24 *Alabama* was ready to commence her twenty-two-month career, during which she destroyed or captured over sixty-four vessels valued at nearly $6 million, including a Union gunboat. *Alabama* penetrated the whaling fleet off the Azores, burning several ships before moving on to the Newfoundland banks where more vessels were captured. After weathering a severe storm, Semmes headed for Martinique to replenish his dwindling supply of coal. Arriving on November 18 to meet up with his supply ship which had been there several months, and fearing that his movements might be known to prowling Union cruisers, he agreed a new rendezvous. As he did so *San Jacinto* arrived and hovered off the harbor, but *Alabama* slipped away.

In newspapers taken from a captured vessel, Semmes learned of an expedition that was about to sail to the Gulf of Mexico and he guessed that its destination would be Galveston. He now planned a daring raid that would take him among the convoy.

Alabama arrived off Galveston at nightfall on January 11, 1863, finding only five blockaders and no troopships. One vessel, its curiosity aroused, headed for the raider as Semmes turned back out to sea. The lone gunboat, *Hatteras*, a converted 1126-ton merchant ship followed him.

Semmes turned on the gunboat at 6.35 p.m., firing five-second fused shells in a broadside at point-blank range of 40 yards. *Hatteras*'s side was lit up, showing glowing rents of 5 or 6 feet in length. It was all over in seventeen minutes, and Semmes rescued 141 survivors.

Alabama was now overcrowded with many prisoners on board, so Semmes was forced to sail for Jamaica to set them ashore on neutral soil.

Slowly *Alabama* made her way to Bahia, reaching there in May after destroying twenty vessels. One captured ship was turned into an armed tender, renamed *Tuscaloosa*, and sent off cruising for likely victims, but without success.

While off the Cape coast, *Alabama* had a narrow escape from the fast Union cruiser *Vanderbilt*. Later Semmes heard that the large cruiser *Wyoming* was patrolling the Straits of Sunda, so he decided to carry out a surprise attack at night — but *Wyoming* could not be found.

Alabama headed for the China Sea where more Union merchant vessels were destroyed. At Singapore the Confederates came across twenty-two US merchant vessels laid up, which gives an idea of the effect the raiders had on US maritime commerce.

Semmes returned to the Cape, where he made his last two captures, then *Alabama* made her way to Cherbourg, France, for much needed repairs. While there, she was blockaded by the US *Kearsage*, with Captain John A. Winslow in command.

On the morning of Sunday, June 19, 1864, *Alabama* steamed out of the harbor for her final action which lasted seventy minutes. *Kearsage* rescued most of the *Alabama*'s survivors, but Semmes managed to escape and eventually arrived back in the Confederacy where he later commanded the James River Flotilla defending Richmond. After the war he practiced law, and died at Mobile on August 20, 1877.

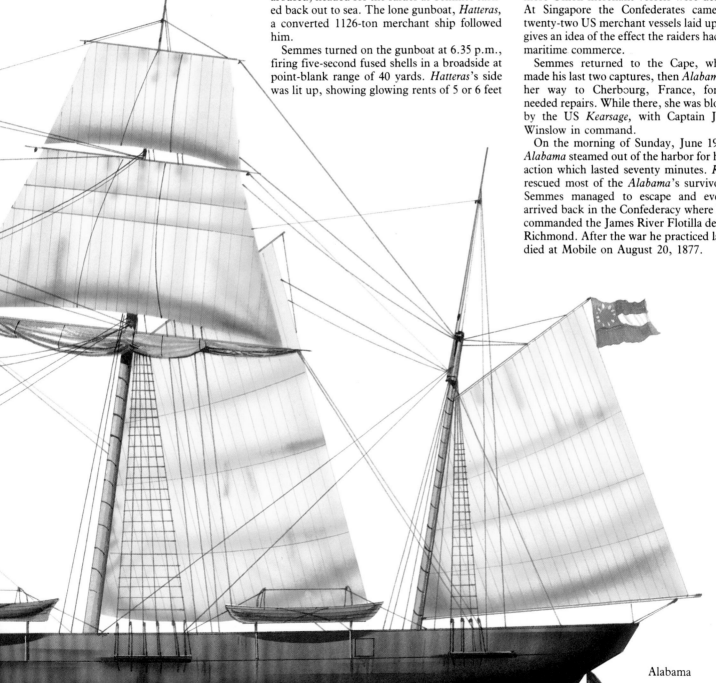

Alabama

CSS *Georgia*

Displacement: 1500 tons, later 1700 tons.
Dimensions: 220ft x 30ft x 16ft. **Speed:** 14 knots. **Armament:** fourteen 30-pdr rifles.

Georgia was one of a quartet of fast corvettes ordered in France for use as commerce raiders. They were split into two pairs, with Arman of Bordeaux building *Mississippi* under the cover name of *Osacca*, and *Louisiana* under the cover name of *Yeddo*. The idea was put about that they were intended for the Japanese.

Arman was also given a contract by Bullock for the other two, and Arman in turn sub-contracted these to J. Voruz of Nantes. *Texas*, code-named *San Francisco*, was built in the shipyard of Jollet & Babin at Nantes; *Georgia*, code-named *Shanghai*, was built by Th. Dubigeon & Sons, also in Nantes. The engines were constructed by Mazeline of Le Havre.

These four vessels were large examples of their type and sturdily built. They had roomy accommodation for long cruises, iron spars to avoid breakages, and a large spread of canvas. All were fine ships, but were never to serve the Confederacy. Nonetheless, all had eventful lives in the navies of their new owners. When nearing completion, it became obvious that, in spite of all the subterfuge, France was not going to allow the vessels to leave, especially as the French–Mexican campaign had caused the Union great alarm.

The Nantes pair were sold to Peru who was then seeking to expand her small capable navy. *Texas* became *America* and fought Spain during the Battle of Abtao on February 7, 1866, when Spain had sent a powerful fleet to fight her former colonies. During a tidal wave at Arica, Chile, on August 3 1868, she was driven ashore and badly damaged. The hulk could not be saved, but the machinery and boilers were removed. Later accounts though, include her as a hulk lost at Callao at the end of Peru's disastrous war with Chile in 1881.

Georgia became the *Union* and also served at the Battle of Abtao. During the 1879–81 war with Chile, she took part in many actions, fighting alongside the ironclad *Huascar* against a stronger force at the Battle of Angamos on October 8, 1879. Under the command of Captain Villavicencio she successfully ran the Chilean blockade of Arica and succeeded in unloading much-needed supplies and to take on coal. During the seven-hour operation, she was constantly under heavy fire. Earlier, on December 17, she had managed to unload provisions at Ylo Ylo, near Arica; in fact, for several hours she had ridden the surf and risked going aground while the supplies were taken ashore. She was saved only by her stout construction and the fine seamanship of her captain. She was finally sunk at Callao to prevent her capture on January 15, 1881.

Prussia purchased *Mississippi* and renamed her SMS *Victoria*. She served on foreign stations from 1868 to 1882 and was later used as a training ship. She was broken up at Hamburg in 1892.

Louisiana became SMS *Augusta* and took part in the Franco–Prussian War of 1870, where she made a brief foray against French trade but without much success. Indeed, she was the only Prussian cruiser to attempt a breach of the French Navy's crippling blockade of German ports where an estimated $3 million of trade per day was lost.

She was ultimately lost with her crew of 223 in the Gulf of Aden during a severe storm on April 2, 1885.

Left: *The ex-Confederate raider* Georgia *as she appeared in the Peruvian Navy under the name of* Union. *She and her sisters carried 340 tons of coal, which enabled them to steam 2500 miles at 12 knots and gave them a good range.*

CSS *Rattlesnake*

Displacement: 1221 tons. **Dimensions:** 225ft 6in x 34ft 6in x 21ft 9in. **Armament:** In 1862 had two 12-pdr guns.

Formerly named *Nashville*, *Rattlesnake* was a brig-rigged passenger steamer of the New York to Charleston Line. She was purchased by the Navy Department and fitted out as a cruiser after the fall of Fort Sumter, when she had been lying at Charleston, North Carolina. Under the command of Lt. R.B. Pegram, she ran the blockade on October 21, 1861, and made her way to Southampton, England, being the first Confederate vessel in European waters. *Georgia* returned to Beaufort, North Carolina, at the end of February 1862, after capturing two prizes worth $66,000 during her cruise.

She was renamed *Thomas L. Wragg*, placed under the command of Captain Baker, and, now acting as a blockade runner, successfully brought arms into Savannah during July 1862.

Baker realized that she could not successfully remain a blockade runner, so he decided to turn her into a privateer. Her name was changed to *Rattlesnake*, she was armed with four more guns, and took on a crew of 130 men. By November 5, 1862, she was ready.

Now painted gray to reduce her visibility, she waited in the Ogeechee River above Fort McAllister for an opportunity of slipping out to sea. Union forces had fixed a tight blockade to the mouth of the river, but tired of waiting for their quarry, they decided late in January 1863 to go up the river to find it.

On February 23 a force of gunboats backed by the monitor *Montauk* moved in to attack but fog delayed them. The delay lasted several days, but eventually the fog lifted on the afternoon of the 28th. *Montauk*, under the command of Commander Worden, was able to move forward, ready to attack the *Rattlesnake* which was now aground. The Confederates made every effort to float the vessel but *Montauk* opened fire at 1500 yards. Soon the range was down to 1200 yards as the monitor closed in, ignoring the fierce fire directed at her by the fort. Only the upper works of the *Rattlesnake* were visible across the low land. Hits were soon scored using seven-second fuses, and *Rattlesnake* was set on fire.

A fog now came down briefly but *Montauk* continued the shelling as the range was preset. Two guns had been landed from the *Rattlesnake* to help in the defense but these inflicted little damage.

Soon *Rattlesnake* was a mass of flames and blew up with tremendous violence. As *Montauk* retired down the river, she struck a mine and began to take on water, so she was grounded to examine the damage. Mud had sealed her leak and later a patch was put over the hole.

Below: Rattlesnake *as she appeared just prior to her planned Atlantic cruise.*

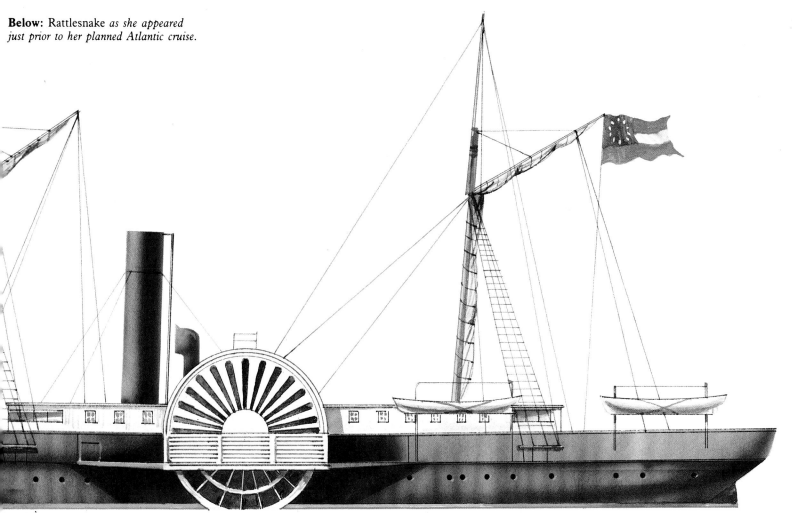

CSS *Shenandoah*

Displacement: 1160 tons. **Dimensions:** 230ft x 32ft x 20ft 6in. **Speed:** 9 knots under steam. **Armament:** Four 8-inch smoothbores, two 32-pdr rifles and two 12-pdr. **Crew:** 109.

By the summer of 1864 Confederate raiders had almost swept the Union merchant flag from the seas. Mallory, however, passed on orders to Bullock to obtain and fit out a suitable cruiser for operations in the Pacific where the Northern whaling fleet was fishing.

By the fall of 1864 Bullock heard of a likely vessel that would suit the pressing need of a badly battered Confederacy. It had to be readily available as it was no longer possible to build a suitable vessel because of the strictly enforced neutrality laws.

The vessel in question was the *Sea King*, newly completed by Stevens & Son of Glasgow, Scotland, and recently returned from a private charter to Bombay as an army transport.

Bullock purchased the vessel and managed to get her out of England on October 8, 1864, in spite of the fact that his plans were known to the Union authorities in England.

She left the Port of London as an unarmed tender. The *Laurel* was employed to carry her guns, ammunition and stores, and meet *Sea King* at Funchal, Madeira. This was accomplished and soon *Sea King* was ready. Lt. James Waddell took over command from the English captain and commissioned the vessel as CSS *Shenandoah*.

Waddell tried to persuade the crew to remain, but only twenty chose to stay on. He was now forced to sail short-handed, but during the first few weeks he managed to enlist men from the ships he captured, thus bringing up the complement to twenty-two officers and fifty-one men.

Shenandoah left Madeira on October 19 and made her first capture on the 30th. Continuing on her way, she captured several more vessels and mid-December saw her rounding the Cape of Good Hope on her way to Australia, arriving there on January 25, 1865. Waddell was forced to wait until February 18 when much needed repairs to the propeller were finished.

Threats were made against the vessel and a rumored plan included hiding American sailors on board who would seize the ship once at sea. More men deserted here but more than enough enlisted to fill the gaps.

Sailing on, the vessel passed through numerous severe storms until arriving at Ascension Island, Ponape, where Waddell

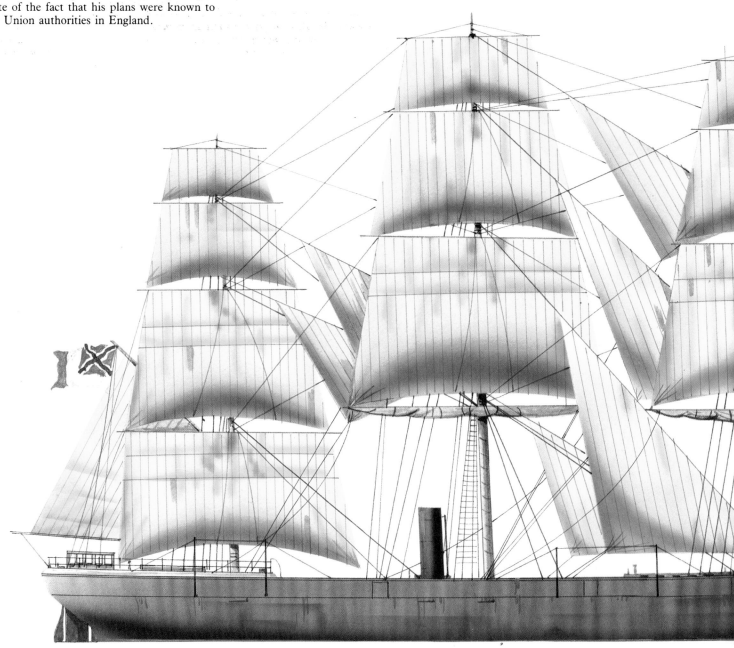

captured four American whalers. These were the first of many.

Unknown to Waddell, the Confederacy was in its death throes as he made plans to enter an area beyond the Arctic Circle where he would find plenty of quarry.

Reaching the Bering Sea on June 16, Waddell steamed through ice and fog and found the New England whaling fleet. In six days he succeeded in capturing twenty-four vessels, burning all but four, which he spared so they could be used to carry all the prisoners the raiders had on their hands.

While the whalers were still burning in the twilight of the Arctic midnight, the *Shenandoah* moved north, slowly pushing her way through drifting ice floes. Indeed for hour after dreary hour she steamed on into the frozen solitude where, as far as the eye could see, there stretched masses of ice which steadily increased in size.

Shenandoah had to take a cautious path as she was not designed for such conditions; if trapped in the ice, she would be crushed and all on board lost. As luck had it, she just managed to navigate the most hazardous area when the ice closed in, sealing the region off.

Through shifting fogs, *Shenandoah* turned South and strong rope mats were hung over the cutwater and bows to protect against the saw-like edges of jagged ice floes.

Waddell had been informed by one of the captured captains that the war was over, but as the distraught man could not produce printed evidence, Waddell refused to believe him. Later he obtained fairly up-to-date newspapers that told of the Confederate government's move to Danville and President Davis's proclamation that the war would still be continued. Armed with this news, Waddell continued with his depreciations and captured nineteen more vessels during the next five days. Again, all but four were burnt and these were used to carry away the prisoners.

Heading south, *Shenandoah* passed through the Bering Strait and forced her way through thickening ice by constantly using her engines. Steaming along the North American coast, Waddell planned a daring raid whereby he would run into San Francisco Bay at night, seize the monitor *Camanche* stationed there, and demand a ransom from the city.

On August 2 he spoke with the British bark *Baracouta* and learned that the war was finally over. The battery was immediately struck down and sail set for Liverpool.

At first there was a threat of mutiny; some officers wanted to go to Cape Town, but eventually matters quietened down and the lonely vessel started on her 17,000-mile run. For two months *Shenandoah* had avoided contact with other ships and ports, preferring to go silently on her way.

At last she anchored in the Mersey on November 6 and surrendered to the British government, who passed the vessel over to the US government. She was then sold to a British merchant, and finally the Sultan of Zanzibar purchased her as a pleasure yacht. Several years later, while on a trip to Bombay, she sank with nearly all on board during a severe storm off the Island of Socotra.

Shenandoah had been the only Confederate vessel to carry the flag right round the world, covering nearly 58,000 miles. She captured thirty vessels during her cruise, many of great value: the bark *Alina* of Searsport, valued at $95,000; the ship *Isaac Howland*, $75,000; the ship *Sophia Thornton*, $70,000; the ship *Hector*, $58,000; the bark *Favorite*, $57,896; the bark *Congress*, $55,000; the whaling barks *Waverly* valued at over $62,000; and the *Jiveh Swift* at just under $62,000. Another fifteen vessels each had a value of between $30,000 and $50,000 placed on them, and the prisoners taken totalled 1053. Most of the vessels were destroyed long after the war, representing the loss of a lifetime's work to their owner-captains.

The small handful of raiders had decimated the American merchant marine, which would not fully recover until 1918. Damage estimates vary between $15 and $25 million, representing a loss of about 200 ships. Of these, *Shenandoah* was responsible for $2,041,000 worth of shipping. Later Britain would have to pay $15 million in damages as a result of the *Alabama* claims, as they were collectively known.

The cruisers employed in searching for the raiders cost the US government $3,325,000. During the fourteen months from January 1, 1863, seventy-seven warships plus twenty-three chartered vessels were engaged in the long, monotonous task of searching miles of heaving ocean without much chance of success.

Shenandoah

CSS *Georgia*

Displacement: 700 tons. **Dimensions:** 212ft x 27ft x 13ft 9in. **Machinery:** Two steeples with a diameter of 54 in and a 4-ft stroke. **Armament:** Two 100-pdr, two 24-pdr and one 32-pdr.

Originally named *Japan*, *Georgia* was a fast screw, brig-rigged, iron merchant steamer. She was purchased on the Clyde at Dumbarton, Scotland, in March 1863 by Commander Mathew Fontaine Maury, who had been sent to England in late 1862 as one of nine Confederate naval officers stationed abroad who had the authority to purchase ships. He had arrived late on the scene and many of the more desirable vessels had already been purchased by other navies eager to acquire them.

Georgia left Greenock with a crew of fifty on the pretext of steaming to Singapore, but once away she rendezvoused with the steamer *Alar* off Ushant, France, and took on guns and supplies ready for a cruise against Union shipping.

She was officially placed in commission under the Confederate flag on April 9 under the command of Commander William Maury, a cousin of her purchaser. First the *Georgia* went to Brazil, then on to the Cape of Good Hope, capturing nine Union merchant ships and burning five of them.

Georgia proved to be a poor sailer and, while cruising in the South Atlantic, her hull became foul with marine growth as a result of the warm water. She succeeded in limping into Cherbourg during the night of October 28 – 29, 1863, to carry out repairs and clean the hull. She remained in dock for several months, but by February 1864 the vessel was judged unfit to carry on. It was arranged for her to meet up with the newly acquired CSS *Rappahannock* off the coast of Morocco to transfer her guns and other hardware, but *Rappahannock* never showed up. *Georgia* waited several weeks, during which time she had a brief skirmish with a large number of hostile Arabs who had fired on a landing party.

Georgia returned to France, then slipped past two patrolling Union warships arriving at Liverpool in May. She was sold to a merchant in June, but while at sea she was captured by USS *Niagara* and sent to Boston, where she was condemned as a prize.

Below: Georgia *at the start of her cruise. Although not a success, she still occupied the attention of numerous Union warships.*

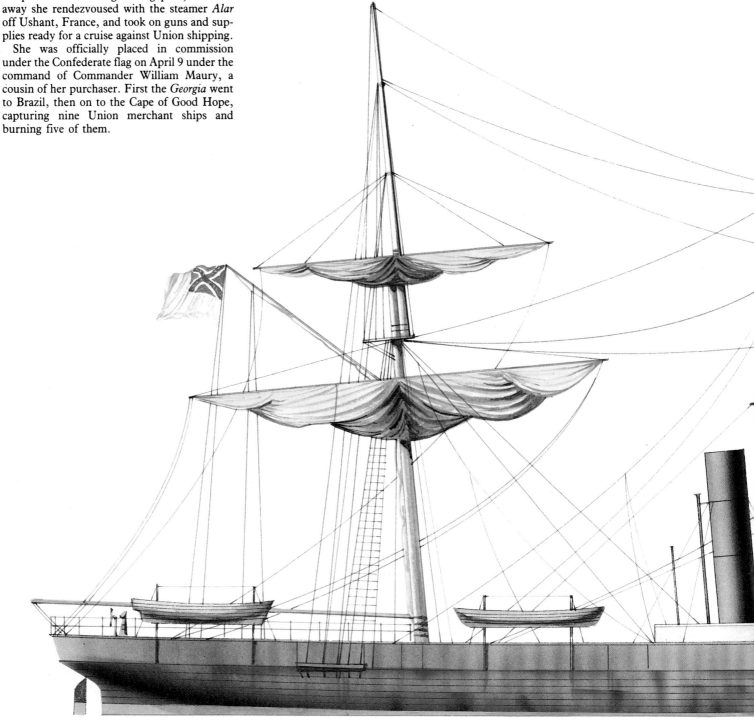

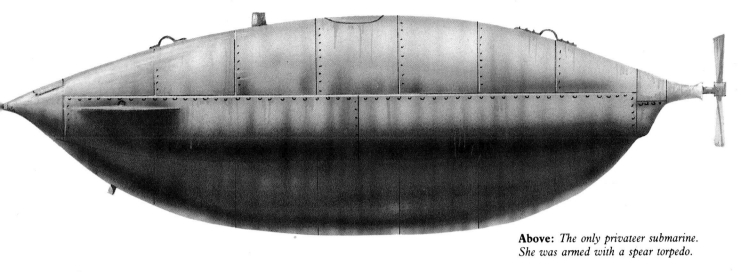

Above: *The only privateer submarine. She was armed with a spear torpedo.*

CSS *Pioneer*

Displacement: 4 tons. **Dimensions:** 34ft x 4ft x 4ft. **Crew:** 2 or 3.

The submarine vessel was almost unique at the time of the Civil War and *Pioneer* was among the first to be built. Considering her early origins, she bore a remarkable resemblance to submarines which were built many years after her.

Oval in shape, with conical ends, *Pioneer* was built at New Orleans by James McClintock and Baxter Watson at the Leeds Foundry. They co-owned the vessel with John K. Scott, who was to take command, and Robbin Barron. All provided the capital to build the craft. Construction began in late 1861 and the vessel was launched at the government yard on New Basin in February 1862. A letter of marque upon the security of H.L. Hunley, later to build his own submarine, and H.J. Leovy, was issued on March 31, 1862.

Such an early and primitive example of the submarine was limited to inshore work. The only possible source of prize money lay in destroying an enemy warship caught unawares, for which the Confederate government had offered a bounty of 20 percent of the value of the destroyed vessel.

Pioneer carried out tests, which were interrupted when New Orleans fell, and she was sunk in a bayou to prevent her capture. She remained lost to view for sixteen years, then was dredged up only to be left abandoned on the riverbank.

In April 1909 she was set up as a monument in the grounds of Camp Nicholls, a retired soldiers' home. She was moved in 1952 to Presbytere Arcade, Louisiana State Museum.

CSS *Calhoun*

Displacement: 509 tons. **Armament:** One 18-pdr, two 12-pdr and two 6-pdr. **Crew:** 85.

Calhoun was originally built at New York in 1851 as the *Cuba*. She was a fast, powerful, low-pressure sidewheel steamer — one of many similar ships that regularly went to the mouth of the Mississippi to tow up to the wharves of New Orleans sailing vessels unable to make any progress in the strong tides of the river.

Privateering created a great interest in many New Orleans businessmen and nine of them formed a syndicate to purchase the tug and obtain a letter of marque.

On May 15, 1861, *Calhoun*, under the command of Captain John Wilson, put down the river during the evening and, off the bar, made her first capture, which was the first privately-armed prize of the war. This was the bark *Ocean Eagle*, which was turned over to a tow boat while Wilson searched for more prizes.

Two days later he seized the 700-ton sailing ship *Milan* and the small schooner *Ella*. The privateer immediately returned to New Orleans with her prizes, arriving on the night of the 19th.

After remaining in port for a short time, *Calhoun* put down the river again and narrowly missed a large prize which had just been seized by a rival privateer. She was now operating in the Gulf, and after cruising for three days captured three New England whalers — *Panama*, *Mermaid*, and *John Adams* — loaded with barrels of oil. After cruising around the Gulf for a few more days *Calhoun* came into contact with USS *Brooklyn* on blockade duty, so she quickly returned to New Orleans.

When the prizes were sold at auction in early July they raised $27,700, which was under half of their true value. Operating at the same time as *Calhoun* were the privately-armed steamers *Music* and *V.H. Ivy*. The *Music* was a fast, 273-ton coast steamer, while *Ivy* was a fast, 454-ton tow boat; both were lightly armed. Like *Calhoun* they had some success, but this was at a time (early 1861) when privateering was at its peak and before enough Union vessels were available for blockade duty.

Calhoun was next chartered by the Confederate Navy with Lt. J.H. Carter in command. She became the flagship of Commodore G.N. Hollins and took part in the successful action on October 11, 1861, against five Union gunboats at the head of the passes on the Mississippi.

Calhoun was captured by the tender to the frigate *Colorado* on January 23, 1862, and taken into Union service. It became one of the most successful blockading ships, taking part in the capture of thirteen vessels by early May before being sent up the Mississippi on patrol, where she captured six more prizes.

She took part in the successful attack on the Confederate cotton-clad steamer *Queen of the West*, where one long-range shot from *Calhoun* set the Confederate vessel on fire, thus removing a serious threat to Union forces. She continued her active service, seizing more prizes, and during the attack on Fort Powell in February 1864 she briefly flew the flag of Admiral Farragut.

She was sold in October 1864 at New Orleans for $14,500. When purchased from the prize court after her capture from the Confederates, the Navy paid $29,000 for what must have been one of the more remarkable vessels to serve on both sides.

CSS *Waccamaw*

Displacement: 972. **Dimensions:** 250ft x 28ft x 15ft 6in.

Waccamaw and her sister ship *Black Prince* were a large pair of vessels ordered by the main Confederate agent James Bullock. They were first intended to run the blockade with sup-plies, then to either be fitted out as raiders, or continue as blockade runners.

While under construction they were given the cover names *Enterprise* and *Adventure*. They were well-proportioned screw steamers built by William Denny & Bros. of Dumbarton, Scotland.

As the situation in the South worsened, Mallory asked Bullock to dispose of the ships and use the funds to build two vessels of light draft that would be more suitable for work in home waters. *Waccamaw* and *Black Prince* were taken back by Denny and disposed of in November 1865.

CSS *Rappahannock*

Displacement: 857 tons. **Dimensions:** 200ft x 30ft 2in x 14ft 6in.

Rappahannock was formerly HMS *Victor*, a steam sloop-of-war built on the River Thames in 1857. She was put up for sale in 1863 and purchased in November for the Confederacy under the cover of plying in the China trade. However, the British authorities suspected her true purpose and ordered her detention. Nevertheless, she was able to escape from Sheerness dockyard at the mouth of the Thames where she was undergoing much needed repairs.

Originally Commander Maury had intended to replace her with the *Georgia*, from which she was to obtain her battery of guns. *Rappahannock* would have made an ideal raider, having a wooden hull, twin engines, bark rig and lifting screw which greatly aided sailing under canvas alone.

When fleeing from Sheerness only hours before her detention order arrived, her bearing burnt out and she had to put into Calais for repairs. Here Lt. C.M. Fauntleroy took command.

After various delays the would-be raider was laid up at Calais and used by the Confederates as a store ship. At the end of the war she was turned over to the United States government.

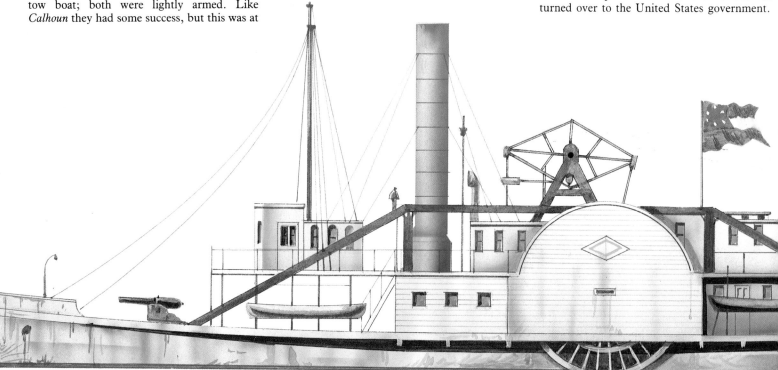

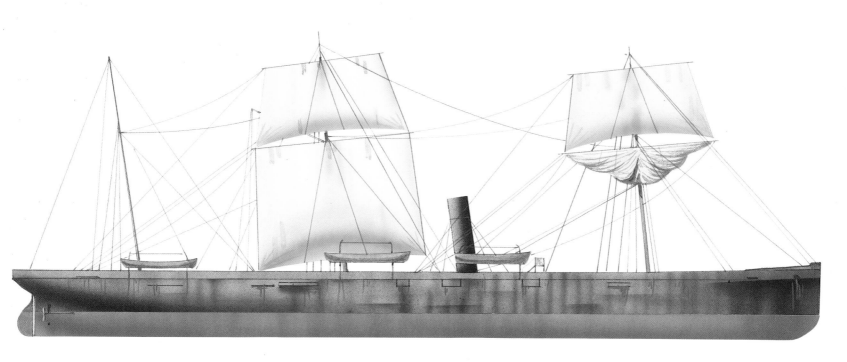

Above: *The sleek lines of the* Waccamaw *were typical of the merchant vessels of the time, which stand in contrast to the steam sloop-of-war.*

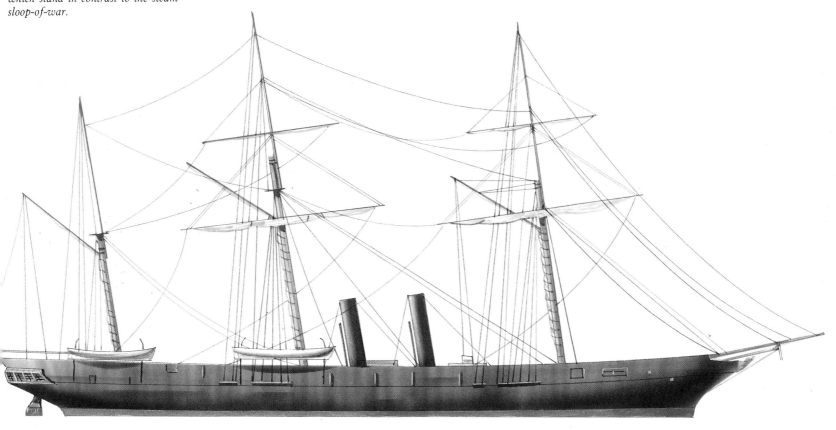

Left: *Sidewheel steamer* Calhoun *in her role as a privateer. After capture by Union forces she went on to be an even more successful blockader, taking many prizes.*

Above: Rappahannock, *with her graceful lines and light rig. This section highlights the many differing types of vessel pressed into service by the Confederates, and also shows up the tremendous problems they faced in trying to organize a cohesive force.*

CSS *Florida*

Displacement: 700 tons. **Dimensions:** 192ft x 27ft 2in x 13ft. **Speed:** 9.5 knots, 12 under canvas. **Armament:** Two 7-inch Blakely rifles, six 6-inch Blakely rifles and one 12-pdr howitzer.

Stephen R. Mallory, secretary of the Confederate States Navy, realized as soon as he took office in 1861 that the South was capable of providing only a few of its desperately needed warships. If it was to have any chance at all against the massive industrial might of the North, he would have to obtain additional vessels abroad.

Europe was the only source able to supply his immediate needs and he lost no time in sending abroad suitable agents empowered to purchase and build warships suitable to the needs of the flagging navy.

His most capable officer was James D. Bullock, who had been an officer in the US Navy, and he was chosen to head up a team of newly appointed officers.

Bullock arrived in England on June 4, 1861, and immediately set up headquarters in Liverpool, where he made contact with the Confederate commercial representative, Charles K. Prioleau of Fraser Trenholm & Company, which was partly owned by businessmen in Charleston, South Carolina.

Bullock learnt that the necessary funds for his activities had not yet arrived from Richmond, but Fraser Trenholm agreed to accept the financial responsibility of any orders placed. Bullock was thus able to start construction on *Oreto*, later known as *Florida*, in June 1861, within a few weeks of arriving.

Efforts were also made to buy existing vessels, particularly wooden ones, that were good sailers, could steam well and had a large coal capacity to enable them to remain at sea for long periods. Wooden ships were preferred because they could be more easily repaired in out of the way places where docking facilities were limited. However, one drawback to this plan was that, in England, wooden vessels were more expensive than iron ones because of the high price of timber.

The blockade made it impossible for Confederate cruisers to use their own ports for supplies, and the neutrality laws of many countries would not allow the raiders to call for coal more than once in ninety days. The longer the raider remained at sea, the more enemy merchant vessels she could destroy, but such ships were not readily available and had to be specially constructed.

After much searching for a suitable builder, Bullock selected William A. Miller & Sons of Liverpool to build the *Florida*, as they had much experience in building wooden vessels for the Royal Navy where heavy weights of guns and supplies were the norm.

Fawcett and Preston & Company, also of Liverpool, were to build the engines and later, when *Florida* was fitted out, they handled all the financial transactions.

It was decided to use a British dispatch boat as the basic model because plans of a suitable ship already existed and needed only slight modifications. The length was increased so that more coal could be carried and, as a bonus, add to her speed. Increased rigging was also provided to increase the amount of sail carried.

Secrecy was of the utmost importance and Bullock knew that his every move was watched

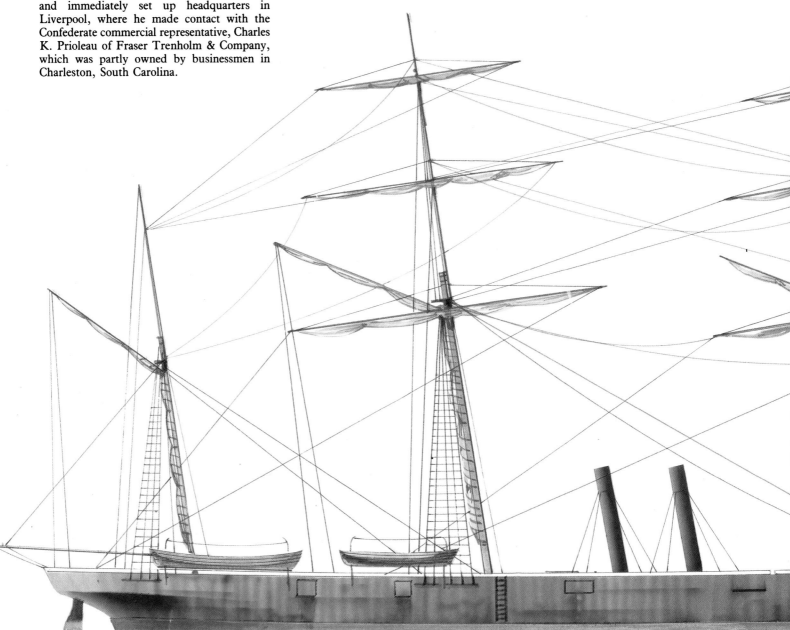

by US officials and their hirelings. *Florida* was therefore given the name *Oreto* and the story was put about that she was meant for an Italian buyer. The ruse worked, and it was not until January 1862 that any evidence of the vessel's true purpose was uncovered by the US officials.

During February the US Consul gained sufficient proof of her true identity when two guns were put aboard. The net began to close in the efforts to have her seized.

Bullock was equal to the situation and quietly got the vessel to sea on March 22, 1862, under the command of James A. Duguid.

Oreto met up at Nassau with the transport *Bahama* who had brought guns and ammunition out from Scotland. While at Nassau under her newly appointed commander, Captain John Newland Maffitt, she was detained and consequently lost nearly all of her 130 crew. Maffitt hastily gathered twenty local men and got out to sea as soon as the legal dispute was settled.

The supplies from the *Bahama* were loaded aboard a small schooner that followed the would-be raider to Green Key, seventy-five miles south of Nassau. Then away from prying eyes and under a blazing August sun, the transshipment of the schooner's cargo was carried out.

By the morning of the 17th the arduous seven-day task was completed and the officially named *Florida* got underway. Unfortunately, she carried the deadly scourge of yellow fever with her and Maffitt had to put into Cardenas, Cuba, for medical help. The situation worsened and five men died, including Maffitt's stepson. After burying the dead at sea, Maffitt headed for Havana where a pilot was picked up who knew the entrance of the nearest Confederate port of Mobile.

Florida avoided contact with cruising Union warships on the lookout for them by keeping close inshore at night off the Cuban coast. Maffitt had been seriously ill himself all this time but was determined to reach Mobile, so heading northwest, with more of the crew stricken down, he made a dash across the open sea towards the Gulf and safety.

Maffitt arrived at Mobile on September 4, only to find three Union vessels off the port. Without hesitation the *Florida*, with her depleted crew, sped past the blockaders, receiving several hits.

Repairs on the *Florida* were not started until October 3 when the quarantine was lifted. The shortage of skilled workers and ordnance supplies caused further delays, and the guns were not ready until early January 1863.

More delay was caused by having to fit out the *Florida* many miles from a dockyard. This was because her deep draft forced her to anchor twenty-eight miles from Mobile in the open bay, which meant that workers had to be taken to and from her in boats. It also meant that machinery and equipment that needed repairs had to be dismantled and shipped to Mobile, then reassembled on the vessel when ready.

Work on *Florida* was also hampered by the bad winter weather which often meant long stoppages. Much of the standing rigging needed replacing, which meant a further demand on limited facilities. The tremendous difficulties involved in getting repairs done and obtaining essential military supplies clearly show the problems faced by the Confederacy in its conduct of the war. At least six weeks were spent in waiting for the necessary items to complete the *Florida* for sea.

At last she was ready on January 10, 1863, but by now a dozen blockading vessels hovered off the port. Maffitt waited for a dark night, but while being moved around Mobile Bay the vessel ran aground. It took two days to float her, and then only after the guns and coal had been taken off. She was finally towed free by the steamers *Morgan* and *Gains*, but went aground a second time, causing a repeat performance of unloading before she was afloat once more.

A northeast storm sprang up, creating ideal conditions for escape. As the rain eased at 2 a.m. on the 17th, the *Florida* slipped out to sea in a thick mist and succeeded in getting past the first two blockaders. When sighted by the third through telltale sparks from her funnel, *Florida* put on steam and set all sails, allowing her to outrun her pursuers, at one stage making 14.5 knots.

At about 5 a.m. that day, *R.R. Culyer*, the one vessel present that could outrun the *Florida*, was spotted only three miles away. Maffitt took in all sails and shut down the engine. As the sea was rough, the high waves hid the low-lying hull of the raider. Once clear, *Florida* steamed on her way. During her two years of operations against Union commerce, she caused $4,051,000 worth of damage destroying (with the tenders outfitted by her crew) fifty-seven vessels, plus one that was recaptured.

During *Florida's* first cruise, which ended in August 1863, she captured twenty-four vessels, including the two barks *Lapwing* and *Clarence*, used as tenders. During the second cruise from March 1864 to September, she made thirteen more captures, including the only steamer, *Electric Spark*. Her tenders, *Clarence* and *Tacony* captured a further twenty-one.

The estimate cost of the *Florida* and the expenses of her cruise came to about $400,000.

Three days after putting into the Brazilian port of Bahia on October 4, 1864 for coal, she was seized by USS *Wachusett*, towed out to sea and sent to the United States as a prize. While anchored at Newport News, she was rammed by the army transport *Alliance* on November 28 and sunk.

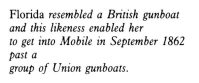

Florida *resembled a British gunboat and this likeness enabled her to get into Mobile in September 1862 past a group of Union gunboats.*

Hercules

CSS *Hercules*

Displacement: 515 tons. **Dimensions:** 170ft x 25ft x 7ft 6in. **Speed:** 12 knots. **Armament:** One 9-inch and one 8-inch rifle.

Hercules and her sister *Ajax* were small iron-screw steamers ordered by Bullock in August 1864 from William Denny & Bros of Dumbarton, Scotland. It was intended first of all to run the ships into Wilmington, North Carolina, loaded with war material, then to arm them for local defense. *Hercules* was completed in February 1865, but she was bought back by Denny when it was seen that she would no longer be needed now that the South's fate was sealed.

Ajax was ready in early January and sailed from Dumbarton on the 12th with Lt. John Low in command. Stopping off briefly at Dublin, Ireland, she proceeded on to Nassau where Low took on a new crew. She then went on to St George's, Bermuda, prior to making a dash for a Confederate port. However, the end of the war stopped this, so she returned to England. She was later sold in September through two ex-Confederate agents in Brazil.

CSS *Savannah*

Displacement: 53 tons. **Dimensions:** 56ft long. **Armament:** One short 18-pdr model 1812. **Crew:** 20.

Savannah, ex-pilot boat No. 7, was one of the rapidly growing bank of private vessels that were pressed into service during the early months of 1861. She played a more prominent role in the war than her diminutive size suggests, her crew being labeled ''pirates'' and threatened with the death penalty when she was finally captured. Only when President Davis intervened and threatened to hang the officers on an ''eye for an eye'' basis did wiser counsel prevail in the Union.

Under the command of Captain Harrison Baker, *Savannah* left Charleston on June 2, 1861, carrying the first letter of marque issued by the Confederacy. After capturing a brig valued at $30,000 and sending her prize into port, *Savannah* continued to cruise, but during a storm part of her rig was carried away. This had fatal repercussions for the speedy schooner, as she fell in with the US brig *Perry* at dusk. *Perry* quickly overhauled the lame vessel, *Savannah* lowered sail so as to reduce her visibility in the murky darkness but without success and she was forced to surrender.

A far more successful raiding captain was Lt. Charles W. Read who, while serving aboard CSS *Florida*, took command of the captured brig *Clarence* and began a career that carried destruction into the heart of Portland. He successfully captured seven vessels, including a revenue cutter, which Read boarded in the harbor and seized.

Privateering was regarded as legal in the South, the United States having been unwilling to sign the Declaration of Paris in 1856 which outlawed such activity. The decision not to sign had been based upon the success of her privateers in the war of 1812.

Cyclone

Cyclone was laid down late as a speculation in 1864 by William Denny & Bros of Dumbarton, Scotland, and P. Henderson & Co. with a view to selling her to the Confederacy who were known to be seeking suitable vessels.

It was quite usual at the time to build standard-type vessels without a particular purchaser in mind as a way of keeping on highly skilled staff when contract work was nearing its end. When a large yard had several slips available, one could easily be set aside for a speculative purchaser. As more definite orders came in workers on the speculation or stand-by ship could be redeployed as needed.

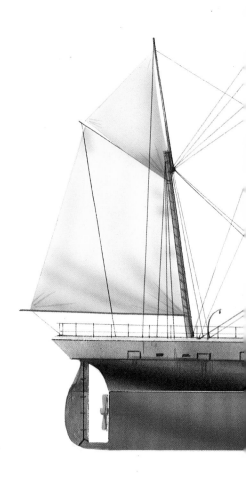

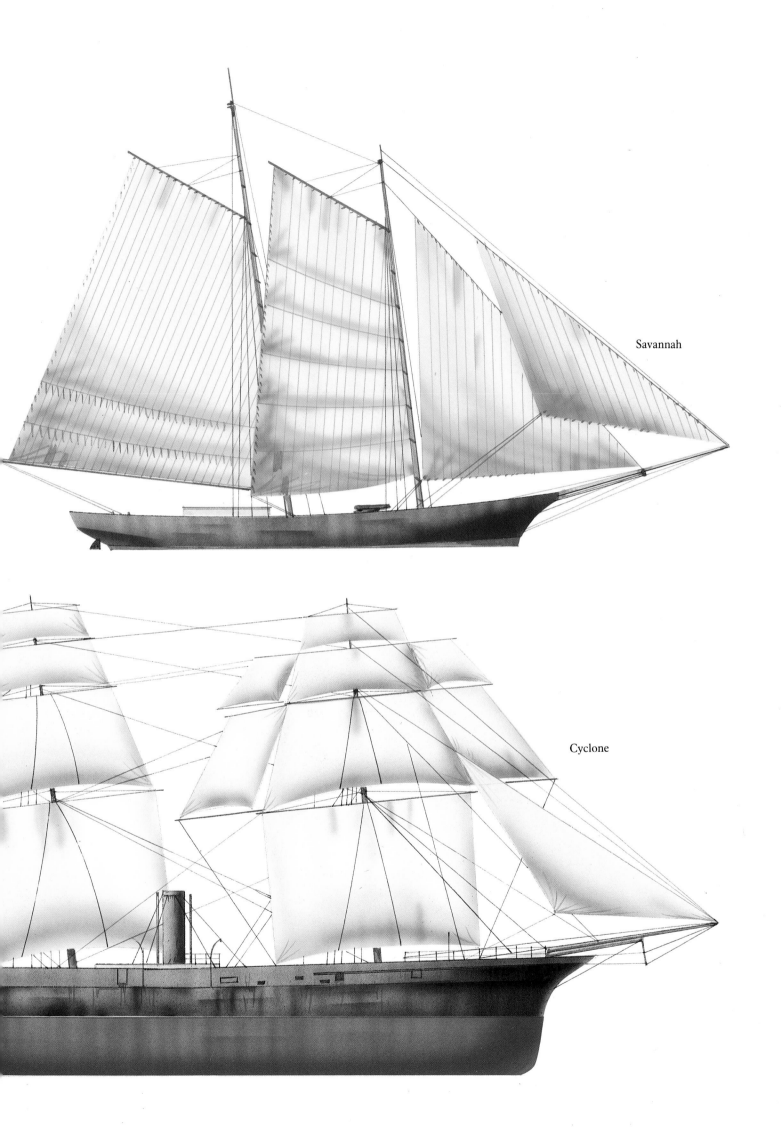

Savannah

Cyclone

CSS *Chickamauga*

Displacement: 586 tons. **Armament:** One 12-pdr, one 32-pdr, and one 64-pdr amidships. **Crew:** 120.

Chickamauga was the former blockade runner *Edith*, partly owned by the government and a group of investors. She was purchased outright by the government in 1864 at Wilmington, North Carolina. In September, when nearly ready for sea, the army tried to retain her for use as a troop and supply ship.

She was more substantially built than most of the blockade runners, and very fast, but Wilkinson, who was to command on her next trip, thought her altogether unfit as a cruiser because of her limited coal supply. She was schooner-rigged, quite unusual for a blockade runner, with short masts. The sails were generally used only for steadying when in a seaway, as she could make only 3 knots under canvas alone in a stiff breeze off the wind. In other even less favorable winds she could not even manage steerage way.

Lt. John Wilkinson took her to sea on the night of October 29 and successfully threw the blockaders into confusion by firing distracting rockets which gave false information about such things as course.

The vessel had shipped a large amount of coal, which was stowed in every available space on the already overcrowded ship; the crew even slept on sacks of the stuff. On this trip six pilots were carried, each qualified for a specific entry point in the South.

Chickamauga cruised north to Long Island Sound, capturing seven vessels. She then headed to Bermuda for repairs and coal, arriving on November 7. Several crew members deserted on arrival, but only to face the horrors of a yellow fever epidemic then raging on the island.

Wilkinson left St George's for Wilmington on the 15th but met only foreign vessels on the way. *Chickamauga* approached the coast in thick weather on the night of the 18th. The crew could dimly see the breakers ahead and close alongside, but it was impossible to distinguish any landmark in such a dense fog. A boat was lowered with one of the bar pilots so that a closer examination could be made, but even this proved unsuccessful. However, from the description of wrecks strewn on the beach by less fortunate seamen, Wilkinson was able to make out their exact position.

The raider was kept under low steam ready for dawn when a dash into port was to be made. As the fog lifted, two blockaders were seen bearing down on the vessel. After a brief exchange of fire, *Chickamauga* was soon under the protective guns of the ever-watchful Fort Fisher, who drove off the Union ships.

During the bombardment of Fort Fisher on December 24 and 25, 1864, some of *Chickamauga*'s crew served at the guns in the fort while the ship transported ammunition. She again aided the fort on January 15 during another heavy attack. When Wilmington finally surrendered, she went up Cape Fear River where she was sunk by her crew.

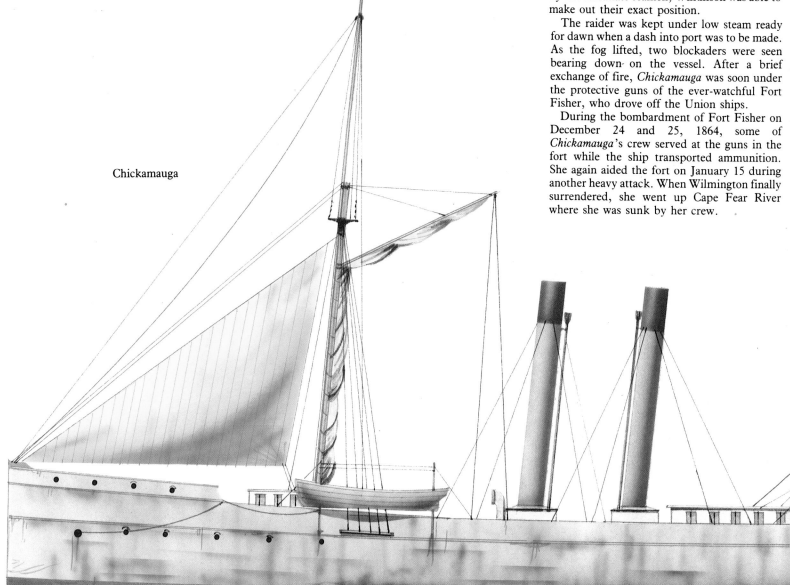

Chickamauga

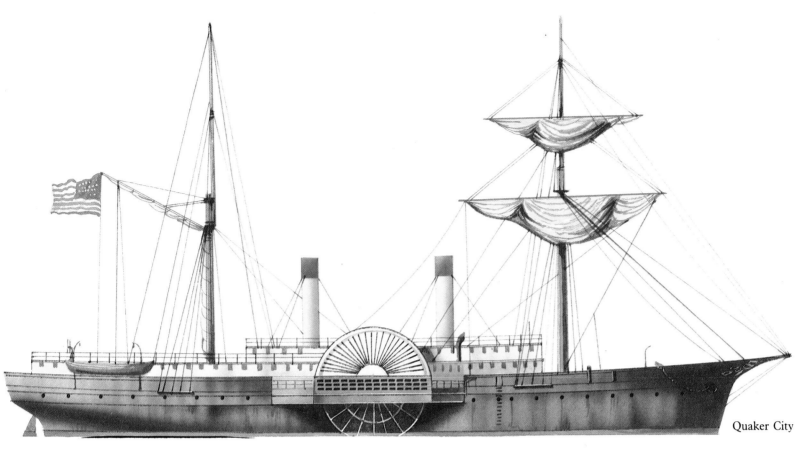

Quaker City

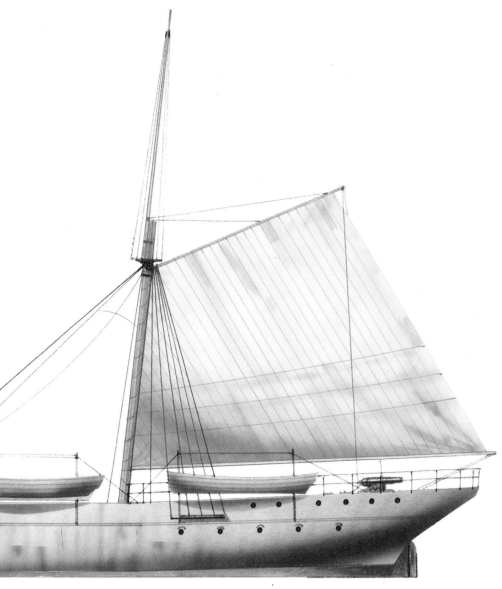

USS *Quaker City*

Displacement: 1600 tons. **Dimensions:** 244ft 8in x 36ft x 13ft. **Machinery:** One side-lever engine with an 8-ft stroke. **Speed:** Maximum 13 knots; 10 average. **Armament:** In April 1861 had two 32-pdr and two 6-pdr rifles. Battery increased later to include eight 32-pdr and 100-pdr Parrott rifles. **Crew:** 99.

Quaker City was a large schooner-rigged sidewheel steamer built at Philadelphia in 1854 and owned by P. Hargous & Co. She was fitted out for sea and armed by means of subscriptions raised at a mass meeting organized by the Union Defense Committee of New York. This committee had become alarmed at the Baltimore riots, where citizens attempted to oppose the movement of Massachusetts' troops through the city, and felt that all sorts of ideas should be explored to help the Union effort.

They chartered *Quaker City* on April 25 for $1000 per day for thirty days, sailing for Hampton Roads with Captain Samuel Mather in command. Not one of her officers held a commission in the US Navy.

The privately-armed vessel cruised in the Chesapeake Bay area and captured four vessels, prompting the committee to hire the vessel for one more month, when it captured two more vessels. The Navy Department then took over the charter and eventually purchased the ship for $117,000. The committee submitted a bill for $15,030 as payment for its armament, but the matter was not satisfactorily settled.

Quaker City served in the North Atlantic Blockading Squadron and the Gulf of Mexico, taking a number of prizes in each.

During her service with the navy, $103,574 was spent on repairs. When sold in June 1865 to Samuel Cook she fetched $35,000. She was sold abroad in 1869.

CSS *Tallahassee*

Displacement: About 500 tons. **Dimensions:** 220ft x 24ft x 14ft. **Speed:** 17 knots. **Armament:** In September 1864 had one 84-pdr, two 24-pdr and two 32-pdr guns; reduced to three guns in November 1864. **Crew:** 120.

Tallahassee was the former blockade runner *Atlanta* built on the River Thames in England. She had twin screws, and was a fast, stable boat — a fine example of the type of craft turned out by her builder, J & W. Dudgeon of Millwall. She had originally been built for the Chatham & Dover Railway as a high-speed ferry capable of making the Calais – Dover crossing in seventy-seven minutes.

After being commissioned, she was taken through the blockade in early August 1864 by her captain, Commander J.T. Wood, to begin a successful cruise that lasted nineteen days and took her along the Atlantic coast right up to Halifax, Nova Scotia. Forced through lack of fuel to end her cruise, she returned to Wilmington on the 26th, having captured or destroyed thirty-three vessels.

Now renamed *Olustee*, she made another successful run through the blockade to capture six vessels before being forced back again through lack of fuel. On the return trip she was attacked by several Union gunboats but successfully evaded capture.

With her guns removed and renamed *Chameleon*, she slipped out of Wilmington with Lt. John Wilkinson in command in order to bring back much needed supplies for the Confederate Army from Bermuda. Unable to break through the blockade on his return, Wilkinson tried, unsuccessfully, to enter two other Southern ports. He reluctantly steamed to Liverpool, England, where he handed the vessel over to Bullock on April 9, 1865. She was seized by the British government, but they were forced to hand her over to the US authorities.

Right: Tallahassee *during the early part of her career. Later the rig was reduced.*

Below: *The graceful lines of* Pampero. *Note the similarity to the* Alabama.

CSS *Pampero*

Displacement: 1000 tons. **Dimensions:** 230ft x 32ft x 20ft.

Pampero was built by James and George Thomson's Clydebank Iron Shipyard in Glasgow, Scotland, and launched in November 1863. She was a composite vessel (iron frames with wood planking), bark-rigged, with iron masts, lifting screw, and telescopic funnel. Her construction was supervised by Commander George Sinclair, who had ordered the vessel in the summer of 1862.

Pampero was seized in December 1863 and not returned to her builders until September 1865.

USS *Hartford*

Displacement: 2900 tons. **Dimensions:** 225ft x 44ft x 17ft 2in. **Machinery:** Two horizontal condensing double-piston engines driving a single screw. **Speed:** 13.5 knots. **Armament:** Varied from twenty 9-inch Dahlgren smoothbore guns in June 1862 to eight Dahlgrens and two 100-pdr Parrott rifles, plus smaller. **Crew:** 310.

Wooden frigates and corvettes were the cruisers of earlier days. They performed the duties of scouts, protecting or destroying commerce, as well as being detached on special service. They all played an important part in the numerous wars of their time and among these units, frigates of the US Navy were reckoned to be some of the best designed and best built vessels in the world.

After the introduction of steam power, and until the early years of the ironclad, many navies neglected the importance of the cruiser-type. Great efforts were made in building up ironclad fleets, so that by the early 1860s America would rank below Britain, France, Russia, Italy, Austria, and Spain.

The situation among cruisers was little better; the duties of scouting and commerce raiding/protection remained with the numerous wood-built, screw-driven frigates. These vessels had both sail and steam propulsion but this combination was unfavorable to their steaming capacity and sailing ability. The early engines were heavy and uneconomical, which resulted in low speed and poor radius of action.

This situation continued until the late 1850s, but then American ingenuity produced some remarkable examples of cruisers, although not all were successful.

Built at the Boston Navy Yard at a cost of $502,650, *Hartford* was slightly smaller than the *Brooklyn*. Laid down on January 1, 1858, launched on November 22, and completed in June 1859, she was considered a strong ship which steered easily, maintaining 9.5 knots under steam and averaging 7.3 knots under sail and steam.

Hartford served initially in the Far East, carrying the American minister, John Elliot Ward, to China where he was to settle American claims in the area.

With the outbreak of the Civil War, she was ordered home, arriving in December 1861 for a partial refit. She then became the flagship of Flag Officer David Farragut who was appointed to command the newly created West Gulf Blockading Squadron.

Late in 1861 it was decided to capture New Orleans as a first step towards driving up the Mississippi to link up with Union forces now forcing their way down the river. After months of toil, Farragut managed to get most of his sea-going ships across the bar at the river's mouth. In the early hours of April 24, the fleet ran past the Confederate forts after a fierce action

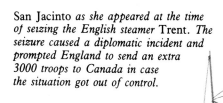

San Jacinto *as she appeared at the time of seizing the English steamer* Trent. *The seizure caused a diplomatic incident and prompted England to send an extra 3000 troops to Canada in case the situation got out of control.*

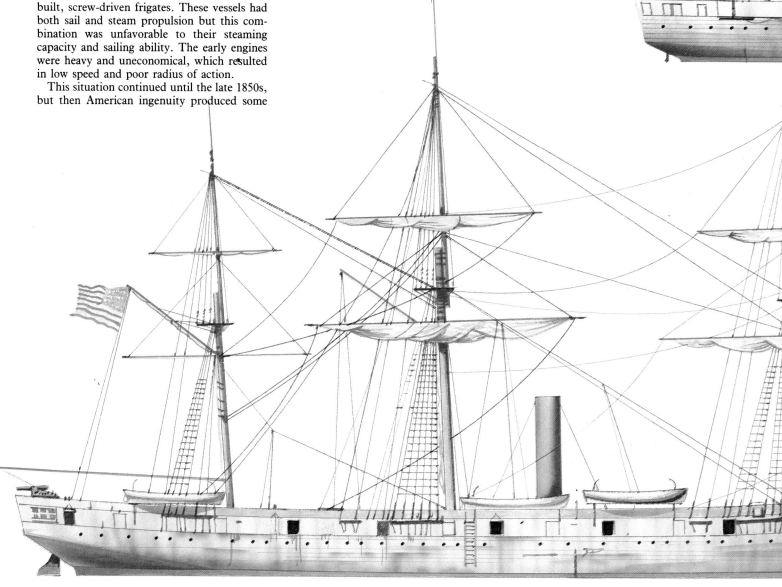

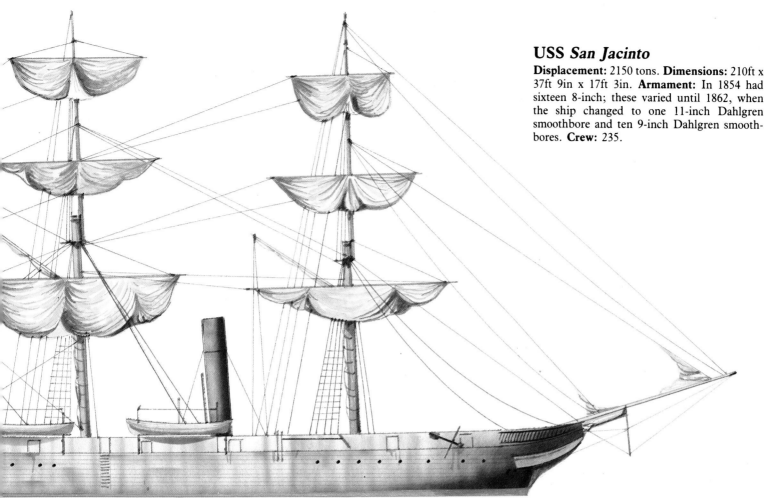

USS *San Jacinto*

Displacement: 2150 tons. **Dimensions:** 210ft x 37ft 9in x 17ft 3in. **Armament:** In 1854 had sixteen 8-inch; these varied until 1862, when the ship changed to one 11-inch Dahlgren smoothbore and ten 9-inch Dahlgren smoothbores. **Crew:** 235.

during which a fire barge set adrift collided with the *Hartford* but was pushed aside just in time.

With the fall of New Orleans the South lost its greatest trading center and its most important outlet to the sea.

Initial thrusts up the Mississippi were successful, but Farragut's fleet could not take Vicksburg without the help of the army. *Hartford* was later withdrawn for repairs but was back on station again by November. After almost ceaseless activity, Vicksburg finally fell in July 1864.

Hartford subsequently led the attack on the Confederate defenses of Mobile, Alabama, and helped defeat the powerful Confederate ironclad *Tennessee*.

In 1880 *Hartford* was fitted with new machinery originally intended for the incomplete sloop *Kewaydin*. In 1887 she was rerigged as a bark, given a new set of 2000 hp compound engines and served as a training ship. Moved to Norfolk Navy Yard, she sank at her berth on November 20, 1956. The remains of one of America's most famous warships were sold the following July.

Hartford as she appeared during her long and arduous service on the Mississippi, far away from her natural surroundings. Working such large vessels in the ever-changing currents and depths of the river called for seamanship of the highest order.

San Jacinto was a wooden-screw sloop laid down at the New York Navy Yard in August 1847 and finally completed in March 1852. Her initial cost was $408,885.

Charles Haswell designed the engine. The hull was designed by Samuel Hartt along the same lines as the *Saranac* in order to test the relative merits of screw and sidewheel propulsion. However, *San Jacinto* was not as successful as her sister because the space allocated to the engines proved too small and added to maintenance problems. The single six-bladed screw was offset from the center line and projected 5 feet beyond the rudder, which was divided into two. The use of the ponderous 7-ton screw was forced upon the designer in order to avoid clashing with any patent rights.

San Jacinto saw service in the Orient, helping to capture several Chinese forts at Canton during one of the many conflicts that flared up in the area.

Under the command of Captain Wilkes, *San Jacinto* seized the English mail steamer *Trent* in late 1861 as it was carrying Confederate Commissioners to Europe. This seizure inevitably led to diplomatic ruptures with England.

San Jacinto subsequently suffered two serious outbreaks of yellow fever while on station, so was forced to cut short her tour while the crew was restored to health.

On New Year's Day, 1865, the veteran warship struck a reef at No Name Key, Great Abaco Island, and she rapidly filled with water. Her guns were saved but efforts to salvage the vessel were unsuccessful. The hulk was later sold at Nassau, New Providence, in May 1871 for $224.61.

New Orleans, *Louisiana*

As the Confederacy's greatest seaport, and the main outlet for the grain and other products of the Midwest, New Orleans was a vital stronghold which the Navy Department was anxious to seize at the earliest opportunity. Unfortunately, no suitable vessels were available to face the two powerful forts; on the left bank stood Fort St Philip, which had been built by the Spaniards and successfully withstood an attack from a British fleet in 1815, while on the right bank stood the more modern Fort Jackson.

The mouth of the Mississippi River was blockaded at the end of 1861 by a force of Union gunboats, but this force was briefly dispersed by a Confederate attack.

A strong Union force under Admiral Farragut assembled below the forts, and on the night of April 23/24, amid smoke and confusion, the Union fleet successfully fought its way past the two powerful forts, thus forcing the city of New Orleans to surrender.

USS *Mississippi*

Displacement: 3220 tons. **Dimensions:** 220ft x 66ft 6in (over paddle boxes) x 21ft 9in. **Machinery:** Two side-lever engines. **Speed:** 11 knots. **Armament:** In 1857 had two 10-inch and eight 8-inch, 63-cwt guns; these later varied. By 1862 carried one 10-inch Dahlgren pivot smoothbore, and nineteen 8-inch, 63-cwt. **Crew:** 257.

In 1839 two boards of officials were convened in Washington to examine proposals for building two or more steam vessels for the US Navy. The results were two large, wooden sidewheel steamers — *Mississippi* and *Missouri*. The former was laid down at Philadelphia Navy Yard in August 1839 and launched in May 1841. *Missouri*, also laid down in 1839, was launched in January 1841 and completed in 1842, but had only a short career, being burnt at Gibraltar in August 1845.

At the time of their construction there was still much apprehension felt against steam power in the navy, and at the time of their completion the navy still had only twenty engineers. Indeed the attitude of conservative officers who were used to handling only sailing ships, caused much friction, which erupted

again many years later. Poor pay and the uncertain tenure of employment were also serious problems.

The hull design was a collaboration between Samuel Hartt, Samuel Humphreys, and John Lenthall, while the engines, constructed by Merrick & Towne, were designed by Charles Copeland. (Although not in the naval service, Copeland had provided much valuable design work on steam engines for the navy.) The original cost of *Mississippi* was $567,408.

The vessels were bark-rigged, spreading 19,000 square feet of canvas. They were very successful and powerful steamers, sailing well in smooth waters, but were rather dull in a head-on sea.

In 1847 *Mississippi* saw action at Vera Cruz. Later, she was flagship of Commodore Perry during his momentous trip to Japan in July 1853, which was the first time Japan had any serious dealings with a foreign power.

While in the Orient she helped to restore order in Shanghai during a period of civil strife. She then joined Farragut's force which was about to attack New Orleans. After several attempts, she and *Pensacola* were successfully maneuvered over the bar at the mouth of the

river on April 7, 1862, the heaviest ships to enter the river at the time.

Mississippi remained off New Orleans for almost a year because of her deep draft which restricted her passage up the river. Ordered into action at Port Hudson on March 14, 1863, against powerful river defenses, the lone vessel, bringing up the rear, was soon enveloped in a pall of smoke. In the confusion she ran aground, thus presenting the Confederate gunners with a perfect target as she was outlined by the bonfires of the enemy on the opposite bank. Her dead and wounded increased by the minute, and although efforts were made to float the vessel off, they were insufficient, so it was decided to abandon the ship, first setting her on fire to avoid capture.

Now deserted, the oldest steamer in the service slid off into deep water and drifted down the river in flames, lighting the water and throwing the banks of the levee into grim relief. When the flames reached the magazines she exploded and sank. She had lost sixty-four men.

USS *Pensacola*

Displacement: 3000 tons. **Dimensions:** 230ft

Mississippi *in 1862. Her executive officer,
Commander George Dewey, was later to become
the famous admiral who defeated the Spanish
fleet at Manila in 1898, thus forcing the US to
take a leading part in events in the Pacific.*

8in x 44ft 5in x 18ft 7in. **Machinery:** Dickerson
engine of 1165 hp. **Speed:** 9.5 knots. **Armament:**
In 1861 had one 11-inch Dahlgren and sixteen
9-inch Dahlgren guns, all smoothbore. **Crew:**
269

Pensacola was laid down in 1858 at the
Warrington Navy Yard, Florida, and launched
in August 1858. Completed in December 1859,
she was a ship-rigged, single-screw, wooden
sloop and originally cost $626,954.

The hull was designed by John Lenthall. The
engine, designed by Edward Dickerson and
Frederick Sickles, was a complete failure. It
was replaced in 1865 by a direct-acting engine
designed by Isherwood, originally intended for
the *Wanaloset*.

Pensacola worked well under sail but was not

as sturdy as her near-sisters. She served on the
Mississippi for two years in the Civil War,
going out of commission in 1864. She was sold
in 1912.

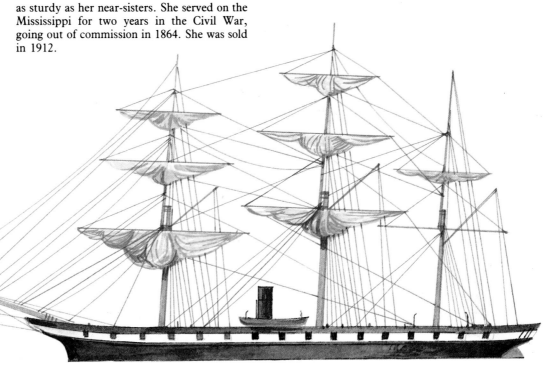

Pensacola

Cruisers

USS *Powhatan*

Displacement: 3765 tons. **Dimensions:** 250ft x 45ft (69ft 6in over paddle boxes) x 20ft 9in. **Machinery:** Two inclined direct-acting engines driving sidewheels. **Speed:** 11 knots. **Armament:** In 1852 had twelve 8-inch, 63-cwt; in November 1861 had one 11-inch Dahlgren smoothbore and ten 9-inch Dahlgren smoothbores, plus smaller; armament then varied for the war period and included several 100-pdr Parrott rifles. **Crew:** 300.

Steam power made slow progress in the navy. Shortage of experience and money inhibited its development, so sail-powered vessels still tended to hold sway.

The boilers of the first steamers used salt water and developed little more than atmospheric pressure, so they frequently had to be blown down to maintain even their limited performance. They consumed much fuel for a modest output of power, and the weight of the machinery equalled about one ton per horsepower. Furthermore, the efficiency of the paddles, which were exposed to bad weather and/or enemy fire, depended on the immersion of the vessel. They also greatly reduced the number of broadside guns that could be carried.

Steam gave warships mobility but the necessary retention of heavy masts and sails greatly cut down on the coal that could be carried. Fuel could be saved by using sail alone but the paddle wheels had to be disconnected or fixed with the lower blades unshipped, which could be hazardous at sea.

In spite of all the negative points, the early paddle steamers marked the beginning of the end of the graceful sailing men-of-war.

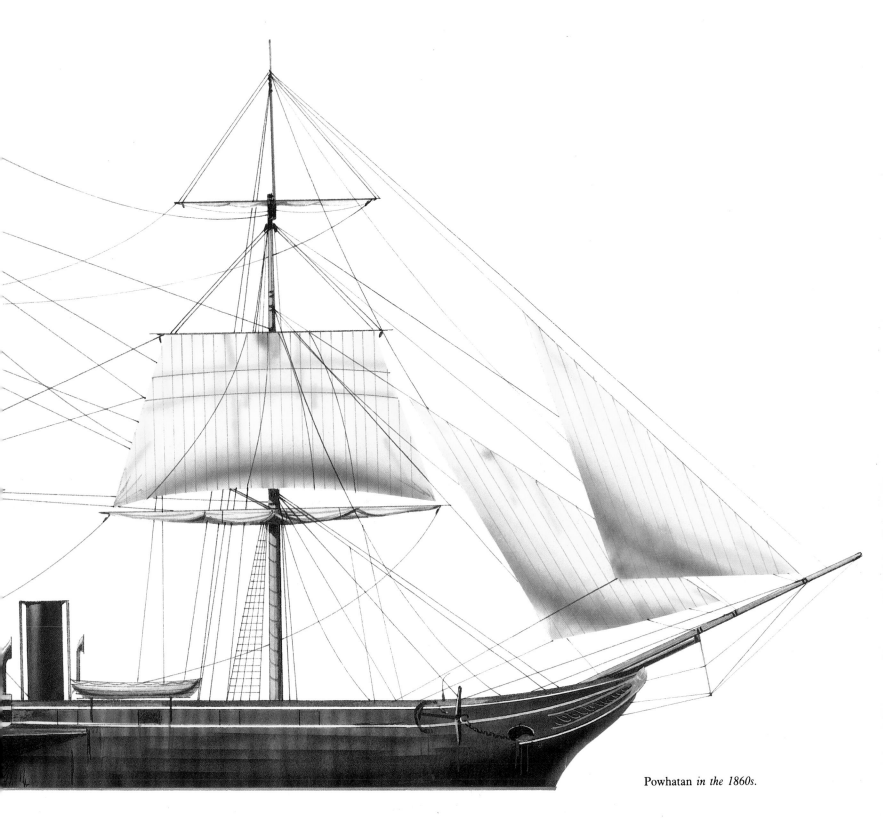

Powhatan *in the 1860s.*

Designed by Francis Grice, *Powhatan* was a graceful, bark-rigged wooden vessel that turned out to be a highly dependable craft that lasted for over thirty years. Charles Haswell designed the engines, which were built by Mehaffy & Co. of Gosport, Virginia. Laid down at Norfolk Navy Yard in July 1847, she was launched in February 1850 and completed in September 1852 at a cost of $795,220.

In service *Powhatan* proved a popular ship, being roomy and comfortable. With ten pounds of steam and her great wheels making ten revolutions a minute she generally made 10 knots, regardless of the weather. In 1878, after she had outlived many newer ships of the navy, she was caught in a fierce cyclone off Hatteras

that at one stage forced *Powhatan*'s fore yard-arm into the sea. During her memorable 3000-mile trip to Japan, when she formed part of Commodore Perry's squadron in 1854, the engines needed hardly any attention, a telling indication of the high standards to which some of these early warships were built.

In August 1855 *Powhatan* took part in a raid with HMS *Rattler* against Chinese pirates. She remained active throughout the Civil War, usually cruising on blockade duty where she made several captures. She also took part in attacks on Fort Fisher towards the end of the war.

Powhatan later served off Valparaiso, Chile, guarding American interests during the Spanish attack. She then saw extended service in home waters and cruised in Cuban waters looking after American interests during the 1880s. Decommissioned in June 1886, *Powhatan* was sold on July 30, 1886, to Burdette Pond of Meridon, Connecticut, for $18,255, and scrapped in August 1887.

Cruisers

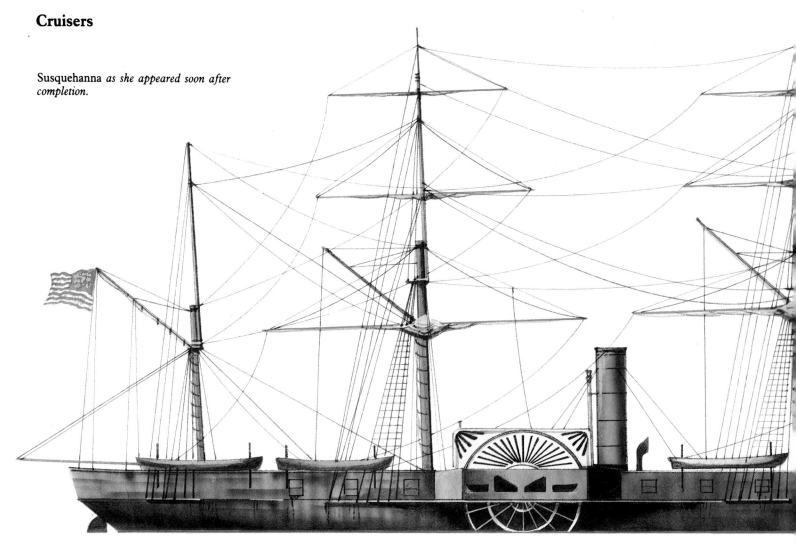

Susquehanna *as she appeared soon after completion.*

USS *Susquehanna*

Displacement: 3824 tons. **Dimensions:** 257ft x 45ft (69ft over the paddle boxes) x 20ft 6in. **Machinery:** Two inclined direct-acting engines driving sidewheels. **Speed:** 12.5 knots maximum, 8 knots average. **Armament:** In 1851 had twelve 8-inch and six 32-pdr; in June 1863 had two 150-pdr Parrott rifles and twelve 9-inch Dahlgren, plus smaller. **Crew:** 300.

Operational experience in the Mexican War clearly demonstrated the advantages of steam warships which could operate without fear of calm weather. As a result, several schemes were put forward. One produced in 1847 called for two large and two smaller steamers, with the larger vessels being modelled on the successful, large sidewheeler, *Mississippi.* The large vessels were to be able to carry sufficient coal and supplies for long voyages to foreign stations, as America lacked overseas bases from which to take on coal while *en route.*

It was decided to build the vessels of wood, but one member of the board, Charles Haswell, the first engineer in the US Navy, favored building at least one in iron. Unfortunately, this farsighted idea was not followed up.

The two larger vessels were to become *Powhatan* and *Susquehanna,* and when completed they were reckoned the most efficient warships afloat.

Susquehanna's hull was designed by John Lenthall and built at the Philadelphia Navy Yard, while the machinery was designed by Charles Copeland and built by Marray & Hazelhurst of Baltimore. The vessel was laid down on September 7, 1847, launched in April 1850, and commissioned the following June.

Within a few months, while on passage from Rio de Janeiro to the Cape of Good Hope, *Susquehanna* encountered a lengthy spell of bad weather. High seas caused the vessel to roll and plunge to such a degree that one of the large

wheels (some 31 feet in diameter) would frequently be 8 or 10 feet out of the water, while the other would be half immersed.

She was an economical steamer. By using just two boilers to keep the paddles idling and relying on sails, she was even more economical, burning only 14 tons of coal a day. (Idling the wheels was preferred to taking off the lower floats as such an action in any sort of a seaway would have fatal results.)

Susquehanna served in the Mediterranean before joining the Atlantic Blockading Squadron when Civil War broke out. She was present at the joint army and navy operation at Hatteras Inlet, North Carolina, and again at Port Royal Sound.

She served on blockade duty before Charleston, South Carolina, then transferred to the West Gulf Blockading Squadron. During her extensive tour of duty she captured several blockade runners. In early 1865 she was present at Wilmington, then the only port left open to the Confederacy for its much needed supplies. When that port finally fell, the Confederacy had only a few months more of life.

After the war, she operated off the South American coast, before being laid up at New York in January 1868. It was planned to convert her into a screw steamer, but after her machinery was removed nothing more was done because of cost, and she was sold in September 1883 to E. Stannard of Westbrook, Connecticut, for $13,143, having originally cost $697,212.

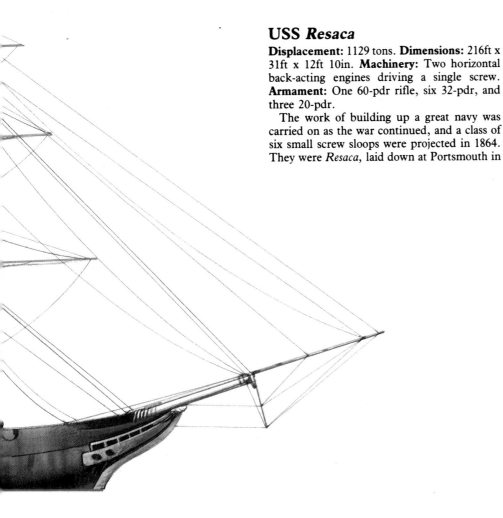

USS *Resaca*

Displacement: 1129 tons. **Dimensions:** 216ft x 31ft x 12ft 10in. **Machinery:** Two horizontal back-acting engines driving a single screw. **Armament:** One 60-pdr rifle, six 32-pdr, and three 20-pdr.

The work of building up a great navy was carried on as the war continued, and a class of six small screw sloops were projected in 1864. They were *Resaca*, laid down at Portsmouth in 1864 and completed in 1866; *Nantasket*, laid down in 1864 and completed in 1869; *Swatara* and *Quinnebaug* also laid down in 1864, and ready by November 1865 and 1869 respectively. These two vessels differed slightly from the rest, being 1 foot narrower and a few tons lighter.

Two more units laid down in 1865, *Alert* and *Epervier*, were never completed.

All were built of unseasoned timber, which rapidly decayed, and all were constructed in naval yards: Portsmouth built two and one each went to Washington, Boston, New York, and Philadelphia.

All the vessels had machinery of the Isherwood design, except for *Quinnebaug*. In order to make a comparison with the American engines, she was fitted with twin, high-expansion engines driving twin screws which were built by Jackson & Watkins in England. The trials were not entirely successful and after about three years she was rebuilt, receiving a pair of Isherwood engines converted for compound use.

Average speed for all the ships was about 12 knots. None lasted for long, however, *Quinnebaug* being broken up in 1872, with *Swatara* following the next year. *Nantasket* was the last to go in 1876.

When sold to Nelson & Perkins in February 1873, after less than seven years in service, *Resaca* made $41,000. She had originally cost $201,229, with an additional $110,048 being spent on her during her career.

Resaca

USS *Vanderbilt*

Displacement: 3360 tons. **Dimensions:** 331ft x 47ft 6in (over hull) x 19ft. **Machinery:** One single-beam engine with a 12-ft stroke. **Armament:** In November 1862 had two 100-pdr Parrott rifles and twelve 9-inch Dahlgren smoothbores. **Speed:** 14 knots.

Vanderbilt was originally a transatlantic passenger steamer built by J. Simonson at Greenpoint, Long Island, New York. Laid down in 1856, and completed the following year for Cornelius Vanderbilt's North Atlantic Mail Steamship Line, she was one of the best appointed liners of the Atlantic.

Shortly after the start of the war the giant wooden sidewheel steamship was offered to the army but was transferred to the navy in March 1862. She first served at Hampton Roads, Virginia, and was intended to be used as a giant ram against the *Marrimack*. Cornelius Vanderbilt suggested filling the bow with concrete and adding iron plating, but the graceful vessel was instead given a heavy battery and sent off in search of the elusive *Alabama*. This cruise lasted until January 1863.

Vanderbilt immediately undertook another year-long search for the Confederate raider, often just missing her quarry by a few hours. She eventually returned to New York in January 1864 for much-needed repairs.

She next cruised on the lookout for blockade runners on the Wilmington, North Carolina, route but without success. Later, she towed the captured Confederate ironclad *Columbia* from Charleston to Norfolk, and at the end of the war spent time in the Pacific to keep up the numbers in the squadron.

She was sold to G. Howes in April 1873 at Mare Island, California, for $42,000. The total cost for repairs and alterations while in navy service was $221,433.

Her new owners removed the machinery and added full rigging. Renamed *Three Brothers*, she spent most of her time in the grain trade, acquiring a reputation for speed and easy handling. She served successive owners, finally ending her days at Gibraltar as a coal hulk. She was sold for scrap in 1899.

USS *Worcester*

Displacement: 3050 tons. **Dimensions:** 296ft 10in x 41ft x 10ft. **Machinery:** Two horizontal back-acting engines driving a single screw. **Armament:** Eight 9-inch Dahlgren smoothbores and one 60-pdr rifle. **Speed:** 13 knots.

Worcester, originally named *Manitou*, was one of the ten-strong class of bark-rigged steamers built as scaled-down versions of the *Wampanoag*, while the engines were of the type used in the larger *Java* class.

The average cost per vessel was about $600,000, but like most of the Civil War ships built of unseasoned timber, their hulls rotted rapidly. *Worcester* was not completed until 1869.

USS *Brooklyn*

Displacement: 2532 tons. **Dimensions:** 233ft x 43ft x 16ft 3in. **Machinery:** Two horizontal condensing cross-head engines driving a single screw. **Speed:** 11.5 knots. **Armament:** In 1861 had twenty-two 9-inch Dahlgren smoothbore guns; in June 1863 one 100-pdr and one 30-pdr Parrott rifles were added. The armament was again slightly altered during the war, then greatly reduced at the end of her career. **Crew:** 335.

In 1857 Congress authorized the construction of five large-screw sloops-of-war. Four were to be built in navy yards: *Pensacola, Lancaster, Hartford,* and *Richmond.*

In order to test the relative qualities of navy-built ships and civilian-built warships, the fifth unit (to be named *Brooklyn*), one of thirteen proposals put forward by private contractors, was awarded to Jacob Westervelt of New York.

The machinery was built by the Fulton Ironworks. *Brooklyn* was laid down in 1857 and launched the following year. She was commissioned on January 26, 1859. On completion she proved to be a good sailer, but was considered somewhat lightly built.

Brooklyn first served in the West Indies and the Gulf of Mexico under the command of Captain David Farragut. During the Civil War she was almost constantly employed in the West Gulf, blockading squadrons and taking part in the capture of New Orleans in early 1862. On August 5 she was selected to lead the squadron into Mobile Bay as she had better ahead fire than the other ships. During this maneuver she took avoiding action to keep away from a group of friendly monitors who had entered a minefield. In stopping she swung across the fairway, nearly dooming the entire assault as she was raked by nearby Fort Morgan. Fortunately, quick action by Farragut, who was leading the assault, saved the situation.

After the war *Brooklyn* had a worldwide range of almost continuous service, ending with the Asiatic Squadron in 1886–89. She was decommissioned at New York in May 1889 and sold in March 1891 at the Norfolk Navy Yard for $13,128, having originally cost $417,921.

Below: Brooklyn *as she appeared at the start of the Civil War. The telescopic funnel is lowered. She also had a two-bladed hoisting screw which, when raised, greatly improved the sailing qualities by reducing drag.*

USS *Kearsage*

Displacement: 1550 tons. **Dimensions:** 198ft 6in x 33ft 10in x 15ft 9in. **Machinery:** Horizontal back-acting engine driving a single screw. **Speed:** 11 knots. **Armament:** In June 1864 had one 28-pdr rifle, two 11-inch Dahlgren smoothbore and four 32-pdr, 42-cwt. Armament later underwent minor changes. **Crew:** 160.

The *Kearsage* was built under the February 1861 emergency program when it was decided to build quickly a group of vessels based on the sloops constructed in 1858. Later, another group of sloops based on the same plans were added, making a total of fourteen, and all were begun in the fall of 1861.

All were to be large, handsome vessels and all gave excellent service in the war. *Kearsage* was a repeat of the *Mohican*, completed in 1859, and was laid down on a marine railroad, transferred to a dry dock at Portsmouth Navy Yard on September 11, 1861, and set afloat on October 5, less than four weeks later. *Kearsage* was commissioned in January 1862 at a cost of $298,049, and sailed for Gibraltar to blockade the raider *Sumter*, forcing that vessel to be decommissioned in December.

She located *Alabama* at Cherbourg, France, in mid-June 1864, and waited outside for the raider to venture out. On June 19 *Alabama* left harbor and *Kearsage*'s commander, Captain John Winslow, took the sloop out of French territorial waters to await the raider who opened fire first. *Kearsage* held her fire until the range was 1000 yards, then, steaming on opposite courses, the two warships moved around in circles as each commander tried to deliver a deadly raking fire. Soon the *Alabama* was in trouble as her long-stored ammunition and powder had badly deteriorated. On his ship, Winslow had taken the added precaution of placing chain cable in tiers over the vital parts of the hull. One shell fired by *Alabama*, had it exploded, would have been a serious threat to *Kearsage* as it lodged in the rudder post.

Kearsage fired 173 shots in the one hour ten-minute battle that ended the career of what is probably the most famous raider of all time.

After the Civil War she served on various stations. The year 1888 found her in the West Indies protecting Americans, but on January 27, 1894, she was ordered to Bluefields, Nicaragua, to safeguard US interests in the struggle between Nicaragua and Honduras. While making the journey, she ran aground on February 2 on the Roncador Reef, which lies 200 miles north of Bluefields. She immediately keeled over on her side and, in an attempt to right her, the masts were cut away. The vessel was to become a total loss, but all the crew were saved.

Congress voted $45,000 to save the vessel but when salvage crews arrived the local natives had burnt the hull to obtain the copper sheathing.

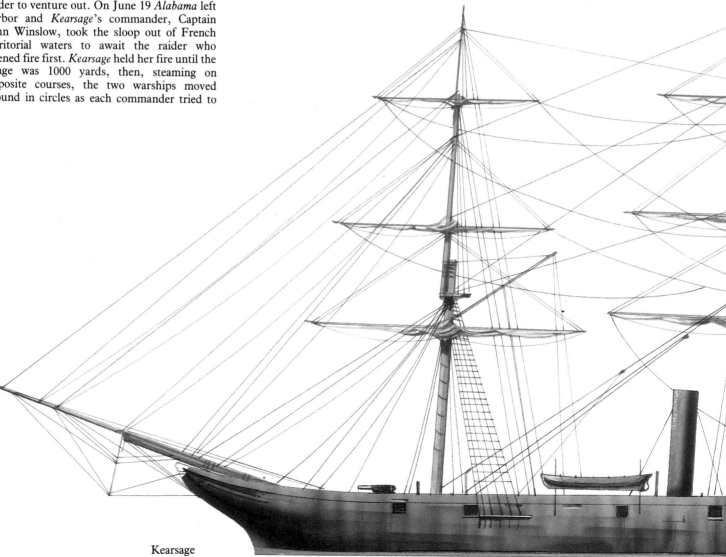

Kearsage

Java's sister Guerriere *soon after completion. The prolific building program entered into by the United States Navy during the Civil War soon exhausted regular supplies of seasoned timber, and new constructions built of green wood promised only a short life.*

USS *Java*

Displacement: 3954 tons. **Dimensions:** 312ft 6in x 46ft x 21ft 5in. **Machinery:** Two horizontal back-acting engines driving a single screw. **Speed:** 13 knots. **Armament:** Two 100-pdr rifles, one 60-pdr rifle, plus smaller. **Crew:** 325.

Java was a large, wooden, bark-rigged steamer, which originally cost $400,000, and formed part of a class of eight units. Seven were laid down in 1864 and one in 1875, but only four were completed; two were ready by 1867, but the remaining vessels were not commissioned until 1870 and 1876.

Three were to have been built at Portsmouth, two at Boston, two at New York and one at Philadelphia — all navy yards now thoroughly choked with new construction.

The four completed vessels were *Antietem, Guerriere, Minnetonka,* and *Piscataqua. Java* and her three sisters, *Illinois, Kewaydin,* and *Ontario,* were eventually broken up on the slips between 1872 and 1884.

The hulls were designed by Delano, and machinery was supplied by Isherwood, who used the well-proven horizontal back-acting type with a 5-foot stroke.

These vessels were not a success in service as the machinery was too heavy and cumbersome. The white oak hulls also quickly deteriorated, as they were made of unseasoned timber, the war having exhausted supplies of correctly seasoned wood.

They were fair sailers, carrying 24,000 square feet of canvas, and were intended to form part of a fleet useful for general cruising purposes at the end of the war. They had long, narrow hulls strengthened with diagonal iron bracing which resembled an enormous iron basket. This held the ships together long after the timbers started to decay. *Guerriere* was sold in 1872 for $54,000, having originally cost a total of $1,324,868, including repairs. The last, *Antietam,* was sold for $6700 in 1888.

USS *Iroquois*

Displacement: 1488 tons. **Dimensions:** 198ft 10in x 33ft 10in x 13ft. **Machinery:** Two horizontal steeple engines driving a single screw. **Speed:** 11.5 knots. **Armament:** In 1863 had one 50-pdr Dahlgren rifle, two 11-inch Dahlgren smoothbores and four 32-pdr, 42-cwt. Armament varied during career, ending in 1889 with two 8-inch rifles, plus several smaller. **Crew:** 123.

Iroquois, designed by John Lenthall, was the first of a trio of steam sloops laid down at navy yards. Begun in New York in August 1858 and launched the following April, she entered service in November 1859, having cost $284,088. Her two near-sisters, *Wachusett* and *Oneida*, were both laid down in June 1861 and completed in early 1862. These two vessels were schooner-rigged, while *Iroquois* carried the more usual bark rig. The machinery, designed by Thomas Main and constructed at the Fulton Ironworks, was similar to that installed on the *Mohican*. Although trials gave over 11 knots, the sea speed was usually about 8 knots.

Iroquois saw extensive service in the Civil War, tracking down the Confederate raider *Sumter* to Gibraltar. She next served on the Mississippi, remaining before Vicksburg prior to the city's surrender. This was followed by blockade duty in the Gulf of Mexico, and later she went in search of the last Confederate raider, *Shenandoah*.

After the war, she looked after US interests in newly opened Japan when local conflicts broke out in the port of Osaka in early 1868. She subsequently served on several foreign stations, taking part in landing operations by US marines needed to protect US interests during the revolutions in Panama in 1885. In 1893 she was transferred to the Marine Hospital Service and eventually sold in 1910.

Her sister *Wachusett* was sold 23 years earlier, while the *Oneida* had been sunk in a collision off Yokohama, Japan, in January 1870.

USS *Idaho*

Displacement: 3241 tons. **Dimensions:** 298ft x 44ft 6in x 17ft. **Armament:** six 32-pdr and one 30-pdr rifle.

Idaho was laid down in 1863 as one of seven large, swift cruisers in the yard of Steers, New York, and was contracted out completely by the Navy Department to Paul Forbes and E.N. Dickerson. The hull was designed by Henry Steers and the machinery, comprising two pairs of engines with 8-foot stroke cylinders driving twin screws, was designed by Dickerson, who had managed to persuade the Navy Department to let him compete with the engineer-in-chief, Isherwood.

The contract called for a continuous sea speed of 15 knots over twenty-four hours, but the vessel's furnaces had only half the usual grate area then needed to develop such power. Launched in October 1864, she was rejected by the trial board in May 1866 after making only 8 knots.

The board recommended refusal of the vessel but, undeterred, Dickerson and Forbes managed to get sufficient support in Congress to have her accepted in spite of her drawbacks.

She was accepted in 1867 and converted into a sailing store-ship and, as such, she was probably one of the fastest vessels afloat, able to make over 18.5 knots.

Idaho originally cost $550,000, but an additional $160,811 was spent on her. She served as store-ship at Yokohama and was ordered home in September 1869, only to be caught in a ferocious typhoon which dismasted the vessel and poured hundreds of tons of water 4 feet deep on the spar deck. The battered ship limped back to Yokohama and was sold there in 1874 for $18,642.

USS *Richmond*

Displacement: 2700 tons. **Dimensions:** 225ft x 42ft 6in x 17ft 5in. **Machinery:** Single direct-acting engine driving a single screw. **Speed:** 9.5 knots. **Armament:** In early 1863 had one 80-pdr Dahlgren rifle, twenty 9-inch Dahlgren smoothbores, and one 30-pdr Parrott rifle; armament varied later. **Crew:** 260.

Laid down at the Norfolk Navy Yard in 1858, *Richmond* was launched in 1860 and completed the same year. The machinery was designed by Samuel Archibald and built at the Washington Navy Yard. The engines featured a series of Sickle's cut-off valves which, through political influence, had been forced on the Navy Department and ultimately proved unsuccessful. At the first available opportunity they were replaced by a new set designed by Benjamin Isherwood in 1866/67.

Richmond and similar vessels were criticized by the Navy Department because of their deep draft, which restricted their use on inshore operations.

She served off the mouth of the Mississippi in the Civil War and took part in the capture of New Orleans. During her run past the Confederate forts, chains were hung over the side to give some protection. She was later present at the battle of Mobile Bay in 1864. After the war, she served in European waters and the Orient, finally cruising in South American waters. She served as a training ship from 1891 to 1893, and as a receiving ship from 1895 to 1915. She was scrapped 1919, having originally cost $566,259.

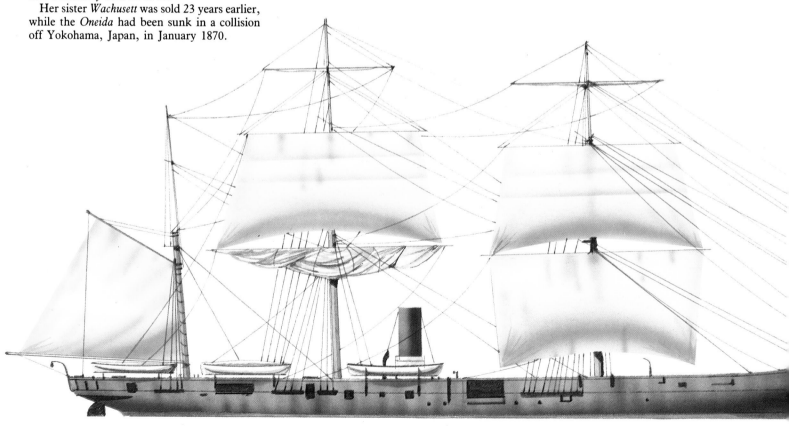

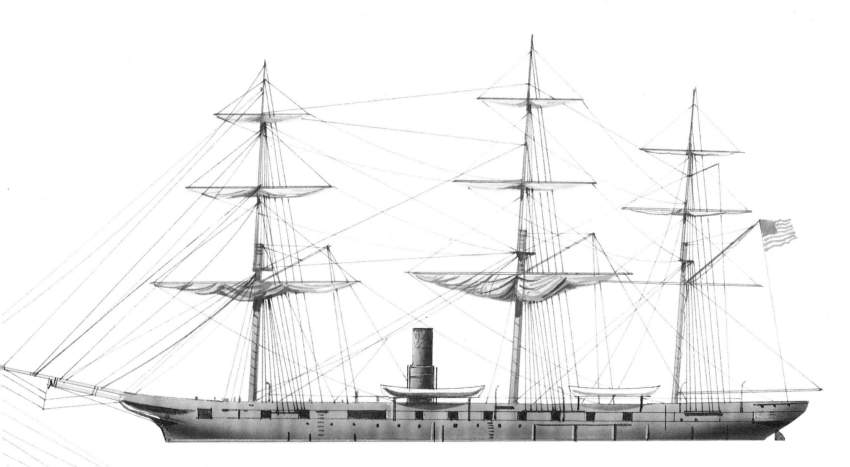

Left: Iroquois *at the start of the Civil War.*

Top: Idaho *as she appeared minus her engines. At one time, while being logged under sail, she recorded 18.5 knots before the sand ran out. In fact, the speed was estimated to be nearer 20 knots, making her one of the fastest sailing ships of her time.*

Above: Richmond *in 1862.*

USS *Wampanoag*

Displacement: 4215 tons: **Dimensions:** 355ft x 45ft 2in x 19ft 10in. **Machinery:** Two horizontal, geared, back-acting engines driving a single screw. **Speed:** 17.5 knots. **Armament:** Ten 9-inch Dahlgren smoothbores, three 60-pdr Parrott rifles, plus smaller. **Crew:** 375.

In 1863 the Secretary of the Navy pointed out that, beside the need for turret vessels and large armored warships for both coastal defense and ocean-going conflicts, there was a pressing need for a group of high-speed cruisers constructed of wood which could sweep the sea and hunt down enemy merchant craft and warships.

The resulting group of vessels, of which *Wampanoag* was the lead ship, were not all of the same design, but when *Wampanoag* was completed, she was an outstanding landmark in US naval and engineering development. At the time of her completion, she was the fastest steamship in the world, and set a new standard that would be hard to beat.

The sleek, wooden hull was designed by Benjamin Delano and the engines by B.F. Isherwood. The engines were connected to the propeller shaft by gearing, and generally proved successful.

Other vessels in the group whose engines were not designed by Isherwood were not so successful. The *Madawaska*, which had lever-type engines without gearing, made only 12.5 knots.

When the Navy Department announced plans for its class of supercruisers, they were already sensitive to accusations of favoritism to Isherwood, so they decided that it would be unwise to have the entire class powered by his machinery. Consequently, the department allowed three of the class to be built by private contractors. Forbes got the *Idaho*, *Chattanooga* went to Cramp & Son, and the *Madawaska* had a hull designed by Delano with engines by Ericsson.

Of the three privately-built vessels, only one, the *Madawaska*, was to have a similar hull to the department's *Wampanoag*, *Ammonoosuc*, and *Neshimany*. Ericsson demanded an identical hull, as he was anxious to compete with the department's geared engine design, and this way Isherwood would have no excuse if *Madawaska* proved to be faster and more economical than the department's vessel. As it turned out, Ericsson's vessel was a disappointment because he had been forced to use large boilers designed by Isherwood, who insisted on large boiler power regardless of engine size.

Unfortunately, in spite of the high speed of some of the ships in the group, they were generally considered failures. Too much had been sacrificed to speed. The weight of the machinery took nearly 30 percent of the displacement, and too little room was left for crew, coal, stores, and so forth. In addition, the lines forward were too fine to allow ahead fire, and the rig was considered too light as steam machinery was not yet sufficiently developed to justify any serious reduction in sail power in a cruising ship.

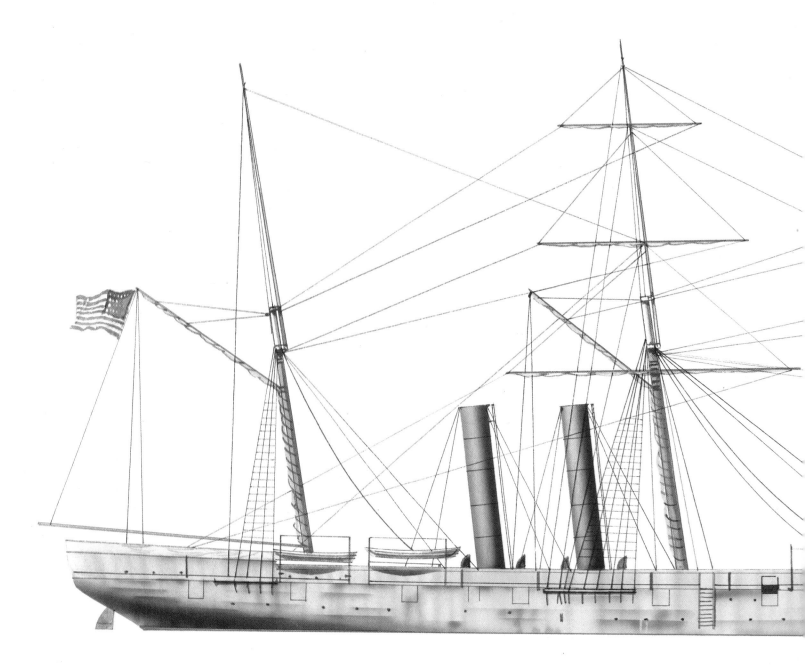

However, *Wampanoag* and her consorts caused great unease in England at a time when diplomatic relations were strained, and fears were expressed over the safety of English merchant vessels. The Admiralty set to work to build a more powerful class of cruiser, the first of which was the *Inconstant* of 1868.

In order to combine good sailing ability with the highest steaming power, it was necessary to work to very large dimensions, so *Inconstant* had a displacement of 5780 tons, which was greater than any other ship of its type. With a speed of 16.5 knots, *Inconstant* was faster than the battleships of her time. Her designer, Sir Edward Reed, realized that such a vessel of great size, length and power could not be given structural strength if made of wood. She was therefore built of iron, thus immediately removing the great barrier that had faced the American designers. However, it would be many years before the US abandoned the use of wood in cruiser construction, and not until the 1880s would she possess steel-built cruisers that came anything near to European models.

In spite of her initial impact on the naval world, *Wampanoag* was laid up until 1874, when she became a receiving ship. Her rival, *Madawaska*, renamed *Tennessee* in 1869, had an extra deck added and a change of engines and boilers. Her appearance also changed, and she had a clipper bow and a funnel fore and aft of the mainmast. She was sold for $34,527 in 1887, having cost a massive $3,800,000 (inclusive of alterations) during her career.

As the *Wampanoag* slowly faded from fame, so Isherwood faced much harsh criticism, particularly from Admiral David Porter who now guided the new naval administration of President Grant. Porter was anxious to turn the clock back to the days of sail and had no time for engineers. During the Civil War he had even said to the Assistant Secretary of the Navy, Gustavus Fox, that he suspected Lenthall of planning to throw as much of the navy as possible into the hands of traitors. This was a totally false accusation, but in the eyes of Porter, Isherwood and Lenthall were linked.

Porter duly had a board appointed to look into the machinery designs of Isherwood, and it happily supplied him with a sweeping condemnation of Isherwood's work. This ensured that, in future, engineers would take second place to line officers, a dearly-held dream of Porter's.

Wampanoag had half her boilers removed and was left to rot away. She was sold in 1885 for $41,508, a pitifully small sum for a vessel that had cost over $1.5 million to build and had been a major landmark of American achievement in naval development.

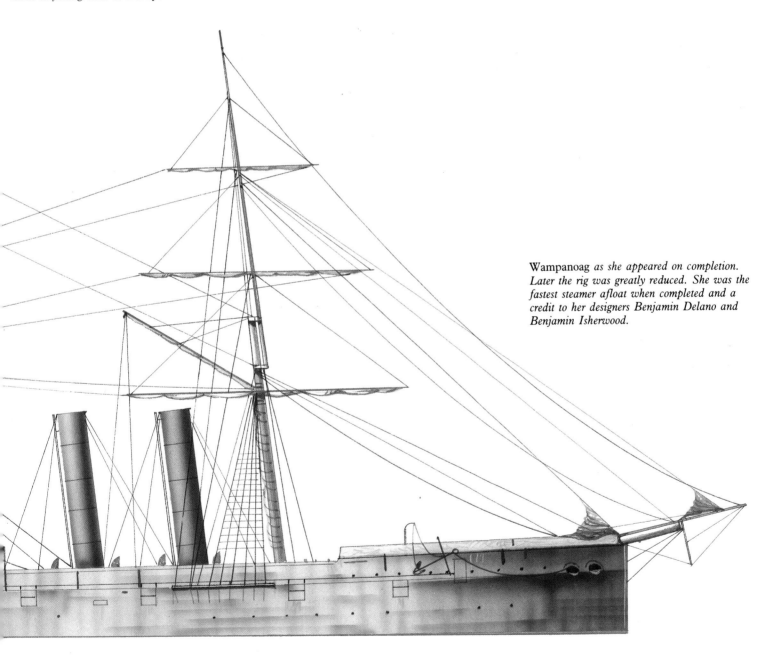

Wampanoag *as she appeared on completion. Later the rig was greatly reduced. She was the fastest steamer afloat when completed and a credit to her designers Benjamin Delano and Benjamin Isherwood.*

Blockade Runners

Hope

Displacement: 1700 tons. **Dimensions:** 281ft 6in x 35ft x 8ft. **Machinery:** Two-cylinder oscillating engines supplied by James Jack & Co. at the Victoria Engine Works, Birkenhead, England. **Speed:** 16 knots.

Blockade runners were an essential part of the Confederate war effort as they brought in a constant supply of military equipment, as well as supplying clothing and other needs of the civilian population. Later, as the Union blockade became more effective, the Confederate government ensured that the majority of the freight space available would be devoted to military needs to bolster the flagging war effort.

It was a formidable task to blockade 3000 miles of hostile coast running from Virginia to the Rio Grande and fringed with a chain of low-lying islands creating an inland waterway. These waters were too shallow for sea-going ships, so were used by smaller, shallow-draft vessels. However, a large number of these were captured in the early part of the war.

Much of the Union effort was placed in blockading the only remaining Southern ports available at the end of 1861. These were Wilmington, North Carolina; Charleston, South Carolina; Mobile, Alabama; New Orleans, Louisiana, and Galveston, Texas.

At first, any suitable merchant vessel was used, but as the war progressed more sophisticated high-speed craft were developed. The main drawback of these lightly built vessels was that they could only carry about 850 bales of cotton. A light steadying rig was usually carried, and some could blow steam off under water to reduce the sight and sound of their presence as they neared a blockade line. Also canvas would be draped round the paddle boxes to deaden the sound of the wheels.

One such craft was the steel-hulled *Hope*, built in 1864 by Jones, Quiggen & Co. of Liverpool. She was a near-sister to *Colonel Lamb*, built at the same yard, and the world's largest steel vessel built up to that time. Steel was used because it made the hulls lighter, and yet had the strength of the standard iron hulls then being built.

Hope was captured off Western Bar, Cape Fear River, Wilmington, after a sixty-five-mile chase by USS *Eolus* on October 22, 1864. Her cargo comprised much needed machinery. She was sold in January 1865 to a private American company and renamed *Savannah*. Purchased in 1866 by the Spanish government at Havana, Cuba, for $76,000, she was taken into the Spanish Navy as the *Churruca* and armed with four guns. She was eventually taken out of service in 1880 and broken up in 1885.

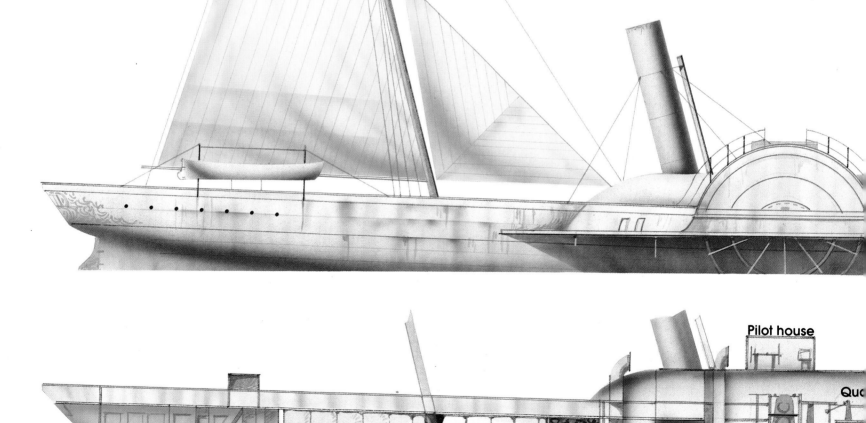

Rudder   Cargo space   Cargo space   Engine   Pilot house   Qua

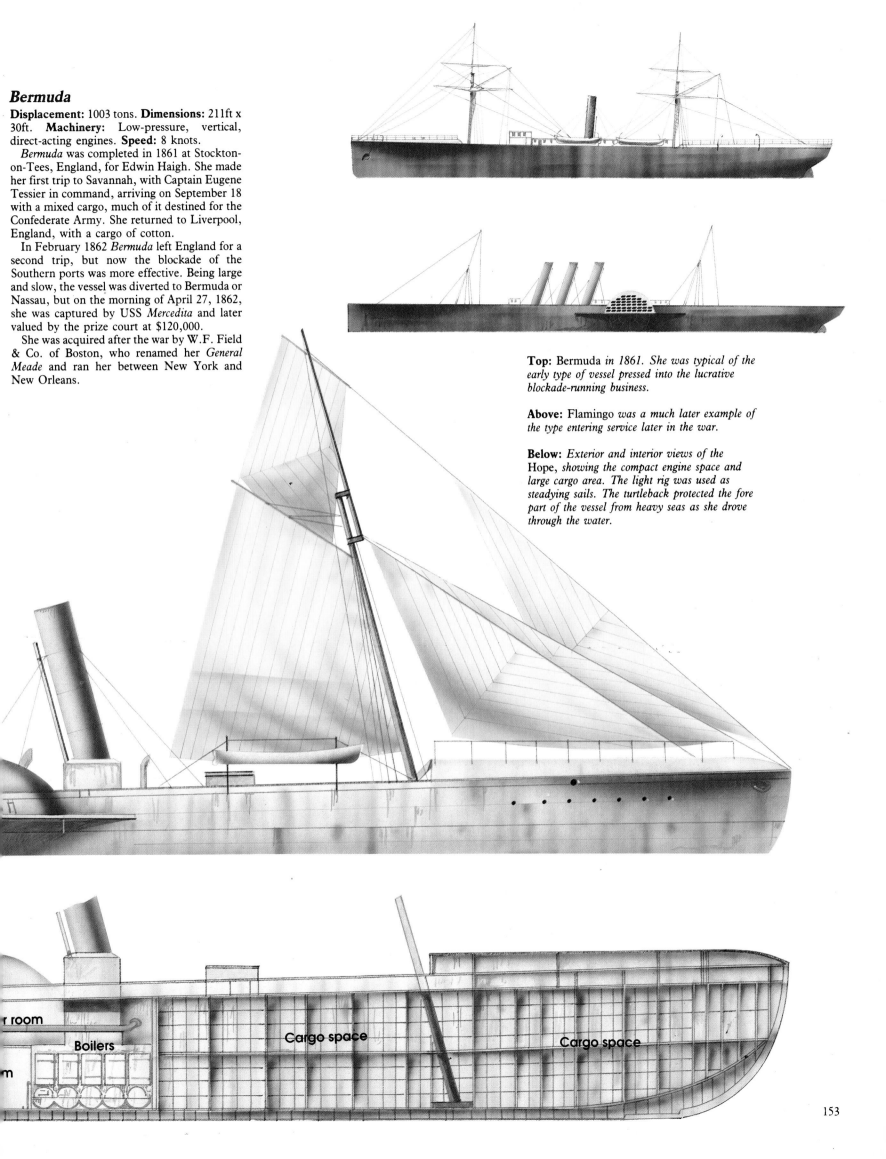

Bermuda

Displacement: 1003 tons. **Dimensions:** 211ft x 30ft. **Machinery:** Low-pressure, vertical, direct-acting engines. **Speed:** 8 knots.

Bermuda was completed in 1861 at Stockton-on-Tees, England, for Edwin Haigh. She made her first trip to Savannah, with Captain Eugene Tessier in command, arriving on September 18 with a mixed cargo, much of it destined for the Confederate Army. She returned to Liverpool, England, with a cargo of cotton.

In February 1862 *Bermuda* left England for a second trip, but now the blockade of the Southern ports was more effective. Being large and slow, the vessel was diverted to Bermuda or Nassau, but on the morning of April 27, 1862, she was captured by USS *Mercedita* and later valued by the prize court at $120,000.

She was acquired after the war by W.F. Field & Co. of Boston, who renamed her *General Meade* and ran her between New York and New Orleans.

Top: Bermuda *in 1861. She was typical of the early type of vessel pressed into the lucrative blockade-running business.*

Above: Flamingo *was a much later example of the type entering service later in the war.*

Below: *Exterior and interior views of the* Hope, *showing the compact engine space and large cargo area. The light rig was used as steadying sails. The turtleback protected the fore part of the vessel from heavy seas as she drove through the water.*

r room

Boilers

Cargo space

Cargo space

153

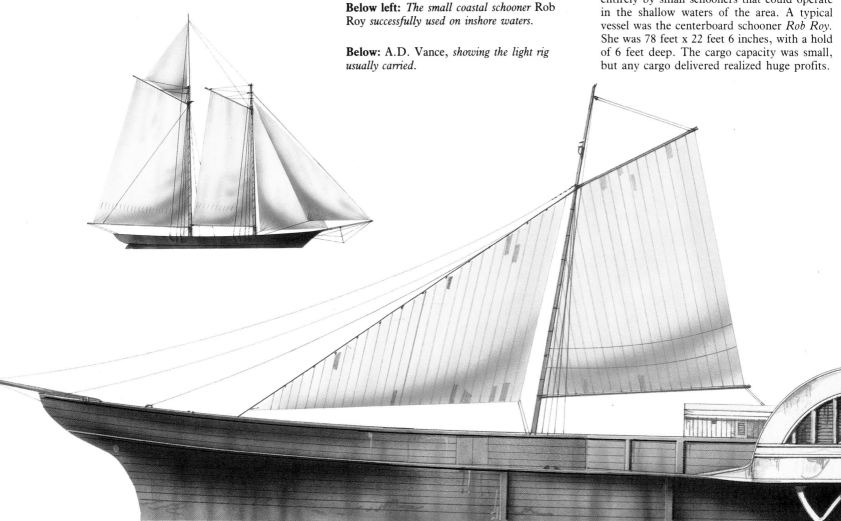

Peterhoff

Displacement: 800 tons. **Dimensions:** 210ft x 28ft x 10ft.

Peterhoff was the former Emperor of Russia's yacht. She was captured by the swift cruiser USS *Vanderbilt* on her first trip from London to Matamaras at the mouth of the Rio Grande River, when she was carrying a valuable cargo which included a large amount of iron and medicines.

After her capture she entered US service and was sunk in a collision off the North Carolina coast on March 6, 1864. She was valued at $80,000.

Lizzie

Dimensions: 230ft x 22ft. **Machinery:** Diagonal oscillating engines. **Speed:** Reputed to be over 20 knots.

Lizzie usually plied between Havana, Cuba, and Galveston, Texas. She was a light-draft vessel able to get over the bar at most states of the tide. She was specially built for the "trade" by Henderson, Coulborn & Co. in 1864.

Many of these runners were built of steel, then coming into use in a limited way. Unfortunately, the powerful engines almost forced the framework through the steel shell, causing it to give way at the rivets against the pressure of the waves. This was because early steel proved difficult to manufacture to a consistently high quality.

Until the very last part of the war, when the blockade of Charleston and Wilmington was effective, the traffic to Matamaras and the Brazos River in Texas was carried on almost entirely by small schooners that could operate in the shallow waters of the area. A typical vessel was the centerboard schooner *Rob Roy*. She was 78 feet x 22 feet 6 inches, with a hold of 6 feet deep. The cargo capacity was small, but any cargo delivered realized huge profits.

The differing shapes and characteristics of blockade runners are clearly shown on these two pages.

Top: *A ready-purchased steamer,* Peterhoff, *was soon captured.*

Above: *The more successful* Lizzie.

Below left: *The small coastal schooner* Rob Roy *successfully used on inshore waters.*

Below: A.D. Vance, *showing the light rig usually carried.*

Salvor

Displacement: 450 tons. **Dimensions:** 161ft x 25ft 6in.

Salvor was the former Great Lakes steamer *M.S. Perry* built at Buffalo, New York, in 1856. In 1861 she was owned by McKay of Key West, Florida, who sent her to Havana, Cuba, for a mixed cargo, including rifles, 6-pdr field guns, 500,000 percussion caps and...400,000 cigars. She was captured by USS *Keystone State* near Tortugas Islands. After the war she served with the Metropolitan Line between Boston and New York.

A.D. Vance

A.D. Vance was a larger and more substantially built vessel than many of the other blockade runners. She was built in 1862 by Caird & Co. on the Clyde in Scotland, and measured 236 feet long by 26 feet wide.

The state of North Carolina owned one quarter interest in the vessel and several others like her. The terms allowed North Carolina one quarter of the outward cargo and all the incoming cargo, which consisted of supplies for the army. No part of the cargo could be used for speculation.

A.D. Vance was captured in 1864 and sold in 1883. She had made more than twenty trips in the Civil War and was one of the most successful blockade runners.

Blockade running

At first the vessels were loaded, usually in England, and sent direct to a port in the Confederacy, but as the blockade tightened, the larger vessels transferred their cargoes to the newly developed runners at Bermuda, about 675 miles from Wilmington, and at Nassau, which became the largest depot and was 515 miles from Charleston. On the return trip cotton only was usually carried, but sometimes tobacco was shipped.

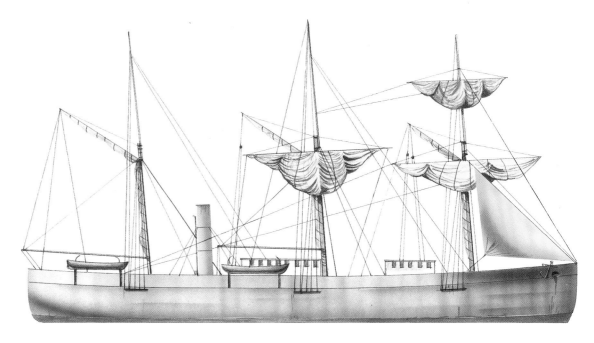

Above: *The* Salvor *was typical of the smaller type of steamer, which at first proved successful.*

Below: *Another example of a standard steamer purchased at the outbreak of the war was* Dawn, *built in 1847 for the Irish cross-Channel service.*

Blockade Runners

The journeys were timed so that the ships arrived off the blockade port at nightfall. However, severe weather was often experienced on the way across and many a blockade runner was lost without trace.

Captains could earn $5000 per round trip and freight rates were high — up to $1000 per ton. The monthly expenses of a runner were about $80,000.

At first the Confederate government had held back all cotton exports in the hope that it would adversely affect the large British cotton industry and persuade Britain to pressurize America into recognizing the South. This did not happen, and the 350,000 or so people then employed in the British textile industry suffered badly. By the end of the war their numbers were reduced to about 46,000.

Not until 1863 did the Confederate government make any effort to export its own cotton and this became necessary to bolster its funds abroad. The entire cost of blockade running cannot be worked out because of the nature of the business, but the Union Navy captured or destroyed 1400 vessels, nearly 300 of which were steamers.

Stag

There were four vessels in the class; *Stag, Owl, Bat,* and *Deer.* All were built by Jones, Quiggin & Co. of Liverpool and measured 230 feet long. They were purchased on the stocks but too late for any major alterations. Even so, they were good vessels and were the backbone of the Confederate government's blockade-running fleet. Their captains received only the usual service pay, but at least it was in gold. *Stag* later became the passenger steamer *Zenobia.*

Banshee

Displacement: 500 tons. **Dimensions:** 214ft x 20ft x 8ft. **Speed:** 11 knots. **Crew:** 36, including three engineers and twelve firemen.

Banshee was typical of the first sleek blockade runners. She was an economical vessel to maintain, using only 30 tons of coal per day and requiring a comparatively small crew.

On the way out to Nassau from England she developed serious leaks through the light decks, which were made of steel sheeting only $\frac{1}{8}$ to $\frac{3}{16}$ of an inch thick. She made eight successful trips, being captured on the ninth, but she had made her owners 700 percent on their investment by the time she was lost.

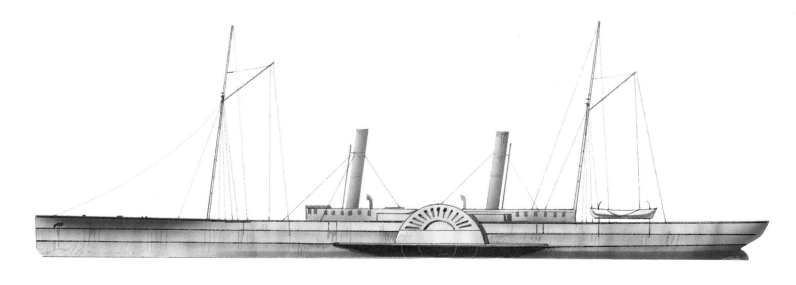

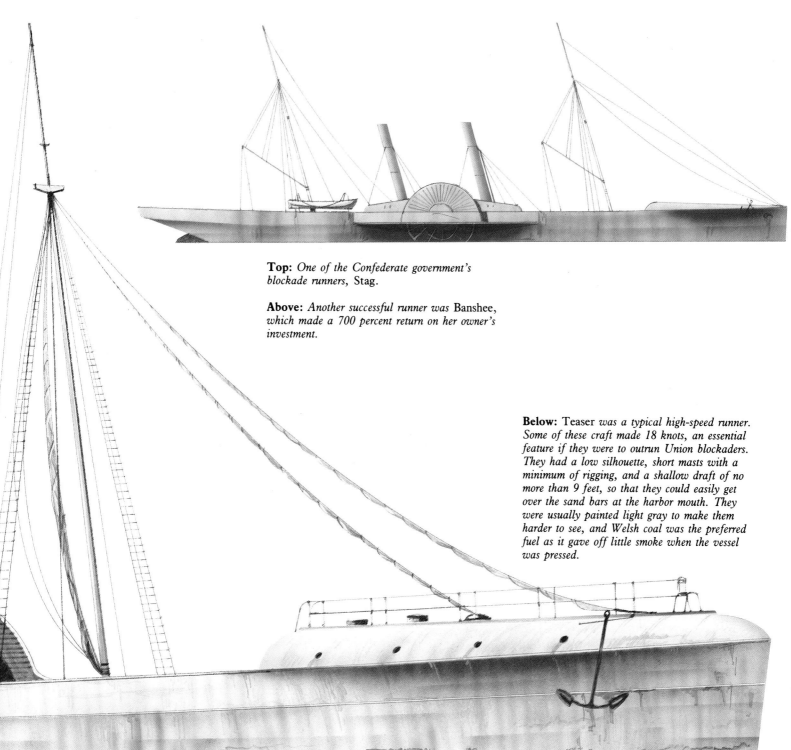

Top: *One of the Confederate government's blockade runners, Stag.*

Above: *Another successful runner was Banshee, which made a 700 percent return on her owner's investment.*

Below: Teaser *was a typical high-speed runner. Some of these craft made 18 knots, an essential feature if they were to outrun Union blockaders. They had a low silhouette, short masts with a minimum of rigging, and a shallow draft of no more than 9 feet, so that they could easily get over the sand bars at the harbor mouth. They were usually painted light gray to make them harder to see, and Welsh coal was the preferred fuel as it gave off little smoke when the vessel was pressed.*

David

As the Confederates could not match the power of the Union squadrons, they developed other methods of counteracting the Union threat, the main one being the development of submarine boats such as *David*. Although these early vessels were rather primitive, they used sophisticated weaponry, spar torpedoes being the most effective.

The Confederate Army had established the first Torpedo Bureau in 1862, and the Confederate Navy soon followed suit. By the end of the war seven ironclads and eleven gunboats had been sunk by mines and many others were damaged.

The early effectiveness of these weapons gave Theodore Stoney an idea for a mine or torpedo that could be carried effectively to the enemy. At his own expense, he built the first *David* and presented it to the navy. By the end of the war over twenty had been built.

The first version, constructed of boiler iron, had a cylindrical form with conical ends and was positioned in the center of the hull.

It measured 54 feet in length and had a beam of 5 feet 6 inches. Mounted forward was a small boiler which generated steam for a marine engine driving a single propeller.

To allow the vessel to reduce its height above water, water ballast was taken into tanks and the whole vessel submerged until it was almost awash. In this condition only about 10 feet of the superstructure length could be seen.

The explosive charge consisted of a 32 x 10-inch copper case which had rounded ends and contained 134 pounds of gunpowder. This was attached to the end of a spar and lowered just below the surface so that it would explode against a ship's hull under water, thus causing maximum damage.

During trials a passing steamer swamped the *David* and sank her. However, she was quickly raised and set off with a volunteer crew under Lt. Glassell to attack a Union warship.

The *New Ironsides* shifted her anchorage every night as a precaution against attack, but around 9 o'clock on October 5, 1863, Glassell was able to get almost alongside before being challenged. He succeeded in exploding the charge against the ironclad's hull but, unfortunately, not far enough below the waterline.

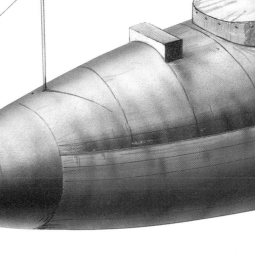

CSS *Hunley*

Dimensions: 40ft x 3ft 6in x 4ft. **Speed:** 2.5 knots.

The submarine *Hunley* was built in 1863 at the workshops of Park & Lyons in Mobile from the designs of H.L. Hunley, James McClintock, and Baxter Watson. The construction was supervised by two Confederate Army engineers, Lt. W.A. Alexander and G.E. Dixon.

The main part of the hull was fashioned from a cylindrical steam boiler which had tapered ends added. *Hunley* was hand powered by a crew of nine: eight were to turn the hand-cranked propeller and one was stationed in the bows to steer and direct the vessel.

Hunley had water ballast tanks at each end which were filled by opening valves and emptied by hand pumps. Iron weights were bolted to the keel as extra ballast and could be released from inside the boat by unscrewing the bolt heads.

The depth of the submarine could be monitored on the mercury depth gauge, and a compass was used to navigate under water. Light was provided by a candle, which also indicated if the air supply was getting too low.

When just under the surface two pipes with stopcocks were raised above the water to let in air, and when on the surface, small glass portholes in the wall of the manhole covers allowed the steersman to see out.

Originally it was planned for *Hunley* to trail torpedoes 200 feet astern, but eventually she was fitted with a spar torpedo, which incorporated 90 pounds of powder in a copper cylinder.

Hunley was successfully tested in Mobile Bay, then transported to Charleston in August on two flat cars. On arrival, the submarine was based at Battery Marshall Breach Inlet, Sullivan's Island, where the smooth waters aided the submarine's performance.

Although several crews were lost on subsequent dives, the Confederates persisted in using her. She patrolled several nights each week but remained on the surface. Time and again she was unable to approach an enemy vessel, but on the night of February 17, 1864, she attacked and sank the *Housatonic* which was anchored in 27 feet of water two miles off Battery Marshall. Unfortunately, the *Hunley* was lost in the at-

tack. Her brave crew were the first to give their lives to the submarine service and the first to destroy a warship with the new-style weapon.

Right: *The US experimental submarine* Intelligent Whale *laid down in the Civil War.*

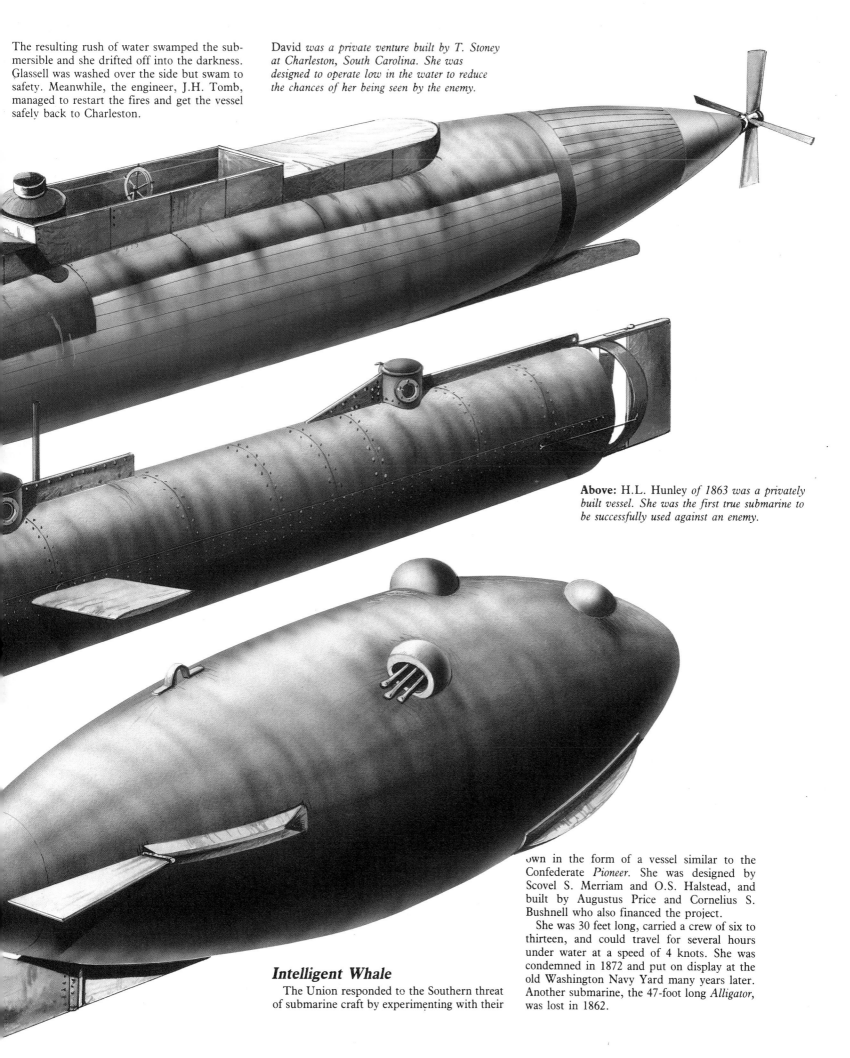

The resulting rush of water swamped the submersible and she drifted off into the darkness. Glassell was washed over the side but swam to safety. Meanwhile, the engineer, J.H. Tomb, managed to restart the fires and get the vessel safely back to Charleston.

David *was a private venture built by T. Stoney at Charleston, South Carolina. She was designed to operate low in the water to reduce the chances of her being seen by the enemy.*

Above: H.L. Hunley *of 1863 was a privately built vessel. She was the first true submarine to be successfully used against an enemy.*

Intelligent Whale

The Union responded to the Southern threat of submarine craft by experimenting with their own in the form of a vessel similar to the Confederate *Pioneer*. She was designed by Scovel S. Merriam and O.S. Halstead, and built by Augustus Price and Cornelius S. Bushnell who also financed the project.

She was 30 feet long, carried a crew of six to thirteen, and could travel for several hours under water at a speed of 4 knots. She was condemned in 1872 and put on display at the old Washington Navy Yard many years later. Another submarine, the 47-foot long *Alligator*, was lost in 1862.

WARSHIPS OF THE US NAVY

KEY: **D** = Dimensions. **A** = Armament. **S** = Speed. **C** = Crew. SB = Smoothbore. R = Rifle. H = Howitzer. M = Mortar.

A. Houghton Bark: 326 tons. **D.** 113′ 4″ x 25′ 3″ x 12′. **A.** 2 32-pdr SB. **S.** 8 knots. Built 1852, sold 1865.

Abeona Sternwheel steamer: 206 tons. **D.** 157′ x 31′ x 4′. **A.** 2 24-pdr R. Built 1831, sold 1865.

Abraham Sidewheel steamer: 800 tons. Captured 1862, sold 1865.

Acacia Screw steamer: 300 tons. **D.** 125′ x 23′ 2″ x 11′ 6″. **A.** 2 30-pdr R, 1 12-pdr R, 1 12-pdr. **S.** 12 knots. Launched 1863, sold 1865.

Adela Sidewheel steamer: 585 tons. **D.** 211′ x 23′ 6″ x 9′ 3″. **A.** 2 20-pdr R, 4 24-pdr SB. **S.** 12 knots. **C.** 70. Captured 1862, sold 1865.

Adirondack Screw sloop: 1240 tons. **D.** 207′ x 38′ x 10′ 2″. **A.** 2 11-in SB, 4 32-pdr SB, 2 24-pdr SB. **S.** 14 knots. Launched 1862. Sank Bahama Islands, August 1862. (See p.82)

Adolph Hugel Schooner: 269 tons. **D.** 114′ x 29′ x 9′. **A.** 1 13-inch M, 2 32-pdr SB. Built 1860, sold 1865.

Advocate Purchased 1863. Sunk as block ship.

Agamenticus Ironclad monitor: 3295 tons. **D.** 250′ x 53′ 8″ x 12′ 3″. **A.** 4 15-in SB. Launched 1863, broken up 1874. (See p.68)

Agawam Sidewheel steamer: 974 tons. **D.** 205′ x 35′ x 8′ 8″. **A.** 2 100-pdr R, 4 9-in SB, 2 24-pdr SB, 1 12-pdr SB, 1 12-pdr R. Built 1863, sold 1867. (See p.104)

A. Holly Schooner. Used as block ship.

A.J. View Schooner. Purchased 1863. Used as coal hulk.

Alabama Sidewheel steamer: 1261 tons. **D.** 214′ 4″ x 35′ 2″ x 14′ 6″. **A.** 8 32-pdr. **S.** 9 knots. Built 1851, sold 1865.

Albany Screw sloop: 2348 tons. **D.** 296′ x 9′ draft. **A.** 8 9-in, 9 60-pdr, 4 24-pdr R. Launched 1864, sold 1872.

Albatross Screw steamer: 378 tons. **D.** 150′ x 30′ x 10′. **A.** 1 8-in SB, 2 32-pdr SB. **S.** 8 knots. Built 1858, sold 1865.

Albemarle Schooner: 200 tons. **D.** 85′ x 25′ 6″ x 7′ 7″. Captured 1862, sold October 1865.

Albemarle Ironclad (ex-Confederate). **D.** 158′ x 35′ 3″ x 9′. **A.** 2 8-in R. Raised April 1865, sold 1867. (See p.58)

Alert Screw steamer: 90 tons. **D.** 62′ x 17′ x 6′ 5″. **A.** 1 24-pdr SB. Built 1861, sold July 1865. Also known as *Watch.* (See p.141)

Alexandria Sidewheel steamer: 60 tons. **D.** 89′ 9″ x 15′ 4″. **A.** 1 24-pdr SB. **S.** 4 knots. Built 1862, sold 1865.

Alfred Robb Sternwheel steamer: 86 tons. **D.** 114′ 9″ x 20′ x 4′ 6″. **A.** 2 12-pdr R, 2 12-pdr SB. **S.** 9½ knots. Built 1860, sold 1865.

Algoma Screw steamer: 1082 tons. Sold 1884.

Algonquin Sidewheel steamer: 974 tons. **D.** 235′ 6″ x 35′ x 4′ 3″. No service. Sold 1869. (See p.104)

Allegheny Steam gunboat: 989 tons. **D.** 185′ x 33′ 4″ x 13′ 6″. **A.** 4 8-in SB. **S.** 6 knots. **C.** 190. Built 1847, sold 1869.

Alligator Submarine. **D.** 47′ x 4′ 6″ x 6′. **A.** 2 spar torpedoes. **C.** 17. Built 1862, sunk 1863.

Alpha Screw tug: 55 tons. **D.** 72′ x 16′ 6″ x 7′. **A.** Spar torpedoes. **S.** 9 knots. **C.** 13. Purchased 1864, sold 1865.

Althea Screw tug: 72 tons. **D.** 70′ x 16′ 4″ x 7′. **A.** 1 12-pdr SB. **S.** 6 knots. Purchased 1863, sold 1866.

Alvarado Schooner. Sunk as block ship.

Amanda Bark: 368 tons. **D.** 117′ 6″ x 27′ 9″ x 12′ 9″. **A.** 6 32-pdr SB, 1 20-pdr R, 1 12-pdr SB. Built 1858, sunk May 1863 at St George's Sound, Fla.

Amaranthus Screw tug: 182 tons. **D.** 117′ x 21′ x 9′. **A.** 3 24-pdr SB. **S.** 9½ knots. Built 1864, sold 1865.

Amazon Bark. Sunk in attempt to block Charleston harbor.

America Sailing ship. Used as block ship.

America Schooner: 100 tons. **D.** 111′ x 25′ x 12′. **A.** 1 12-pdr R, 2 24-pdr SB. Built 1851, captured 1862, scrapped 1945. (See pp76,77)

American Sailing ship. Used as block ship.

Ammonoosuc Screw cruiser: 2190 tons. **D.** 335′ x 44′ 4″ x 10′ 6″. **A.** 10 9-in SB, 3 60-pdr R, 2 24-pdr SB. Built 1864, sold 1883. (See p.150)

Anacostia Screw steamer: 217 tons. **D.** 129′ x 23′ x 5′. **A.** 1 30-pdr R, 1 12-pdr SB, 1 9-in SB. **S.** 7½ knots. Built 1858, sold 1865.

Anemone Screw tug: 156 tons. **D.** 99′ x 20′ 5″ x 11′. **A.** 2 24-pdr SB, 2 12-pdr SB. **S.** 11 knots. Built 1864, sold 1865.

Anna Schooner: 27 tons. **D.** 46′ 2″ x 14′ 9″ x 5′. **A.** 1 12-pdr SB. Captured 1863. Sunk by explosion December 1864.

Antelope Sidewheel steamer: 173 tons. D. 264′ x 34′ x 3′. **A.** 2 30-pdr R, 4 24-pdr SB. Purchased 1861. Sunk in Mississippi River September 1864.

Antietam Screw sloop: 2354 tons. **D.** 310′ x 46′ x 18′ 3″. Launched 1875, sold 1888. (See p.147)

Antona Screw steamer: 549 tons. **D.** 13′ draft **A.** 2 32-pdr SB, 1 20-pdr R, 2 24-pdr SB. **S.** 8 knots. Captured 1863, sold 1865.

Arapahoe Screw steamer: 3050 tons. **D.** 296′ 10″ x 41′ x 9′ 9″. **A.** 8 9-in, 1 60-pdr. Never built.

Archer Sailing ship: 322 tons. Sunk it attempt to block Charleston harbor.

Arethusa Screw tug: 195 tons. **D.** 110′ x 22′ x 8′ 8″. **A.** 2 12-pdr. Purchased 1864, sold 1866.

Argosy Sternwheel steamer: 219 tons. **D.** 156′ 4″ x 33′ x 4′ 6″. **A.** 6 24-pdr SB, 2 12-pdr R. **S.** 5 knots. Built 1863, sold 1865.

Argosy See *Wave.*

Ariel Schooner: 20 tons. **D.** 4′ draft. **A.** 1 12-pdr SB. Captured 1862, sold 1865.

Aries Screw steamer: 820 tons. **D.** 210′ x 27′ 10″ x 16′.. **A.** 4 8-in SB, 1 30-pdr R, 1 12-pdr R. **S.** 12 knots. **C.** 90. Built 1861, sold 1865.

Arizona See *Neshaminy.*

Arizona Sidewheel steamer: 950 tons. **D.** 200′ x 34′ x 8′. **A.** 4 32-pdr SB, 1 30-pdr R, 1 12-pdr R. **C.** 91. Built 1859, accidentally destroyed by fire February 1865 at New Orleans.

Arkansas Screw steamer: 752 tons. **D.** 191′ x 30′ x 10′. **A.** 4 32-pdr SB, 1 12-pdr R. **S.** 15 knots. **C.** 88. Built 1863, sold 1865.

Arletta Schooner: 200 tons. **D.** 103′ x 27′ x 10′. **A.** 1 13-in M, 2 32-pdr SB, 2 12-pdr SB. **S.** 10½ knots. **C.** 21. Built 1860, sold 1865.

Aroostook Screw gunboat: 507 tons. **D.** 158′ x 28′ x 10′ 6″. **A.** 1 11-in SB, 1 20-pdr R, 2 24-pdr SB. **S.** 11 knots. **C.** 90. Built 1862, sold 1869. (See p.84)

Ascutney Sidewheel gunboat: 974 tons. **D.** 205′ x 35′ x 6′ 5″. **A.** 2 100-pdr R, 4 9-in, 2 24-pdr H, 2 12-pdr H. In service 1864, sold 1868. (See p.104)

Ashuelot Sidewheel gunboat: 1039 tons. **D.** 255′ x 35′ x 9′. **A.** 4 8-in SB, 2 60-pdr R, 2 24-pdr H, 2 20-pdr R. Completed 1866. Sank after striking Lamock Rock near Swatow, February 18, 1883.

Aster Screw tug: 285 tons. **D.** 122′ 6″ x 23′ x 10′. **A.** 1 30-pdr R, 2 12-pdr R. Purchased 1864. Wrecked on Carolina Shoals, October 8, 1864.

Atalanta See *Sumpter.*

Atlanta Ironclad: 1006 tons. **D.** 204′ x 41′ x 15′ 9″. **A.** 2 150-pdr R, 2 100-pdr SB. **S.** 10 knots. **C.** 162. Captured June 17, 1864, sold 1869. (See p.45)

Augusta Sidewheel steamer: 1310 tons. **D.** 220′ x 35′ 4″ x 13′ 8″. **A.** 8 32-pdr SB. **S.** 11 knots. Built 1852, sold 1868.

Augusta Dinsmore Screw steamer: 834 tons. **D.** 169′ x 32′ 6″ x 12′ 6″. **A.** 2 12-pdr R. **S.** 11 knots. Built 1863, sold 1865.

Avenger Bark: 554 tons. **D.** 138′ x 31′ 5″ x 14′ 1″. **A.** 6 32-pdr SB. **S.** 5 knots. Purchased 1861, sold 1865.

Avenger Sidewheel ram: 409 tons. **D.** 210′ x 6′ draft. **A.** 6 24-pdr SB, 2 12-pdr R. Built 1863, sold 1865.

Azalea Screw steamer: 176 tons. **D.** 110′ x 21′ 6″ x 10′. **A.** 1 30-pdr R, 1 20-pdr R. **S.** 9 knots. Built 1864, sold 1865.

Bainbridge Brig: 259 tons. **D.** 100′ x 25′ x 14′. **A.** 12 32-pdr on carriages. **S.** 11½ knots. **C.** 100 Launched 1842. Sunk off Cape Hatteras in storm, August 21, 1863.

Baltimore Sidewheel steamer: 500 tons. **D.** 200′ x 26′ 8″ x 10′. **A.** 1 32-pdr SB. Built 1848, sold 1865.

Banshee Sidewheel steamer: 533 tons. **D.** 220′ x 20′ 4″ x 10′. **A.** 1 30-pdr R, 2 24-pdr SB. **S.** 15 knots. **C.** 89. Built 1862, captured 1863, sold 1865. (See p.156)

Baron de Kalb Ironclad: 512 tons. **D.** 175′ x 51′ 2″ x 6′. **A.** 2 8-in SB, 4 42-pdr R, 7 32-pdr SB. **S.** 9 knots. **C.** 251. Built 1861. Sunk by mine on Yazoo River, July 13, 1863. Formerly named *St Louis.*

Barrataria Ironclad: 400 tons. **A.** 2 guns. Captured by US Army. On April 7, 1863 struck snag in Lake Maurepas, La., and destroyed to avoid capture. Known in US Navy as *Barataria.*

Bat Sidewheel steamer: 750 tons. **D.** 230′ x 26′ x 8′. **A.** 1 30-pdr R, 2 12-pdr SB. **S.** 16 knots. Captured October 1864, sold 1865.

Bazely Tug: 50 tons. **D.** 70′ x 16′ x 7′. **S.** 10 knots. **C.** 14. Purchased June 1864. Sunk by mine on Roanoke River, December 1864.

Beaufort Tug: 80 tons. **D.** 85′ x 17′ 5″ x 5′. Captured May 1865, sold September 1865.

Beauregard Schooner: 101 tons. **A.** 1 30-pdr R, 2 12-pdr H. Captured November 1861, sold 1865.

Bella Screw steamer: 52 tons. **D.** 61′ 4″ x 15′ x 8′. **A.** 1 24-pdr SB, 1 12-pdr R. **S.** 10 knots. **C.** 19. Built 1864, sold 1865.

Ben Morgan Ship: 407 tons. **D.** 15′ draft. **C.** 26. Built 1826, sold 1865.

Benton Ironclad: 1033 tons. **D.** 202′ x 72′ x 9′. **A.** 2 9-in SB, 7 32-pdr SB, 7 32-pdr R. **S.** 5½ knots. **C.** 176. Converted 1861, sold November 1865. (See p.13)

Berberry Screw steamer: 160 tons. **D.** 99′ 6″ x 20′ 6″ x 8′ 6″. **A.** 2 24-pdr SB, 2 12-pdr SB. **S.** 5 knots. **C.** 31. Built 1864, sold 1865.

Bermuda Screw steamer: 1238 tons. **D.** 211′ x 21′ 7″ x 16′ 8″. **A.** 1 9-in SB, 2 30-pdr R. **S.** 11 knots. Captured 1862, sold 1865. (See p.153).

Bibb (See p.76)

Bienville Sidewheel steamer: 1558 tons. **D.** 253′ x 38′ x 16′ 2″. **A.** 8 32-pdr SB, 1 32-pdr R. **S.** 15 knots. **C.** 185. Built 1860, sold 1867.

Bignonia Screw tug: 321 tons. **D.** 131′ x 22′ x 10′ 8″. **A.** 1 30-pdr R, 2 12-pdr SB. **S.** 10 knots. **C.** 50. Built 1863, sold 1865.

Black Hawk Sidewheel steamer: 902 tons. **D.** 260′ x 45′ 6″ x 8′. **A.** 4 32-pdr SB, 2 30-pdr R, 1 12-pdr R, 1 12-pdr SB. Built 1848. Accidentally burnt near Cairo, April 22, 1865.

Bloomer Sidewheel steamer: 130 tons. **A.** 1 32-pdr SB, 1 12-pdr R. **C.** 49 Built 1856. Wrecked off Florida Coast, June 1865.

Blue Light Screw tug: 103 tons. **A.** 1 gun. Built 1863, sold 1883.

Bohio Brig: 197 tons. **D.** 100′ x 24′ 9″ x 7′. **A.** 2 32-pdr SB. Built 1856, sold 1865.

Bon Homme Richard Screw steamer: 3713 tons. **A.** 20 guns. Never built.

Brandywine Frigate: 1708 tons. **D.** 175′ x 45′ x 22′. **A.** 44 guns. **S.** 13 knots. **C.** 467. Built 1825. Destroyed by fire at Norfolk, September 3, 1864.

Braziliera Bark: 541 tons. **D.** 135′ 8″ x 28′ 7″ x 10′. **A.** 6 32-pdr SB. **S** 10 knots. Built 1856, sold 1865.

Brilliant Sternwheel steamer: 227 tons. **D.** 154′ 8″ x 33′ 6″ x 5′. **A.** 2 12-pdr R. 2 12-pdr SB. **S.** 6 knots. Built 1862, sold 1865.

Britannia Sidewheel steamer: 495 tons. **D.** 189′ x 26′ x 8′. **A.** 1 30-pdr R, 2 12-pdr R, 2 24-pdr H. **S.** 12½ knots. Built 1862, sold 1865.

Brooklyn Screw steamer: 2532 tons. **D.** 233′ x 43′ x 16′ 3″. **A.** 1 10-in SB, 20 9-in SB. **S.** 11½ knots. **C.** 335. Built 1858, sold 1891. (See p.145)

Buckthorn Screw steamer: 128 tons. **D.** 87′ x 226′ x 6′. **A.** 1 30-pdr R, 2 12-pdr SB. **S.** 8½ knots. Built 1863, sold 1869.

Buena Vista Canal boat. Purchased 1864 for use as block ship.

C.P. Williams Schooner: 210 tons. **D.** 103′ 8″ x 28′ 3″ x 6′. **A.** 1 13-in M, 2 32-pdr. **S.** 10 knots. **C.** 35. Purchased 1861, sold 1865.

Cactus Sidewheel steamer: 176 tons. **D.** 110′ x 22′ 6″ x 7′. **A.** 1 30-pdr, 2 12-pdr. **S.** 15 knots. Built 1863, transferred to Lighthouse Board 1865.

Cairo Ironclad: 512 tons. **D.** 175′ x 51′ 2″ x 6′. **A.** 4 42-pdr R, 3 8-in SB, 6 32-pdr SB. **S.** 8 knots. **C.** 251. Built 1861. Sunk by mine off Haines Bluff, Miss., December 12, 1862. (See p.16)

Calhoun Sidewheel steamer: 508 tons. **A.** 2 32-pdr, 1 32-pdr R. Built 1851, captured January 1862, sold to US Army 1864. (See p.122)

Calypso Screw steamer: 630 tons. **D.** 175′ 2″ x 26′ 6″ x 12′. **A.** 2 30-pdr R, 4 24-pdr R. **S.** 12 knots. **C.** 70. Captured June 1863, sold 1865.

Camanche Ironclad monitor: 800 tons. **D.** 200′ x 46′ x 11′. **A.** 2 15-in SB. **C.** 76. Built 1863, sold 1899. (See p.26)

Cambria Schooner. Purchased 1861 for use as block ship.

Cambridge Screw steamer: 868 tons. **D.** 200′ x 32′ x 13′ 6″. **A.** 2 8-in R. **S.** 10 knots. **C.** 96. Built 1860, sold 1865.

Camelia Screw tug: 198 tons. **D.** 111′ x 19′ 6″ x 10′ 6″. **A.** 2 20-pdr. **S.** 10 knots. **C.** 40. Built 1862, sold 1865.

Canandaigua Screw sloop: 1395 tons. **D.** 228′ x 38′ 5″ x 15′. **A.** 2 11-in SB, 1 8-in SB, 3 20-pdr R. **S.** 10 knots. Launched 1862, broken up 1884.

Canonicus Ironclad monitor: 1034 tons. **D.** 225′ x 43′ 8″ x 13′ 6″. **A.** 2 15-in SB. **S.** 7 knots. **C.** 85. Built 1863, sold 1908. (See p.30)

Carmita Schooner: 61 tons. **D.** 65′ 2″ x 20′ 2″ x 5′ 6″. Captured December 1862, sold 1866.

Carnation Screw tug: 82 tons. **D.** 73′ 6″ x 17′ 6″ x 7′ 6″. **A.** 1 20-pdr R, 1 12-pdr R. **S.** 10 knots. **C.** 19. Built 1863, sold 1865.

Carondelet Ironclad: 512 tons. **D.** 175′ x 51′ 2″ x 6′. **A.** 3 8-in SB, 6 32-pdr, 4 42-pdr R, 1 12-pdr H. **S.** 4 knots. **C.** 251. Built 1861, sold 1865. (See p.16)

Carrabasset Sidewheel steamer: 202 tons. **D.** 155′ x 31′ 7″ x 4′ 7″. **A.** 2 32-pdr, 4 24-pdr SB. **C.** 45. Purchased 1864, sold 1865.

Casco Ironclad monitor: 614 tons. **D.** 208′ 9″ x 37′ x 6′ 6″. **A.** 1 11-in SB. Launched 1864, broken up 1875. (See p.38)

Catalpa Screw tug: 191 tons. **D.** 105′ 3″ x 22′ 2″ x 9′. **A.** 2 24-pdr SB, 1 12-pdr SB. **C.** 37. Built 1864, sold 1894.

Catawba Ironclad monitor: 1034 tons. **D.** 235′ x 46′ x 13′ 6″. **A.** 2 15-in SB. **S.** 10 knots. **C.** 85. Built 1864, sold 1868 to Peru, renamed *Athualpa*. (See p.30)

Catskill Ironclad monitor: 1875 tons. **D.** 200′ x 46′ x 11′ 6″. **A.** 1 15-in SB. 1 11-in SB. **S.** 4 knots. Built 1862, sold 1901. (See p.26)

Cayuga Screw steamer: 507 tons. **D.** 158′ x 28′ x 10′ 3″. **A.** 1 11-in SB, 1 20-pdr R, 2 24-pdr SB. **S.** 10 knots. Built 1861, sold 1865. (See p.84)

Ceres Sidewheel steamer: 150 tons. **D.** 108′ 4″ x 22′ 4″ x 6′ 3″. **A.** 1 30-pdr R, 1 32-pdr SB. **S.** 9 knots. **C.** 45. Built 1856, sold 1865.

Champion Sidewheel steamer: 115 tons. **D.** 145′ 8″ x 26′ 5″ x 3′ 6″. **A.** 2 30-pdr R, 1 24-pdr SB. **S.** 4 knots. Built 1859, sold 1865.

Charles Phelps Ship: 363 tons. **D.** 110′ x 27′ 4″ x 18′. **A.** 1 32-pdr SB. **C.** 23. Built 1848, sold 1865.

Charlotte Schooner: 70 tons. **A.** 2 guns. **C.** 14. Captured April 1862, sold 1867.

Chatham Sidewheel steamer: 198 tons. **D.** 120′ x 26′ x 7′ 7″. Built 1836, captured December 1863, sold 1865.

Chattanooga Screw steamer: 3233 tons. **D.** 315′ x 46′ x 20′ 6″. **A.** 17 guns. **S.** 14 knots. Built 1863. Sunk by ice at League Island, January 1872.

Chenango Sidewheel steamer: 974 tons. **D.** 205′ x 35′ x 6′ 6″ **A.** 2 100-pdr, 4 9-in SB, 2 20-pdr R, 2 24-pdr SB. **S.** 11 knots. **C.** 171. Launched March 1863, sold 1868. (See p.104)

Cherokee Screw steamer: 606 tons. **D.** 194′ 6″ x 25′ 2″ x 11′ 6″. **A.** 2 20-pdr R, 2 24-pdr SB. **S.** 13 knots. **C.** 92. Captured May 1863, sold 1865.

Chickasaw Ironclad monitor: 970 tons. **D.** 230′ x 56′ x 6′. **A.** 4 11-in SB. **C.** 138. Launched February 1864, sold 1874. (See p.12)

Chicopee Sidewheel steamer: 974 tons. **D.** 205′ x 35′ x 6′ 6″. **A.** 2 100-pdr R, 4 9-in SB. Launched March 1863, sold 1867. (See p.104)

Childs Hull sold 1865.

Chillicothe Ironclad: 385 tons. **D.** 162′ x 50′ x 4′. **A.** 2 11-in SB. **S.** 7 knots. Built 1862, sold 1865. (See p.48)

Chimo Ironclad monitor: 614 tons. **D.** 225′ x 37′ x 6′ 6″. **A.** 1 150-pdr R. **C.** 65. Launched May 1864, sold 1874. (See p.38).

Chippewa Screw gunboat: 507 tons. **D.** 158′ x 29′ x 8′. **A.** 1 11-in SB, 1 20-pdr R, 2 24-pdr SB. **S.** 4 knots. Built 1861, sold 1865. (See p.84)

Choctaw Ironclad: 1004 tons. **D.** 260′ x 45′ x 8′. **A.** 1 100-pdr R, 3 9-in SB, 2 30-pdr R, 2 24-pdr SB. Built 1853, sold 1866. (See p.47)

Chocura Screw steamer: 507 tons. **D.** 158′ x 28′ x 10′ 5″. **A.** 1 11-in SB, 2 24-pdr SB. **S.** 6 knots. Built 1861, sold 1867.

Chotank Schooner: 53 tons. **D.** 56′ x 17′ x 6′. **A.** 2 9-in SB, 1 11-in SB. Captured July 1861, sold 1865.

Cimarron Sidewheel steamer: 860 tons. **D.** 205′ x 35′ x 9′. **A.** 1 100-pdr R, 1 9-in SB, 6 24-pdr SB H. **S.** 10 knots. Launched March 1862, sole 1865.

Cincinnati Ironclad: 512 tons. **D.** 175′ x 51′ x 6′. **A.** 3 8-in SB, 6 32-pdr, 4 42-pdr R. **C.** 251. Built 1861, sold 1866. (See p.16)

Circassian Screw steamer: 1750 tons. **D.** 241′ x 39′ x 18′. **A.** 4 9-in SB, 1 100-pdr R, 1 12-pdr R. Captured May 1862, sold 1865.

Clara Dolsen Sidewheel steamer: 939 tons. **D.** 268′ x 42′ x 7′. **A.** 1 32-pdr. Captured June 1862, returned to owner 1864.

Clematis Screw tug: 297 tons. **D.** 127′ x 22′ x 10′. **A.** 1 30-pdr R, 2 12-pdr SB. **S.** 12 knots. **C.** 46. Built 1863, sold 1866.

Clifton Sidewheel steamer: 892 tons. **D.** 210′ x 40′ x 10′. **A.** 2 9-in SB, 4 32-pdr. Built 1861. Captured by Confederates September 1863, burnt March 1864.

Clinton Screw tug: 50 tons. **D.** 58′ 8″ x 15′ 10″ x 7′. **C.** 16. Purchased 1864, sold 1870.

Clover Screw tug: 129 tons. **D.** 92′ x 19′ x 9′. **A.** 1 12-pdr R, 1 12-pdr SB. **S.** 7 knots. Purchased 1863, sold 1865.

Clyde Sidewheel steamer: 294 tons. **D.** 200′ 6″ x 18′ 6″ x 6′. **A.** 2 24-pdr H. **S.** 9 knots. **C.** 67. Captured June 1863, sold 1865.

Coeur de Lion Sidewheel steamer: 110 tons. **D.** 100′ x 20′ 6″ x 4′ 6″. **A.** 1 30-pdr, 1 12-pdr R, 1 12-pdr SB. **C.** 29. Loaned in 1861 by the Lighthouse Board, returned in 1865.

Cohasset Screw tug: 100 tons. **D.** 82′ x 18′ 10″ x 6′. **A.** 1 20-pdr R. **S.** 8 knots. **C.** 12. Built 1860, sold 1892.

Cohoes Ironclad monitor: 1175 tons. **D.** 225′ x 45′ x 9′. **A.** 2 11-in SB. **S.** 9 knots. **C.** 69. Built 1865, sold 1875. (See p.38)

Collier Sternwheel steamer: 177 tons. **D.** 158′ x 30′ x 3′. **A.** 2 20-pdr R, 1 12-pdr R, 6 24-pdr H. Purchased 1864, sold 1865.

Colonel Kinsman Sidewheel steamer. Captured 1862. Sank off Brashear City, La., after striking underwater obstruction, February 1863.

Colorado Steam screw frigate: 3425 tons. **D.** 263′ 8″ x 52′ 6″ x 22′ 1″. **A.** 2 10-in, 28 9-in, 14 8-in. **S.** 9 knots. **C.** 646. Built 1856, sold 1885.

Colossus Sternwheel steamer: 183 tons. **D.** 155′ 2″ x 31′ 9″ x 4′. **A.** 2 30-pdr, 1 12-pdr SB, 4 24-pdr H. **S.** 5 knots. Built 1864, sold 1865.

Columbia Frigate: 1726 tons. **D.** 175′ x 45′ x 22′. **A.** 4 8-in SB, 28 32-pdr, 22 42-pdr. **S.** 12 knots. **C.** 480. Laid down 1825, completed 1838. Scuttled at Norfolk Navy Yard to avoid capture, April 21, 1861.

Columbia Screw steamer: 503 tons. **D.** 168′ x 25′ x 11′. **A.** 6 24-pdr SB, 1 30-pdr R. **C.** 100. Captured August 1862. Wrecked off Mosonboro Inlet, January 14, 1863.

Columbia Ironclad: 216′ x 51′ 2″ x 13′ 6″. Captured at Charleston February 1865, sold 1867. (See p.52)

Columbine Sidewheel tug: 133 tons. **D.** 117′ x 36′ x 4′. **A.** 2 20-pdr R. **C.** 25. Built 1850. Captured on St Johns River and burnt, May 23, 1863.

Columbus Ship-of-the-line: 2480 tons. **D.** 191′ 10″ x 53′ 6″ x 25′. **A.** 68 32-pdr, 24 42-pdr. Completed 1819. Scuttled at Norfolk Navy Yard to avoid capture, April 20, 1861.

Commodore Sidewheel steamer: 80 tons. **A.** 1 20-pdr R, 1 12-pdr R, 1 24-pdr H, 1 12-pdr H. **C.** 56. Purchased 1863, sold 1865.

Commodore Barney Sidewheel ferry: 512 tons. **D.** 143′ x 33′ x 9′. **A.** 1 100-pdr R, 3 9-in SB. **S.** 8 knots. **C.** 96. Built 1859, sold 1865.

Commodore Hull Sidewheel ferry: 376 tons. **D.** 141′ x 28′ 4″ x 9′. **A.** 2 30-pdr R, 4 24-pdr SB. **S.** 10 knots. Built 1860, sold 1865.

Commodore Jones Sidewheel ferry: 542 tons. **D.** 154′ x 32′ 6″ x 10′. **A.** 4 9-in SB, 1 50-pdr R, 2 30-pdr R, 4 24-pdr. **S.** 12 knots. **C.** 88. Purchased 1863. Sunk by mine on James River, May 6, 1864.

Commodore McDonough Sidewheel ferry: 532 tons. **D.** 8′ 6″ draft. **A.** 1 9-in SB, 1 20-pdr R, 4 24-pdr SB. **S.** 8 knots. **C.** 75. Purchased 1862. Sunk while under tow, August 23, 1865. (See p.110)

Commodore Morris Sidewheel ferry: 532 tons. **D.** 8′ 6″ draft. **A.** 1 100-pdr R, 1 9-in SB, 4 24-pdr H. **S.** 7 knots. **C.** 106. Built 1862, sold 1865.

Commodore Perry Sidewheel ferry: 512 tons. **D.** 143′ x 33′ x 10′. **A.** 2 9-in, 2 32-pdr SB, 1 12-pdr H. **S.** 7 knots. **C.** 125. Built 1856, sold 1865. (See p.110)

Commodore Read Sidewheel ferry: 659 tons. **D.** 179′ x 33′ 6″ x 6′ 3″. **A.** 2 100-pdr R, 4 24-pdr SB. **C.** 84. Built 1857, sold 1865.

Commodore Truxtun No details available, but existed in 1863.

Commodore Stockton Canal boat. Purchased for use as block ship.

Conemaugh Sidewheel steamer: 955 tons. **D.** 233′ 9″ x 34′ 10″ x 8′. **A.** 1 100-pdr R, 1 11-in SB, 6 24-pdr SB, 1 12-pdr SB. **S.** 11 knots. **C.** 125. Launched 1862, sold 1867.

Conestoga Sidewheel steamer: 572 tons. **A.** 4 32-pdr. Purchased 1861. Sunk after colliding with gunboat *General Price*, March 8, 1864. (See p.73)

Confiance Screw steamer: 1380 tons. **A.** 7 guns. Mentioned 1865; not completed.

Congress Frigate: 1867 tons. **D.** 179′ x 47′ 10″ x 22′ 6″. **A.** 8 8-in SB, 42 32-pdr. **C.** 480. Launched 1841. Sunk by *Merrimack* at Hampton Roads, March 8, 1862.

Connecticut Sidewheel steamer: 1725 tons. **D.** 251′ 6″ x 38′ 2″ x 18′. **A.** 4 32-pdr, 1 12-pdr R. **S.** 10 knots. **C.** 166. Built 1861, sold 1865.

Constellation Frigate: 1265 tons. **D.** 164′ x 40′ 6″ x 19′. **A.** 16 8-in SB, 4 32-pdr, 1 30-pdr R, 2 12-pdr SB. **C.** 340. Launched 1797, now preserved.

Constitution Frigate: 2200 tons. **D.** 175′ x 43′ 6″ x 23′ 6″. **A.** 16 32-pdr. **S.** 13 knots. **C.** 450. Launched 1797, in commission 1863.

Contoocook Screw sloop: 2348 tons. **D.** 296′ x 9′ draft. **A.** 8 9-in, 9 60-pdr, 4 24-pdr R. Launched 1864, sold 1872.

Corea Ship. Purchased for use as block ship.

Cornubia Sidewheel steamer: 589 tons. **D.** 102′ x 24′ 6″ x 11′. **A.** 1 20-pdr R, 2 24-pdr SB. **S.** 13 knots. **C.** 76. Captured November 1863, sold 1865.

Corypheus Schooner: 82 tons. **A.** 1 30-pdr R, 1 24-pdr H. **C.** 28. Captured May 1862, sold 1865.

Cossack Bark. Purchased for use as block ship.

Courier Ship: 556 tons. **D.** 135′ x 30′ x 12′. **A.** 2 32-pdr. **C.** 82. Purchased 1861. Wrecked on Abaco Island, Bahamas, June 14, 1864.

Courier Ship. Purchased for use as block ship.

Covington Sidewheel steamer: 224 tons. **D.** 126′ x 37′ x 6′ 6″. **A.** 4 24-pdr SB, 2 30-pdr R, 2 50-pdr R. **C.** 76. Purchased 1863. Burnt to prevent capture 25 miles below Alexandria on Red River, April 1864.

Cowslip Sidewheel steamer: 220 tons. **D.** 123′ x 24′ x 7′. **A.** 1 20-pdr R, 2 24-pdr SB. **C.** 36. Built 1863, sold 1866.

Cricket Sternwheel steamer: 176 tons. **D.** 154′ 1″ x 28′ 2″ x 4′. **A.** 6 24-pdr H. **S.** 6 knots. Built 1861, sold 1865.

Crocus Screw tug: 122 tons. **D.** 79′ x 18′ 6″ x 6′. **A.** 2 guns. **S.** 8 knots. Built 1862. Wrecked at Bodies Island, N.C., August 17, 1863.

Crusader Screw steamer: 545 tons. **D.** 169′ x 28′ x 12′ 6″. **A.** 4 32-pdr, 1 12-pdr. **S.** 8 knots. **C.** 92. Chartered 1858, sold 1865.

Cumberland Frigate: 1726 tons. **D.** 175′ x 45′ x 21′ 1″. **A.** 22 9-in SB, 1 10-in SB, 1 70-pdr R. **C.** 400. Launched 1842. Sunk in action with *Merrimack*, March 8, 1862.

Curlew Sternwheel steamer: 196 tons. **D.** 159′ x 32′ 1″ x 4′. **A.** 8 24-pdr H. **S.** 4 knots. Built 1862, sold 1865.

Curlew Screw steamer: 380 tons. Purchased 1861.

Currituck Screw steamer: 195 tons. **D.** 120′ x 23′ x 6′. **A.** 32-pdr, 1 20-pdr R. **C.** 52. Purchased 1861, sold 1865.

Cyane Frigate: 539 tons. **D.** 110′ x 39′ 6″ x 6′. **A.** 36 guns. **C.** 180. Built 1796. Sunk at moorings in Philadelphia Navy Yard, 1885.

Cyane Sloop: 792 tons. **D.** 132′ x 35′ 4″ x 16′ 6″. **A.** 14 32-pdr, 4 8-in SB. **C.** 200. Launched 1837, sold 1887.

Dacotah Steam sloop: 996 tons. **D.** 198′ 5″ x 32′ 9″ x 14′ 8″. **A.** 1 100-pdr R, 4 32-pdr, 1 10-in, 1 12-pdr R, 1 12-pdr. **S.** 11 knots. Launched 1859, sold 1873.

Daffodil Sidewheel steamer: 173 tons. **D.** 110′ 6″ x 22′ 6″ x 5′ 6″. **A.** 2 32-pdr R. **S.** 8 knots. **C.** 35. Built 1862, sold 1867.

Dahlia Sidewheel tug: 50 tons. **D.** 6′ draft. **S.** 10 knots. Built 1862, sold 1865.

Dai Ching Screw steamer: 520 tons. **D.** 170′ 6″ x 29′ 4″ x 9′ 6″. **A.** 1 100-pdr R, 4 24-pdr, 2 20-pdr. **S.** 6 knots. **C.** 83. Built 1863. Set on fire to avoid capture after running aground in Combahee River, Carolina, January 26, 1865.

Daisy Screw tug: 50 tons. **D.** 73′ 4″ x 13′ 10″ x 6′. **S.** 10 knots. Built 1850, sold 1865.

Dale Sloop: 566 tons. **D.** 117′ x 32′ x 15′ 6″. **A.** 14 32-pdr, 1 12-pdr H. **S.** 10 knots. **C.** 150. Built 1839, transferred to Coast Guard 1906.

Dan **A.** 1 20-pdr R, 1 12-pdr. Captured October 1862. Sunk February 1863 on Mississippi River.

Dan Purchased for use as block ship.

Dan Smith Schooner: 150 tons. **D.** 87′ 9″ x 25′ 2″ x 10′. **A.** 2 32-pdr. **C.** 33. Purchased 1861, sold 1865.

Dandelion Steam tug: 111 tons. **D.** 90′ x 19′ x 6′. **A.** 2 12-pdr H. **S.** 19 knots. **C.** 21. Built 1862, sold 1865.

Darlington Sidewheel steamer: 300 tons. **A.** 1 H. **C.** 23. Captured March 1862, transferred to army September 1862.

Dart Schooner: 94 tons. **A.** 12-pdr H. Captured July 1861. Dismantled October 1861.

Dawn Screw steamer: 399 tons. **D.** 154′ x 28′ x 12′. **A.** 2 32-pdr. **S.** 8 knots. **C.** 60. Built 1857, sold 1865.

Daylight Screw steamer: 682 tons. **D.** 170′ x 30′ 6″ x 13′. **A.** 4 32-pdr. **S.** 5 knots. **C.** 57. Built 1859, sold 1865.

Daylight Purchased for use as block ship.

Decatur Sloop: 566 tons. **D.** 117′ x 32′ x 15′ 6″. **A.** 4 8-in SB, 20 32-pdr. **S.** 10 knots. **C.** 150. Built 1838, sold 1865.

Delaware Ship-of-the-line: 2633 tons. **D.** 196′ 2″ x 53′ x 26′ 2″. **A.** 74 guns. **C.** 820. Launched 1820. Burnt at Norfolk Navy Yard to prevent capture, April 20, 1861.

Delaware Sidewheel steamer: 357 tons. **D.** 161′ x 27′ x 6′. **A.** 4 32-pdr, 1 12-pdr R. **S.** 13 knots. **C.** 65. Purchased 1861. Sold to Treasury Dept, 1865.

Delaware Farmer Schooner. Purchased for use as block ship.

Delight Purchased for use as block ship.

Delta Screw tug: 50 tons. **D.** 66′ x 14′ x 7′ 8″. **S.** 9 knots. Purchased 1864, sold 1865.

De Sota Sidewheel steamer: 1675 tons. **D.** 253′ x 38′ x 16′. **A.** 8 32-pdr, 1 30-pdr R. **S.** 8 knots. **C.** 130. Purchased 1861, sold 1868. (See p.79)

Detroit Screw steamer. Laid down 1865, never completed.

Diana Sidewheel steamer. Captured April 1862. Recaptured at Grand Lake, La., March 28, 1863.

Dick Fulton Steamer. Converted to a ram.

Dictator Ironclad monitor: 3033 tons. **D.** 312′ x 50′ x 20′. **A.** 2 15-in SB. **S.** 10 knots. **C.** 174. Launched 1863, sold 1883. (See p.64)

Dolphin Brig: 224 tons. **D.** 88′ x 25′ x 13′. **A.** 2 9-pdr, 8 24-pdr. **C.** 80. Built 1836. Burnt at Norfolk Navy Yard to prevent capture, April 21, 1861.

Don Screw steamer: 390 tons. **D.** 162′ x 23′ x 6′. **A.** 2 20-pdr, 6 24-pdr. **C.** 94. Captured March 1862, sold 1868.

Donegal Sidewheel steamer: 1080 tons. **D.** 200′ x 36′ x 8′. **A.** 2 30-pdr R, 2 12-pdr SB. **S.** 10 knots. **C.** 130. Built 1860, sold 1865.

Dove Bark. Purchased for use as block ship.

Dragon Screw steamer: 118 tons. **D.** 17′ beam, 7′ 6″ draft. **A.** 1 30-pdr R, 1 24-pdr SB. **C.** 42. Purchased 1861, sold 1865.

Dryad Gunboat. **A.** 8 24-pdr.

Dumbarton Sidewheel steamer: 636 tons. **D.** 204′ x 29′ x 10′. **A.** 2 32-pdr, 2 12-pdr H. **S.** 10 knots. Captured June 1864, sold 1867.

Dunderberg Ironclad: 5090 tons. **D.** 376′ x 73′ x 15′ 5″. **A.** 15-in SB, 12 11-in SB. **S.** 11½ knots. **C.** 590. Launched 1865, sold to France 1867. (See p.71)

E.B. Hale Screw steamer: 220 tons. **D.** 117′ x 28′ x 8′ 6″. **A.** 4 32-pdr. **S.** 8 knots. **C.** 50. Purchased 1861, sold 1865.

E.D. Thompson Schooner. Purchased for use as block ship.

Eastport Ironclad: 700 tons. **D.** 280′ x 6′ 6″ draft. **A.** 1 100-pdr R, 6 9-in SB. **C.** 150. Captured incomplete at Cerro Gordo, February 7, 1862. Destroyed to prevent recapture, April 26, 1864. (See p.14)

Edward Bark: 340 tons. Purchased 1861 for use as block ship.

Elfin Steamer: 192 tons. **D.** 155′ x 31′ x 4′ 4″. **A.** 8 24-pdr H. **C.** 50. Purchased 1864. Burnt to prevent capture, November 4, 1864.

Elk Sidewheel steamer: 162 tons. **D.** 156′ x 29′ x 3′ 10″. **A.** 2 32-pdr, 4 24-pdr SB. **C.** 65. Purchased 1863, sold 1865.

Ella Sidewheel steamer: 230 tons. **D.** 150′ x 23′ x 8′ 6″. **A.** 2 24-pdr H. **S.** 8 knots. **C.** 39. Captured November 1862, sold 1865.

Ellen Sidewheel steamer: 341 tons. **D.** 125′ x 28′ x 7′. **A.** 2 32-pdr, 2 30-pdr R. **C.** 50. Purchased 1861, sold 1865.

Ellen Goldsboro Schooner. Purchased 1861 for use as block ship.

Ellis Sidewheel steamer: 100 tons. **D.** 6′ draft. **A.** 1 32-pdr R, 1 12-pdr H. **C.** 28. Captured at Elizabeth City, N.C., February 10, 1862. Destroyed November 25, 1862 to prevent capture.

Emerald Ship: 518 tons. Purchased 1861 for use as block ship.

Emma Screw steamer: 350 tons. **D.** 156′ x 21′ x 9′ 4″. **A.** 6 24-pdr H, 2 12-pdr R. **S.** 12 knots. Captured July 1863, sold 1865.

Eolus Sidewheel steamer: 368 tons. **D.** 140′ x 25′ x 7′. **A.** 1 30-pdr R, 2 24-pdr H. **S.** 16 knots. Built 1864, sold 1865.

Epervier Screw steamer: 831 tons. Authorized November 1864 but never built. (See p.141)

Epsilon Screw tug: 55 tons. **D.** 66′ x 15′ x 7′ 6″. **S.** 9 knots. Purchased 1864, sold 1865.

Essex Ironclad: 614 tons. **D.** 159′ x 47′ 6″ x 6′. **A.** 3 9-in SB, 1 10-in SB, 1 32-pdr. Built 1856, sold 1865. (See p.15)

Estrella Sidewheel steamer: 438 tons. **A.** 1 30-pdr R, 2 32-pdr, 2 24-pdr H. Transferred 1862, sold 1867.

Ethan Allen Bark: 556 tons. **D.** 153′ 6″ x 35′ 1″ x 13′. **A.** 6 32-pdr. **S.** 12 knots. **C.** 90. Built 1859, sold 1865.

Etlah Ironclad monitor: 614 tons. **D.** 225′ 8″ x 45′ 6″. **A.** 1 11-in SB. **S.** 9 knots. **C.** 69. Launched 1865, sold 1874. (See p.38)

Eugene Schooner: 150 tons. Captured 1862, sold 1864.

Eureka Screw steamer: 50 tons. **D.** 85′ x 12′ 8″ x 3′ 6″. **A.** 2 12-pdr. **C.** 19. Captured 1862, sold 1865.

Eutaw Sidewheel steamer: 955 tons. **D.** 205′ x 35′ x 8′ 6″. **A.** 4 9-in SB, 2 100-pdr R, 2 20-pdr R. **S.** 13 knots. Commissioned July 1863, sold 1867. (See p.104)

Exchange Sternwheel steamer: 211 tons. **D.** 155′ 3″ x 33′ 5″. **A.** 2 32-pdr, 4 24-pdr H. **S.** 6 knots. **C.** 81. Built 1862, sold 1865.

Express Merchant vessel purchased for use as block ship.

Fahkee Screw steamer: 660 tons. **D.** 163′ x 29′ 6″ x 13′ 3″. **A.** 2 24-pdr H, 1 10-pdr R. **S.** 12 knots. **C.** 73. Built 1862, sold 1865.

Fairplay Sidewheel steamer: 156 tons. **D.** 5′ draft. **A.** 4 12-pdr H. **S.** 5 knots. Built 1859, captured 1862, sold 1865.

Fairy Sternwheel steamer: 211 tons. **D.** 157′ x 31′ 6″ x 5′. **A.** 8 24-pdr H. **S.** 6 knots. Built 1861, sold 1865.

Falmouth Sloop: 703 tons. **D.** 127′ x 33′ 9″ x 16′. **A.** 4 8-in, 16 32-pdr. **C.** 190. Launched 1827, sold October 1863.

Farallones Screw steamer: 765 tons. **D.** 161′ x 31′ 10″ x 15′. **A.** 6 32-pdr. Built 1849, sold 1867.

Fawn Sternwheel steamer: 174 tons. **D.** 158′ 8″ x 30′ 5″ x 3′ 6″. **A.** 6 24-pdr H. **S.** 4 knots. Launched 1863, sold 1865.

Fearnot Ship: 1012 tons. **D.** 178′ x 35′ x 23′ 6″. **A.** 6 32-pdr R. Built 1861, sold 1866.

Fern Screw tug: 50 tons. **D.** 6′ draft. **A.** 1 12-pdr H. **S.** 12 knots. Transferred 1862, sold 1865.

Fernandina Bark: 297 tons. **D.** 115′ x 29′ x 10′. **A.** 6 32-pdr. **S.** 8 knots. **C.** 86. Purchased 1861, sold 1865.

Flag Screw steamer: 938 tons. **D.** 193′ x 30′ 10″ x 15′. **A.** 6 8-in SB. Purchased 1861, sold 1865.

Flambeau Screw steamer: 850 tons. **D.** 180′ x 30′ x 11′. **A.** 1 30-pdr R, 1 20-pdr R. Built 1861, sold 1865.

Florida Sidewheel steamer: 1261 tons. **D.** 214′ x 35′ 3″ x 22′ 4″. **A.** 8 32-pdr, 1 20-pdr R. Purchased 1861, sold 1868.

Flusser Schooner. **D.** 66′ x 21′ x 5′ 11″. Captured 1864, sold 1865.

Forest Rose Sternwheel steamer: 260 tons. **D.** 155′ x 32′ 3″ x 5′. **A.** 2 30-pdr R, 4 24-pdr H. **S.** 6 knots. Built 1862, sold 1865.

Fort Canal boat: 112 tons. Purchased 1864 for use as block ship.

Fort Donelson Sidewheel steamer: 900 tons. **D.** 283′ x 20′ x 10′. **A.** 5 12-pdr, 2 30-pdr. Captured November 1863, sold 1865. Formerly known as *R.E. Lee*.

Fort Gaines Sidewheel steamer: 80 tons. **A.** 1 20-pdr R, 2 12-pdr, 1 24-pdr. Captured 1864, sold 1865.

Fort Henry Sidewheel steamer: 519 tons. **D.** 150′ 6″ x 32′ x 10′. **A.** 2 9-in SB, 4 32-pdr. Purchased 1862, sold 1865.

Fort Hindman Sidewheel steamer: 286 tons. **D.** 150′ x 37′ x 2′ 2″. **A.** 6 8-in. Purchased 1863, sold 1865. (See p.87)

Fort Jackson Sidewheel steamer: 1850 tons. **D.** 250′ x 38′ 6″ x 18′. **A.** 1 100-pdr R, 2 30-pdr R, 8 9-in SB. **S.** 14 knots. Purchased 1863, sold 1865. (See p.108)

Fort Morgan Screw steamer: 1249 tons. **D.** 220′ x 34′ 6″ x 10′ 2″. **A.** 1 30-pdr R, 2 12-pdr R, 2 24-pdr H. Built 1863, sold 1865.

Fortune Bark: 292 tons. Purchased 1861 for use as block ship.

Fortune Screw steamer: 450 tons. **D.** 137′ x 26′ x 9′ 6″. **A.** 2 32-pdr. **S.** 10 knots. Launched 1865, sold 1922.

Fox Schooner: 80 tons. **D.** 8′ 6″ draft. **A.** 1 12-pdr H, 1 12-pdr R. Built 1859, captured April 1863, sold 1865.

Frances Henrietta Bark: 407 tons. Purchased 1861 for use as block ship.

Franklin Screw frigate: 5170 tons. **D.** 265′ x 53′ 8″ x 17′. **A.** 1 11-in SB, 34 9-in SB, 4 100-pdr R. Laid down 1854, commissioned June 1867, sold 1915.

Fredonia Bark: 800 tons. **D.** 160′ x 32′ 11″ x 16′ 6″. **A.** 4 24-pdr. **C.** 37. Built 1845. Destroyed in earthquake at Arica, Peru, August 13, 1868.

Friendship Schooner. Purchased 1861 for use as block ship.

Frolic Sidewheel steamer: 880 tons. **D.** 230′ x 26′ x 11′ 8″. **A.** 4 24-pdr H SB, 1 20-pdr H R. **S.** 12 knots. **C.** 107. Built 1862, captured 1864, sold 1877.

Fuchsia Screw tug: 240 tons. **D.** 98′ 3″ x 21′ 9″ x 8′. **A.** 1 30-pdr R, 1 24-pdr H. Built 1863, sold 1865. (See p.76)

Fulton Sidewheel steamer: 698 tons. **D.** 10′ 2″ draft. **S.** 11 knots. Built 1837. Destroyed at Pensacola Navy Yard by Confederates to prevent recapture, May 10, 1862.

G.L. Brockenboro Sloop. Captured October 1862. Wrecked on west coast of Florida, May 27, 1863.

G.W. Blunt Schooner: 121 tons. **D.** 76′ 6″ x 20′ 6″ x 8′ 9″. **A.** 2 12-pdr. **S.** 10 knots. Purchased 1861, sold 1865.

Galatea Screw steamer: 1244 tons. **D.** 209′ 6″ x 35′ 6″ x 20′ 8″. **A.** 1 100-pdr R, 8 32-pdr, 2 30-pdr. **S.** 10 knots. Built 1862, sold to Haitian government 1865.

Galena Ironclad: 738 tons. **D.** 210′ x 36′ x 11′. **A.** 4 9-in SB, 2 100-pdr R. **S.** 8 knots. **C.** 164. Launched February 1862. Broken up 1872 at Norfolk Navy Yard. (See p.41)

Gamage Sidewheel steamer: 187 tons. **D.** 148′ 6″ x 30′ 3″ x 4′ 6″. **A.** 2 20-pdr, 1 12-pdr. Built 1864, sold 1865. Renamed *Southern Belle*. Burnt at Plaquemine, La., October 11, 1876.

Gamma Screw steamer: 36 tons. **D.** 65′ x 14′ x 6′. **A.** 1 torpedo. **S.** 12 knots. Built 1863, sold 1865. Renamed *Peter smith*. Burnt at New York, May 9, 1893.

Garland Bark: 243 tons. **D.** 92′ 5″ x 24′ 4″ x 12′ 2″. Built 1815 as privateer. Purchased 1861 for use as block ship but transferred to army in January 1862 for use as depot ship.

Garonne Schooner: 14 tons. Captured December 1861. Used as block ship.

Gazelle Sidewheel steamer: 117 tons. **D.** 135′ x 23′ x 4′. **A.** 6 12-pdr R. **S.** 4 knots. Built 1863, sold 1865. Renamed *Plain City* and abandoned 1869.

Gem of the Sea Bark: 371 tons. **D.** 116′ x 26′ 3″ x 13′ 5″. **A.** 6 32-pdr. **C.** 65. Purchased 1861, sold 1865.

Gemsbok Bark: 622 tons. **D.** 141′ 7″ x 31′ x 17′. **A.** 4 8-in, 2 32-pdr. Purchased 1861, sold 1865.

General Bragg Sidewheel steamer: 1043 tons. **D.** 208′ x 32′ 8″ x 12′. **A.** 1 30-pdr, 1 32-pdr, 1 12-pdr R. Built 1851, captured June 6, 1862, sold 1865.

General Burnside Sidewheel steamer: 201 tons. **D.** 171′ x 26′ x 4′ 9″. **A.** 2 20-pdr, 3 24-pdr H. Built 1862, returned to army 1865.

General Grant Sidewheel steamer: 201 tons. **D.** 171′ x 26′ x 4′ 9″. **A.** 2 30-pdr, 2 24-pdr H. Built 1863, returned to army 1865. Lost when stranded in ice at Portsmouth, Nebr., March 1866.

General Lyon Sidewheel steamer: 1200 tons. **A.** 2 12-pdr R. Built 1860, captured at Island No. 10 April 1862, sold 1865. Renamed *Alabama*. Destroyed by fire at Grand View, La., April 1, 1867.

General Pillow Sidewheel steamer: 38 tons. **D.** 81′ 5″ x 17′ 1″ x 3′. **A.** 2 12-pdr H. Captured June 1862, sold 1865.

General Price Sidewheel steamer: 633 tons. **D.** 182′ x 30′ x 13′. **A.** 4 9-in SB. Built 1856, captured June 1862, sold 1865. (See p.98)

General Sherman Sidewheel steamer: 187 tons. **D.** 168′ x 26′ x 4′ 6″. **A.** 2 20-pdr R, 3 24-pdr H. Built 1864, returned to army 1865.

General Thomas Sidewheel steamer: 184 tons. **D.** 165′ x 26′ x 4′ 6″. **A.** 2 20-pdr R, 4 24-pdr H. Built 1864, returned to army 1865.

Genesee Sidewheel steamer: 803 tons. **D.** 209′ x 34′ 11″ x 10′ 6″. **A.** 1 10-in SB, 1 100-pdr R, 6 24-pdr H. **S.** 8½ knots. Built 1862, sold 1867. (See p.94)

George Mangham Schooner: 274 tons. **D.** 110′ x 28′ x 10′. **A.** 1 13-in M, 2 32-pdr. **S.** 10 knots. Built 1854, purchased 1861, sold 1865.

George P. Upshur Schooner. Purchased 1861 for use as block ship.

George W. Rodgers Schooner: 87 tons. **D.** 76′ x 22′ x 6′. **A.** 2 20-pdr R. Captured July 1861, sold 1865.

George Washington Parke Curtis Coal barge: 120 tons. **D.** 14′ 6″ beam, 4′ draft. Built mid-1850s, purchased 1861 for use as balloon ship.

Geranium Sidewheel steamer: 223 tons. **D.** 128′ 6″ x 23′ 3″ x 5′. **A.** 1 20-pdr R, 2 12-pdr R. Purchased 1863, sold 1865.

Germantown Sloop: 939 tons. **D.** 150′ x 36′ x 16′ 8″. **A.** 4 8-in, 18 32-pdr. **S.** 11 knots. Built 1846. Scuttled at Norfolk Navy Yard, April 20, 1861. Hulk raised and sold 1864.

Gertrude Screw steamer: 350 tons. **D.** 156′ x 21′ x 10′ 6″. **A.** 2 12-pdr R, 6 24-pdr H. Captured April 1863, sold 1865. Renamed *Gussie Telfair.* No longer listed in 1878.

Gettysburg Sidewheel steamer: 950 tons. **D.** 221′ x 26′ 3″ x 10′. **A.** 1 30-pdr, 2 12-pdr R, 4 24-pdr H. **S.** 15 knots. Built 1858, captured November 1863, sold 1879.

Gipsey Schooner. Served in 1862.

Gladiolus Screw tug: 81 tons. **D.** 88′ x 18′ 6″ x 8′. **A.** 2 12-pdr R, 1 24-pdr H. Purchased 1864, sold 1865, lost 1887.

Glance Screw tug: 81 tons. **D.** 75′ x 8′ draft. **S.** 8 knots. Built 1863, purchased 1864, sold 1883.

Glasgow Sidewheel steamer: 252 tons. **D.** 7′ 2″ draft. **A.** 1 12-pdr R, 1 12-pdr H. Captured May 1863, sold 1869.

Glaucus Screw steamer: 1244 tons. **D.** 209′ x 35′ 6″ x 20′ 8″. **A.** 1 100-pdr R, 2 30-pdr R, 8 8-in. **S.** 10 knots.

Glide Sternwheel steamer: 137 tons. **A.** 6 24-pdr H. Built 1862. While at Cairo under repair, she caught fire and was completely destroyed.

Governor Buckingham Screw steamer: 806 tons. **D.** 177′ 6″ x 32′ 2″ x 13′ 6″. **A.** 1 20-pdr R, 2 24-pdr H, 1 12-pdr H. Purchased 1863, sold 1865.

Grampus Sidewheel steamer: 230 tons. **D.** 180′ x 27′ x 5′. Purchased 1863, sold 1868.

Grand Gulf Screw steamer: 1200 tons. **D.** 210′ 4″ x 34′ 6″ x 20′. **A.** 1 100-pdr R, 2 30-pdr R, 5 8-in. **S.** 11½ knots. Purchased 1863, sold 1865. Burnt and sank alongside wharf at new Orleans, April 19, 1869.

Granite Sloop: 75 tons. **A.** 1 32-pdr R, 1 30-pdr R. Transferred from Lighthouse Board January 1862 and returned 1865.

Granite City Sidewheel steamer: 450 tons. **D.** 160′ x 23′ x 5′ 6″. **A.** 6 24-pdr H, 1 12-pdr R. Captured March 1863. Recaptured by Confederates, April 28, 1864. Ran aground and lost, January 20, 1865.

Great Western Sidewheel steamer: 800 tons. **A.** 1 12-pdr, 1 32-pdr, 1 6-pdr R. Built 1857. Transferred to navy September 1862, sold 1865.

Grossbeak Sidewheel steamer: 196 tons. **D.** 164′ x 28′ x 46′ 6″. **A.** 2 20-pdr R, 2 30-pdr R, 1 12-pdr SB. Purchased February 1865, sold 1865.

Guerriere Screw sloop: 3954 tons. **D.** 319′ 3″ x 45′ x 17′ 11″. **A.** 2 100-pdr R, 1 60-pdr R, 6 9-in SB, 4 20-pdr H. Launched 1865, sold 1872. (See p.147)

Harcourt Screw tug: 75 tons. **D.** 66′ x 16′ 3″ x 7′ 9″. **S.** 13 knots. Purchased 1864, sold 1867.

Harriet Lane Sidewheel steamer: 600 tons. **A.** 3 9-in, 1 30-pdr R. Built in 1857 for Treasury Department, transferred to navy 1861. Captured at Galveston, Texas, January 1, 1865. Lost in Caribbean Sea, May 13, 1884. (See p.82)

Hartford Screw sloop: 2900 tons. **D.** 225′ x 44′ x 17′ 2″. **A.** 20 9-in SB, 2 20-pdr R, 2 12-pdr R. **S.** 13½ knots. **C.** 302. Launched November 1858. Sank at berth in Norfolk Navy Yard 1956. (See p.132)

Harvest Bark: 314 tons. Purchased 1861 for use as block ship.

Harvest Moon Sidewheel steamer: 275 tons. **D.** 152′ x 30′ x 8′. **A.** 4 24-pdr H. **S.** 15 knots. Built 1863. Struck mine on February 29, 1865 in Winyah Bay, S.C. Abandoned after removing machinery and equipment on April 21. Attempts were made to raise the vessel in 1963.

Hastings Sidewheel steamer: 293 tons. **D.** 173′ x 34′ 2″ x 5′ 4″. **A.** 2 30-pdr R, 2 32-pdr, 2 24-pdr. Built 1860, sold 1865. Served as river freighter until 1872.

Hatteras Sidewheel steamer: 1126 tons. **D.** 210′ x 34′ x 18′. **A.** 4 32-pdr, 1 20-pdr R. **S.** 8 knots. **C.** 126. Purchased 1861. Sunk by *Alabama* January 11, 1863 off Galveston, Tex.

Heliotrope Sidewheel steamer: 239 tons. **D.** 134′ x 24′ 6″ x 5′. **A.** 1 12-pdr. **S.** 6 knots. Purchased December 1863, sold to Lighthouse Service 1865.

Hendrick Hudson Screw steamer: 460 tons. **D.** 171′ x 29′ 11″ x 9′ 6″. **A.** 4 8-in, 2 20-pdr. **S.** 11 knots. Built 1859, captured April 1862, sold 1865, lost 1867.

Henry Andrew Screw steamer: 177 tons. **D.** 150′ x 26′ x 7′ 6″. **A.** 2 32-pdr, 1 20-pdr R. Built 1847, purchased 1861. Driven ashore in heavy weather off Cape Henry, August 24, 1862. Total loss.

Henry Brinker Screw steamer: 108 tons. **D.** 82′ x 26′ 7″ x 7′. **A.** 1 30-pdr. **S.** 7 knots. Purchased 1861, sold 1865.

Henry Janes Schooner: 260 tons. **D.** 109′ 9″ x 29′ 8″ x 9′. **A.** 1 13-in M, 2 32-pdr. Purchased 1861, sold 1865.

Herald Ship: 274 tons. Purchased 1861 for use as block ship.

Hero Schooner. Purchased 1861 for use as block ship.

Hetzel Sidewheel steamer: 200 tons. **A.** 1 9-in SB, 1 80-pdr R. Built 1861 for Coast Guard Service and returned 1865. (See p.105)

Hibiscus Screw steamer: 490 tons. **A.** 2 30-pdr R, 2 24-pdr. **S.** 9 knots. Purchased 1864, sold 1866.

Hollyhock Sidewheel steamer: 352 tons. **D.** 135′ x 26′ 9″ x 7′. **A.** 1 20-pdr R, 2 12-pdr H. **S.** 14 knots. Purchased 1863, sold 1865.

Home Screw steamer: 725 tons. **D.** 165′ x 29′ 9″ x 13′ 6″. **A.** 2 24-pdr H, 1 12-pdr R. **S.** 6 knots. Purchased 1862, sold 1865. Renamed *Key West.* Stranded off Cape Hatteras and became total loss, October 12, 1870.

Honduras Sidewheel steamer: 376 tons. **D.** 150′ x 27′ x 9′. **A.** 2 12-pdr R. **S.** 12 knots. Purchased 1863, sold 1865. Stranded in 1870 off Key West.

Honeysuckle Screw steamer: 234 tons. **D.** 123′ x 20′ 2″ x 10′. **A.** 2 20-pdr R. **S.** 12 knots. Purchased 1863, sold 1865, remained in service until 1900.

Hope Schooner: 134 tons. **D.** 85′ x 20′ 9″ x 9′. **A.** 1 20-pdr R. **S.** 10 knots. Purchased 1861, sold 1865.

Horace Beals Barkentine: 296 tons. **D.** 121′ 6″ x 30′ 8″ x 11′ 8″. **A.** 1 32-pdr, 1 30-pdr R. Purchased 1861, sold 1865.

Housatonic Screw sloop: 1240 tons. **D.** 207′ x 38′ x 8′ 7″. **A.** 1 100-pdr R, 3 30-pdr R, 1 11-in SB, 2 32-pdr, 2 24-pdr H. Launched 1861. Sunk by submarine *H.L. Hunley* off Charleston, February 17, 1864. (See p.82)

Howquah Screw steamer: 460 tons. **D.** 120′ x 22′ 10″ x 12′. **A.** 2 30-pdr R, 1 12-pdr R, 1 12-pdr. **S.** 10 knots. Purchased 1863, sold 1865.

Hoyt Screw tug: 20 tons. **D.** 45′ x 10′ 5″ x 6′. **A.** 1 spar torpedo. **S.** 7 knots. Purchased 1864, sold 1865.

Hunchback Sidewheel steamer: 517 tons. **D.** 179′ x 29′ x 9′. **A.** 3 9-in SB, 1 100-pdr R. **S.** 12 knots. Built 1852, purchased 1861, sold 1865. Served as ferry until 1880.

Huntress Sternwheel steamer: 211 tons. **D.** 131′ x 31′ 3″ x 5′. **A.** 2 30-pdr R, 4 24-pdr H. **S.** 5 knots. Purchased 1864, sold 1865. Lost after being stranded near Alexandria, La., December 30, 1865.

Huntsville Screw steamer: 860 tons. **D.** 196′ 4″ x 29′ 6″ x 19′ 5″. **A.** 1 64-pdr, 2 32-pdr. **S.** 11 knots. **C.** 64. Purchased 1861, sold 1865.

Huron Screw steamer: 507 tons. **D.** 158′ x 28′ x 10′ 6″. **A.** 1 11-in SB, 1 20-pdr R, 2 24-pdr H. Launched 1861, sold 1869. (See pp. 84, 85)

Hyacinth Screw tug: 50 tons. **D.** 6′ draft. **S.** 8 knots. Sold 1865.

Hydrangea Screw tug: 224 tons. **D.** 120′ x 20′ 3″ x 9′ 6″. **A.** 1 20-pdr R, 2 12-pdr H. **S.** 11 knots. Built 1862, sold 1865. Lost after being stranded on Cape May, N.J., November 17, 1886.

I.N. Seymour Sidewheel steamer: 133 tons. **D.** 100′ x 19′ 8″ x 6′. **A.** 1 30-pdr R, 1 20-pdr R. **S.** 11 knots. **C.** 30. Purchased 1861, transferred to Lighthouse Board 1865, sold 1882. Served foreign owners until 1888.

Ibex Sidewheel steamer: 235 tons. **D.** 157′ x 33′ x 4′ 6″. **A.** 2 30-pdr R, 2 12-pdr R, 4 24-pdr H. Purchased 1861, sold 1865. Renamed *Harry Dean.* Lost through explosion, January 3, 1868.

Ice Boat Steamer. **A.** 4 32-pdr. **C.** 50. Offered as a free boat in 1861. Returned to owners November 1861.

Ida Steam tug: 104 tons. **A.** 1 gun. Purchased 1863. Sunk by mine in Mobile Bay, April 13, 1865.

Idaho Steam sloop: 3241 tons. **D.** 298′ x 44′ 6″ x 16′. **A.** 6 32-pdr, 1 30-pdr R, 1 12-pdr H. Launched October 1864, sold 1874. (See p.148)

Illinois Steam sloop: 3954 tons. **D.** 312′ 6″ x 46′ x 21′ 5″. **A.** 2 100-pdr R, 16 9-in SB. Laid down 1864, never completed. Broken up 1872. (See p.147)

Independence Ship-of-the-line: 3270 tons. **D.** 190′ 10″ x 54′ 7″ x 24′ 4″. **A.** 90 32-pdr. **C.** 790. Launched June 1814. Burnt on the Hunters Point mudflats, California, to recover her metal fittings, September 20, 1919.

India Ship: 366 tons. Purchased 1861 for use as block ship.

Indianola Ironclad: 511 tons. **D.** 174′ x 50′ x 5′. **A.** 2 11-in SB, 2 9-in SB. **S.** 9 knots. Built 1862, captured February 24, 1863 but destroyed by Confederates to prevent recapture. (See p.48)

Ino Ship: 895 tons. **D.** 160′ 6″ x 34′ 11″ x 18′ 9″. **A.** 8 32-pdr. **S.** 14 knots. **C.** 144. Purchased 1861, sold 1867.

Intelligent Whale (See p.159)

Iosco Sidewheel steamer: 974 tons. **D.** 205′ x 35′ x 9′ 3″. **A.** 2 100-pdr R, 4 9-in SB, 2 24-pdr H. **S.** 9 knots. **C.** 173. Launched 1863. Used as coal hulk from 1868. (See p.104)

Iris Screw steamer: 159 tons. **D.** 87′ x 19′ x 9′. **A.** 2 20-pdr R. **S.** 10 knots. **C.** 34. Purchased 1863, transferred to Lighthouse Dept, 1865.

Iron Age Screw steamer: 424 tons. **D.** 144′ x 25′ x 12′ 6″. **A.** 6 8-in SB, 3 30-pdr R. Built 1862, purchased 1863. Destroyed to prevent capture after running aground at Lockwoods Folly Inlet, Wilmington, January 10, 1864.

Ironsides Bark. Used as store ship from August 1863 to June 1864.

Iroquois Steam sloop: 1016 tons. **D.** 198′ 11″ x 33′ 10″ x 13′. **A.** 1 50-pdr R, 2 11-in SB, 4 32-pdr. **S.** 11 knots. Launched 1859. No longer listed in 1910.

Isaac Smith Screw steamer: 453 tons. **D.** 171′ 6″ x 31′ 4″ x 9′. **A.** 8 8-in SB, 1 30-pdr R. **C.** 56. Built 1851, purchased 1861. Captured January 30, 1863. Renamed *Stono* and destroyed at Charleston.

Isilda Schooner. **D.** 8′ draft. **A.** 1 24-pdr. Captured September 1861, sold 1863.

Island Belle Sidewheel steamer: 123 tons. **D.** 100′ x 20′ 4″ x 6′ 7″. **A.** 1 32-pdr, 1 12-pdr R. Purchased 1861. Ran aground on Appomattox River, June 27, 1862 and burnt June 28 to prevent capture.

Isonomia Sidewheel steamer: 593 tons. **D.** 212′ x 30′ x 9′. **A.** 1 30-pdr R, 2 24-pdr H. **S.** 12 knots. Purchased 1864, sold 1865.

Itasca Screw steamer: 507 tons. **D.** 158′ x 28′ x 12′. **A.** 1 10-in SB, 2 32-pdr, 1 20-pdr R. **C.** 70. Commissioned 1861, sold 1865. (See p.84)

Iuka Sidewheel steamer: 944 tons. **D.** 200′ x 31′ 6″ x 20′. **A.** 1 100-pdr R, 2 8-in, 2 30-pdr R. Purchased 1864, sold 1865.

Ivy Screw tug: 50 tons. **D.** 10′ draft. **S.** 10 knots. Built 1862, sold 1892.

J.C. Kuhn Bark: 888 tons. **D.** 153′ x 35′ x 13′ 5″. **A.** 4 32-pdr. **S.** 10 knots. **C.** 61. Built 1859, purchased 1861, sold 1869.

J.J. Crittenden Schooner. Captured Newbegun Creek, N.C., April 10, 1862 and used as block ship.

J.W. Wilder Schooner. Captured off Mobile Bay, January 20, 1862. Used as a tender.

Jacob Bell Sidewheel steamer: 229 tons. **D.** 141′ 3″ x 21′ x 8′. **A.** 1 8-in SB, 1 32-pdr. **C.** 49. Built 1842, purchased 1861. Lost at sea while under tow, May 13, 1865. (See p.82)

James Adger Sidewheel steamer: 1152 tons. **D.** 215′ x 33′ 6″ x 21′. **A.** 8 32-pdr. **S.** 11 knots. **C.** 120. Built 1851, purchased 1861, sold 1866.

James L. Davis Bark: 461 tons. **D.** 133′ x 30′ 7″ x 12′. **A.** 4 8-in. **C.** 75. Purchased 1861, sold 1865.

James S. Chambers Schooner: 401 tons. **D.** 124′ 6″ x 29′ 3″ x 12′. **A.** 4 32-pdr. **C.** 62. Purchased 1861, sold 1865.

Jamestown Sloop: 1150 tons. **D.** 163′ 6″ x 32′ 2″ x 17′ 3″. **A.** 6 8-in, 14 32-pdr. **C.** 186. Launched 1844. Destroyed by fire at Norfolk Navy Yard, January 3, 1913.

Jasmine Screw tug: 120 tons. **D.** 79′ x 18′ 3″ x 7′ 6″. **A.** 1 20-pdr R, 1 12-pdr H. **C.** 19. Purchased 1863, sold 1866.

Java Screw sloop: 3954 tons. **D.** 312′ 6″ x 46′ x 21′ 5″. **A.** 2 100-pdr R, 16 9-in SB. **S.** 13 knots. **C.** 325. Laid down 1864, never completed. Broken up 1884. (See p.147)

Jean Sands Screw tug: 139 tons. **D.** 102′ x 22′ 8″ x 6′. Built 1863, sold 1892.

Jeff Davis Sloop. Captured March 1862. Used as coal hulk.

John Adams Frigate: 700 tons. **D.** 139′ x 32′ x 16′ 4″. **A.** 2 30-pdr R, 2 8-in, 4 32-pdr. **C.** 220. Built 1799, rebuilt 1830, sold 1867.

John Alexander Schooner. Purchased 1861 for use as block ship.

John Griffith Schooner: 240 tons. **D.** 113′ 8″ x 8′ draft. **A.** 1 13-in M, 2 32-pdr. **C.** 39. Purchased 1861, sold 1865.

John Hancock Screw steamer: 382 tons. **D.** 151′ x 22′ x 13′. **A.** 2 guns. **S.** 9 knots. **C.** 20. Launched 1850, sold 1865.

John L. Lockwood Sidewheel steamer: 180 tons. **D.** 114′ x 24′ x 6′ 6″. **A.** 1 80-pdr, 1 12-pdr R, 1 12-pdr H. Built 1854, purchased 1861. Purchased by army 1876.

John McHale Canal boat: 122 tons. Purchased 1864 for use as block ship in James River.

John Mitchell Canal boat: 114 tons. Purchased 1864 for use as block ship in James River.

John P. Jackson Sternwheel steamer: 750 tons. **D.** 192′ x 36′ 6″ x 12′. **A.** 1 9-in SB, 4 32-pdr, 1 6-in R. **C.** 99. Purchased 1861, sold 1865, abandoned 1871.

Jonquil Screw steamer: 90 tons. **D.** 69′ 4″ x 17′ 6″ x 7′. **A.** 2 12-pdr R. **S.** 8 knots. **C.** 15. Purchased 1863, sold 1865.

Jubilee Bark: 233 tons. Purchased 1861 for use as block ship.

Judge Torrence Sidewheel steamer: 700 tons. **D.** 179′ 1″ x 45′ 6″ x 9′. **A.** 2 24-pdr H. **S.** 7 knots. Purchased 1862, sold 1865. Sank after striking obstruction off Ozark Island, February 19, 1868.

Julia Sloop: 10 tons. Purchased 1863 for use as tender.

Juliet Sternwheel steamer: 157 tons. **D.** 155′ 6″ x 30′ 2″ x 5′. **A.** 6 24-pdr H. **S.** 4 knots. Built 1862, sold 1865. Stranded December 31, 1865, and abandoned.

Juniata Screw sloop: 1934 tons. **D.** 15′ 3″ draft. **A.** 1 100-pdr R, 1 11-in SB, 4 30-pdr. **S.** 9 knots. Launched 1862, sold 1891. (See p.82)

Juniper Screw tug: 116 tons. **D.** 79′ 6″ x 18′ 4″ x 9′. **A.** 1 20-pdr R. **S.** 12 knots. Purchased 1864, sold to Lighthouse Board 1865.

Kalamazoo Ironclad monitor: 6160 tons. **D.** 354′ 5″ x 56′ 8″ x 17′ 6″. **A.** 4 15-in SB. Laid down 1863, never completed. Broken up 1884. (See p.70)

Kalmia Screw steamer: 112 tons. **D.** 85′ x 19′ 6″ x 8′. **A.** 2 guns. **S.** 12 knots. Purchased 1863, sold 1865. Destroyed by fire June 14, 1905 at Bartlett's Point, N.Y.

Kanawha Screw steamer: 507 tons. **D.** 158′ x 28′ x 7′ 8″. **A.** 1 11-in SB, 1 20-pdr R, 2 24-pdr H. **C.** 87. Launched 1861, sold 1866. (See p.84)

Kansas Screw steamer: 625 tons. **D.** 129′ 6″ x 29′ x 10′ 6″. **A.** 1 150-pdr R, 2 9-in SB, 2 12-pdr R, 2 20-pdr R. **S.** 12 knots. **C.** 108. Launched 1863, sold 1883.

Katahdin Screw steamer: 507 tons. **D.** 158′ x 28′ x 10′ 3″. **A.** 1 11-in SB, 1 20-pdr R, 2 24-pdr H. **S.** 9 knots. **C.** 78. Launched 1861, sold 1866. (See p.84)

Kate Sternwheel steamer: 242 tons. **D.** 5′ 6″ draft. **A.** 2 20-pdr R, 6 24-pdr H, 2 12-pdr H. Purchased 1864, sold 1866. Stranded 300 miles below Fort Benton, June 21, 1867.

Kearsage Screw steamer: 1031 tons. **D.** 201′ 4″ x 33′ 10″ x 146′ 3″. **A.** 2 11-in SB, 1 28-pdr R, 4 32-pdr. **S.** 11 knots. Launched 1861. Wrecked on Roncador Reef, February 2, 1894. (See p.146)

Kennebec Screw steamer: 507 tons. **D.** 158′ x 28′ x 9′ 6″. **A.** 1 11-in SB, 1 20-pdr R, 2 24-pdr H. Launched 1861, sold 1865. (See p.84)

Kenosha Screw steamer. Purchased 1858, broken up 1884.

Kensington Screw steamer: 1053 tons. **D.** 195′ x 31′ 10″ x 18′. **A.** 2 32-pdr, 1 30-pdr R. Built 1858, purchased 1862, sold 1865. Sank January 27, 1871 after colliding with unknown sailing vessel.

Kensington Ship: 357 tons. Purchased 1861 for use as block ship.

Kenwood Sternwheel steamer: 232 tons. **D.** 5′ 6″ draft. **A.** 2 32-pdr, 4 24-pdr H. **S.** 7 knots. Purchased 1863, sold 1865. Exploded and sank at Shawneetown, Ill., August 14, 1869.

Keokuk Ironclad: 677 tons. **D.** 159′ 6″ x 36′ x 8′ 6″. **A.** 2 11-in SB. **S.** 9 knots. Launched 1862. Sank off Morris Island as a result of damage sustained in attack on forts, April 8, 1863. (See p.40)

Keosauqua Screw frigate: 3050 tons. **D.** 296′ 10″ x 41′ x 9′ 9″. **A.** 8 9-in SB, 1 60-pdr R. **S.** 13 knots. **C.** 250. Never built.

Keystone State Sidewheel steamer: 1364 tons. **D.** 220′ x 35′ x 14′ 6″. **A.** 4 12-pdr. **S.** 9½ knots. **C.** 163. Built in 1853, purchased 1861, sold 1865. Operated in merchant service until 1879.

Key West Sternwheel steamer: 207 tons. **D.** 156′ x 32′ x 4′ 6″. **A.** 6 24-pdr H. Purchased 1863. Set on fire to avoid capture November 1864.

Kewaydin Screw steamer. Broken up 1884. (See p.147)

Kickapoo Ironclad: 970 tons. **D.** 220′ x 57′ x 7′. **A.** 4 11-in SB. **C.** 123. Built 1864, sold 1874. (See p.12)

Kineo Screw steamer: 507 tons. **D.** 158′ x 28′ x 10′ 3″. **A.** 1 11-in SB, 1 20-pdr R, 2 24-pdr H. Built 1861, sold 1866. (See p.84)

Kingfisher Bark: 451 tons. **D.** 121′ 4″ x 28′ 8″ x 14′. **A.** 4 8-in SB. **C.** 97. Purchased 1861. Grounded on Combahee Bank in St Helena Sound, March 28, 1864, and abandoned April 5.

King Philip Sidewheel steamer: 500 tons. **D.** 204′ x 22′ 11″ x 8′. Transferred 1861, sold 1865.

Kinsman Sidewheel steamer. Captured 1862. Struck obstruction and sank at Berwick Bay near Brasher City, February 23, 1863.

Kittatinny Schooner: 450 tons. **D.** 129′ x 29′ x 11′ 6″. **A.** 4 32-pdr. **C.** 66. Purchased 1861, sold 1865.

Klamath Ironclad monitor: 1175 tons. **D.** 225′ x 45′ 6″ x 9′. **A.** 1 11-in SB. Completed 1866, sold 1874. (See p.38)

Koka Ironclad monitor: 1175 tons. **D.** 225′ x 45′ x 9′. **A.** 11-in SB. Completed 1865, scrapped 1874. (See p.38)

Kosciusko Sidewheel steamer: 257 tons. Built 1855. Part of Ellet's Ram Fleet. Sunk at Vicksburg, March 25, 1863. Also known as *Lancaster.*

L.C. Richmond Ship: 341 tons. Purchased 1861 for use as block ship.

Laburnum Screw tug: 181 tons. **D.** 110′ x 22′ x 9′. **A.** 2 20-pdr R, 2 24-pdr H. **S.** 10 knots. **C.** 29. Built 1864, sold 1866. Purchased by foreign owners 1878.

Lackawanna Screw sloop: 1533 tons. **D.** 237′ x 38′ 2″ x 16′ 3″. **A.** 1 150-pdr R, 2 11-in SB, 4 9-in SB, 2 24-pdr H, 2 12-pdr H, 2 12-pdr R. **S.** 10½ knots. Launched 1862, sold 1887.

Lady Sterling Sidewheel steamer: 835 tons. **D.** 242′ x 26′ 6″ x 13′. Captured October 1864, sold 1869.

Lafayette Ironclad: 1193 tons. **D.** 280′ x 45′ x 8′. **A.** 2 11-in SB, 4 9-in SB, 2 100-pdr R. **S.** 4 knots. Built 1848, converted 1862, sold 1866. (See p.47)

Lancaster Screw sloop: 2362 tons. **D.** 235′ 8″ x 46′ x 18′ 6″. **A.** 24 9-in SB, 2 11-in SB, 2 30-pdr R. **S.** 10 knots. **C.** 367. Launched 1858. Broken up 1933.

Larkspur Screw tug: 121 tons. **D.** 90′ 9″ x 19′ 2″ x 7′ 3″. **A.** 1 12-pdr H, 1 12-pdr R. **S.** 9 knots. **C.** 26. Built 1863, sold 1865, abandoned 1905.

Laurel Screw tug: 50 tons. **D.** 6′ draft. **S.** 5 knots. Built 1862, sold 1865, abandoned 1903.

Lavender Screw tug: 173 tons. **D.** 112′ x 22′ x 7′ 6″. **A.** 2 24-pdr H, 2 12-pdr R. **C.** 23. Built 1864. Struck reef off North Carolina during storm and lost, June 12, 1864.

Lavinia Logan Steamer: 145 tons. Purchased 1864 for use as block ship.

Lehigh Ironclad monitor: 1875 tons. **D.** 200′ x 45′ x 10′ 6″. **A.** 1 15-in SB, 1 11-in SB. **S.** 7 knots. Launched 1863, sold 1904. (See p.26)

Lenapee Sidewheel steamer: 974 tons. **D.** 205′ x 35′ x 7′ 7″. **A.** 2 100-pdr R, 4 9-in SB, 2 24-pdr H, 2 20-pdr R. Launched 1863, sold 1868. (See p.104)

Leonidas Bark: 231 tons. Purchased 1861 for use as block ship.

Leslie Screw tug: 100 tons. Loaned by army for use as tender 1861, returned 1865.

Levant Sloop: 792 tons. **D.** 132′ 3″ x 35′ 3″ x 16′ 6″. **A.** 4 24-pdr, 13 32-pdr. **S.** 12 knots. **C.** 200. Built 1837. Lost in Pacific Ocean, May 1860.

Lewis Ship: 308 tons. Purchased 1861 for use as block ship.

Lexington Sidewheel steamer: 448 tons. **D.** 177′ 7″ x 36′ 10″ x 6′. **A.** 4 8-in SB, 2 32-pdr. Built 1861, sold 1865. (See p.72)

Leyden Screw tug: 350 tons. **A.** 2 guns. Launched 1865. Foundered off Block Island, January 21, 1903.

Lightning Schooner. Captured March 1865, sold 1865.

Lilac Screw tug: 129 tons. **D.** 92′ x 19′ x 8′. **A.** 1 12-pdr R, 1 12-pdr SB. **S.** 9 knots. **C.** 17. Built 1863, sold 1865. Served in merchant marine until abandoned 1888.

Lillian Sidewheel steamer: 630 tons. **D.** 225′ 6″ x 26′ x 8′ 2″. **A.** 1 30-pdr R, 1 20-pdr R. **S.** 14 knots. Captured 1863, sold 1865. Served in merchant marine until 1868.

Lily Steam tug: 50 tons. Built 1862. Sank in Yazoo River after colliding with *Choctaw*, May 28, 1863.

Linden Sidewheel steamer: 177 tons. **D.** 154′ x 31′ x 4′. **A.** 6 24-pdr H. Built 1860, purchased 1862. Sank after striking obstruction in Arkansas River, February 22, 1864.

Little Ada Screw steamer: 150 tons. **D.** 112′ x 12′ 6″ x 8′. **A.** 2 20-pdr R. **S.** 10 knots. Captured 1864, transferred to army 1865.

Little Rebel Screw steamer: 161 tons. **D.** 12′ draft. **A.** 3 12-pdr R. **S.** 12 knots. Built 1859, captured 1862. Remained in merchant service until 1874.

Lodona Screw steamer: 750 tons. **D.** 210′ x 27′ 6″ x 11′ 6″. **A.** 1 100-pdr R, 1 9-in SB, 1 30-pdr R, 4 24-pdr. Built 1862, captured 1862, sold 1865.

Louisiana Screw steamer: 295 tons. **D.** 143′ 2″ x 27′ 3″ x 8′ 6″. **A.** 1 8-in SB, 1 32-pdr, 1 12-pdr. Purchased 1861. Loaded with powder and blown up at Fort Fisher, Wilmington, N.C., December 24, 1864.

Louisville Ironclad: 512 tons. **D.** 175′ x 51′ 2″ x 6′. **A.** 3 8-in SB, 4 42-pdr. **S.** 9 knots. **C.** 251. Built 1861, sold 1865.

Lupin Screw tug: 68 tons. **D.** 69′ x 16′ x 6′. Built 1861, sold 1865, still in service 1884.

Lynnhaven Captured 1863 and used as block ship.

Macedonian Sloop: 1341 tons. **D.** 164′ x 41′ x 21′ 6″. **A.** 2 10-in SB, 16 8-in SB, 4 32-pdr. **C.** 306. Captured from British 1812, rebuilt 1836.

Mackinaw Sidewheel steamer: 974 tons. **D.** 205′ x 35′ x 9′ 6″. **A.** 2 100-pdr R, 4 9-in SB, 2 24-pdr SB, 2 12-pdr. Built 1863, sold 1867. (See p.104)

Madawaska Screw frigate: 4170 tons. **D.** 355′ x 45′ 2″ x 21′ 8″. **A.** 10 9-in SB, 3 60-pdr. **S.** 11 knots. **C.** 480. Launched 1865, sold 1886. (See p.150)

Madgie Screw steamer: 220 tons. **D.** 122′ 6″ x 22′ 7″ x 8′. **A.** 1 8-in SB, 1 20-pdr. Built 1858, purchased 1861. Sank off Frying Pan Shoals, October 11, 1863.

Mognolia Sidewheel steamer: 843 tons. **D.** 8′ draft. **A.** 1 20-pdr R, 4 24-pdr. **S.** 12 knots. **C.** 95. Built 1857. Impressed into Confederate Navy 1862. Captured February 1862, sold 1865, abandoned at sea 1866.

Mahaska Sidewheel steamer: 1070 tons. **D.** 228′ 2″ x 33′ 10″ x 10′ 4″. **A.** 1 100-pdr R, 1 9-in SB, 4 24-pdr. **S.** 9 knots. Built 1861, sold 1868.

Mahopac Ironclad monitor: 2100 tons. **D.** 223′ x 43′ 8″ x 13′ 6″. **A.** 2 15-in SB. **S.** 8 knots. **C.** 85. Launched 1864, sold 1902.

Mail Schooner. Captured 1862, sold 1865. Used as divers' depot ship.

Majestic Ship: 297 tons. Purchased 1861 for use as block ship.

Malvern Sidewheel steamer: 1477 tons. **D.** 240′ x 23′ x 8′ 5″. **A.** 4 20-pdr R, 8 12-pdr. Seized by Confederate forces and used as blockade runner. Captured November 8, 1863, sold 1865. Wrecked on Colorado Reef off Cuba in February 1895. (See p.103)

Manhattan Ironclad monitor: 2100 tons. **D.** 223′ x 43′ 8″ x 13′ 6″. **A.** 2 15-in SB. Launched 1863, sold 1902. (See p.30)

Manhattan Steamer: 326 tons. **D.** 129′ x 28′ x 6′.

Manayunk Ironclad monitor: 2100 tons. **D.** 235′ x 43′ 8″ x 13′ 6″. **A.** 2 15-in SB. Launched 1864, sold 1899. (See p.30)

Marataza Sidewheel steamer: 786 tons. **D.** 209′ x 32′ x 9′ 6″. **A.** 1 100-pdr R, 1 9-in SB, 4 24-pdr. **S.** 10 knots. Built 1861, sold 1868. (See p.99)

Marblehead Screw steamer: 691 tons. **D.** 158′ 4″ x 28′ x 10′ 6″. **A.** 1 11-in SB, 2 24-pdr, 1 20-pdr R. **S.** 11 knots. **C.** 81. Built 1861, sold 1868. (See p.84)

Marcia Bark: 343 tons. Purchased 1861 for use as block ship.

Margaret and Rebecca Canal boat: 125 tons. Purchased 1864 for use as block ship.

Margaret Scott Ship: 330 tons. Purchased 1861 for use as block ship.

Maria Screw tug: 170 tons. **A.** 2 guns. Built 1864. Sunk in collision with monitor *Miaotomah*, January 4, 1870.

Maria A. Wood Schooner: 334 tons. **D.** 125′ x 28′ 6″ x 9′. **A.** 2 32-pdr. Purchased 1861, sold 1866.

Maria Denning Sidewheel steamer: 870 tons. Built 1858, purchased 1861, later served as army transport until 1863.

Maria J. Carlton Schooner: 178 tons. **D.** 98′ x 27′ x 7′ 8″. **A.** 1 13-in M, 2 12-pdr R. Purchased 1861. Sunk in action against Forts Jackson and St Philip, April 19, 1862.

Maria Theresa Ship: 330 tons. Purchased 1861 for use as block ship.

Marietta Ironclad: 479 tons. **D.** 170′ x 50′ x 5′. **A.** 2 11-in SB. Launched 1865, sold 1873. (See p.63)

Marigold Screw tug: 115 tons. **D.** 84′ 7″ x 18′ 9″ x 7′. **A.** 2 12-pdr. Built 1863, sold 1866. Destroyed by fire at New York, November 30, 1875.

Marion Screw steamer: 566 tons. **D.** 117′ x 32′ x 15′. **A.** 14 32-pdr, 1 12-pdr H. **S.** 11½ knots. Built 1838, sold 1907.

Marmora Sternwheel steamer: 207 tons. **D.** 155′ x 33′ 5″ x 4′ 6″. **A.** 8 24-pdr, 2 12-pdr, 6 14-pdr. **S.** 7 knots. Built 1862, sold 1865. (See p.100)

Martin Screw tug: 25 tons. **D.** 45′ 3″ x 11′ 3″ x 5′ 9″. **S.** 6 knots. **C.** 9. Built 1864, sold 1865.

Mary Ann Canal boat. Purchased 1864 for use as block ship.

Mary Francis Schooner. Purchased 1861 for use as block ship.

Mary and Hetty Schooner. Purchased 1861 for use as block ship.

Mary Linda Canal boat: 116 tons. Purchased 1864 for use as block ship.

Mary Sandford Screw steamer: 457 tons. **D.** 102′ x 31′ 6″ x 12′ 6″. **A.** 2 24-pdr. **S.** 9 knots. Built 1862, sold 1865. Operated in merchant service until 1871.

Massachusetts Screw steamer: 765 tons. **D.** 178′ x 32′ 2″ x 156′. **A.** 1 32-pdr, 4 8-in. Built 1845, transferred to navy 1862, sold 1867.

Massasoit Sidewheel steamer: 974 tons. **D.** 205′ x 35′ x 8′ 8″. **A.** 2 100-pdr R, 4 9-in SB, 2 24-pdr, 2 12-pdr. **S.** 8½ knots. Launched 1863, sold 1867. (See p.104)

Mattabesett Sidewheel steamer: 1173 tons. **D.** 205′ x 35′ x 8′ 6″. **A.** 2 100-pdr R, 4 11-in SB, 4 24-pdr, 1 12-pdr. **S.** 14 knots. Completed 1864, sold 1865. (See p.104)

Matthew Vassar Schooner: 216 tons. **D.** 93′ 7″ x 27′ 2″ x 8′ 6″. **A.** 1 13-in M, 2 32-pdr. Purchased 1861, sold 1865.

Maumee Screw steamer: 593 tons, **D.** 190′ x 29′ x 11′ 3″. **A.** 1 100-pdr R, 1 30-pdr, 4 24-pdr, 1 120-pdr R. **S.** 11½ knots. Launched 1863, sold 1869.

Mayflower Screw tug: 420 tons. **D.** 137′ x 26′ x 9′ 6″. **S.** 10½ knots. Built 1866, sold 1893.

Mechanic Ship: 335 tons. Purchased 1861 for use as block ship.

Memphis Screw steamer: 791 tons. **D.** 227′ x 30′ 1″ x 15′ 6″. **A.** 4 24-pdr, 2 12-pdr, 1 30-pdr R. **S.** 14 knots. Built 1861, captured July 1862, sold 1869. Operated as freighter until destroyed by fire at Seattle, Washington, May 13, 1883. (See p.94)

Mendota Sidewheel steamer: 974 tons. **D.** 205′ x 35′ x 8′ 9″. **A.** 2 100-pdr R, 4 9-in SB, 2 24-pdr, 2 20-pdr. **S.** 11 knots. Launched 1863, sold 1867. (See p.104)

Mercedita Screw steamer: 1000 tons. **D.** 183′ 6″ x 30′ 3″ x 12′ 9″. **A.** 8 32-pdr. **S.** 11½ knots. Built 1861, sold 1865. Converted to brigantine 1879.

Mercury Sidewheel steamer: 187 tons. **D.** 128′ x 22′ x 5′ 6″. **A.** 1 20-pdr, 1 30-pdr R. Purchased 1861, sold 1873.

Merrimac Sidewheel steamer: 684 tons. **D.** 230′ x 30′ x 8′ 6″. **A.** 2 30-pdr R, 4 24-pdr, 2 12-pdr. Built 1862, captured July 1863. Foundered at sea during gale, February 15, 1865.

Merrimack Screw frigate: 3200 tons. **D.** 275′ x 38′ 6″ x 24′ 3″. **A.** 14 8-in, 2 10-in, 24 9-in SB. **S.** 12 knots. **C.** 519. Launched 1855. Burnt and sunk at Norfolk Navy Yard to prevent capture, April 20, 1861. Later raised and rebuilt as Confederate ironclad *Virginia*. Original cost in 1855 was $685,842. (See p.22)

Messenger Bark: 216 tons. Purchased 1861 for use as block ship.

Metacomet Sidewheel steamer: 1173 tons. **D.** 205′ x 35′ x 8′ 6″. **S.** 2 100-pdr R, 4 9-in SB, 2 24-pdr. **S.** 12½ knots. Launched 1863, sold 1865. (See p.104)

Meteor Ship: 324 tons. Purchased 1861 for use as block ship.

Meteor Sidewheel steamer: 221 tons. **D.** 156′ x 33′ 6″ x 4′ 3″. **A.** 2 32-pdr, 2 24-pdr. Built 1863, sold 1865.

Miami Sidewheel steamer: 730 tons. **D.** 208′ 2″ x 33′ 2″ x 8′ 6″. **A.** 1 80-pdr R, 1 9-in SB, 4 24-pdr. **S.** 8 knots. Launched 1861, sold 1865. Served as merchant vessel until 1869. (See p.107)

Miantonomoh Ironclad monitor: 3401 tons. **D.** 250′ x 50′ x 14′ 9″. **A.** 4 15-in SB. **S.** 9 knots. Launched 1864, broken up 1874. (See p.69)

Michigan Sidewheel steamer: 865 tons. **D.** 163′ 3″ x 27′ 1″ x 9′. **A.** 1 30-pdr R, 5 20-pdr R. **S.** 8 knots. Built 1842, scrapped 1949. She was the US Navy's first iron-hulled warship.

Midnight Bark: 387 tons. **D.** 126′ x 27′ 10″ x 11′. **A.** 6 32-pdr, 1 20-pdr R. **C.** 70. Purchased 1861, sold 1865.

Mignonette Sidewheel steam tug: 50 tons. Purchased 1861, sold 1873.

Milwaukee Ironclad monitor: 1500 tons. **D.** 229′ x 56′ x 6′. **A.** 4 11-in SB. **S.** 9 knots. Launched 1864. Mined on Blakely River, Fla., March 28, 1865. (See p.12)

Mingo Sternwheel steamer: 300 tons. **S.** 12 knots. Transferred to army 1862 for use in Ellet's Ram Fleet. Sank accidentally at Cape Girardeau, Mo., November 1862.

Mingoe Sidewheel steamer: 974 tons. **D.** 205′ x 35′ x 6′ 5″. **A.** 4 9-in SB, 2 100-pdr R, 2 24-pdr, 2 12-pdr. Launched 1863, sold 1867. (See p.104)

Minnesota Steam frigate: 3307 tons. **D.** 23′ 10″ draft. **A.** 1 10-in, 28 9-in SB, 14 8-in. **S.** 12 knots. Completed 1857. Sold 1901 and burnt at Eastport, Me.

Minnetonka Screw sloop: 2354 tons. **D.** 313′ 6″ x 46′ x 17′. **A.** 18 9-in SB, 2 100-pdr R, 1 60-pdr R, 2 20-pdr SB. Launched 1867, sold 1875. (See p.147)

Mississippi Sidewheel steamer: 3220 tons. **D.** 229′ x 40′ x 19′. **A.** 1 9-in SB, 10 8-in. Completed 1849. Grounded March 14, 1863 while attempting to pass forts at Port Hudson, and set on fire to prevent capture.

Missouri Ironclad: 399 tons. **D.** 183′ x 53′ 8″ x 8′ 3″. **A.** 2 11-in SB, 4 9-in SB, 2 32-pdr. Surrendered by Confederates June 1865, sold 1865. (See p.56)

Mist Sternwheel steamer: 232 tons. **D.** 157′ 3″ x 30′ 4″ x 4′. **A.** 2 20-pdr, 4 24-pdr, 1 12-pdr. **S.** 5½ knots. Built 1864, sold 1865. Served as merchant ship until 1874.

Mistletoe Steam tug: 50 tons. Built 1861, sold 1871.

Moccasin Screw tug: 192 tons. **D.** 104′ 5″ x 22′ 3″ x 9′. **A.** 3 12-pdr R. **S.** 10 knots. Built 1864. Sold to Treasury Dept 1865.

Modoc Ironclad monitor: 1175 tons. **D.** 225′ 8″ x 45′ 1″ x 9′. **A.** 1 spar torpedo. Launched 1865, scrapped 1875. (See p.38)

Mohawk Screw steamer: 464 tons. **D.** 162′ 4″ x 24′ x 14′. **A.** 4 32-pdr. **S.** 9 knots. **C.** 90. Built 1853, sold 1864.

Mohican Steam sloop: 1461 tons. **D.** 198′ 9″ x 33′ x 13′. **A.** 2 11-in SB, 4 32-pdr. Completed 1859. Sank at moorings Mare Island 1872, towed onto mudflats and broken up 1873.

Mohongo Sidewheel steamer: 1034 tons. **D.** 225′ x 35′ x 9′ 6″. **A.** 2 100-pdr R, 4 9-in SB, 2 20-pdr, 2 24-pdr. **S.** 13 knots. **C.** 190. Launched 1864, sold 1870.

Monadnock Ironclad monitor: 3295 tons. **D.** 250′ x 53′ x 12′ 3″. **A.** 4 15-in SB. Launched 1864, broken up 1874. (See p.69)

Monitor Ironclad: 987 tons. **D.** 179′ x 41′ 6″ x 10′ 6″. **A.** 2 11-in SB. Launched 1862, foundered off Cape Hatteras, N.C., December 31, 1862. (See p.24)

Monocacy Sidewheel steamer: 1370 tons. **D.** 265′ x 35′ x 9′. **A.** 6 guns. **S.** 11 knots. Launched 1864, sold 1903.

Monongahela Screw sloop: 2078 tons. **D.** 227 ′ x 38′ x 17′ 6″. **A.** 1 200-pdr R, 2 11-in SB, 2 24-pdr, 4 12-pdr. **S.** 8½ knots. Launched 1862. Destroyed by fire Guantanamo Bay, Cuba, March 17, 1908.

Montauk Ironclad monitor: 1875 tons. **D.** 200′ x 46′ x 11′ 9″. **A.** 1 15-in SB, 1 11-in SB. Launched 1862, sold 1904. (See p.26)

Monterey Screw tug: 87 tons. **D.** 75′ x 18′ x 7′. **A.** 1 24-pdr, 1 12-pdr. Built 1862, scrapped 1892.

Montezuma Ship: 424 tons. Purchased 1861 for use as block ship.

Montgomery Screw steamer: 787 tons. **D.** 201′ 6″ x 28′ 7″ x 15′ 6″. **A.** 1 8-in, 4 32-pdr. **S.** 8 knots. Built 1858, purchased 1861, sold 1865. In merchant service until 1877.

Monticello Screw steamer: 655 tons. **D.** 180′ x 29′ x 12′ 10″. **A.** 1 9-in SB, 2 32-pdr. **S.** 11½ knots. Built 1859, sold 1865. Served in merchant marine until foundering off Newfoundland, April 29, 1872.

Moose Sternwheel steamer: 189 tons. **D.** 154′ 8″ x 32′ 2″ x 5′. **A.** 6 24-pdr. **S.** 6 knots. Built 1863, sold 1865. Destroyed by fire at Clarendon, Ark., December 23, 1867.

Morning Light Ship: 937 tons. **D.** 172′ x 34′ 3″ x 19′. **A.** 8 32-pdr. Built 1853, purchased 1861. Surrendered January 21, 1863, wreck burnt January 23.

Morse Sidewheel steamer: 514 tons. **D.** 143′ x 33′ x 8′ 6″. **A.** 2 9-in SB. **S.** 9 knots. Built 1861, purchased 1861, sold 1865, abandoned 1885.

Mosholu Screw sloop. **D.** 290′ x 41′ x 13′. Completed 1869, sold 1877.

Mound City Ironclad: 512 tons. **D.** 175′ x 50′ x 6′. **A.** 3 8-in, 4 42-pdr, 6 32-pdr. **S.** 9 knots. **C.** 251. Built 1861, sold 1865. (See p.16)

Mount Vernon Screw steamer: 625 tons. **D.** 175′ 7″ x 22′ 6″ x 14′. **A.** 1 32-pdr. Built 1859, purchased 1861, sold 1865.

Mount Washington Sidewheel steamer: 500 tons. **D.** 200′ x 24′ x 6′ 6″. **A.** 1 32-pdr. **S.** 12 knots. Built 1846, sold 1865. Served in merchant marine until 1880.

Musadora Canal boat: 123 tons. Purchased 1864 for use as block ship.

Muscoota Sidewheel steamer: 1030 tons. **D.** 255′ x 35′ x 9′ 4″. **A.** 2 100-pdr R, 4 11-in SB, 2 20-pdr R. **S.** 13½ knots. Completed 1864, sold 1869.

Myrtle Screw tug: 60 tons. **D.** 75′ x 16′ 3″ x 6′. **S.** 10 knots. Purchased 1862, sold 1865.

Mystic Screw steamer: 541 tons. **D.** 157′ x 24′ x 13′ 6″. **A.** 4 32-pdr, 1 24-pdr. Built 1849, commissioned 1858, sold 1865.

Nahant Ironclad monitor: 1875 tons. **D.** 200′ x 46′ x 11′ 9″. **A.** 1 11-in SB, 1 15-in SB. Launched 1862, sold 1904. (See p.26)

Naid Sternwheel steamer: 183 tons. **D.** 156′ 10″ x 30′ 4″ x 6′. **A.** 8 24-pdr. Purchased 1863, sold 1865.

Nansemond Sidewheel steamer: 340 tons. **D.** 146′ x 26′ x 8′ 3″. **A.** 1 30-pdr R, 2 24-pdr. Built 1862, sold 1897.

Nantasket Screw steamer: 1129 tons. **D.** 216′ x 31′ x 12′. **A.** 6 9-pdr. **S.** 10½ knots. **C.** 114. Launched 1876, sold 1883. (See p.141)

Nantucket Ironclad monitor: 1875 tons. **D.** 200′ x 46′ x 11′ 6″. **A.** 1 11-in SB, 1 15-in SB. Launched 1862, sold 1899. (See p.26)

Napa Ironclad monitor: 1175 tons. **D.** 225′ x 45′ x 9′. **A.** 1 11-in SB. Launched 1864, scrapped 1875. (See p.38)

Narcissus Screw tug: 101 tons. **D.** 81′ 6″ x 18′ 9″ x 6′. **A.** 1 20-pdr, 1 12-pdr. **S.** 14 knots. **C.** 19. Built 1863. Sank off Egmont Key, Fla., January 4, 1866.

Narragansett Screw sloop: 1235 tons. **D.** 188′ x 30′ 4″ x 11′ 6″. **A.** 1 11-in, 4 32-pdr. Built 1858, sold 1883.

Nashville Captured Confederate ironclad, May 10, 1865. Sold 1867. (See p.43)

Nathaniel Taylor Schooner. Captured 1863. Used as block ship.

National Guard Ship: 1049 tons. **D.** 162′ 6″ x 38′ x 16′. **A.** 4 32-pdr. Purchased 1861, sold 1865. Used as coal hulk.

Naubuc Ironclad monitor: 1175 tons. **D.** 225′ x 45′ 3″ x 9′. **A.** 1 11-in. Launched 1864, scrapped 1876. (See p.38)

Naugatuk Screw steamer: 192 tons. **D.** 110′ x 20′ x 6′. **A.** 1 rifled gun. Loaned to the navy in 1862, sold 1889. She was lightly armored and had been built as a test bed for the much larger *Stevens Battery*. *Naugatuk* was also known as the *Stevens Battery*.

Naumkeag Sternwheel steamer: 148 tons. **D.** 154′ 4″ x 30′ 5″ x 5′ 6″. **A.** 2 30-pdr R, 2 24-pdr. **S.** 6 knots. Built 1863, sold 1865. Destroyed by fire at Erie, Ala., January 19, 1867.

Nausett Ironclad monitor: 1175 tons. **D.** 225′ x 45′ x 9′. **A.** 1 11-in. Launched 1865, scrapped 1875. (See p.38)

Neosho Ironclad monitor: 523 tons. **D.** 180′ x 45′ x 4′. **A.** 2 11-in SB. **S.** 12 knots. **C.** 100. Launched 1863, sold 1873. (See p.57)

Neptune Screw steamer: 1244 tons. **D.** 209′ x 34′ 6″ x 13′ 9″. **A.** 1 100-pdr R, 2 30-pdr R, 8 32-pdr. **S.** 11 knots. **C.** 173. Purchased 1863, sold 1865.

Nereus Screw steamer: 1244 tons. **D.** 209′ x 34′ x 13′ 9″. **A.** 1 100-pdr R, 2 30-pdr R, 6 32-pdr, 2 12-pdr. **S.** 11 knots. **C.** 164. Built 1863, sold 1865. Remained in merchant service until 1881.

Neshaminy Screw frigate: 3850 tons. **D.** 335′ x 44′ 4″ x 11′ 4″. **A.** 2 100-pdr, 10 8-in SB. Launched 1865. Never completed; guns not mounted. Handed over in 1874 to John Roach as part payment for new monitor *Puritan*. (See p.150)

Nettle Sidewheel tug: 50 tons. Purchased by army, transferred to navy 1862. Sank after colliding with an ironclad, October 20, 1865.

New Berne Screw steamer: 948 tons. **D.** 195′ x 32′ x 13′ 6″. **A.** 2 24-pdr, 2 12-pdr. **S.** 13 knots. **C.** 92. Purchased 1863, transferred to army 1868.

Newburyport Ship: 341 tons. Purchased 1861 for use as block ship.

New England Ship: 375 tons. Purchased 1861 for use as block ship.

New Era Sternwheel steamer: 157 tons. **D.** 137′ 1″ x 29′ 6″ x 4′. **A.** 6 24-pdr H. Built 1862, sold 1865.

New Hampshire Ship-of-the-line: 2633 tons. **D.** 203′ 8″ x 52′ 4″ x 17′ 5″. **A.** 4 100-pdr R, 6 9-in. Laid down as 74-gun ship in 1819. Remained on stocks until 1864, when she was launched for service in Civil War as store ship. Caught fire on Hudson River and sank at her pier, May 23, 1921. Raised 1922 but hulk caught fire and sank July 1922 after towline parted in storm off Half Way Rock, Massachusetts Bay.

New Ironsides Ironclad: 4120 tons. **D.** 232′ x 57′ 6″ x 15′ 8″. **A.** 2 150-pdr R, 14 11-in SB, 2 50-pdr R. **S.** 8 knots. **C.** 460. Launched 1862. Destroyed by fire at League Island, December 16, 1865. (See p.32)

New London Screw steamer: 221 tons. **D.** 125′ x 25′ x 9′ 6″. **A.** 1 20-pdr R, 4 32-pdr. **S.** 9½ knots. **C.** 47. Built 1859, purchased 1861, sold 1865. Served in merchant marine until 1910.

New National Sidewheel steamer: 1000 tons. **A.** 1 12-pdr R. Seized 1861. Returned to owner 1865.

New Orleans Ship-of-the-line: 2805 tons. **D.** 204′ x 56′. **A.** 87 32-pdr. Laid down 1815. Construction halted after peace had been signed with Britain and she remained on the stocks until sold 1883. Guns never mounted.

New York Ship-of-the-line: 2633 tons. **D.** 197′ 1″ x 53′ x 22′. **A.** 74 guns. Laid down 1820 at Norfolk Navy Yard. Kept on stocks and burnt April 21, 1861 to prevent capture.

Niagara Screw frigate: 5540 tons. **D.** 328′ 10″ x 55′ x 24′ 5″. **A.** 12 11-in SB. **C.** 251. Launched 1855, sold 1885.

Nightingale Ship: 1066 tons. **D.** 177′ x 36′ x 16′. **A.** 4 32-pdr. **S.** 12 knots. **C.** 186. Built 1851. Captured April 1861 near mouth of Congo River, Angola. Sold 1865. Foundered while in merchant service in North Atlantic, April 17, 1893. When captured she was registered at Boston and had 961 Negro slaves chained below deck and was waiting for more.

Nina Screw tug: 420 tons. **D.** 137′ x 26′ x 9′ 10″. **S.** 10 knots. Built 1864, lost in storm, March 15, 1910.

Niphon Screw steamer: 475 tons. **D.** 153′ 2″ x 24′ 9″ x 11′ 3″. **A.** 1 20-pdr R, 2 12-pdr R, 4 32-pdr. **S.** 12½ knots. **C.** 70. Built 1862, sold 1865.

Nipsic Screw steamer: 592 tons. **D.** 179′ 6″ x 30′ x 11′ 6″. **A.** 1 150-pdr R, 2 9-in SB, 1 30-pdr R, 2 24-pdr H, 2 12-pdr. **S.** 11 knots. Built 1863, sold 1913. She was driven ashore and badly damaged in a hurricane at Apia Harbor, Samoa, March 16, 1889.

Nita Sidewheel steamer: 210 tons. **D.** 146′ x 22′ 4″ x 5′. **A.** 1 12-pdr H, 2 12-pdr SB. **C.** 46. Built 1856, captured 1863, sold 1865.

Noble Bark: 274 tons. Purchased 1861 for use as block ship.

Norfolk Packet Schooner: 349 tons. **D.** 108′ x 28′ 2″ x 11″. **A.** 1 13-in M, 2 32-pdr. Purchased 1861, sold 1865.

North Carolina Ship-of-the-line: 2633 tons. **D.** 196′ 3″ x 53′ 6″ x 20′. **A.** 4 9-in SB, 1 30-pdr R. Launched 1820 as 74-gun ship, sold 1867. Served as receiving ship at New York.

Norwich Screw steamer: 450 tons. **D.** 132′ 5″ x 24′ 6″ x 10′. **A.** 4 8-in, 1 30-pdr R. **S.** 9½ knots. Built 1861, sold 1865. Served in merchant marine until 1873. (See p.86)

Nyack Screw steamer: 836 tons. **D.** 179′ 6″ x 29′ 8″ x 11′ 6″. **A.** 2 9-in SB, 1 30-pdr R, 2 24-pdr. **S.** 10 knots. Built 1863, sold 1883.

Nyanza Sidewheel steamer: 203 tons. **A.** 6 24-pdr H. Built 1863, sold 1865. Served in merchant marine until 1873.

Nymph Sternwheel steamer: 171 tons. **D.** 161′ 2″ x 30′ 4″ x 5′. **A.** 8 24-pdr. Built 1863, sold 1865. (See p.96)

O.H. Lee Schooner: 199 tons. **D.** 100′ 9″ x 28′ 4″ x 8′. **A.** 1 13-in M, 2 32-pdr. Purchased 1861, sold 1865.

O.M. Pettit Sidewheel tug: 165 tons. **D.** 106′ x 24′ x 6′. **A.** 1 30-pdr, 1 20-pdr R. Purchased 1861, sank in collision 1865.

Octorara Sidewheel steamer: 829 tons. **D.** 193′ 2″ x 34′ 6″ x 4′ 10″. **A.** 1 80-pdr R, 1 9-in SB, 4 24-pdr. **S.** 11 knots. **C.** 102. Launched 1861, sold 1866.

Ohio Ship-of-the-line: 2724 tons. **D.** 197′ x 53′ x 22′. **A.** 1 8-in R, 4 100-pdr R, 12 32-pdr. **C.** 840. Launched 1820, sold 1883.

Oleander Sidewheel steamer: 246 tons. **D.** 143′ x 22′ 6″ x 6′. **A.** 2 20-pdr R. **S.** 11 knots. **C.** 35. Built 1862, sold 1865.

Oneida Screw steamer: 1488 tons. **D.** 201′ 5″ x 33′ 10″ x 8′. **A.** 2 9-in SB, 3 30-pdr R, 4 32-pdr. **S.** 12 knots. **C.** 186. Built 1861. Sunk near Saratoga Spit, Yokohama, Japan, after colliding with the British P&O steamer *City of Bombay,* January 24, 1870. The British vessel did not stop to render aid, but steamed on, leaving 125 men to drown. Wreck sold 1872. (See p.147)

Oneota Ironclad monitor: 2100 tons. **D.** 225′ x 43′ 8″ x 136′ 6″. **A.** 2 15-in SB. **S.** 8 knots. **C.** 85. Launched 1864, sold to Peru 1868 and renamed *Manco Capac.* Sank at Arica on June 7, 1880 in war with Chile to prevent capture. (See p.30)

Onondaga Ironclad monitor: 1250 tons. **D.** 226′ x 49′ 3″x 12′. **A.** 2 15-in SB, 2 150-pdr R. **S.** 9 knots. **C.** 150. Launched 1864, sold back to builder 1867, who sold her on to France. (See p.36)

Ontario Screw frigate: 3953 tons. **D.** 312′ 6″ x 47′ x 21′ 5″. **A.** 16 9-in SB, 2 100-pdr R, 1 60-pdr R. **S.** 13 knots. **C.** 325. Laid down 1864, never completed. Sold while still on stocks, 1888. (See p.147)

Onward Ship: 874 tons. **D.** 159′ x 34′ 8″ x 16′. **A.** 8 32-pdr. **S.** 11 knots. **C.** 103. Built 1852, purchased 1861, sold 1884.

Oriole Sidewheel steamer: 137 tons. **D.** 125′ x 26′ 5″ x 6′ 3″. **A.** 2 30-pdr R, 6 24-pdr. Purchased 1864, sold 1865.

Orion Schooner. Purchased 1861 for use as block ship.

Orvetta Schooner: 199 tons. **D.** 93′ x 27′ 2″ x 6′. **A.** 1 13-in M, 2 12-pdr. Purchased 1861, sold 1865.

Osage Ironclad monitor: 532 tons. **D.** 180′ x 45′ x 4′ 6″. **A.** 2 11-in SB. **S.** 7½ knots. **C.** 100. Launched 1863. Sunk by mine during attack on Spanish Fort, Mobile, Ala., March 28, 1865. Hulk sold 1867. (See p.57)

Osceola Sidewheel steamer: 974 tons. **D.** 205′ x 35′ x 8′ 8″. **A.** 2 100-pdr R, 4 9-in SB, 2 12-pdr, 1 24-pdr. **S.** 15 knots. Launched 1863, sold 1867. (See p.104)

Ossipee Screw steamer: 1240 tons. **D.** 207′ x 38′ x 16′. **A.** 1 100-pdr R, 1 11-in SB, 3 30-pdr, 6 32-pdr, 2 12-pdr. **S.** 10 knots. **C.** 141. Built 1861, sold 1891. (See p.82)

Otsego Sidewheel steamer: 974 tons. **D.** 205′ x 35′ x 9′. **A.** 2 100-pdr, 4 9-in SB, 2 24-pdr, 2 24-pdr R. **S.** 14 knots. **C.** 145. Launched 1863. Sunk by two mines in Roanoke River near Jamesville, N.C., December 9, 1864. (See p.104)

Ottowa Screw steamer: 691 tons. **D.** 158′ 4″ x 9′ 2″. **A.** 1 11-in SB, 1 20-pdr R, 2 24-pdr. **S.** 11 knots. Built 1861, sold 1865. (See p.84)

Ouachita Sidewheel steamer: 720 tons. **D.** 227′ 6″ x 38′ x 7′. **A.** 5 30-pdr R, 8 24-pdr, 1 12-pdr. Captured 1863, sold 1865.

Owasco Screw steamer: 507 tons. **D.** 158′ x 28′ x 6′ 9″. **A.** 1 11-in SB, 1 20-pdr, 1 20-pdr R, 2 24-pdr H. **S.** 9 knots. **C.** 91. Built 1861, sold 1865. (See p.84)

Ozark Ironclad monitor: 578 tons. **D.** 180′ x 50′ x 5′. **A.** 2 11-in SB, 1 10-in SB, 3 9-in SB. **S.** 2½ knots. **C.** 120. Built 1862, sold 1865. (See p.62)

Palos Screw tug: 420 tons. **D.** 137′ x 26′ x 9′ 10″. **A.** 2 guns. **S.** 10 knots. Built 1865, sold 1893.

Pampero Ship: 1375 tons. **D.** 202′ 3″ x 38′ 2″ x 20′. **A.** 4 32-pdr. **C.** 50. Built 1853, purchased 1861, sold 1867.

Pansy Screw tug: 46 tons. **A.** 1 12-pdr. Built 1861, sold 1868.

Para Schooner: 200 tons. **D.** 98′ x 24′ x 9′. **A.** 1 13-in M, 2 32-pdr. Purchased 1861, sold 1865.

Passaconaway Ironclad monitor: 5600 tons. **D.** 345′ 5″ x 56′ 8″ x 17′ 6″. **A.** 4 15-in SB. Laid down 1863, never completed. Broken up on stocks 1884. (See p.70)

Passaic Ironclad monitor: 1875 tons. **D.** 200′ x 46′ x11′ 6″. **A.** 1 15-in SB, 1 11-in SB. Launched 1862, sold 1899. (See p.26)

Patapsco Ironclad monitor: 1875 tons. **D.** 200′ x 46′ x 11′ 6″. **A.** 1 15-in SB, 1 150-pdr R. Launched 1862. Sunk by mine at Charleston, S.C., January 15, 1865. (See p.26)

Patriot Schooner. Purchased 1861 for use as block ship.

Patroon Screw steamer: 183 tons. **D.** 113′ x 22′ 5″ x 6′. **A.** 4 8-in, 1 30-pdr R. **C.** 49. Built 1859, purchased 1861 and sold to army 1863.

Paul Jones Sidewheel steamer: 1210 tons. **D.** 216′ 10″ x 35′ 4″ x 8′. **A.** 11-in SB, 2 9-in SB, 1 100-pdr R, 2 50-pdr R. **S.** 10 knots. **C.** 148. Launched 1862, sold 1867. (See p.97)

Paul Jones Jr Steam launch: 30 tons. **A.** 1 gun. Built 1862, sold 1865. (See p.97)

Pawnee Screw steamer: 1533 tons. **D.** 221′ 6″ x 47′ x 10′. **A.** 8 9-in SB, 2 12-pdr. **S.** 10 knots. **C.** 181. Launched 1859, sold 1884. (See p.90)

Paw Paw Centerwheel steamer: 175 tons. **D.** 120′ x 34′ x 6′. **A.** 2 30-pdr R, 6 24-pdr H. **S.** 4 knots. Purchased 1863, sold 1865.

Pawtucket (Pawtuxet) Sidewheel steamer: 974 tons. **D.** 205′ x 35′ x 9′ 3″. **A.** 4 9-in SB, 2 100-pdr R, 2 20-pdr R, 2 24-pdr H. Launched 1864, sold 1867. (See p.104)

Pembina Screw steamer: 507 tons. **D.** 171′ x 31′ 6″ x 10′. **A.** 1 11-in SB, 1 20-pdr R, 2 24-pdr H. **S.** 10 knots. Built 1861, sold 1865. (See p.84)

Penguin Screw steamer: 389 tons. **D.** 155′ x 30′ 8″ x 8′. **A.** 1 8-in, 2 32-pdr. **S.** 10 knots. Built 1861, sold 1865.

Penobscot Screw steamer: 691 tons. **D.** 158′ 4″ x 28′ x 10′ 6″. **A.** 1 11-in SB, 1 20-pdr R, 2 24-pdr H. Built 1861, sold 1869. (See p.84)

Pennsylvania Ship-of-the-line: 3105 tons. **D.** 210′ x 56′ 9″ x 24′. **A.** 16 8-in, 104 32-pdr. **C.** 1100. Laid down 1821; lack of funds delayed launch until 1837. Burnt to prevent capture at Norfolk Navy Yard, April 20, 1861. Pierced for 136 guns on four decks, *Pennsylvania* was the largest sailing ship built for the US Navy.

Pensacola Screw sloop: 3000 tons. **D.** 130′ 5″ x 44′ 5″ x 18′ 7″. **A.** 1 11-in SB, 16 9-in SB. **S.** 9½ knots. Launched 1859. Stricken from list 1911 and burnt near Hunters Point, San Francisco Bay, May 1912. (See p.137)

Peony Screw steamer: 180 tons. **D.** 104′ 6″ x 20′ 6″ x 8′ 6″. **A.** 1 24-pdr. Purchased 1864, sold 1865.

Peoria Sidewheel steamer: 974 tons. **D.** 235′ 6″ x 35′ x 9′ 3″. **A.** 4 8-in SB, 2 60-pdr R, 2 24-pdr, 2 20-pdr. Built 1863, sold 1868. (See p.104)

Peosta Sidewheel steamer: 233 tons. **D.** 151′ 2″ x 34′ 3″ x 6′. **A.** 3 30-pdr R, 2 32-pdr, 2 12-pdr, 6 24-pdr H. Purchased 1863, sold 1865. (See p.92)

Pequot Screw steamer: 593 tons. **D.** 190′ x 29′ x 12′. **A.** 1 50-pdr, 1 30-pdr R, 6 32-pdr, 2 24-pdr, 2 12-pdr. **S.** 11 knots. **C.** 130. Launched 1863, sold 1869.

Percy Drayton Sloop. Captured 1863, sold 1865.

Peri Sternwheel steamer: 209 tons. **D.** 147′ 6″ x 28′ 2″ x 5′ 6″. **A.** 1 30-pdr R, 6 24-pdr H. Purchased 1864, sold 1865.

Peri Ship: 265 tons. Purchased 1861 for use as block ship.

Perwinkle Screw tug: 383 tons. **D.** 140′ x 28′ x 10′. **A.** 2 24-pdr. Built 1864. Lost while carrying provision for expedition to North Pole. She had reached the highest latitude ever made by a vessel, but on return journey in October 1872 was caught in ice and crushed.

Perry Brig: 280 tons. **D.** 105′ x 25′ 6″ x 13′ 2″. **A.** 6 32-pdr. **C.** 67. Built 1843, sold 1865.

Peter Demill Bark: 300 tons. Purchased 1861 for use as block ship.

Peterhoff Sidewheel steamer: 800 tons. **D.** 210′ x 28′ x 10′. Captured 1863. Sank after colliding with *Monicello* off Wilmington, N.C., on March 6, 1864; wreck destroyed next day to prevent salvage by Confederates. (See p.154)

Petrel Steamer: 226 tons. **A.** 8 24-pdr H. Purchased 1862, captured near Yazoo City and burnt by Confederates to prevent recapture, April 22, 1864.

Philadelphia Sidewheel steamer: 500 tons. **D.** 200′ x 30′ x 7′ 6″. **A.** 2 12-pdr R. Seized 1862, sold 1865.

Philippi Sidewheel steamer: 311 tons. **D.** 140′ x 24′ x 6′. **A.** 2 12-pdr R. **C.** 41. Captured 1863. Set on fire and destroyed in action against Confederate forts at Mobile Bay, August 5, 1864.

Phlox Sidewheel steamer: 317 tons. **D.** 145′ x 24′ x 6′. **S.** 12 knots. Purchased 1864, later served at the Naval Academy, Annapolis, until 1873.

Pheonix Ship: 404 tons. Purchased 1861 for use as block ship.

Picket Boat No. 1 **D.** 40′ x 9′ 6″ x 3′. **S.** 7 knots. Built 1864.

Picket Boat No. 2 Boat captured by Confederates on October 18, 1864 in Great Wicomico River, Md.

Picket Boat No. 3 Screw steamer. Cut adrift February 19, 1885 and drifted out to sea.

Picket Boat No. 4 Screw steamer: 20 tons. **D.** 3′ 6″ draft. **A.** 1 12-pdr H. **S.** 8 knots. Built 1864.

Picket Boat No. 5 Screw steamer. **D.** 3′ 6″ draft. **A.** 1 12-pdr SB. **S.** 8 knots. Built 1864.

Picket Boat No. 6 Screw steamer. **D.** 3′ 8″ draft. **A.** 1 12-pdr H. Built 1864.

Pilgrim Canal boat: 126 tons. Purchased 1864 for use as block ship.

Pilgrim Screw tug: 170 tons. **D.** 6′ draft. **S.** 12 knots. Built 1864, sold 1891.

Pink Screw tug: 184 tons. **D.** 110′ 4″ x 24′ 6″ x 6′. **A.** 1 30-pdr R, 2 12-pdr SB. Built 1863. Rank aground on Dauphin Island and abandoned, September 22, 1865.

Pinola Screw steamer: 507 tons. **D.** 158′ x 28′ x 10′ 6″. **A.** 1 11-in SB, 1 20-pdr R, 2 24-pdr H. Built 1861, sold 1865. (See p.84)

Pinta Screw tug: 306 tons. **D.** 127′ x 26′ x 11′. **A.** 2 30-pdr R, 1 12-pdr H. Built 1864, sold 1908.

Piscataqua Screw steamer: 2400 tons. **D.** 312′ 6″ x 46′ x 16′ 8″. **A.** 20 9-in SB. **S.** 12 knots. Launched 1866. Sank at New York Navy Yard 1876; hulk sold 1877. (See p.147)

Pittsburgh Ironclad: 512 tons. **D.** 175′ x 51′ 2″ x 6′. **A.** 3 8-in, 4 24-pdr R, 6 32-pdr. Built 1861, sold 1865. (See p.16)

Planter Sidewheel steamer: 300 tons. **D.** 147′ x 30′ x 3′ 9″. **A.** 1 32-pdr, 1 24-pdr H. Built 1860. Surrendered by crew to Union forces 1862, lost at sea July 1876. (See p.106)

Plymouth Sloop: 189 tons. **D.** 147′ x 38′ 1″ x 14′. **A.** 4 8-in, 18 32-pdr. Built 1844. Burnt and scuttled at Norfolk Navy Yard to prevent capture, April 20, 1861.

Plymouth Screw steamer: 1122 tons. **D.** 250′ 6″ x 38′ x 16′. **A.** 1 11-in SB, 10 9-in SB, 1 60-pdr, 2 20-pdr R. Laid down 1867, scrapped 1884.

Pompanoosuc Screw frigate: 4446 tons. **D.** 335′ x 48′ x 21′. **A.** 2 100-pdr R, 12 9-in SB, 2 60-pdr R. Laid down 1864, never completed. Broken up on stocks 1884.

Pontiac Sidewheel steamer: 974 tons. **D.** 205′ x 35′ x 6′ 6″. **A.** 2 100-pdr R, 4 9-in SB, 4 24-pdr H, 4 12-pdr. **S.** 11 knots. **C.** 172. Delivered 1864, sold 1867. (See p.104)

Pontoosuc Sidewheel steamer: 974 tons. **D.** 205′ x 35′ x 9′. **A.** 2 100-pdr R, 4 9-in SB, 2 24-pdr H., 2 20-pdr R. Delivered 1864, sold 1866 (See p.104)

Poppy Screw tug: 93 tons. **D.** 88′ x 19′ x 7′ 3″. **A.** 2 12-pdr. Purchased 1863, sold 1865.

Port Fire Screw tug: 103 tons. Built 1863. Served as powder tug. Sold 1878.

Port Royal Sidewheel steamer: 805 tons. **D.** 209′ x 35′ x 9′. **A.** 1 100-pdr R, 1 10-in SB, 6 24-pdr H. **S.** 9 knots. Built 1861, sold 1866. (See p.96)

Portsmouth Screw sloop: 1022 tons. **D.** 153′ x 38′ 1″ x 16′ 6″. **A.** 16 8-in, 1 12-pdr. **C.** 200. Launched 1843, sold 1915.

Potomac Frigate: 1726 tons. **D.** 177′ 10″ x 46′ 2″ x 20′ 6″. **A.** 10 8-in, 40 32-pdr. Launched 1822, completed 1831, sold 1877.

Potomac Ship: 356 tons. Purchased 1861 for use as block ship.

Potomska Screw steamer: 287 tons. **D.** 134′ 6″ x 27′ x 11″. **A.** 4 32-pdr, 1 20-pdr R. Purchased 1861, sold 1865.

Powhatan Sidewheel steamer: 3765 tons. **D.** 250′ x 45′ x 20′ 9″. **A.** 1 11-in SB, 10 9-in SB, 4 12-pdr. Launched 1850, sold 1887. (See p.138)

Prairie Bird Sternwheel steamer: 171 tons. **D.** 159′ 10″ x 29′ 3″ x 5′. **A.** 8 24-pdr. Purchased 1862, sold 1865.

Preble Sloop: 566 tons. **D.** 117′ x 32′ x 12′. **A.** 16 32-pdr. Launched 1839. Destroyed by fire at Pensacola, April 27, 1863.

Preston Screw steamer: 428 tons. **D.** 170′ x 23′ 1″ x 10′. Captured 1864, sold 1865.

Primrose Screw tug: 94 tons. **D.** 83′ x 17′ 6″ x 7′. Purchased 1863, sold 1871.

Princess Royal Screw steamer: 829 tons. **D.** 196′ 9″ x 27′ 3″ x 11′. **A.** 1 9-in SB, 2 30-pdr R. Captured 1863, sold 1865.

Princeton Screw steamer: 1370 tons. **D.** 177′ 6″ x 32′ 8″ x 25′ 9″. **A.** 4 8-in, 6 32-pdr. **S.** 8 knots. Launched 1851 as clipper ship partly using timber from previous *Princeton* of 1842. Machinery added 1852. Sold 1866.

Proteus Screw steamer: 1244 tons. **D.** 203′ x 36′ x 13′ 9″. **A.** 1 100-pdr R, 2 30-pdr R, 6 32-pdr. Purchased 1863, sold 1865.

Pulaski Sidewheel steamer: 395 tons. **A.** 3 12-pdr. Built 1854. Condemned and sold in Montevideo 1863.

Puritan Ironclad monitor: 4912 tons. **D.** 340′ x 50′ x 21′. **A.** 2 20-in SB. Laid down 1863, never completed. Broken up 1874. Used as part payment for new 6060-ton *Puritan* laid down in 1875. (See p.64)

Pursuit Bark: 600 tons. **D.** 144′ x 34′ 10″ x 12′. **A.** 6 32-pdr. Purchased 1861, sold 1865.

Pushmataha Screw sloop: 3003 tons. **D.** 290′ x 41′. **A.** 14 9-in SB, 1 60-pdr, 3 12-pdr. **C.** 480. Launched 1868, sold 1883.

Quaker City Sidewheel steamer: 1600 tons. **D.** 244′ 8″ x 36′ x 13′ 8″. **A.** 1 20-pdr, 8 32-pdr. **S.** 13 knots. **C.** 163. Built 1854, chartered 1861, sold 1869. (See p.129)

Queen Screw steamer: 630 tons. **D.** 168′ 8″ x 28′ 4″ x 9′ 9″. **A.** 3 32-pdr. **C.** 83. Captured 1863, sold 1865.

Queen City Sidewheel steamer: 212 tons. **A.** 2 30-pdr R, 2 32-pdr, 4 24-pdr H. Purchased 1863. Captured in dawn attack by Confederate cavalry, June 24, 1863, and blown up to prevent recapture. (See p.80)

Queen of the West Sidewheel steamer: 406 tons. **D.** 180′ x 37′ 6″ x 6′. **A.** 1 30-pdr, 3 12-pdr. One of General Ellet's Ram Fleet. Captured February 14, 1863 in Black River. Set on fire in action April, 14, 1863 and blown up. (See p.111)

Quinnebaug Screw sloop: 1113 tons. **D.** 216′ x 30′ x 12′. **A.** 1 60-pdr R, 4 32-pdr. Launched 1866, broken up 1871. (See p.141)

Quinsigamond Ironclad monitor: 5600 tons. **D.** 345′ 5″ x 56′ 8″ x 17′ 6″. **A.** 4 15-in SB. Laid down 1864, never completed. Broken up on stocks 1884. (See p.70)

R.B. Forbes Screw steamer: 329 tons. **D.** 121′ x 25′ 6″ x 12′ 3″. **A.** 2 32-pdr. **S.** 11 knots. Built 1845, purchased 1861. Driven ashore off Cape Henry during storm February 8, 1862. Wreck burnt to prevent capture.

R.R. Cuyler Screw steamer: 1200 tons. **D.** 237′ x 33′ 3″ x 17′. **A.** 8 32-pdr R. **S.** 14 knots. Built 1860, purchased 1861, sold 1865. Blown from her moorings during a storm in September 1867 and grounded on a coral reef at Cartagena, where she was abandoned.

Racer Schooner: 252 tons. **D.** 105′ x 28′ x 9′ 10″. **A.** 1 13-in M, 2 32-pdr. Purchased 1861, sold 1865.

Rachel Seaman Schooner: 303 tons. **D.** 115′ x 30′ x 9′. **A.** 2 32-pdr. Purchased 1861, sold 1865.

Raritan Frigate: 1708 tons. **D.** 174′ 10″ x 45′ x 22′ 8″. **A.** 44 guns. Laid down 1820, launched 1843. Burnt at Norfolk Navy Yard to prevent capture, April 20, 1861.

Rattler Sidewheel steamer: 165 tons. **A.** 2 30-pdr, 4 24-pdr. Purchased 1862. Anchor cable parted during heavy gale near Grand Gulf, Miss., and vessel sank after striking underwater obstruction, December 30, 1864. Confederates later burnt wreck. (See p.102)

Rebecca Sims Ship. Purchased 1861 for use as block ship.

Red Rover Sidewheel steamer: 786 tons. **D.** 256′ x 8′ draft. **A.** 1 32-pdr. Built 1859, used as a hospital ship. Captured 1862, sold 1865.

Reindeer Sternwheel steamer: 212 tons. **D.** 154′ x 32′ 9″ x 6′. **A.** 6 24-pdr H. Purchased 1863, sold 1865. Stranded and destroyed at Decatur, Ala., May 8, 1867.

Release Bark: 327 tons. **D.** 113′ x 27′ 2″ x 11′ 9″. **A.** 2 32-pdr. Purchased 1855, sold 1865.

Relief Ship: 468 tons. **D.** 109′ x 30′ x 12′. **A.** 2 32-pdr. Launched 1836, sold 1883.

Reliance Screw steamer: 90 tons. **D.** 88′ 2″ x 17′ x 6′. **A.** 1 24-pdr H. Purchased 1861, captured August 23, 1863, destroyed on August 28 to prevent recapture.

Renshaw Schooner: 75 tons. **D.** 68′ x 20′ x 6′ 6″. Captured 1862, sold 1865.

Republic Screw steamer: 225 tons. **D.** 104′ 6″ x 20′ 6″ x 8′ 6″. **A.** 1 24-pdr. Purchased 1864, sold 1865.

Resaca Screw sloop: 1129 tons. **D.** 216′ x 31′ x 12′. **A.** 1 150-pdr R, 6 32-pdr, 3 24-pdr H. Launched 1865, sold 1873. Rebuilt as passenger steamer able to carry 145 passengers. Renamed *Ventura*, she was wrecked off Santa Cruz on April 20, 1875 and lost. (See p.141)

Rescue Screw steamer: 111 tons. **D.** 80′ x 18′ x 8′. **A.** 1 20-pdr R. Built in 1861 as a speculation. Purchased 1861, sold 1891.

Resolute Screw tug: 90 tons. **D.** 88′ 2″ c 17′ x 6′ 6″. **A.** 1 24-pdr, 1 12-pdr. Built 1860, sold 1865. Served in merchant marine until abandoned in 1899.

Restless Bark: 265 tons. **D.** 108′ 8″ x 27′ 8″ x 8′. **A.** 4 32-pdr. Purchased 1861, sold 1865.

Rhode Island Sidewheel steamer: 1517 tons. **D.** 236′ 6″ x 36′ 8″ x 15′. **A.** 4 32-pdr. **S.** 16 knots. **C.** 257. Built 1860, burnt and rebuilt 1861, sold 1867. Served in merchant marine until abandoned in 1885. (See p.102)

Richard Vaux Canal boat: 120 tons. Purchased 1864 for use as block ship.

Richmond Steam sloop: 2604 tons. **D.** 225′ x 42′ 6″ x 17′ 5″. **A.** 1 80-pdr SB, 20 9-in SB. **C.** 259. Launched 1860, broken up 1919. (See p.148)

Roanoke Steam frigate: 3435 tons. **D.** 263′ 8″ x 52′ 6″ x 23′ 6″. **A.** 2 10-in SB, 28 9-in SB, 14 8-in. **S.** 11 knots. **C.** 674. Launched 1855. Rebuilt as monitor 1862, sold 1883. (See p.36)

Robin Hood Ship: 395 tons. Purchased 1861 for use as block ship.

Rocket Screw tug: 187 tons. **D.** 85′ 8″ x 18′ 10″ x 7′. Built 1862, sold 1899.

Rodolph Sidewheel steamer: 217 tons. **A.** 2 32-pdr, 2 24-pdr. Purchased 1863. Struck a mine and sank in Mobile Bay, April 1, 1865.

Roebuck Bark: 455 tons. **D.** 135′ x 27′ x 12′. **A.** 4 32-pdr. **C.** 69. Built 1856, purchased 1861, sold 1865.

Rolling Wave Canal boat: 112 tons. Purchased 1864 for use as block ship.

Roman Ship: 350 tons. **D.** 112′ x 26′ 3″ x 18′. **A.** 1 32-pdr. Built 1835, purchased 1861, used as ordnance ship, sold 1865. Resumed role of whaler and crushed by ice near Bering Sea, September 7, 1871.

Romeo Sternwheel steamer: 175 tons. **D.** 154′ 2″ x 31′ 2″ x 4′ 6″. **A.** 6 24-pdr. Purchased 1862, sold 1865.

Rosalie Sloop: 29 tons. **D.** 45′ x 17′ x 3′ 6″. **A.** 1 12-pdr. Captured 1863, sold 1865.

Rose Screw steamer: 96 tons. **D.** 84′ x 18′ 2″ x 6″. **A.** 1 20-pdr R. Purchased 1863, sold 1883.

Sabine Frigate: 1726 tons. **D.** 202′ 6″ x 47′ x 21′ 6″. **A.** 2 10-in SB, 10 9-in SB, 36 32-pdr. **S.** 12 knots. **C.** 400. Laid down as a 50-gun ship in 1822. Launched 1855 after being lengthened 20 ft. Sold 1883.

Sachem Screw steamer: 197 tons. **D.** 121′ x 23′ 6″ x 6′. **A.** 1 20-pdr R, 4 32-pdr. **C.** 52. Built 1844, purchased 1861. Captured at Sabine Pass, September 7, 1863. Fitted out as blockade runner.

Saco Screw steamer: 593 tons. **D.** 179′ 6″ x 30′ 6″ x 11′ 6″. **A.** 1 100-pdr R, 1 30-pdr, 6 32-pdr. **C.** 127. Launched 1863, sold 1883.

Sacramento Screw sloop: 2100 tons. **D.** 29′ 6″ x 38′ x 8′ 10″. **A.** 1 150-pdr R, 2 11-in SB, 1 30-pdr, 2 24-pdr. Launched 1862. Ran onto reefs near Godavary River in Madras and wrecked, June 19, 1867.

Saffron Screw tug: 78 tons. **D.** 8′ draft. Built 1863, sold 1865, lost at sea 1885.

Sagamore Screw steamer: 507 tons. **D.** 158′ x 28′ x 7′. **A.** 1 20-pdr, 2 24-pdr. Launched 1861, sold 1865. (See p.84)

Saginaw Sidewheel steamer: 453 tons. **D.** 4′ 5″ draft. **A.** 1 50-pdr R, 1 32-pdr, 2 24-pdr R. Launched 1859. Ran onto reef at Ocean Island in Pacific and wrecked, October 29, 1870. She was the first of the many vessels built at Mare Island Navy Yard, California.

St Clair Sternwheel steamer: 203 tons. **D.** 156′ x 32′ x 2′ 4″. **A.** 4 12-pdr. Built 1862, purchased 1862, sold 1865. Served in merchant marine until abandoned in 1869.

St Lawrence Frigate: 1726 tons. **D.** 175′ x 45′ x 23′. **A.** 10 8-in, 40 32-pdr. **S.** 12 knots. **C.** 480. Laid down 1826, launched 1848, sold 1875.

St Louis Sloop: 700 tons. **D.** 127′ x 33′ 9″ x 16′. **A.** 4 8-in, 14 32-pdr. Laid down 1827, launched 1828, scrapped 1907.

St Louis Ironclad: 512 tons. **D.** 175′ x 51′ 2″ x 6′. **A.** 2 8-in, 4 24-pdr R, 7 32-pdr. (See p.16)

St Mary's Sloop: 958 tons. **D.** 149′ 3″ x 37′ 4″ x 18′. **A.** 6 8-in, 16 32-pdr. **C.** 195. Built 1844, scrapped 1908.

Sallie Woods Sidewheel steamer: 256 tons. Built 1860, captured 1862. Driven ashore by enemy fire on July 21, 1862 at Island No. 82, forcing the crew to abandon the vessel. Confederate forces later set her on fire.

Sam Houston Schooner: 66 tons. **A.** 1 12-pdr SB. Captured 1861, sold 1865.

Samson Steam tug. Transferred from army 1862. Former Ellet Ram Fleet vessel. Sold 1865.

Samuel Rotan Schooner: 212 tons. **D.** 110′ x 28′ 6″ x 9′. **A.** 2 32-pdr. Purchased 1861, sold 1865.

Sandusky Ironclad monitor: 479 tons. **D.** 170′ x 50′ x 5′. **A.** 2 11-in SB. Built 1864, sold 1873. (See p.63)

Sangamon Ironclad monitor: 1875 tons. **D.** 200′ x 46′ x 11′ 6″. **A.** 1 15-in SB, 1 11-in SB. Launched 1862, sold 1904. Also known as *Conestoga*.

San Jacinto Screw frigate: 1567 tons. **D.** 234′ x 37′ 9″ x 16′ 6″. **A.** 1 11-in SB, 10 9-in SB, 1 12-pdr. **S.** 8 knots. Laid down in 1847, launched 1850. Struck reef near Great Abaco Island and became total loss, January 1, 1865. Wreck sold 1871. (See p.133)

Santee Frigate: 1726 tons. **D.** 175′ x 45′ x 16′. **A.** 2 64-pdr, 10 8-in, 36 32-pdr. Laid down as 44-gun vessel 1820. Launched 1855. Served at Naval Academy, Annapolis, until she sank at her moorings, April 2, 1912. Raised, taken to Boston and burnt for the metal in her hull.

Santiago de Cuba Sidewheel steamer: 1567 tons. **D.** 229′ x 38′ x 16′ 2″. **A.** 2 20-pdr R, 8 32-pdr. **S.** 14 knots. **C.** 114. Built and purchased 1861, sold 1865. Served in merchant marine. Engines removed in 1866 and rigged as schooner. (See p.109)

Sarah Bibbey Schooner. Purchased 1861 for use as block ship.

Sarah and Caroline Schooner. Captured 1863, sold 1865.

Sarah Bruen Schooner: 233 tons. **D.** 105′ 6″ x 26′ 7″ x 9′ 6″. **A.** 1 13-in, 2 32-pdr. Purchased 1861, sold 1865.

Sarah M. Kemp Schooner. Purchased 1861 for use as block ship.

Saranac Sidewheel steamer: 1446 tons. **D.** 215′ 6″ x 37′ 9″ x 26′ 6″. **A.** 9 8-in. Launched 1848, sunk in Seymour Narrows off Vancouver Island, June 18, 1875.

Saratoga Sloop: 882 tons. **D.** 146′ 4″ x 35′ 3″ x 13′. **A.** 8-in, 18 32-pdr. **C.** 210. Launched 1843, sold 1907.

Sassacus Sidewheel steamer: 974 tons. **D.** 205′ x 35′ x 9′. **A.** 2 100-pdr R, 4 9-in SB, 2 24-pdr. Launched 1862, sold 1868. (See p.104)

Satellite Sidewheel tug: 217 tons. **D.** 120′ x 22′ 9″ x 6′. **A.** 2 8-in. Built 1854, purchased 1861. Captured on August 22/23, 1863, and destroyed August 28 to prevent recapture.

Saugus Ironclad monitor: 2100 tons. **D.** 235′ x 43′ 8″ x 13′ 6″. **A.** 2 15-in SB. Launched 1863, sold 1899. (See p.30)

Savannah Sloop: 1708 tons. **D.** 47′ beam. **A.** 2 10-in SB, 8 8-in, 14 32-pdr. **S.** 11 knots. **C.** 480. Begun 1820, launched 1842, sold 1883.

Sciota Screw steamer: 507 tons. **D.** 158′ x 28′ x 7′. **A.** 1 20-pdr R, 2 24-pdr, 1 11-in SB. Built 1861, mined in Mobile Bay, April 14, 1865. Hulk sold 1865. (See p.84)

Sea Bird Schooner: 58 tons. **D.** 59′ 8″ x 18′ 4″ x 7′ 6″. **A.** 1 12-pdr. Captured. Sold 1865.

Sea Foam Brig: 251 tons. **D.** 112′ 6″ x 26′ x 6″. **A.** 1 13-in M, 2 32-pdr. Purchased 1861, sold 1865.

Sebago Sidewheel steamer: 832 tons. **D.** 228′ 2″ x 33′ 10″ x 9′ 3″. **A.** 1 100-pdr R, 1 9-in SB, 4 24-pdr. Launched 1861, sold 1867.

Selma Sidewheel steamer. **D.** 252′ x 30′ x 6′. Captured in Mobile Bay, August 1864, sold 1865. (See p.101)

Seminole Screw steamer: 801 tons. **D.** 188′ x 30′ 6″. **A.** 1 11-in SB, 6 32-pdr, 1 30-pdr R. **S.** 11 knots. **C.** 120. Launched 1859, sold 1870.

Seneca Screw steamer: 507 tons. **D.** 158′ 4″ x 28′ x 10′ 6″. **A.** 1 11-in SB, 1 20-pdr R, 2 24-pdr. Built 1861, sold 1868. (See p.84)

Shakamaxon Ironclad monitor: 5600 tons. **D.** 345′ 5″ x 56′ 8″ x 17′ 6″. **A.** 4 15-in SB. Laid down 1863, never completed. Broken up on stocks 1874; took 14 months to dismantle the vessel. (See p.70)

Shamokin Sidewheel steamer: 1030 tons. **D.** 255′ x 35′ x 9′. Launched 1865, sold 1869.

Shamrock Sidewheel steamer: 974 tons. **D.** 205′ x 356′ x 8′ 10″. **A.** 2 100-pdr R, 4 9-in SB, 2 20-pdr R, 2 24-pdr H. Launched 1863, sold 1868. (See p.104)

Shawmut Screw steamer: 593 tons. **D.** 179′ 6″ x 30′ x 11′ 3″. **A.** 1 100-pdr R, 2 9-in SB, 1 30-pdr R. Built 1863, sold 1877.

Shawnee Ironclad monitor: 1175 tons. **D.** 225′ x 45′ x 9′. **A.** 1 11-in. Launched 1865, sold 1875. (See p.38)

Shawnsheen Sidewheel tug: 180 tons. **D.** 118′ x 22′ 6″ x 66′. **A.** 2 20-pdr R. Built 1855. Badly damaged in action at Chaffin's Bluff, James River on May 7, 1864 and blown up to prevent capture.

Shenandoah Screw sloop: 1375 tons. **D.** 225′ x 38′ 4″ x 15′. **A.** 1 150-pdr R, 2 11-in SB, 1 30-pdr R, 2 24-pdr H. **S.** 15 knots. **C.** 175. Built 1862, sold 1887.

Shepherd Knapp Ship: 838 tons. **D.** 160′ 10″ x 33′ 8″ x 13′. **A.** 8 guns. Purchased 1861. Wrecked on coral reef at Cape Haitien in the Caribbean on May 8, 1863 and abandoned.

Shiloh Ironclad monitor: 1175 tons. **D.** 225′ x 456′ x 96′. **A.** 1 11-in. Launched 1865, transferred to Lighthouse Board same year. (See p.38)

Shokokon Sidewheel steamer: 709 tons. **D.** 181′ x 32′ x 8′ 7″. **A.** 2 30-pdr R, 4 24-pdr. Built 1862, purchased 1863, sold 1865. Rejoined merchant marine until abandoned in 1886.

Sibyl Sidewheel steamer: 176 tons. **A.** 2 30-pdr R, 2 24-pdr. Built 1863, sold 1865, abandoned 1876. (See p.76)

Sidney C. Jones Schooner: 254 tons. **D.** 98′ x 27′ x 6′. **A.** 1 13-in M, 2 32-pdr. Purchased 1861. Ran aground June 1863 and destroyed to avoid capture.

Signal Sternwheel steamer: 190 tons. **D.** 157′ x 30′ x 1′ 10″. **A.** 2 30-pdr R, 4 24-pdr H, 2 12-pdr R. Built 1862. Disabled in action in Red River, May 5, 1864. Ran aground and set alight to avoid capture. (See p.75)

Silver Cloud Sternwheel steamer: 236 tons. **D.** 155′ x 32′ x 6′. **A.** 6 24-pdr H. Built 1862, sold 1865. Converted to sidewheel steamer. Lost after striking obstruction in Buffalo Bayou, Tex., February 27, 1866.

Silver Lake Sternwheel steamer: 236 tons. **D.** 155′ x 326′ 2″ x 6′. **A.** 6 24-pdr H. Built 1862, sold 1865. Converted to sidewheel in 1865 and destroyed by fire in the Red River, February 27, 1866. (See p.98)

Siren Sternwheel steamer: 214 tons. **D.** 154′ 7″ x 32′ 3″ x 5′. **A.** 2 24-pdr H. **S.** 7 knots. Built 1862, sold 1865, abandoned 1867.

Snowdrop Screw tug: 125 tons. **D.** 91′ x 17′ 6″ x 8′. **A.** 2 guns. **S.** 12 knots. Built 1863, broken up 1884.

Somerfield Schooner. Purchased 1861 for use as block ship.

Somerset Sidewheel steamer: 521 tons. **D.** 151′ x 32′ 4″. **A.** 2 9-in SB, 4 32-pdr. Built 1862, sold 1865. Served as ferry boat until 1914.

Sonoma Sidewheel steamer: 955 tons. **D.** 233′ 9″ x 34′ 10″ x 8′ 7″. **A.** 1 100-pdr, 1 11-in SB, 6 24-pdr H, 2 12-pdr R. Launched 1862, sold 1867.

Sophronia Schooner: 217 tons. **D.** 104′ 6″ x 28′ 4″ x 6′. **A.** 1 13-in M, 2 32-pdr. Purchased 1861, sold 1865.

Sorrel Steam tug: 68 tons. **D.** 77′ x 16′ 6″ x 5′. Purchased 1864, sold 1883.

South America Bark. Purchased 1861 for use as block ship but beached instead at Tybee Island, Ga., for use as wharf.

South Carolina Screw steamer: 1165 tons. **D.** 218′ x 33′ 6″ x 14′ 6″. **A.** 4 8-in, 1 32-pdr. **S.** 12 knots. Built 1860, purchased 1861, sold 1866. Served in merchant marine before being reduced to a schooner barge in 1893 as machinery was beyond economical repair.

Southerner Schooner. Purchased 1861 for use as block ship.

Southfield Sidewheel steamer: 750 tons. **D.** 200′ x 34′ x 66′ 6″. **A.** 1 100-pdr R, 3 8-in SB. **S.** 12 knots. **C.** 61. Built 1857, purchased 1861. Sunk in action with *Albemarle* on Roanoke River, N.C., April 19, 1863.

South Wind Schooner. Purchased 1861 for use as block ship.

Sovereign Sidewheel steamer: 336 tons. Built 1855, captured at Island No. 10 in April 1862. Sold 1865.

Speedwell Screw tug: 350 tons. **D.** 137′ x 26′. Built 1865, sold 1891.

Spirea Sidewheel steamer: 409 tons. **A.** 2 30-pdr R, 4 24-pdr SB. Built 1864, sold 1866, lost at sea 1867.

Springfield Sternwheel steamer: 146 tons. **D.** 134′ 9″ x 27′ x 4′. **A.** 6 24-pdr H. Purchased 1862, sold 1865. Served as a river transport until 1875.

Spuyten Duyvil Screw steamer: 116 tons. **D.** 75′ x 19′ 6″ x 8′. **A.** 1 spar torpedo. **S.** 8 knots. **C.** 22. Built in 1864 from designs of William Wood, chief engineer of the US Navy, and John Lay. The vessel had a wooden hull with a 1-in covering of iron sheeting. On going into action, water was taken into buoyancy tanks, thus increasing the draft by 2 ft and leaving only 1 ft of hull showing above water. The torpedo was run out from a tube in the bows. Removed from Navy List 1880.

Squando Ironclad monitor: 1175 tons. **D.** 225′ 5″ x 45′ 2″ x 9′. **A.** 2 11-in. Launched 1864, scrapped 1874. (See p.38)

Standfish Screw tug: 350 tons. **D.** 137′ x 26′ x 9′ 6″. **A.** 2 guns. Built 1865. Later served at Naval Academy, Annapolis. Sold 1921.

Stars and Stripes Screw steamer: 407 tons. **D.** 124′ 3″ x 34′ 6″ x 10′. **A.** 4 8-in, 1 20-pdr R. Purchased 1861, sold 1865. Served in merchant marine. Wrecked on outer bar of Currituck Beach, N.C:, January 31, 1878.

State of Georgia Sidewheel steamer: 1204 tons. **D.** 200′ x 336′ x 14′. **A.** 6 8-in, 2 32-pdr, 1 30-pdr R. Built 1851, purchased 1861, sold 1865. Driven ashore during hurricane at Currituck Inlet, N.C., October 5, 1866, and became total loss.

Stephen Young Brig: 200 tons. Purchased 1861 for use as block ship.

Stepping Stones Sidewheel steamer: 226 tons. **D.** 110′ x 24′ x 4′ 6″. **A.** 1 12-pdr H.P **S.** 14 knots. Purchased 1861, sold 1865. Converted to a barge 1871.

Stettin Screw steamer: 600 tons. **D.** 164′ x 28′ x 12′. **A.** 1 30-pdr R, 4 24-pdr H. Captured 1862, sold 1865, lost at sea 1866.

Stevens Battery Ironclad: 4683 tons. **D.** 250′ x 40′ x 28′. Laid down in 1854 but never completed. Broken up on the slip 1880. This vessel, designed by Robert Stevens, was the first ironclad authorized for any navy. A new design had a 5000-ton vessel measuring 420′ x 53′ x 20′ 6″, with armor increased from 4½ in to nearly 7 in. Armament was increased to two 10-in rifles and five 15-in SB. Stevens died in 1856 and his two brothers, Edwin and John, offered to complete the vessel at their own expense in 1861, but this generous offer was refused.

On the death of Edwin Stevens the vessel became the property of the State of New Jersey. The $1 million he left to complete the vessel was exhausted by 1874, and still the ship was not ready. A new design, prepared by George B. McClellan and Isaac Newton, called for a 6000-ton vessel measuring 390′ x 45′ x 22′, with a speed of 16½ knots, and carrying a single massive turret.

Stockdale Sidewheel steamer: 188 tons. **A.** 2 30-pdr R, 4 24-pdr H. Purchased 1863, sold 1865.

Stonewall Schooner: 30 tons. **A.** 12-pdr. Captured 1863, sold 1865.

Stonewall Ironclad. Ex-Confederate warship turned over to US by the Captain-General of Cuba in July 1865. Sold 1867 to Japan for service in the Imperial Japanese Navy. Sold to a fishing company 1891.

Sumpter Screw steamer: 465 tons. **D.** 163′ x 24′ 4″ x 11′ 9″. **A.** 1 20-pdr R, 1 12-pdr, 4 32-pdr. Built 1853, purchased 1859. Sunk in collision with transport steamer *General Meigs* off Smith Island, June 24, 1863.

Sumter Steamer: 400 tons. **A.** 2 32-pdr. Captured June 1862. Ran ashore off Bayou Sara, La., and abandoned in August 1862. Later burned by the Confederates.

Suncook Ironclad monitor: 1175 tons. **D.** 225′ x 45′ x 9′. **A.** 1 11-in. Launched 1864, scrapped 1874. (See p.38)

Sunflower Screw steamer: 294 tons. **D.** 104′ 5″ x 20′ 9″ x 12′. **A.** 2 30-pdr R. **S.** 10½ knots. Purchased 1863, sold 1865.

Supply Ship: 547 tons. **D.** 16′ draft. **A.** 4 24-pdr. Purchased 1846, sold 1884.

Susan A. Howard Schooner. **D.** 50′ x 17′ 4″ x 4′. Captured 1863, sold 1864.

Susquehanna Sidewheel steamer: 3824 tons. **D.** 257′ x 45′ x 20′ 6″. **A.** 12 8-in, 6 32-pdr. Launched 1850, sold 1883. (See p.140)

Suwanee Sidewheel steamer: 1030 tons. **D.** 255′ x 35′ x 9′. **A.** 2 100-pdr R, 4 9-in SB, 2 24-pdr, 2 20-pdr. Launched 1864. Wrecked in Shadwell Passage, Queen Charlotte Sound, British Columbia, July 9, 1868.

Swatara Screw steamer: 1113 tons. **D.** 216′ x 30′ x 13′. **A.** 1 60-pdr, 6 32-pdr, 3 20-pdr. Launched 1865, decommissioned in 1871 and used as part payment under the guise of "repairs" for a new 1900-ton *Swatara.* (See p.141)

Sweet Brier Screw tug: 240 tons. **D.** 120′ x 21′ 3″ x 9′ 6″. **A.** 1 20-pdr, 1 12-pdr. Purchased 1863, sold 1865. Served in merchant marine until 1900.

Swift Schooner: 12 tons. **A.** 2 12-pdr H. Captured 1864, sold 1865.

Switzerland Sidewheel steamer: 500 tons. Acquired by army. Transferred to navy 1862 and sunk by Vicksburg batteries, March 25, 1863. (See p.108)

T.A. Ward Schooner: 284 tons. **D.** 114′ 6″ x 28′ 2″ x 10′ 6″. **A.** 1 13-in M, 2 32-pdr. Purchased 1861, sold 1865.

T.D. Horner Sternwheel steamer: 123 tons. **A.** 2 12-pdr. Built 1859, purchased by army 1862 and formed part of the Ellet Ram Fleet. Sold 1865. Ran into bridge at Louisville, Ky., and damaged beyond economical repair on January 1, 1868.

Tacony Sidewheel steamer: 974 tons. **D.** 205′ x 35′ x 8′ 10″. **A.** 2 11-in SB, 3 9-in SB, 1 24-pdr. Launched 1863, sold 1868. (See p.104)

Tahoma Screw steamer: 507 tons. **D.** 158′ x 28′ x 10′ 6″. **A.** 1 10-in SB, 2 20-pdr R, 2 24-pdr. Built 1861, sold 1867. (See p.84)

Tallahatchie Sidewheel steamer: 171 tons. **A.** 2 32-pdr, 4 24-pdr. Purchased 1865 and destroyed by fire at Licking River, Ky., July 7, 1869.

Tallahoma Sidewheel steamer: 974 tons. **D.** 35′ beam, 4′ 6″ draft. **A.** 10 guns. Launched 1863, sold 1868. Converted to a barge 1870. (See p.104)

Tallapoosa Sidewheel steamer: 974 tons. **D.** 205′ x 35′ x 6′ 6″. **A.** 2 100-pdr, 4 9-in SB, 2 20-pdr. Built 1862, sold 1892. (See p.79)

Tawah Sidewheel steamer: 108 tons. **D.** 114′ x 336′ x 36′ 9″. **A.** 4 24-pdr, 2 30-pdr R. Purchased 1863. Sunk November 4, 1864 off Johnsonville, Tennessee River, and burned same day to prevent capture.

Teaser Screw tug: 90 tons. **D.** 80′ x 18′ x 6′. **A.** 1 32-pdr, 1 12-pdr R. Seized July 4, 1862, sold 1865. Served in merchant marine until 1878. While in Confederate service was used as a balloon ship.

Tecumseh Ironclad monitor: 2100 tons. **D.** 223′ x 43′ 4″ x 13′ 6″. **A.** 2 15-in SB. Launched 1863. Sunk by mine in Mobile Bay on August 5, 1864. (See p.30)

Tempest Sidewheel steamer: 161 tons. **A.** 2 30-pdr R, 2 24-pdr H. Built 1862, purchased 1864, sold 1865. Served in merchant marine until 1870.

Tenedos Bark: 245 tons. **D.** 12′ draft. Purchased 1861 for use as block ship.

Tennessee Ironclad: 1273 tons. **D.** 209′ x 48′ x 14′. **A.** 2 7-in R, 4 6-in R, 1 12-pdr. Captured August 5, 1865. Sold 1867. (See p.44)

Tennessee Sidewheel steamer: 1275 tons. **A.** 2 32-pdr, 1 30-pdr R, 1 12-pdr R. Captured April 1862 at New Orleans. Sold 1865.

Tensas Sidewheel steamer: 41 tons. **D.** 91′ x 22′ 5″ x 4′. **A.** 2 24-pdr H. Built 1860, captured 1863, sold 1865.

Texas Ironclad. **D.** 217′ x 48′ x 13′ 6″. **A.** 6 guns. Captured April 4, 1865. Laid up at Norfolk Navy Yard, sold 1867.

Thistle Sidewheel tug: 50 tons. **A.** 1 12-pdr. Transferred 1862, sold 1865.

Thomas Freeborn Sidewheel steamer: 269 tons. **D.** 143′ x 25′ 6″ x 6′. **A.** 2 32-pdr. Purchased 1861, sold 1865. Served in merchant marine until 1887.

Thunder Sloop. Captured 1862, sold 1865.

Ticonderoga Screw sloop: 2526 tons. **D.** 237′ x 38′ 2″ x 17′ 6″. **A.** 1 150-pdr R, 6 9-in SB, 1 50-pdr R, 2 24-pdr H, 4 12-pdr. **S.** 11 knots. Launched 1862, sold 1887.

Tigress Screw tug. **A.** 1 H. Built 1858, purchased 1861. Sank after colliding with steamer *State of Maine* off Indian Head, Md., September 20, 1861.

Timor Ship: 289 tons. Purchased 1861 for use as block ship.

Tioga Sidewheel steamer: 819 tons. **D.** 209′ x 34′ 11″ x 10′ 2″. **A.** 1 10-in SB, 1 100-pdr R, 6 24-pdr H. **S.** 11½ knots. **C.** 105. Launched 1862, sold 1867.

Tippecanoe Ironclad monitor: 2100 tons. **D.** 224′ x 43′ x 13′ 6″. **A.** 2 15-in SB. Launched 1864, never commissioned. Served as training ship, sold 1899. (See p.30)

Tonawanda Ironclad monitor: 3400 tons. **D.** 259′ 6″ x 52′ 10″ x 13′ 5″. **A.** 4 15-in SB. Launched 1864, broken up 1874. (See p.68)

Trefoil Screw steamer: 370 tons. **D.** 145′ 7″ x 23′ 9″ x 11′ 2″. **A.** 1 30-pdr R, 1 12-pdr. **C.** 44. Built 1864, purchased 1865, sold 1867.

Triana Screw tug: 450 tons. **D.** 137′ x 26′ x 9′ 6″. **S.** 10 knots. Built 1865, sold 1891.

Tristram Shandy Sidewheel steamer: 444 tons. **D.** 222′ x 23′ 6″ x 6′ 4″. **A.** 3 32-pdr, 1 20-pdr R. Built 1864, captured 1864, sold 1865. Served in merchant marine until she ran aground and became a total loss off Havana, Cuba, in 1874.

Tritonia Sidewheel steamer: 202 tons. **D.** 178′ x 22′ 4″ x 7′. **A.** 2 12-pdr. Purchased 1863, sold 1865, lost at sea 1880.

Tulip Screw steamer: 183 tons. **D.** 97′ 3″ x 21′ 9″ x 8′. **A.** 2 24-pdr, 1 20-pdr R. Built 1863 for Chinese Navy, purchased 1863. Blew up as a result of defective boilers off Ragged Point, Inigoes Creek, St Mary's County, Md., November 11, 1864.

Tuscarora Screw sloop: 1457 tons. **D.** 198′ 6″ x 33′ 2″ x 14′ 10″. **A.** 2 11-in SB, 6 32-pdr, 1 30-pdr. Built 1861, sold 1883.

Tuscumbia Ironclad: 915 tons. **D.** 178′ x 75′ x 7′. **A.** 6 11-in SB, 2 9-in SB. Built 1862, sold 1865. (See p.48)

Tuxis Ironclad monitor: 1175 tons. **D.** 225′ x 45′ x 9′. **A.** 1 150-pdr R, 1 11-in SB. Launched 1864, scrapped 1874. (See p.38)

Two Sisters Schooner: 54 tons. **A.** 1 12-pdr. Built 1856, captured 1862, sold 1865.

Tyler Sidewheel steamer: 575 tons. **D.** 180′ x 45′ 4″ x 6′. **A.** 6 8-in, 1 32-pdr. **S.** 8 knots. Purchased 1861 by army, transferred 1862, sold 1865. (See p.73)

Umpqua Ironclad monitor: 1175 tons. **D.** 225′ x 45′ x 9′. **A.** 1 11-in. Launched 1865, sold 1874. (See p.38)

Unadilla Screw steamer: 507 tons. **D.** 158′ x 28′ x 9′ 6″. **A.** 1 11-in SB, 1 20-pdr R, 2 24-pdr. Built 1861, sold 1869. (See p.84)

Uncas Screw steamer: 192 tons. **D.** 118′ 6″ x 23′ 4″ x 6′. **A.** 1 20-pdr R, 2 32-pdr. **S.** 11 knots. Built 1843, purchased 1861, sold 1863 owing to poor condition, but remained in merchant service until abandoned in 1886.

Underwriter Sidewheel steamer: 341 tons. **D.** 170′ x 23′ 7″ x 6′. **A.** 1 80-pdr R, 1 8-in SB. Built 1852, purchased 1861. Captured off New Berne by Confederates on February 2, 1864, and set on fire to prevent recapture.

Undine Sternwheel steamer: 179 tons. **A.** 8 24-pdr. Built 1863, purchased 1864. Captured by Confederates on Tennessee River, October 30, 1864. Burnt one mile above Reynolds Island to prevent recapture on November 4.

Union Screw steamer: 1114 tons. **D.** 220′ x 34′ x 16′. **A.** 1 12-pdr R. **S.** 13½ knots. Purchased 1861, sold 1865. Served in merchant marine until destroyed by fire in the Bahamas on October 22, 1872.

Unit Screw tug: 57 tons. **D.** 8′ draft. Built 1862, sold 1865. Served in merchant marine until 1902.

United States Frigate: 1576 tons. **D.** 175′ x 43′ 6″ x 23′ 6″. **A.** 32 24-pdr, 24 32-pdr. **S.** 11 knots. **C.** 364. Launched 1797. Taken out of service at Norfolk Navy Yard in 1849 but was not thought worth destroying when the city fell in April 1861. Used by Confederates as a harbor defense ship armed with 19 guns. Recaptured and broken up in 1865 for the sale of her timbers.

Valley City Screw steamer: 190 tons. **D.** 127′ 6″ x 21′ 10″ x 8′ 4″. **A.** 4 32-pdr. **S.** 10 knots. Built 1859, purchased 1861, sold 1865. Lost at sea off Cape San Blas, Fla., January 30, 1882.

Valparaiso Ship: 402 tons. **D.** 117′ 6″ x 27′ 6″. Built 1836, purchased 1861, sold 1865.

Vandalia Screw sloop: 614 tons. **D.** 127′ 4″ x 34′ 6″ x 16′ 6″. **A.** 4 8-in, 16 32-pdr. **C.** 150. Launched 1828. Taken out of service 1863 and broken up 1872.

Vanderbilt Sidewheel steamer: 3360 tons. **D.** 331′ x 47′ 6″ x 19′. **A.** 2 100-pdr R, 12 9-in SB. **S.** 14 knots. Built 1856, transferred to navy 1862, sold 1873. Ended her days as a coal hulk and scrapped 1899. (See p.142)

Varuna Screw steamer: 1300 tons. **D.** 218′ x 34′ 8″ x 12′. **A.** 8 8-in, 2 30-pdr R. Built 1861, sunk during an action with Confederate vessels while running past the defenses of New Orleans, April 24, 1862.

Velocity Schooner: 87 tons. **A.** 12-pdr. Captured 1862, recaptured by Confederates at Sabine Pass, Tex., January 21, 1863.

Verbena Screw steamer: 104 tons. **D.** 74′ 10″ x 17′ 6″ x 8′ 10″. **A.** 1 20-pdr R, 1 12-pdr. **S.** 12 knots. Built and purchased 1864, sold 1865. Served in the merchant marine until 1900.

Vermont Ship-of-the-line: 2633 tons. **D.** 197′ 2″ x 53′ 6″ x 20′. **A.** 4 8-in, 20 32-pdr. Laid down 1818, completed 1825 but kept on the stocks until 1848, when she was launched because the space was needed. She was originally to have been armed with 20 8-in and 64 32-pdr, and to have a crew of 820. Sold 1902.

Vicksburg Screw steamer: 886 tons. **D.** 185′ x 336′ x 13′ 8″. **A.** 1 100-pdr R, 2 20-pdr. Built and purchased 1863, sold 1865. Served in merchant marine until 1868.

Victoria Screw steamer: 254 tons. **D.** 113′ x 22′ x 12′. **A.** 1 30-pdr R, 2 8-in. **S.** 12 knots. Built 1855, purchased 1861, sold 1865. Served until 1871 in merchant marine.

Victory Sternwheel steamer: 160 tons. **D.** 157′ x 306′ x 5″. **A.** 6 24-pdr H. Built and purchased 1863, sold 1865, and converted soon after into a barge.

Vincennes Sloop: 700 tons. **D.** 127′ x 33′ 9″ x 16′ 6″. **A.** 4 8-in, 14 32-pdr. Launched 1826, sold 1867.

Vindicator Sidewheel steamer: 750 tons. **D.** 6′ draft. **A.** 1 100-pdr R, 2 24-pdr H. Acquired by army 1863, transferred to navy 1864, sold 1866. (See p.90)

Violet Screw tug: 166 tons. **D.** 85′ x 19′ 9″ x 7′. **A.** 2 12-pdr. Purchased 1862. Wrecked and lost at Western Bar Inlet, Cape Fear River, N.C., August 7/8, 1864.

Virginia Ship-of-the-line: 2633 tons. **A.** 74 guns. Laid down 1822, completed 1825 but kept on stocks and broken up 1874 to 1884.

Virginia Screw steamer: 581 tons. **D.** 170′ x 26′ 2″ x 12′. **A.** 6 24-pdr H, 1 12-pdr R. Captured 1863, sold 1865. Converted to barge 1885.

Vixen Sidewheel steamer: 300 tons. **A.** 2 20-pdr R. Acquired 1861 from Coast Survey Dept and returned 1864.

Volunteer Sternwheel steamer: 209 tons. **D.** 5′ draft. **A.** 1 12-pdr. Captured 1863, sold 1865.

W.L. Bartlett Schooner. Purchased 1861 for use as block ship.

W.W. Burns Schooner. Purchased 1861 for use as block ship. Not all vessels purchased for this use, usually referred to as the "Stone Fleet", actually ended up blocking various entrances to river mouths and channels. A number remained at Hampton Roads slowly rotting away and their ultimate fate is unrecorded.

Wabash Screw frigate: 4808 tons. **D.** 301′ 6″ x 51′ 4″ x 23′. **A.** 2 10-in SB, 28 9-in SB, 14 8-in. **S.** 9 knots. Launched 1855, sold 1912.

Wachusett Screw sloop: 1032 tons. **D.** 201′ 4″ x 33′ 11″ x 14′. **A.** 2 11-in SB, 2 30-pdr R, 1 20-pdr R, 4 32-pdr, 1 12-pdr. **S.** 11½ knots. Launched 1862, sold 1887. (See p.147)

Walter Forward Revenue cutter: 150 tons. **A.** 6 9-pdr. Built 1841, sold 1865.

Wampanoag Screw sloop: 4215 tons. **D.** 355′ x 45′ 2″ x 19′ 10″. **A.** 10 9-in SB, 3 60-pdr R. **S.** 17½ knots. Launched 1864, sold 1885. When completed, *Wampanoag* was the fastest steamer afloat and a credit to her designers who had produced an outstanding milestone in the development of the US Navy. (See p.150)

Wamsutta Screw steamer: 270 tons. **D.** 129′ 3″ x 26′ 8″ x 11′. **A.** 1 20-pdr R, 4 32-pdr. Built 1853, purchased 1861, sold 1865.

Wanderer Schooner-rigged yacht: 300 tons. **D.** 106′ x 25′ 6″ x 9′ 6″. **A.** 1 20-pdr R, 2 24-pdr H. **S.** 20 knots. Built 1857, seized 1858 as a suspected slave trader, but released. Turned over by her crew in 1859 after being used as a slaver. Sold 1865 in an unseaworthy condition. Lost at sea off Cape Maisi, Cuba, January 21, 1871.

Wando Sidewheel steamer: 645 tons. **D.** 230′ x 26′ x 7′. **A.** 1 20-pdr R, 2 12-pdr. Captured 1864, sold 1865.

Warren Sloop: 697 tons. **D.** 127′ x 33′ 9″ x 10′ 10″. **A.** 20 24-pdr. **C.** 190. Completed 1827, sold 1863. Ended her days as a coal hulk in 1874.

Washington Revenue cutter. **A.** 10 guns. Built 1837. Taken over by Louisiana State Authorities at New Orleans, January 1861.

Wasp Sidewheel steamer: 521 tons. **D.** 212′ x 256′ 2″ x 6′. **A.** 1 30-pdr R, 2 24-pdr. Captured 1864, sold 1876.

Wassuc Ironclad monitor: 1175 tons. **D.** 225′ x 45′ x 9′. **A.** 1 11-in. Launched 1865, sold 1875. (See p.38)

Watch Screw steamer: 90 tons. **D.** 62′ x 17′ x 6′ 5″. **A.** 1 24-pdr H. Purchased 1861. Built at Norfolk Navy Yard 1863 under the name of *Alert*; rebuilt and sold 1865.

Water Witch Sidewheel steamer: 378 tons. **D.** 150′ x 23′ x 7′ 3″. **A.** 1 8-in, 2 32-pdr. **S.** 9 knots. Completed 1853. Captured in Ossabaw Sound, Ga., June 3, 1864. Burnt by the Confederates at White Bluff, Ga., to prevent recapture. *Water Witch* was the third vessel to carry that name. The first, a 100-ton vessel built in 1845, had a unique propulsion system designed by Lt. W.W. Hunter comprising horizontally-mounted paddle wheels operating in a drum-like structure below water, thereby allowing more guns to be mounted on the broadside, as well as keeping the paddle wheels away from enemy fire.

In 1843 Hunter also proposed fitting a curved lower deck to protect the machinery. In this idea he was years ahead of his time. It would be over forty years later that such decks were given to warships around the world, especially cruisers not fitted with side armor, so that the machinery should be effectively protected.

Unfortunately the propulsive system was not a success, so this vessel was rebuilt in 1845 and emerged as a 255-ton gunboat with the length increased by 30 ft to 131 ft. The machinery, which was the more conventional type, was removed in 1851 and used in the third *Water Witch*. (See p.104)

Wateree Sidewheel steamer: 974 tons. **D.** 205′ x 35′ x 4′ 4″. **A.** 2 100-pdr, 4 9-in SB, 2 24-pdr H, 4 12-pdr. Launched 1863. Driven 500 yards inland by a tidal wave at Arica, Peru, on August 13, 1868. Sold and converted into living quarters. (See p.104)

Wave Sidewheel steamer: 229 tons. **A.** 6 guns. Built and purchased in 1863. Captured May 6, 1864 and used by Confederates as a transport until destroyed to prevent recapture.

Waxsaw Ironclad monitor: 1175 tons. **D.** 225′ x 45′ x 9′. **A.** 1 11-in. Launched 1865, scrapped 1875. (See p.38)

Weehawken Ironclad monitor: 1875 tons. **D.** 200′ x 46′ x 11′ 6″. **A.** 1 15-in SB, 1 11-in SB. Launched 1862. Foundered off Morris Island, Charleston, on December 6, 1863 while loading ammunition which had been stowed forward in too large a quantity and altered the trim. Unfortunately, the forward hatch being open, water found its way below. Ordinarily all water ran aft and was thrown out by the pumps in the engine-room, but with the changed trim this did not happen and a large quantity of water accumulated forward which brought down the bow even more.

This fatal condition was not discovered until nearly fifteen minutes before she sank. Desperate efforts were made to save her but the reserve buoyancy of 125 tons was reached before the pumps began gaining on the rising water and *Weehawken* went down. Thirty crew died in her, including two engineer officers who went back below to try to save the vessel. (See p.26)

Western World Screw steamer: 441 tons. **D.** 178′ x 34′ 3″ x 8′ 6″. **A.** 1 30-pdr R, 2 32-pdr R. Built 1856, purchased 1861, sold 1865.

Westfield Sidewheel steamer: 822 tons. **D.** 215′ x 35′. **A.** 1 100-pdr R, 1 9-in SB, 4 8-in SB. Purchased 1861. Blown up to prevent capture on January 1, 1863 at Galveston, Tex. (See p.78)

Whitehall Sidewheel steamer: 326 tons. **D.** 126′ x 28′ 2″ x 8′. **A.** 4 32-pdr. Built 1850, purchased 1861. Destroyed by flash fire at Old Point, Va., March 10, 1862.

Whitehead Screw steamer: 136 tons. **D.** 93′ 2″ x 19′ 9″ x 8″. **A.** 1 30-pdr R. **S.** 8 knots. Built and purchased 1861, sold 1865. Served in merchant marine until destroyed by fire at New London, Conn., September 1, 1872.

Wild Cat Schooner: 30 tons. Captured 1862, sold 1865.

Wilderness Sidewheel steamer: 390 tons. **D.** 137′ x 25′ x 6′. **A.** 4 24-pdr. **S.** 13 knots. Purchased 1864, sold 1891.

William Bacon Schooner: 183 tons. **D.** 95′ x 26′ x 8′ 10″. **A.** 1 13-in M, 2 32-pdr. Purchased 1861, sold 1865.

William Badger Whaler: 334 tons. **D.** 106′ x 26′ x 14′. Purchased 1861, sold 1865 and broken up soon after. She was used as a depot ship.

William G. Anderson Bark: 593 tons. **D.** 149′ 7″ x 30′ 1″ x 14′. **A.** 6 32-pdr, 1 24-pdr. Built 1859, purchased 1861, sold 1866.

William G. Putnam Screw tug: 149 tons. **D.** 103′ 6″ x 22′ x 7′. **A.** 1 32-pdr R, 24-pdr. Built 1857, purchased 1861, transferred to Treasury Dept and broken up 1885.

William H. Brown Sidewheel steamer: 800 tons. **A.** 2 12-pdr. Transferred to navy 1862, served as transport. Sold 1865.

William L. Jones Schooner. Purchased 1861 for use as block ship.

William Lee Ship: 418 tons. Purchased 1861 for use as block ship. She was the last wooden-built whaler constructed at Newport, R.I.

Winnebago Ironclad monitor: 1500 tons. **D.** 229′ x 56′ x 6′. **A.** 4 11-in SB. Launched 1863, sold 1874. (See pp 12, 13)

Winnipec Sidewheel steamer: 1030 tons. **D.** 225′ x 35′ x 5′ 8″. Built 1864, sold 1869.

Winona Screw steamer: 507 tons. **D.** 158′ x 28′ x 10′ 6″. **A.** 1 11-in SB, 1 20-pdr R, 2 24-pdr H. Built 1861, sold 1865. (See p.84)

Winooski Sidewheel steamer: 974 tons. **D.** 205′ x 35′ x 12′. **A.** 10 guns. Launched 1863, sold 1868. (See p.104)

Wissahickon Screw steamer: 507 tons. **D.** 158′ x 28′ x 10′ 8″. **A.** 1 11-in SB, 1 20-pdr R, 2 24-pdr H. Built 1861, sold 1865. (See pp 84, 85)

Worcester Screw sloop: 3050 tons. **D.** 296′ 10″ x 41′ x 9′ 9″. **A.** 4 12-pdr. Laid down 1863, launched 1866, sold 1888. (See p.142)

Wyalusing Sidewheel steamer: 974 tons. **D.** 205′ x 35′ x 9′. **A.** 2 100-pdr R, 4 9-in SB, 4 24-pdr H, 2 12-pdr R. Launched 1863, sold 1867. (See p.104)

Wyandank Sidewheel steamer: 400 tons. **D.** 132′ 5″ x 31′ 5″ x 8′. **A.** 2 12-pdr. Built 1847, purchased 1861, broken up 1879. Ended her career as floating barracks.

Wyandotte Screw steamer: 464 tons. **A.** 4 32-pdr, 1 24-pdr H. **S.** 7 knots. Built 1853, purchased 1861, sold 1865. Stranded and damaged beyond economical repair when she ran aground off Duxbury, Mass., on January 26, 1866.

Wyoming Screw sloop: 1457 tons. **D.** 198′ 6″ x 33′ 2″ x 14′ 10″. **A.** 2 11-in SB, 1 60-pdr R, 3 32-pdr. Launched 1859, sold 1892. Spent last ten years of career as practice ship at Naval Academy, Annapolis.

Yankee Sidewheel steamer: 328 tons. **D.** 146′ x 25′ 7″ x 9′. **A.** 2 32-pdr. Built 1860, purchased 1861, sold 1865.

Yanctic Screw steamer: 836 tons. **D.** 179′ x 30′ x 13′ 9″. **A.** 1 100-pdr R, 1 30-pdr R, 2 9-in SB, 2 24-pdr H. **S.** 9½ knots. **C.** 154. Launched 1864. Sank at dockside on October 22, 1929 at Townsend Avenue, Detroit, Mich.

Yazoo Ironclad monitor: 1175 tons. **D.** 225′ x 45′ x 9′. **A.** 1 11-in. Launched 1865, sold 1874. (See p.38)

Young America Screw tug: 173 tons. **D.** 10′ 6″ draft. **A.** 1 30-pdr R, 1 32-pdr, 1 12-pdr. Captured 1861, sold 1865.

Young Rover Screw steamer: 418 tons. **D.** 141′ x 28′ 1″ x 11′. **A.** 1 12-pdr R, 4 32-pdr. **S.** 13 knots. Purchased 1861, sold 1865.

Yucca Screw steamer: 373 tons. **D.** 145′ 7″ x 23′ 7″ x 10′. **A.** 1 30-pdr R, 1 12-pdr. Built 1864, purchased 1865, sold 1868.

Yuma Ironclad monitor: 1175 tons. **D.** 225′ x 45′ x 9′. **A.** 1 11-in. Launched 1865, sold 1874. (See p.38)

Zeta Screw steamer: 60 tons. **D.** 58′ x 13′ x 7′ 6″. **A.** 1 torpedo. **S.** 8½ knots. Built 1844, purchased 1864, sold 1865.

Zouave Screw tug: 127 tons. **D.** 9′ draft. **A.** 2 30-pdr R. **S.** 14 knots. Built and purchased 1861, sold 1865.

WARSHIPS OF THE CONFEDERATE STATES NAVY

KEY: **D.** = Dimensions. **A.** = Armament. **S.** = Speed. **C.** = Crew. SB. = Smoothbore. R. = Rifle. H. = Howitzer. M. = Mortar.

A.B. Seger Sidewheel steamer: 30 tons. **D.** 55′ long. **A.** 2 guns. Purchased 1862. Captured after being run aground and abandoned near Berwick Bay, November 1, 1862.

A.C. Gunnison Screw tug: 54 tons. **D.** 70′ x 15′ x 7′. **A.** 2 6-pdr, 1 spar torpedo. **C.** 10. Served as privateer from May 1861. Taken over by Confederate Navy 1862 and surrendered April 1865.

A.D. Vance Sidewheel steamer. Used as blockade runner. Captured September 10, 1864 after making over twenty successful dashes through the blockade.

Aiken Revenue cutter: 82 tons. **A.** 2 guns. Surrendered to South Carolina Authorities December 1860. Became privateer July 1861. Renamed *Petre*, and sunk 28 July.

A.S. Ruthven Sidewheel steamer: 144 tons. **D.** 127′ x 30′ x 4′ 8″. **Built** 1860, chartered October 1863 by Texas Marine Dept for use as transport. Lost 1869.

A.W. Baker Sidewheel steamer: 112 tons. **D.** 95′ x 256′ x 4′ 6″. Built 1856, used as cargo ship. Captured by *Queen of the West* after being run ashore in the Red River, February 2, 1863.

Acacia Steamer. Used as transport. Captured June 1862, sunk August 1862.

Admiral Sidewheel steamer. Used as picket boat. Captured New Madrid April 7, 1862.

Adventure Screw steamer: 972 tons. **D.** 250′ x 28′ x 12′. Cover name for *Waccamaw* which was built in England as a raider. Sold 1865.

Agrippina Bark: 285 tons. **D.** 97′ x 24′ 4″ x 16′. Built 1834. Chartered 1862 for use as tender to *Alabama*. (See p.114)

Aid Schooner. Captured off Mobile on June 5, 1861. Used as block ship off Santa Rosa Island, August 1861.

Aid Steamer. **A.** 1 42-pdr. Privately purchased 1861. Engines used on *Chicora* in November 1862.

Ajax Screw steamer: 515 tons. **D.** 170′ x 256′ x 7′ 6″. **A.** 1 9-in R, 1 8-in R. **S.** 12 knots. Built in England 1864, sold 1865.

Alabama Screw sloop: 1050 tons. **D.** 220′ x 31′ 8″ x 14′. **A.** 1 110-pdr, 1 68-pdr, 6 32-pdr. **S.** 13 knots. **C.** 145. Built 1862. Sunk off Cherbourg, France, by *Kearsage*, June 19, 1864. (See p.114)

Alamo Steamer. Used as transport; served with Texas Marine Dept in 1863.

Alar Sidewheel steamer: 150 tons. **D.** 134′ x 17′ x 9′ 3″. Built 1847. Chartered as tender to *Georgia*.

Albatross Sternwheel steamer: 1063 tons. **D.** 240′ x 30′ x 10′. A fast steamer built in England early 1865. Sold and renamed *Isabel*.

Albemarle Sternwheel steamer: 183 tons. Built 1855. Used as a transport. Captured off New Berne by *Delaware*, March 15, 1862. Sank after running onto piling at New Berne, April 5, 1862.

Albemarle Ironclad. **D.** 152′ x 34′ x 9′. **A.** 2 6, 4-in R. Completed 1864, sunk by torpedo boat at 3 a.m. on October 28, 1864 at Plymouth, N.C. (See pp.58, 59)

Alena Sloop. Used as a transport. Captured June 1861 in Pamunkey River.

Alert Schooner. **A.** 1 32-pdr. Seized at Mobile, Ala., 1861. Served until 1862.

Alexandra Screw steamer: 124 tons. **A.** 4 guns. Built in UK as gift from Fraser, Trenholm to Confederate government. Launched March 7, 1863. Seized by UK authorities.

Alfred Robb Sternwheel steamer: 79 tons. **D.** 114′ 9″ x 20′ x 4′. **S.** 9 knots. Built 1860. Used as a transport. Captured at Florence, Ala., April 19, 1862.

Alliance Schooner. Captured by Confederates at Eastville, Va., September 19, 1863. Driven ashore by Union vessels at Old Haven Creek and burnt to prevent recapture, September 23, 1863.

Alliance Steamer. Blockade runner, 1863. Captured May 1864.

Allison Steamer. Used as a transport on James River.

Alonzo Child Sidewheel steamer: 493 tons. **D.** 222′ x 36′ x 6′. **A.** 8-in, 10-in, 6-in R. Built 1857. Engines used for *Tennessee* in May 1863 and hull used as obstruction in Yazoo River. Raised by Union forces.

Amazon Sidewheel steamer: 372 tons. **D.** 2′ draft. Built 1856; used as a transport. Surrendered at Savannah, March 2, 1865.

Anglo-Norman Sidewheel steamer: 558 tons. **D.** 176′ 2″ x 29′ 5″ x 9′. **A.** 1 32-pdr. **C.** 35. Built 1850; taken into Confederate service January 1862 and captured April 1862.

Anglo-Saxon Sidewheel steamer: 558 tons. **D.** 120′ 3″ x 28′ x 8′. Built 1848, taken over 1862. Struck by mortar fire and set alight, April 24, 1862, and repaired but then captured by Union forces.

Anna Dale Schooner: 70 tons. **A.** 1 12-pdr. Privateer. Captured February 1865 off Pass Cavallo, Tex; she was then run aground and set on fire.

Anna Perrette Sternwheel steamer: 173 tons. **D.** 130′ x 32′ x 4′ 6″. Built 1857. Used to transport cotton.

Appleton Belle Sternwheel steamer: 103 tons. Built 1856. Burnt at Paris, Tenn., to prevent capture, February 7, 1862.

Appomattox Tug. **A.** 2 guns. Purchased 1862. Unable to pass through the lock into Dismal Swamp Lake, she was blown up.

Arladia Transport. Burnt and scuttled on Yazoo River to prevent capture, July 1863.

Archer Schooner: 90 tons. **A.** 1 12-pdr H. Captured off Long Island by bark *Tacony*, June 24, 1863. Abandoned off Portland, Me., and recaptured.

Arctic Ironclad floating battery. **A.** 3 guns. Built at Wilmington 1863; sunk in channel as obstruction December 24, 1864.

Argo Sternwheel steamer: 99 tons. Built 1859. Burnt 1863.

Argosy Steamer. Destroyed to prevent capture on Sunflower River, Miss., 1863.

Argus Sternwheel steamer. Used as army transport. Captured October 7, 1863 and destroyed by Union forces to prevent recapture.

Arizona Sidewheel steamer: 578 tons. **D.** 200′ x 34′ x 8′. Built 1858 and taken over 1862. Used as a blockade runner until captured off Mobile, October 28, 1862. Burnt near New Orleans, February 27, 1865.

Arkansas Ironclad. **D.** 165′ x 35′ x 11′ 6″. **A.** 9-in SB, 2 9-in, 2 9-in shell guns, 2 6-9in R, 2 30-pdr. Completed 1862. Drifted ashore near Baton Rouge, August 6, 1862 and burnt to prevent capture. (See p.54)

Arrow Steamer. **A.** 1 32-pdr. Seized 1861. Burnt in West Pearl River to prevent capture, June 4, 1862.

Arrow Steam tug. Used as a picket boat in 1861.

Atlanta Ironclad: 1006 tons. **D.** 204′ x 41′ x 156′ 9″. **A.** 2 7-in R, 2 6, 4-in R. Built 1861, converted 1862. Captured in Wassaw Sound, Ga., by monitors *Weehawken* and *Nahant*, June 17, 1863. (See p.45)

Atlantic Sidewheel steamer: 623 tons. Seized 1862. Used as blockade runner until grounded at Lockwoods Folly in the Cape Fear River, Wilmington, September 24, 1863. She was later burnt.

Austin Sidewheel steamer: 1150 tons. **D.** 200′ x 34′ x 86′. **S.** 10 knots. Built 1859, seized 1862 and used as a blockade runner until captured on June 6, 1864. Returned to owners, Southern Steam Ship Co., 1865.

B.M. Moore Sternwheel steamer: 38 tons. **D.** 81′ 5″ x 17′ 1″ x 3′ 8″ **A.** 2 12-pdr H. Captured September 30, 1862, sold 1865.

Bahama Screw steamer: 888 tons. **D.** 226′ x 29′ 2″ x 19′. Built 1862. Still in service 1863. Tender at one time to *Alabama*.

Baltic Ironclad: 624 tons. **D.** 186′ x 38′ x 66′ 5″. **A.** 6 guns. Built 1860, converted 1862, surrendered May 10, 1865, sold December 1865. (See p.42)

Banshee (See pp.156, 157)

Barataria Sternwheel steamer: 400 tons. **D.** 125′ x 3′ 6″ draft. **A.** 2 guns. Plated with 1-in iron 1861, captured April 1862, destroyed after striking obstruction on Lake Maurepas, Amite River, April 7, 1863.

Bartow Schooner: 74 tons. **A.** 1 24-pdr, 1 6-pdr.

Bat Sidewheel steamer: 771 tons. **D.** 230′ x 26′ x 7′ 6″. **S.** 16 knots. Blockade runner. Captured October 8, 1864.

Bayou City Steamer. **D.** 3′draft. **A.** 1 32-pdr. Chartered by Texas Marine Dept. from 1861 to 1865.

Beaufort Screw tug: 85 tons. **D.** 85′ x 17′ 5″ x 56′. **A.** 1 gun. Built 1854, taken over 1861, surrendered April 3, 1865, sold 1865.

Beauregard Schooner: 101 tons. **A.** 1 24-pdr. Privateer 1861. Captured November 12, 1861.

Beauregard Sternwheel steamer. Used as transport. Captured January 1865.

Beauregard Schooner. Used as transport. Burnt May 4 1862.

Beauregard Steamer. Used as transport. Captured on Red River June 6, 1864.

Belle Algerine Steamer. Sunk in collision with *Governor Moore* April 24, 1862.

Ben McCullock Sternwheel steamer: 80 tons. Built 1860. Burnt on Tchula Lake to prevent capture, July 1863.

Bermuda Screw steamer: 888 tons. **D.** 226′ x 29′ x 16′. Built 1861. (See p.153)

Berosa Steamer. Built 1840s. Sank April 8 1863 after springing leak.

Berwick Bay Steamer: 64 tons. Used as transport. Captured and destroyed February 3, 1863.

Bienville Sidewheel steamer. **A.** 5 42-pdr. Built 1861. Sunk to prevent capture on Lake Pontchartrain, April 21, 1862.

Black Diamond Sternwheel steamer. **D.** 156′ x 48′ x 36′ 6″. Built 1865, surrendered May 1865.

Black Prince (See p.122)

Black Warrior Schooner. **A.** 2 32-pdr. Burnt to prevent capture, February 10, 1862.

Blue Wing Sternwheel steamer: 170 tons. Seized December 1862 by Union forces but ran aground soon after and taken back into Confederate service.

Bombshell Steamer. **D.** 90′ x 3′ 6″ draft. **A.** 3 H, 1 20-pdr. Sunk by Confederate batteries April 18, 1864 and raised. Recaptured in Albermarle Sound, May 5, 1864.

Boston Screw tug. **D.** 9′ draft. Captured June 8, 1863, recaptured July 8, 1864.

Bracelet Sternwheel steamer: 169 tons. Built 1857.

Bradford Steamer. Used as transport. Destroyed 1862.

Breaker Schooner. Run ashore and set alight August 12, 1862. Rebuilt by Union forces and used as tender.

Caleb Cushing Schooner: 153 tons. **D.** 100′ 4″ x 23′ x 9′ 7″. **A.** 1 32-pdr, 1 12-pdr. Used as revenue cutter. Seized June 27, 1863, blown up later same day.

Calhoun Sidewheel steamer; 509 tons. **A.** 1 18-pdr, 2 12-pdr, 2 6-pdr. Built 1851, became privateer May 1861, taken over by Confederate Navy, captured January 23, 1862. (See p.122)

Capitol Sidewheel steamer: 499 tons. **D.** 244′ x 32′ x 6′. Built 1855. Burnt June 1862 and used as obstruction in Yazoo River July 1862.

Carondelet Sidewheel steamer. **A.** 5 42-pdr, 1 32-pdr. Built 1862. Sunk on Lake Pontchartrain, April 4, 1862.

Castor Bark: 252 tons. Built 1851. Used as a tender.

Caswell Sidewheel steamer. Burnt at Wilmington 1865.

Catawba Steamer. Surrendered 1865.

Charleston Ironclad. **D.** 180′ x 34′ x 10′. **A.** 4 R, 2 9-in SB. **C.** 150. Built 1863, set on fire to prevent capture February 18, 1865. (See p.50)

Charm Sidewheel steamer: 223 tons. Built 1860, sunk 1863.

Chattahoochee Sidewheel steamer. **D.** 150′ x 25′ x 8′. **D.** 150′ x 25′ x 8′. **A.** 5 32-pdr, 1 9-in. Built 1862, destroyed to prevent capture on Apalachicola River, December 1864.

Cheney Steamer. Operated on Mississippi River 1861 to 1863.

Cheops Ironclad: 900 tons. **D.** 171′ 10″ x 32′ 8″ x 14′ 14″. **A.** 1 300-pdr, 2 6-in. Built 1863–65. Sold to Prussians and renamed *Prinz Adalbert.* Broken up 1878.

Chesapeake Screw steamer. Built 1853, rebuilt 1857. Seized December 7, 1863. Restored to owners and remained in service until 1881.

Chesterfield Sidewheel steamer: 204 tons. Built 1853, chartered as transport 1861.

Chickamauga Screw steamer: 585 tons. **A.** 3 R. Purchased 1864, sunk to prevent capture on Cape Fear River, January 1865. (See p.128)

Chicora Ironclad. **D.** 150′ x 35′. **A.** 2 9-in, 4 32-pdr R. Built 1862; destroyed to prevent capture February 18, 1865 at Charleston. (See p.50)

City of Richmond Steamer. Used to transport stores to *Stonewall* off Quiberon, France, January 1865.

Clara Dolsen Sidewheel steamer: 939 tons. **D.** 268′ x 42′ x 6′. Built 1861, captured on White River, June 14, 1862.

Clarence Brig: 253 tons. **D.** 114′ x 24′ x 11′. **A.** 1 12-pdr. Built 1857, captured May 6, 1863 by *Florida,* burnt to prevent recapture June 12, 1863.

Clarendon Steamer: 143 tons. Built 1860. Seized by Union forces off Fort Fisher and burnt March 14, 1865.

Clifton Sidewheel steamer: 892 tons. **D.** 210′ x 40′ x 7′ 6″. **A.** 4 32-pdr, 2 9-in SB, 1 30-pdr. Built 1861 as ferry boat. Purchased for US Navy 1861, captured Sabine Pass, Tex., September 8, 1863. Grounded and set on fire, March 21, 1864.

Colonel Hill Steamer. Used as transport. Boarded and burnt by Union forces July 20, 1863 near Tarborough, Tar River, N.C.

Colonel Lamb Sidewheel steamer: 1788 tons. **D.** 281′ x 36′ x 10′. Built 1864 as blockade runner. At end of war blew up at Liverpool, England, after loading explosives for Brazil.

Colonel Lovell Sidewheel steamer: 521 tons. **D.** 162′ x 30′ 10″ x 11′. Built 1843, sunk off Memphis, Tenn., June 6, 1862. (See p.92)

Colonel Stell Sidewheel steamer: 199 tons. **D.** 138′ x 24′ x 4′. Built 1860, accidentally sunk off Pelican Island in Galveston Bay on February 10, 1864, but raised. Surrendered 1865, sold 1866, lost at sea December 21, 1867.

Columbia Ironclad. **D.** 216′ x 51′ 4″ x 13′ 6″. **A.** 6 guns. Built 1864, run onto sunken wreck in Charleston Harbor, January 12, 1865. Raised April 26, 1865, sold 1865. (See p.52)

Condor Sidewheel steamer: 300 tons. **D.** 270′ x 24′ x 7′. Used as blockade runner. Ran aground on Swash Channel Bar, Wilmington, N.C., October 1, 1864, Rose Greenhow, a famous writer, was lost while trying to escape in the surf.

Coquette Sternwheel steamer: 238 tons. Built 1859. Blockade runner 1864.

Coquette Screw steamer: 300 tons. **D.** 220′ x 25′ x 10′. **S.** 13½ knots. Built 1863, turned over to US government December 1865.

Cornubia Sidewheel steamer: 411 tons. **D.** 190′ x 24′ 6″ x 9′. **S.** 18 knots. Built 1858. Ran ashore off Wilmington but towed off by Union vessels, November 8, 1863.

Corpus Christi Served with Texas Marine Dept, 1864.

Corypheus Schooner: 81 tons. **D.** 72′ x 20′ x 6′. Built 1859, taken over by Confederates 1861. Seized by Union forces, May 13, 1862.

Cotton Sidewheel steamer: 549 tons. **A.** 1 32-pdr, 1 9-pdr. Built 1861, purchased 1862 and partly covered with iron. Burnt to prevent capture off Brashear City, La., January 15, 1863.

Cotton Plant Sidewheel steamer: Built 1859. Used as transport. Burnt to prevent capture on Tallahatchie River, July 1863.

Cotton Plant Sternwheel steamer: 85 tons. **D.** 107′ x 18′ 9″ x 4′ 5″. Built 1860, turned over to US authorities May 1865.

Countess Sidewheel steamer: 198 tons. **D.** 150′ x 30′ x 4′. Built 1860. Ran aground near Alexandria and burnt to prevent capture.

Curlew Sidewheel steamer: 260 tons. **D.** 150′ x 4′ 6″ draft. **A.** 2 guns. **S.** 12 knots. Built 1856. Sunk to prevent capture on Roanoke River, February 8, 1862.

Curlew Sidewheel steamer: 645 tons. **D.** 225′ x 24′ x 6′. Used as blockade runner. Laid down 1864, completed 1865, too late for use in war.

Currituck Steam tug. Saw service along N. Carolina waters, 1862–63.

Curtis Peck Sidewheel steamer: 446 tons. Built 1842, Used as block ship at Drewry's Bluff, September 1862.

Cyclone (See p.126)

D. Bentley Built 1840s. Fitted out as gunboat 1863 for service on Red River.

Dalman Served Mobile Bay. Surrendered May 4, 1865.

Damascus Transport. Sunk to obstruct James River 1862.

Dan Steamer: 112 tons. Built 1858, captured October 1862 on Calcasieu River, sunk on Mississippi February 1863.

Danube Floating battery: 980 tons. **D.** 170′ 4″ x 30′ 11″ x 16′ 11″. **A.** 4 42-pdr. Built 1854, seized Mobile Bay 1861. Used as part of bay defense, then sunk November 1864 in upper line of obstructions in Spanish River.

Darby Steamer. Used as transport. Sunk at Bayou Teche, April 14, 1863.

Darlington Sidewheel steamer: 298 tons. Built 1849, captured off Fernandinda, Fla., March 3, 1862.

David Submarine. **D.** 50′ x 6′ x 5′. **A.** 1 spar torpedo. Built 1863. Captured Charleston 1865 along with several other vessels of the same type. (See p.159)

De Sota Sidewheel steamer. Used as transport. Surrendered May 1862 at Island No. 10.

Deer Sidewheel steamer: 857 tons. **D.** 238′ x 26′ 2″ x 7′ 6″. Last of group of four units built in UK, 1864. Captured off Charleston February 18, 1865. Sold to Argentina 1869.

Defiance Sidewheel steamer: 544 tons. **D.** 178′ x 29′ 5″ x 6′. **A.** 1 32-pdr. Built 1849, purchased 1861. Burnt to prevent capture at New Orleans, La., April 28, 1862.

Delight Schooner. Captured off Cat Island Passage in Mississippi Sound, December 9, 1861.

Dew Drop Sidewheel steamer: 184 tons. Built 1858. Burnt on Sunflower River to prevent capture, May 30, 1863.

Diana Steamer. **D.** 3′ 2″ draft. **A.** 2 12-pdr. bows plated with 1-in armor. Served with Texas Marine Dept.

Diana Sidewheel steamer: 239 tons. **A.** 5 guns. Seized at New Orleans April 27, 1862. Recaptured at Bayou Teche near Pattersonville, La., March 28, 1863. Burnt to prevent capture at Bayou Teche, April 12, 1863.

Dick Keys Steamer. Captured off Mobile, May 8, 1861. Used as a transport.

Dime Steamer. Served with Texas Marine Dept, 1863–64.

Dixie Schooner: 110 tons. **A.** 3 guns. Built 1856. Privateer 1861. Captured off Georgetown, S.C., April 15, 1862.

Dodge Schooner: 153 tons. **D.** 100′ 4″ x 23′ x 6′. **A.** 1 9-pdr. Used as revenue cutter. Seized March 1861. Became blockade runner 1864. Captured off Galveston, Tex., April 4, 1864.

Dollie Webb Sternwheel steamer: 139 tons. **A.** 5 guns. Built 1859, converted to gunboat 1861.

Dolly Steamer. Seized at Edwards Ferry 1865. Reported sunk in canal May 1865.

Don Screw steamer: 390 tons. **D.** 162′ x 23′ x 6′. **S.** 14 knots. **C.** 43. Captured off Wilmington, N.C., March 4, 1864.

Doubloon Sidewheel steamer: 293 tons. **D.** 165′ x 33′ x 5′. Built 1859, burnt to prevent capture on Red River in May 1863.

Dr Beatty Sidewheel steamer: 281 tons. **D.** 171′ x 28′ 9″ x 4′. **A.** 1 20-pdr. Built 1850. Used as a transport and boarding ship for 250 men from 1862. Still in service July 1863.

Drewry Steamer: 166 tons. **D.** 106′ x 21′ x 5′. **A.** 1 6, 4-in R, 1 7-in R. Iron V-shaped shield fitted to foredeck. Destroyed by magazine explosion at Trents Reach, January 24, 1865.

Duane Schooner: 153 tons. **D.** 102′ x 23′ x 9′ 7″. Used as revenue cutter. Seized April 1861.

Dunbar Sidewheel steamer: 213 tons. Built 1859.

Eastport Ironclad: 700 tons. **D.** 280′ x 6′ 3″ draft. Built 1852. Partly converted into ironclad before being seized by Union forces February 7, 1862. Sunk by mine in Red River, April 15, 1864.

Edward J. Gay Sidewheel steamer: 823 tons. Built 1859. Seized February 1863 and scuttled to avoid capture on Yazoo River July 1863.

Egypt Mills Screw steamer: 70 tons. Built 1856. Seized and served as transport. Captured in Roanoke River, May 22 1865. Served in merchant marine until 1869.

Eliza G Steamer. Used as a transport. Sunk as obstruction in White River near St Charles, Ark., June 16, 1862.

Ellis Sidewheel tug. **A.** 1 32-pdr R, 1 H. Purchased 1861, captured Elizabeth City February 10, 1862. Grounded New River, N.C., November 12, 1862, and set on fire to prevent recapture.

Elma Schooner. Taken into Confederate Army service July 1862. Grounded in Nueces Bay, August 11, 1862. Fired next day to prevent capture.

Elmira Sternwheel steamer: 139 tons. **D.** 125′ x 27′ x 4′ 6″. Built 1858, purchased 1861, captured in Tensas River July 13, 1863.

Emma Betts Steamer: 79 tons. Built 1858. Served as transport until captured and burnt in Quiver Bayou, May 30, 1863.

Empire Steamer. Chartered 1861.

Empire Parish Sidewheel steamer: 279 tons. **D.** 56′ x 31′ x 6′. Built 1859, captured April 1862 at New Orleans.

Enterprise Screw steamer: 972 tons. **D.** 250′ x 28′. Built 1864, sold 1865.

Equator Sidewheel tug. **A.** 1 gun. Converted to gunboat March 1864. Sunk to prevent capture at Wilmington, 1865.

Era No. 3 Steamer: 144 tons. **D.** 129′ x 28′ 4″ x 4′. Built 1858. Served with Texas Marine Dept.

Era No. 5 Sternwheel steamer: 115 tons. Built 1860, chartered 1863, captured on Black River, February 14, 1863.

Etiwan Sidewheel steamer: 132 tons. Built 1834, wrecked Charleston Harbor 1865. Repaired and used to clear mines by Union forces.

Express Sloop. Served as privateer, December 1861.

Fairplay Sidewheel steamer: 156 tons. **D.** 5′ draft. Built 1859, captured August 18, 1862, sold 1865.

Falcon Sidewheel steamer: 285 tons. **D.** 270′ x 24′ x 7′. **S.** 18 knots. Built 1864. Used as a blockade runner. Made 20 knots on trials.

Fanny Screw steamer. **A.** 1 32-pdr, 1 8-pdr R. US Army transport. Captured October 1861, ran aground and blown up to prevent recapture at Elizabeth City, N.C., February 10, 1862.

Fanny Morgan Yacht: 8 tons. **D.** 26′ x 11′. Loaned October 1861; joined Texas Marine Dept.

Ferd Kennet Sidewheel steamer: 591 tons. Built 1861, seized May. Burnt and scuttled July 1863 at Yalobusha River to prevent capture.

Firefly Sidewheel steamer. **A.** 1 gun. Purchased 1861. Burnt at Savannah to prevent capture, December 21, 1864.

Fisher Sidewheel steamer: 66 tons. Captured while being built at Edwards Ferry, N.C. Sold 1865, lost at sea 1873.

Flamingo Sidewheel steamer: 284 tons. **D.** 270′ x 24′ x 7′. **S.** 16 knots. **C.** 45. Built 1864, run ashore at Charleston Harbor 1865.

Florida Screw steamer: 460 tons. **D.** 171′ x 29′11″ x 8′. **A.** 4 guns. Built 1859, captured March 1862.

Florida Schooner. **A.** 1 6-pdr. Privateer 1861.

Florida Screw sloop. **D.** 191′ x 27′ 2″ x 13′. **A.** 6 6-in R, 2 7-in R, 1 12-pdr. **S.** 9½ knots, 12 under canvas. Built 1861. Seized while in neutral port, October 1864. Rammed and sunk at Newport News, November 28, 1864. (See p.124)

Florilda Steamer. Used as a transport 1863.

Warships of the Confederate States Navy

Flycatcher Screw steamer: 37 tons. Sunk as obstruction in Atchafalaya River, La., November 1862.

Forrest Steam tug. **A.** 3 guns. Purchased 1861, damaged in action at Roanoke Island February 7, 1862. While being repaired on slip at Elizabeth City, set on fire to prevent capture.

Fredericksburg Ironclad. **D.** 188′ x 40′ 3″ x 9′ 6″. **A.** 1 11-in SB, 1 8-in R, 2 6-in R. Built 1862–63. Blown up to prevent capture below Richmond, April 4, 1865. (See p.68)

Frolic Sidewheel steamer: 296 tons. Built 1860. Served on Red River 1864.

Fulton Sidewheel steamer: 698 tons. **D.** 180′ x 34′ 8″ x 10′ 6″. **A.** 4 32-pdr. **S.** 10 knots. **C.** 130. Built 1837, captured at Pensacola Navy Yard January 1861. Destroyed while still in yard to prevent recapture, May 10, 1862.

G.H. Smoot Schooner: 36 tons. Used as a transport. Captured May 18, 1862.

Gaines Sidewheel steamer: 863 tons. **D.** 202′ x 38′ x 6′. **A.** 1 8-in R, 5 32-pdr. **S.** 10 knots. **C.** 130. Built of unseasoned timber 1861–62. Run aground to prevent capture at Mobile Bay, Ala., August 5, 1864. (See p.92)

Gallatin Schooner: 112 tons. **D.** 73′ 4″ x 20′ 6″ x 6′. Built 1831; sister to revenue cutter *Caleb Cushing*. Seized April 1861. Among first to become privateers.

Gallego Schooner: 596 tons. **D.** 144′ x 30′ x 12′. Built 1855. Used as cargo ship until run aground at Drewry's Bluff because of poor condition, 1864. Floated off and turned over to army, January 18, 1865.

General Beauregard Sidewheel steamer. Part of River Defense Fleet. Blown up and sunk off Memphis, June 6, 1862.

General Beauregard Sidewheel steamer. **A.** 4 guns. Served at Mobile 1863.

General Bee Sidewheel steamer. Guard whip at Corpus Christi Bay 1862.

General Bragg Sidewheel steamer: 1043 tons. **D.** 208′ x 32′ 8″ x 12′. **A.** 1 30-pdr R, 1 32-pdr, 1 12-pdr. **S.** 10 knots. Built 1851, captured off Memphis June 6, 1862. (See p.101)

General Breckinridge Sidewheel steamer. **A.** 1 24-pdr. **C.** 35. Formed part of River Defense Fleet. Burnt to prevent capture at New Orleans, April 24, 1862.

General Clinch Sidewheel steamer: 256 tons. **A.** 2 guns. Built 1839, acquired 1861, sank Charleston Harbor 1864. Raised for possible use as blockade runner.

General Earl Van Dorn Sidewheel steamer. **A.** 1 32-pdr. Part of Mississippi Defense Force. Burnt in Yazoo River to prevent capture, June 26, 1862.

General Lee Sidewheel steamer. Used as transport. Captured at Savannah, December 1864.

General Lovell Sidewheel tug. **A.** 1 32-pdr. Part of River Defense Fleet. Burnt to prevent capture below New Orleans, April 24, 1862.

General M. Jeff Thompson Sidewheel steamer. Part of River Defense Fleet. Blew up after running aground June 6, 1862.

General Polk Sidewheel steamer: 390 tons. **A.** 5 guns. Built 1852, purchased 1861. Burnt to prevent capture on Yazoo River, June 26, 1862.

General Quitman Sidewheel steamer: 946 tons. **D.** 233′ 3″ x 34′ 3″ x 9′. **A.** 2 32-pdr. **C.** 90. Built 1857, acquired 1861. Burnt to prevent capture at New Orleans, April 1862.

General Quitman Sidewheel steamer: 1076 tons. **D.** 246′ x 366′ x 6′. Built 1859. Used as transport. Sank at New Texas Landing near Morganza, La., October 1868.

General Rusk Sidewheel steamer: 750 tons. **D.** 200′ x 31′ x 5′ 7″. Built 1857, seized 1861. Ran aground near Marianao, Cuba, October 1862, and destroyed by fire.

General Scott Steamer. Used as guard boat on York River. Set alight to prevent capture May 1862.

General Sterling Price Sidewheel steamer: 633 tons. **D.** 182′ x 30′ x 6′. Built 1856, sunk off Memphis, June 6, 1862.

General Sumter Sidewheel steamer: 525 tons. **D.** 182′ x 28′ 4″ x 6′. **A.** 1 32-pdr. Built 1851. Captured at Memphis, June 6, 1862.

General Sumter Sidewheel steamer. Captured at Lake George, Fla., March 23, 1864.

George Buckhart Schooner. **A.** 1 6-pdr. Served with Texas Marine Dept. Captured March 1865.

George Page Sidewheel steamer: 410 tons. **A.** 2 guns. Built 1853. Captured from US Army May 1861. Destroyed to prevent recapture at Quantico Creek, March 9, 1862.

Georgia Screw steamer: 600 tons. **D.** 212′ x 27′. **A.** 2 100-pdr, 2 24-pdr, 1 32-pdr. Built 1862, sold at Liverpool, England, June 1864. (See p.116)

Georgia Ironclad floating battery. **D.** 250′ x 60′. **A.** (1864) 2 9-in SB, 3 32-pdr. Built 1862–63. Destroyed when Savannah fell, December 21, 1864.

Georgian Screw steamer: 350 tons. Purchased 1864 in Canada and seized by Canadian authorities April 1865.

Georgiana Screw steamer: 519 tons. **D.** 205′ 6″ x 25′ 2″. Built 1862. Forced aground and set alight by Union forces off Charleston, March 19, 1865.

Germantown Sloop: 939 tons. **D.** 150′ x 36′ 9″ x 17′. Former 22-gun sloop built 1846. Scuttled at Norfolk Navy Yard April 1862. Raised in June by Confederates and sunk as obstruction in Elizabeth River. Raised April 1863 by Union forces.

Gibraltar Schooner: 60 tons. **A.** 2 guns. Privateer at Mobile 1864.

Golden Age Steamer. Sunk May 1863 as obstruction in Yazoo River.

Gordon Grant Steam tug. Stationed at Columbus, Ky., 1861.

Gossamer Sternwheel steamer. Used as transport 1863.

Governor Aiken Ship. Used as lighthouse tender. Seized at Charleston, December 1860.

Governor Milton Sidewheel steamer: 68 tons. **D.** 85′ x 20′ x 4′. Used as transport. Captured near Hawkinsville, Fla., October 7, 1862.

Governor Moore Sidewheel steamer: 1215 tons. **A.** 2 32-pdr. **C.** 93. Built 1854. Destroyed to prevent capture below New Orleans, April 24, 1862. (See p.78)

Governor Moorehead Sternwheel steamer. Used as a transport. Sunk by Union forces in Pamlico River area, July 1863.

Grampus Sternwheel steamer: 352 tons. **A.** 2 12-pdr. Used as transport. Sunk to prevent capture at Island No. 10, April 7, 1862. Raised by Union forces, but burnt January 1863.

Grand Bay Sternwheel steamer: 135 tons. **D.** 121′ x 26′ x 4′. Built 1857. Served with Texas Marine Dept.

Grand Duke Sidewheel steamer: 508 tons. **D.** 205′ x 35′ x 7′ 6″. Built 1859, acquired 1863. Burnt at Shreveport, La., 1863.

Grand Era Steamer. Served as tender in Red River.

Granite City Sidewheel steamer: 450 tons. **D.** 160′ x 23′ x 56′ 6″. **A.** 6 24-pdr H, 1 24-pdr R, 1 20-pdr R. Captured off Bahamas, March 1863. Recaptured by Confederates May 6, 1864, but run aground January 21, 1865 and broke up.

Great Republic Steamer. Captured by Union forces 1864.

Grey Cloud Steamer. Used as a transport. Captured July 1862.

Greyhound Screw steamer: 290 tons. Used as blockade runner. Captured May 10, 1864. Blown up by bomb off Bermuda Hundred, 1864.

H.D. Mears Sternwheel steamer: 338 tons. Built 1860. Scuttled, Sunflower River to prevent capture August 1863.

H.L. Hunley Submarine. Built early 1863. Sunk in attack on *Housatonic* February 17, 1864. This was the first time a submarine had successfully destroyed a warship.

H.R.W. Hill Sidewheel steamer: 602 tons. Built 1852. Captured at Memphis June 6, 1862.

Halifax Screw tug. **D.** 91′ long. Seized May 12, 1865 while being completed on the stocks at Confederate Navy Yard, Halifax, N.C.

Hallie Jackson Brig. Used as privateer. Built 1860, captured April 1861.

Hampton Screw steamer: 166 tons. **D.** 106′ x 21′ x 5′. Built 1862, burnt at Richmond, Va., to prevent capture April 3, 1865. She was one of 100 small gunboats planned by Cdr. Matthew Fontaine Maury.

Hannah Schooner. Run aground and burnt to prevent capture at Corpus Christi, Tex., October 1862.

Hansa Sidewheel steamer: 257 tons. **S.** 12 knots. Served initially as blockade runner 1863.

Harmony Sidewheel tug: 78 tons. **A.** 2 32-pdr. Built 1859.

Harriet Lane Sidewheel steamer: 674 tons. Built 1857–58 for US Revenue Service. Captured Galveston, Tex., January 1, 1863. (See p.82)

Harriet Pickney Brig: 715 tons. **D.** 190′ x 28′ 5″. Served as blockade runner.

Hart Steamer. Partly covered in iron. Sunk to prevent capture April 14, 1863.

Hartford City Steamer: 150 tons. Built 1856. Burnt by Union forces July 18, 1863.

Hawley Schooner. Used as transport in 1861.

Helen Steamer. Burnt at Pensacola to prevent capture May 1862.

Helen Sloop. Captured April 1863 and set alight off Bayport.

Henry J. King Steamer. Captured at Coosa River, Ala., April 14, 1865.

Hercules Screw steamer: 515 tons. **D.** 170′ x 25′ x 7′ 6″. **A.** 1 9-in R, 1 8-in R. **S.** 12 knots. Under construction in Europe at end of war. (See p.126)

Hibben Steamer. Used as transport, Charleston Harbor.

Hope Sidewheel steamer: 193 tons. **D.** 128′ x 34′ x 5′. Used as blockade runner. Captured October 1864. (See p.152)

Hornet Steamer. **D.** 46′ x 6′ 3″ x 4′. **A.** 1 18-in spar torpedo. Fitted out 1864. Sank after colliding with steamer *Alison*, January 26, 1865.

Hunley (See p.159)

Huntress Sidewheel steamer: 500 tons. **D.** 230′ x 24′ 6″ x 6′ 6″. **A.** 3 guns. Built 1838, purchased 1861, became blockade runner. Renamed *Tropic*. Accidentally burnt off Charleston, January 18, 1863.

Huntsville Ironclad. **D.** 150′ x 7′ draft. **A.** 4 32-pdr. Built 1862. Sunk to prevent capture at Spanish River, Mobile, April 12, 1865. (See p.35)

Ida Sidewheel steamer. Used as transport. Captured and burnt at Argyle Island, Savannah, December 10, 1864.

Indian Chief Receiving and torpedo ship. Burnt to prevent capture at Charleston, February 18, 1865.

Iron King Steamer. Used as coal transport 1864.

Isabella Sloop. Captured by Union forces at Waccassa Bay, Fla., May 22, 1863.

Isabella Ellis Schooner: 340 tons. Captured by Union forces 1864.

Island City Sidewheel steamer: 245 tons. Served with Texas Marine Dept.

Isondiga Sternwheel steamer. **D.** 6′ 6″ draft. **A.** 1 9-in, 1 6.4-in R. **S.** 5 knots. **C.** 60. Burnt near Savannah to prevent capture January 1865.

Ivy Sidewheel steamer: 454 tons. **D.** 191′ x 28′ x 6′. **A.** 1 8-in, 1 32-pdr, 2 24-pdr. Privateer. Destroyed May 1863 to prevent capture.

J.D. Clarke Sidewheel steamer. Used as transport. Captured by Union forces on Red River April 9, 1863.

J.D. Swaim Sidewheel steamer: 350 tons. **D.** 150′ 6″ x 30′ x 5′. Built 1859, acquired 1862, sunk 1862. Raised by Union forces April 1864.

J.H. Jarvis Steamer. Built 1863–64.

J.J. Crittenden Schooner. Captured by Union forces at Newbegan Creek, N.C., and sunk as obstruction 1862.

J.O. Nixon Schooner: 95 tons. **A.** 1 18-pdr, 2 6-pdr. Privateer. Operated out of New Orleans July 1863.

Jackson (Muscogee) Ironclad. (See p.60)

Jackson Sidewheel steamer: 297 tons. **A.** 2 32-pdr. Built 1849, sunk at New Orleans to prevent capture April 1862.

Jacob Musselman Sternwheel steamer: 144 tons. Built 1860. Captured by Confederates who sank her at Bradley's Landing, January 6, 1863.

James Battle Sidewheel steamer: 407 tons. Blockade runner. Captured off Mobile July 18, 1863.

James Funk Steamer: 120 tons. Pilot boat. Captured off Montauk Point August 11, 1864. Later burnt to avoid recapture.

James Johnson Sidewheel steamer: 526 tons. Built 1856, purchased 1861 for conversion into gunboat, but destroyed February 1862 before work completed.

James L. Day Sidewheel steamer: 414 tons. **D.** 187′ x 25′ 6″ x 6′. Built 1843.

James Woods Sidewheel steamer: 585 tons. Built 1860. Under conversion at Nashville when destroyed to prevent capture in February 1862.

Jamestown Sidewheel steamer: 1300 tons. **D.** 250′ x 34′ x 12′. **A.** 2 guns. Built 1853. Sunk as obstruction off Drewry's Bluff, May 1862.

Jeff Davis Steamer. Captured at Memphis, June 6, 1862.

Jeff Davis Steamer. Transport with Texas Marine Dept.

Jeff Davis Schooner. Captured off New Berne, N.C., June 1864.

Jeff Davis Steamer. Tender to ironclad *Georgia*.

Jefferson Davis Brig. **D.** 187′ x 10′ 6″ draft. **A.** 2 32-pdr, 2 24-pdr, 1 18-pdr. **C.** 75. Built 1845. Captured off Cuba as the slaver *Echo*, August 1858. Became privateer 1861. Wrecked at St Augustine, Fla., August 18, 1861.

Jenny Lind Steamer. Union Army transport. Captured June 1863.

Jenny Lind Schooner. Captured June 16, 1864.

John B. White Steam tug. Surrendered to Union Army May 8, 1862.

John F. Carr Steamer. Cottonclad serving with Texas Marine Dept.

John Roach Transport. Sunk as obstruction in James River, October 1862.

John Simonds Steamer: 1024 tons. Built 1852. Sunk at Island No. 10, 1862.

John Walsh Sidewheel steamer: 809 tons. D. 275' x 38' x 6'. Built 1858. Sunk to block Yazoo River, July 1863.

Josiah A. Bell Sidewheel steamer: 412 tons. D. 4' 6" draft. A. 1 8-in converted to 6-in R.

Judah Schooner: 250 tons. A. 5 guns. Privateer. Destroyed Pensacola Navy Yard, September 14, 1861.

Julia A. Hodges Steamer: 8 tons. Captured off Indianola, Tex., April 6, 1864.

Julius Steamer. Burnt to prevent capture at Florence, Ala., February 7, 1862.

Junaluska Screw tug: 79 tons. A. 2 guns. Built 1860, dismantled 1862.

Juno Sternwheel steamer. D. 4' draft. A. 1 H. C. 50. Captured off Wilmington, September 22, 1863.

Kahukee Screw tug: 100 tons. D. 95' x 17'. S. 9 knots. Built 1855.

Kanawha Valley Steamer. Used as hospital ship. Captured at Madrid Bend, Mo., March 1862.

Kaskaskia Sidewheel steamer: 49 tons. Built 1859. Captured at Little Red River, August 14, 1863.

Kate Bruce Schooner: 310 tons. A. 2 guns. Sunk as obstruction Chattahoochee River, 1862.

Kentucky Sidewheel steamer: 500 tons. Captured June 1862.

Lady Davis Screw tug: 250 tons. A. 24-pdr, 1 12-pdr R. Built 1858. Machinery used in ironclad *Palmetto State*. Hull later captured at Charleston 1865. (See p.111)

Lady Walton Sternwheel steamer: 150 tons. Built 1858. Captured June 6, 1863.

Landis Sidewheel steamer: 377 tons. D. 190' x 30' x 7'. Built 1853, acquired 1862, surrendered below New Orleans, April 1862.

Lapwing Bark. Captured by *Florida*, March 28, 1863. Used as armed tender and burnt June 20, 1863.

Launch No. 1 Served in Berwick Bay.

Launch No. 3 Steam launch. A. 1 H. Captured below New Orleans April 1862.

Launch No. 6 Steam launch. A. 1 H. Destroyed below New Orleans, April 24, 1862.

Laura Schooner. Crew deserted at Key West, October 1861. Vessel handed over to US authorities.

Laurel Screw steamer: 386 tons. D. 11' draft. S. 13 knots. Purchased 1864, sold 1865.

Le Grand Sidewheel steamer: 235 tons. Built 1856.

Lecompt Schooner. Captured Matagorda Bay, February 1862. Recaptured by Confederates, January 1863. Ran aground on Bird Key Spit, Galveston Bay, May 24, 1865.

Leesburg Steamer. Used as transport on Savannah River.

Leviathan Screw tug. D. 11' draft. US Army transport. Captured September 22, 1863; recaptured a few hours later.

Lewis Cass Schooner. A. 1 68-pdr. Used as revenue cutter. Seized January 1861.

Little Rebel Steamer: 159 tons. D. 12' draft. A. 3 12-pdr R. S. 10 knots. Built 1859. Captured Memphis, Tenn., June 6, 1862.

Livingston Sidewheel steamer. D. 180' x 40' x 9'. A. 6 guns. Built 1861. Burnt to prevent capture on Yazoo River, June 26, 1862.

Logan Sidewheel steamer: 296 tons. Built 1855. Burnt to prevent capture at Barretts Landing, Va.

Lone Star Sidewheel steamer: 126 tons. Built 1854. Used as transport.

Lorton Schooner: 95 tons. A. 1 gun. Privateer 1861.

Louis d'Or Sidewheel steamer: 343 tons. D. 180' x 32' x 6'. Built 1860. Used as transport.

Louisiana Ironclad: 1400 tons. D. 264' x 62'. A. 2 7-in R, 3 9-in, 4 8-in, 7 32-pdr. C. 300. Built 1861. Scuttled below New Orleans, April 1862. (See p.10)

Louisiana Steam frigate. (See p.116)

Louisville Sidewheel steamer: 743 tons. D. 231' 5" x 38' 6" x 6'. Captured Little River, La., July 13, 1863. Sold 1869.

Lucy Gwin Sternwheel steamer: 152 tons. Built 1859. Surrendered 1865 at end of war.

Lynx Sidewheel steamer. Used as blockade runner. Acquired 1864. Driven ashore and burnt off Wilmington, N.C., September 25, 1864.

M.C. Etheridge Schooner: 144 tons. D. 92' x 24' x 7'. A. 2 guns. Built 1859. Burnt to prevent capture, February 10, 1862.

M.E. Dowing Steamer. Dispatch boat 1861.

Macon Sternwheel steamer. D. 150' x 25' x 8'. A. 6 guns. Fitted out as gunboat 1864. Served at Savannah.

Magenta Sidewheel steamer: 782 tons. D. 269' x 39' x 6'. Built 1861. Burnt to prevent capture on Yazoo River, July 1863.

Magnolia Sidewheel steamer: 843 tons. S. 12 knots. Built 1857, sold 1865.

Magnolia Sidewheel steamer: 824 tons. Built 1859. Destroyed off Yazoo City to prevent capture, April 1863.

Manassas Schooner. Used as US revenue cutter. Seized August 1861, dismantled 1862.

Manassas Ironclad: 387 tons. D. 143' x 33'. A. 1 64-pdr. Built 1855, converted 1861, sunk below New Orleans, April 24, 1862.

Marianna Sidewheel steamer. D. 3' 3" draft. Used as tow boat for sailing vessels.

Mariner Screw steamer. 135 tons. A. 2 12-pdr. Privateer 1861.

Marion Sidewheel steamer: 258 tons. Built 1850. Sunk accidentally on Ashley River after drifting from moorings, April 6, 1863.

Mars Sidewheel steamer: 329 tons. Built 1856. Captured by Union forces at Island No. 10, April 1862.

Mary E. Keene Sidewheel steamer: 659 tons. D. 238' x 38' x 6'. Built 1860. Scuttled to prevent capture off Yazoo City, July 1863.

Mary Hill Sidewheel steamer: 234 tons. D. 2' draft. A. 1 24-pdr, 1 12-pdr. Built 1859.

Mary Patterson Steamer. Built 1859. Sunk as obstruction in White River, Ark., June 16, 1862.

Matagorda Sidewheel steamer: 1250 tons. D. 220' x 30' x 8'. Built 1858. Captured while running blockade, September 10, 1864.

Matilda Bark: 400 tons. A. 6 guns. Served out of New Orleans 1861.

Maurepas Sidewheel steamer: 399 tons. D. 180' x 34' x 7'. A. 6 guns. Built 1858, purchased 1861. Sunk to prevent capture on White River, Ark., June 16, 1862.

May Steamer. Used as transport.

McRae Steam sloop: 830 tons. A. 1 9-in, 6 32-pdr, 1 6-pdr. Purchased 1861. Sunk on Mississippi River, New Orleans, April 28, 1862.

Memphis Schooner: 208 tons. D. 111' x 25' x 12'. A. 1 12-pdr, 2 24-pdr SB. Built 1851 as racing schooner *America*. Acquired 1861. Seized by Union forces March 1862. Served as school ship at Naval Academy, Annapolis, 1863 – 73. Presented to academy 1921, scrapped 1945.

Memphis Floating battery. A. 18 guns. Converted from floating dry dock at New Orleans 1861. Destroyed when city fell April 1862.

Merite Steamer. Served on Mississippi.

Merrimac Sidewheel steamer: 635 tons. D. 230' x 30' x 8' 6". S. 18 knots. Blockade runner 1862. Captured off Cape Fear, July 24, 1863.

Milledgeville Ironclad. D. 175' x 35' 3" x 9'. A. 4 guns. Built by Willink 1864. Burnt to water's edge and sunk to prevent capture Savannah, Ga., December 1864. (See p.51)

Mississippi Ironclad: 1400 tons. D. 260' x 58' x 12' 6". A. designed for 20 guns. Built 1861. Fired, incomplete at New Orleans to prevent capture, April 1862. (See p.11)

Mississippi Steam frigate. (See p.116)

Mississippi Ironclad: 2750 tons. (See p.66)

Missouri Ironclad. D. 183' x 53' 8" x 8' 6". A. 1 32-pdr, 1 11-in SB, 1 9-in SB. Built 1862/63. Surrendered at Shreveport, La., June 3, 1865. (See p.56)

Mobile Steamer. D. 283' long. A. 3 32-pdr, 1 8-in SB. Built 1860. When ready for armor plating, sunk on Yazoo River to prevent capture, May 21, 1863. (See p.61)

Mohawk Sternwheel steamer. Sunk at Island No. 10, April 7, 1862.

Morgan Schooner. A. 3 guns. US revenue cutter. Seized 1861.

Morgan Sidewheel steamer: 863 tons. D. 202' x 38' x 7' 2". A. 1 7-in R, 1 6-in R, 4 32-pdr. S. 10 knots. Purchased 1861. Burnt to prevent capture 1865.

Morning Light Ship: 937 tons. D. 172' x 34' 3" x 19'. A. 8 32-pdr. Built 1853, purchased by US Navy 1861. Captured at Sabine Pass, Tex., January 21, 1863. Burnt to prevent recapture January 23, 1863.

Moro Sidewheel steamer: 132 tons. D. 122' x 24' 10" x 4'. Built 1858. Used as transport. Captured on Red River, February 4, 1863.

Mosher Screw tug: 49 tons. C. 40. Built 1857. Sunk while towing fire boat against a Union sloop off Forts Jackson and St Philip, New Orleans, April 24, 1862.

Mosquito Launch. Part of naval defenses of Virginia, N.C., 1861.

Moultrie Steamer. Served at Charleston until 1863.

Muscle Steamer: 125 tons. Built 1856. Captured by Union forces February 1862 but sprang a leak and sank on Tennessee River.

Muscogee *(Jackson)* Ironclad. Burnt to prevent capture while still incomplete, 1865. Wreck discovered 1961. (See p.60)

Music Sidewheel steamer: 330 tons. D. 172' x 29' x 4'. A. 2 6-pdr. Built 1857. Privateer 1861.

Nansemond Screw steamer: 166 tons. D. 106' x 21' x 5'. A. 2 8-in. Built 1862, destroyed at Richmond to prevent capture, April 3, 1865.

Nashville Sidewheel steamer: 1221 tons. D. 215' 6" x 34' 6". A. 2 12-pdr. C. 40. Seized at Charleston 1861; renamed *Rattlesnake*. Sunk on Ogeechee River, Ga., February 1863. (See p.43)

Nashville Ironclad. D. 271' x 62' 6" x 10' 9". A. 3 7-in R, 1 24-pdr. Built 1864. Surrendered at Anna Hubba Bluff, Tombigbee River, Ala., May 10, 1865. Sold 1867.

Natchez Sidewheel steamer: 800 tons. D. 273' x 38' x 6'. Built 1860. Burnt to prevent capture in Yazoo River, April 1863.

Neafie Sidewheel steamer. D. 8' draft. S. 6 knots. C. 60. Captured by Union forces, February 1863.

Nelms Steamer. Sunk at Mobile.

Nelson Steamer. Served on Red River 1863.

Neptune Steamer. A. 2 guns. Sunk at Galveston, Tex., January 1, 1863.

Neuse Ironclad. D. 152' x 34' x 9'. Built 1863–64. Grounded off Kingston and finally burnt March 1865 to prevent capture. (See p.34)

New Falls City Sidewheel steamer: 880 tons. D. 301' 4" x 39' 9" x 6'. Built 1858. Sunk as obstruction on Red River, March 1864.

New National Steamer. Used as transport. Captured at Memphis, June 1862.

New Orleans Floating battery. A. 17 8-in, 1 9-in, 2 32-pdr R. Sunk at Island No. 10 to avoid capture.

Nina Simms Sidewheel steamer: 327 tons. D. 177' x 33' x 6'. Built 1860. Used as transport at New Orleans, 1861.

Norfolk Screw steamer: 166 tons. D. 106' x 21' x 5'. A. 1 9-in, 1 32-pdr. Burnt on building ways to prevent capture, May 10, 1862.

North Carolina Ironclad. D. 150' x 32' x 12'. Built 1863. Sank at anchor off Smithville, Cape Fear River, September 27, 1864. (See p.55)

North Carolina Ironclad: 2750 tons. (See p.67)

Northampton Sidewheel steamer: 405 tons. Built 1860. Sunk as obstruction in James River, 1862.

Ohio Belle Sidewheel steamer: 406 tons. Built 1855. Captured at Island No. 10, April 7, 1862.

Oregon Sidewheel steamer: 532 tons. D. 216' 10" x 26' 6". A. 1 8-in, 1 32-pdr H. Built 1846. Sunk to prevent capture at New Orleans, April 1862.

Orizaba Sidewheel steamer: 595 tons. Blockade runner. Lost at sea 1865.

Osceola Sidewheel steamer: 157 tons. Built 1858. Used as block ship in Red River 1864.

Osceola Sloop. Captured by Union forces in Mississippi Sound, December 9, 1861.

Owl Sidewheel steamer: 771 tons. D. 230' x 26' x 7' 6". S. 16 knots. Built 1864, sold 1865.

Palmetto State Ironclad. D. 150' x 34' x 12'. A. 2 7-in R, 2 9-in SB. S. 6 knots. Built 1862. Burnt in Charleston Harbor to prevent capture, February 18, 1865. (See p.50)

Pamlico Sidewheel steamer: 218 tons. D. 3' 8" draft. A. 1 6,4-in R. Purchased July 1861. Burnt to prevent capture on Lake Pontchartrain, La., April 1862.

Pampero (See p.131)

Pargoud Sidewheel steamer: 523 tons. D. 319' x 36' x 6'. Built 1860. Scuttled on Yazoo River to prevent capture, July 1863.

Patrick Henry Sidewheel steamer: 1300 tons. D. 250' x 34' x 13'. A. 1 10-in SB. Built 1859. Burnt to prevent capture at Richmond, April 3, 1865. (See p.74)

Warships of the Confederate States Navy

Paul Jones Sidewheel steamer: 353 tons. **D.** 172′ x 34′ x 6′. Built 1855, lost 1863. Her remains could be seen in 1963 at low water in Mississippi River.

Pauline Steamer. Used as transport in Louisiana waters 1863–64.

Peedee Screw sloop. **D.** 170′ x 26′ x 8′. **A.** 1 7-in R, 1 6.4-in R, 1 9-in SB. **S.** S. 9 knots. **C.** 91. Built 1862. Destroyed to prevent capture in Peedee River, February 18, 1865.

Penguin Sidewheel steamer: 1063 tons. **D.** 240′ x 30′ x 10′. Built 1865 but completed too late for service.

Paytona Sidewheel steamer: 685 tons. **D.** 256′ x 37′ x 6′. Built 1859. Burnt and scuttled on Yazoo River to prevent capture, July 1863.

Phantom Screw steamer: 500 tons. **D.** 190′ x 22′ x 8′ 6″. **S.** 18 knots. C. 33. Blockade runner, built 1862. Driven ashore by Union forces off Fort Fisher, Wilmington, and fired by her crew to prevent capture, September 23, 1863.

Philo Parsons Steamer. Seized on Lake Erie in an attempt to free Confederate prisoners on Johnson Island but the plan failed and the vessel was scuttled to prevent recapture, September 1864.

Phoenix Ironclad floating battery. **A.** 6 guns. Built 1863, destroyed at Mobile to prevent capture, August 1864.

Phoenix Sidewheel tug. **C.** 75. Sunk near Forts St Philip and Jackson, New Orleans, April 24, 1862.

Pickens Schooner. **A.** 3 guns. US revenue cutter. Seized 1861. Served at New Orleans.

Pine Sloop: 40 tons. Used as transport.

Pioneer Submarine: 4 tons. Privateer two-man submarine built 1861; abandoned at New Orleans. Moved to Presbytere Arcade, Louisiana State Museum in 1957. (See p.121)

Pioneer II Submarine. **D.** 36′ x 3′ x 4′. **A.** Clockwork torpedo. **S.** 2½ knots. Built 1863.

Planter Sidewheel steamer: 313 tons. **D.** 4′ draft. **A.** 1 32-pdr, 1 24-pdr H. Built 1860. Seized by her own crew at 4 a.m. on May 12, 1862, and once out of Charleston Harbor was handed over to Union warships. (See p.106)

Plover Sidewheel steamer: 645 tons. **D.** 225′ x 24′ x 6′. Built 1865 but not completed in time.

Plymouth Sloop: 974 tons. **D.** 147′ 6″ x 38′ 1″ x 12′. **A.** 22 guns. Built 1843. Scuttled at Norfolk Navy Yard by Union forces, April 1861. Raised by Confederates who planned to take her to Richmond, but scuttled once more upon recapture of yard by Union forces, May 10, 1862.

Pontchartrain Sidewheel steamer: 454 tons. **D.** 204′ x 36′ 6″x 10′. **A.** 6 guns. Purchased 1861. Burned to prevent capture off Little Rock, Arkansas River, October 9, 1863.

Portsmouth Sidewheel steamer: 166 tons. **D.** 106′ x 21′ x 56′. **A.** 1 9-in, 1 32-pdr. Built 1862 but burnt to prevent capture in same year while still on stocks at Norfolk Navy Yard.

Post Boy Steamer. Tow boat in North Carolina waters 1861–62.

Powhatan Screw tug. Acquired 1862.

Prince Sidewheel steamer: 223 tons. Built 1859. Used as transport. Sunk to prevent capture in early April 1862 at Island No. 10.

Prince of Wales Sternwheel steamer: 572 tons. Built 1860. Burnt at Yazoo City to prevent capture, July 1863.

Ptarmigan Sidewheel steamer: 284 tons. **D.** 270′ x 24′ x 7′. **S.** 18 knots. **C.** 50. Blockade runner. Built 1864.

Queen Mab Sidewheel steamer. Used as transport. Surrendered at Charleston, February 1865, and condemned unfit.

Queen of the West Sidewheel steamer: 406 tons. **D.** 180′ x 37′ 6″ x 6′. **A.** 1 30-pdr, 1 20-pdr, 3 12-pdr H. **C.** 120. Built 1854, purchased in 1862 by US Army and converted into a ram. Sunk February 14, 1863 off Fort de Russy, La., and raised by Confederates. Set on fire in action on Atchafalaya River April 14, 1863 and exploded. (See p.111)

R.J. Lockland Sidewheel steamer: 710 tons. **D.** 265′ x 40′ x 6′. Built 1857, set on fire July 1863 and sunk as obstruction in Yazoo River.

Raleigh Screw steamer: 65 tons. **A.** 2 guns. Transferred 1862. Destroyed at Richmond, Va., to prevent capture, April 4, 1865.

Raleigh Ironclad. **D.** 150′ x 32′ x 12′. **A.** 4 6-in R. Built 1862/63. Ran aground and broke her back at Wilmington Bar, May 7, 1864. (See p.55)

Randolph Steamer. Served at Charleston 1863–64.

Rappahannock Sidewheel steamer: 1200 tons. **A.** 1 gun. Captured by Confederates posing as passengers near Point Lookout, Potomac River, June 28, 1861. Burnt at Fredericksburg, April 1862.

Rappahannock Steam sloop: 857 tons. **D.** 200′ x 30′ 2″ x 12′. Built 1857. Detained at Calais, France. Turned over to US authorities at end of war. (See p.122)

Rattlesnake (See p.117)

Raven Yawl. Served at Mathews County, Va.

Rebel Sidewheel steamer. Used as transport.

Red Rover Sidewheel steamer: 786 tons. **D.** 8′ draft. **S.** 8 knots. Built 1859. Captured at Island No. 10 by Union forces, April 7, 1862. Served as hospital ship.

Reliance Screw steamer: 90 tons. **D.** 88′ 2″ x 17′ x 6′. **A.** 1 30-pdr R, 1 24-pdr H. Built 1860. Captured by Confederates August 19, 1863. Sunk to prevent recapture, August 28.

Renshaw Schooner: 75 tons. **D.** 68′ x 20′ x 4′. Captured by Union forces, May 20, 1863.

Republic Sidewheel steamer: 699 tons. **D.** 249′ x 40′ x 7′ 3″. Built 1855. Burnt to prevent capture at Yazoo City, May 21, 1863.

Rescue Schooner: 120 tons. **D.** 150′ x 27′ 6″. **A.** 1 gun.

Resolute Sidewheel steamer. **A.** 3 32-pdr. **C.** 40. Sunk at New Orleans to prevent capture, April 24, 1861.

Resolute Sidewheel tug: 322 tons. Built 1858. Ran aground after colliding with two gunboats during an action on Savannah River, December 12, 1864. Captured same day by Union forces.

Richmond Ironclad. **D.** 172′ 6″ x 34′ x 12′. **A.** 6 guns. **C.** 150. Built 1862, scuttled at Richmond to prevent capture, April 4, 1865. (See p.34)

Roanoke Steamer. Served on Nansemond River, 1861.

Robert E. Lee Sidewheel steamer: 900 tons. **D.** 283′ x 20′ x 10′. **S.** 13½ knots. Built 1862. Used as blockade runner. Captured November 9, 1863.

Robert Fulton Sidewheel steamer: 158 tons. Built 1860. Used as transport. Captured on Red River, October 7, 1863, and burnt by Union forces to prevent capture.

Robert Habersham Sidewheel steamer: 173 tons. Built 1860. Used as transport at Savannah.

Roebuck Sidewheel steamer: 164 tons. **D.** 147′ x 23′ x 5′. Built 1857. Served with Texas Marine Dept.

Rosina Sidewheel steamer: 1391 tons. **D.** 260′ x 33′ x 9′. **S.** 14 knots. Built 1865 but not completed in time to serve as an intended blockade runner capable of carrying 1500 bales of cotton.

Roundout Sidewheel steamer. Used as transport. Captured in Rappahanock River April 1862.

Royal Yacht Schooner: 40 tons. **D.** 6′ 6″ draft. **A.** 1 12-pdr. Captured and set alight November 8, 1861. Recaptured and fire extinguished. Captured by Union forces, April 15, 1863.

Ruby Sidewheel steamer: 1391 tons. **D.** 260′ x 33′ x 9′. **S.** 14 knots. Blockade runner ordered late 1864 but not completed by end of war.

Sachem Screw steamer: 197 tons **D.** 121′ x 23′ 6″ x 5′ 4″. **A.** 2 32-pdr, 2 24-pdr. **C.** 50. Built 1844. Served with Texas Marine Dept.

St Francis No. 3 Sidewheel steamer: 219 tons. Built 1858. Used was transport. Sunk 1863.

St Mary Sidewheel steamer: 60 tons. **D.** 89′ 9″ x 15′ x 4′. **A.** 1 24-pdr, 1 12-pdr. Built 1862. Captured at Yazoo City, Miss., July 13, 1863.

St Patrick Submarine torpedo boat. **D.** 30′ long. **A.** 1 spar torpedo. **C.** 6. Privately built in 1864 by John P. Halligan. Served at Mobile.

St Philip Sidewheel steamer: 1172 tons. **D.** 228′ 4″ x 32′ 8″ x 18′. **A.** 2 68-pdr, 4 32-pdr. Built 1852 at a cost of $250,000. Captured by Confederates April 17, 1862. Sunk as an obstruction at Fort Pemberton above mouth of Yalobusha River in Tallahatchie River, Miss., March 1863.

Sallie Schooner: 170 tons. **A.** 1 gun. Served as privateer at Charleston.

Sallie Wood Sternwheel steamer: 256 tons. Built 1860. Captured at Chickasaw, Ala., February 8, 1862.

Sam Kirkman Sternwheel steamer: 271 tons. Built 1857. Burnt to prevent capture at Florence, Ala., February 8, 1862.

Sampson Sidewheel steamer. **D.** 8′ draft. **A.** 1 32-pdr, 1 12-pdr. Purchased 1861. Receiving ship at Savannah.

Samuel Hill Steamer. Used as transport.

Samuel Orr Steamer. Used as hospital ship. burnt to prevent capture at Duck River, February 7, 1862.

Sand Fly Launch.

San Francisco (See p.116)

Santa Maria Ironclad: 3200 tons. **D.** 270′ x 50′. Laid down 1862 but sold to Denmark. She was also known as "North's Ship" after Lt James H. North, who was responsible for her creation. (See p.67)

Satellite Sidewheel steamer: 217 tons. **D.** 120′ 7″ x 22′ 9″. **A.** 1 8-in, 1 30-pdr. Captured on Rappahanock River, August 23, 1863. Scuttled nine days later to prevent recapture.

Savannah Sidewheel steamer: 406 tons. **A.** 1 32-pdr. Built 1856. Sank at sea in bad weather while acting as a blockade runner, August 8, 1863.

Savannah Ironclad. **D.** 150′ x 34′ x 12′ 6″. **A.** 2 7-in R, 2 6.4-in R. Built 1863. Burnt at the evacuation of Savannah, December 21, 1864. (See p.60)

Savannah Schooner: 53 tons. **D.** 56′ x 17′ x 6′. **A.** 1 gun. Served as privateer 1861. Captured June 3, 1861. (See p.126)

Schultz Sidewheel steamer: 164 tons. Accidentally blown up by mine on James River.

Scorpion Steamer. **D.** 46′ x 6′ 3″. **A.** 1 spar torpedo. Acquired 1864. Ran ashore in James River and severely damaged by an exploding Confederate vessel which was nearby. Subsequently abandoned and seized by Union forces.

Scotland Sidewheel steamer: 567 tons. **D.** 230′ x 27′ x 6′. Built 1855. Burnt July 1863 and hulk sunk as obstruction in Yazoo River.

Sea Bird Sidewheel steamer: 202 tons. **A.** 1 32-pdr, 1 30-pdr. Built 1854. Rammed and sunk in action with Union forces at Elizabeth City, February 10, 1862.

Seabird Sidewheel tug: 59 tons. Built 1859. Captured on James River at Tree Hillbridge near Richmond, April 4, 1865.

Sealine Brig: 179 tons. **A.** 1 gun. Served as privateer 1861.

Selma Sidewheel gunboat. **D.** 252′ x 30′ x 6′. **A.** 2 9-in SB, 1 8-in SB, 1 6.4-in R. **S.** 9 knots. Built 1856. Captured at Mobile, August 5, 1864.

Sharp Steamer. Used as transport. Burnt and scuttled to prevent capture on Sunflower River, August 1863.

Shenandoah Screw steamer: 1160 tons. **D.** 230′ x 32′ **A.** 4 8-in SB, 2 32-pdr, 2 12-pdr. Purchased 1864. Handed over to British authorities, November 1865. (See p.118)

Shrapnel Steamer. Used as tender. Burned to prevent capture at Richmond, Va., April 4, 1865.

Skirwan Steamer. Seized by Union forces at Halifax, N.C., May 1865.

Slidell Steamer. **A.** 8 guns. Built 1862. Destroyed on Tennessee River early 1863.

Snipe Sidewheel steamer: 645 tons. **D.** 225′ x 24′ x 6′. Blockade runner. Built 1865 but not completed in time for service in war.

Sovereign Sidewheel steamer: 336 tons. Built 1855. Run ashore at Island No. 37 on Mississippi River and captured by Union forces, June 5, 1862.

Spray Sternwheel steamer. **A.** 2 guns. Used as tender. Sunk on St Mary's River May 1865.

Squib Torpedo boat. **D.** 46′ x 6′ 3″. **A.** 1 spar torpedo. Built 1864. Served on James River.

Stag Sidewheel steamer: 771 tons. **D.** 230′ x 26′ x 7′ 6″. **S.** 16 knots. Blockade runner, built 1864. Captured off Wilmington, January 20, 1865. Sold 1867. Served in merchant marine until 1885. (See p.156)

Star Steam tug: 250 tons. Sunk at New Orleans, April 24, 1862.

Starlight Steamer. Used as transport. Captured at Thompsons' Creek near Port Hudson, May 26, 1863.

Stonewall Ironclad: 900 tons. **D.** 171′ 10″ x 32′ 8″ x 14′ 4″. **A.** 1 300-pdr R, 2 70-pdr R. Built 1863–64. Turned over to US authorities May 1865. Sold to Japan. (See p.66)

Stonewall Jackson **A.** 1 32-pdr. Sunk below New Orleans, April 24, 1862.

Stonewall Jackson. Schooner: 150 tons, **A.** 3 guns.

Stono Sidewheel steamer: 453 tons. **D.** 171′ 6″ x 31′ 4″ x 6′. **A.** 8 8-in, 1 30-pdr R. Captured on Stono River, January 30, 1863. Used as blockade runner. Ran ashore on breakwater near Fort Moultrie, S.C., June 5, 1863.

Sumter Screw steamer: 499 tons. **D.** 184' x 30'. **A.** 1 8-in, 4 32-pdr. Built 1859. Sold at Gibraltar, December 9, 1862. (See p.112)

Sumter Screw tug: 90 tons. **D.** 80' x 18' x 5'. Served on James River.

Sumter Sidewheel steamer. Used as transport. Sunk at Charleston Harbor, September 22, 1863.

Sunflower Sidewheel steamer: 105 tons. **D.** 121' 6" x 25' x 36' 9". Built 1857. Used as transport.

Superior Barge. **A.** 4 guns.

Swan Steamer: 487 tons. Used as transport. Captured off Key West, May 24, 1862.

Swan Yawl. Part of "Volunteer Coast Guard." Manned by a group led by John Yates Beal, captured several Union merchant vessels until part of the group was captured during a raid ashore. One prisoner was immediately hung to force the rest to reveal Beal's hiding place. When caught, Beal was secretly executed on February 18, 1865.

T.D. Hine Sidewheel steamer: 205 tons. **D.** 147' x 30' x 4' 6". Built 1860. Captured on Red River during 1865.

Tacony Bark: 296 tons. **A.** 1 12-pdr H. Built 1856. Captured by *Clarence*, a tender to *Florida*, June 12, 1863. *Tacony* was burnt June 25, 1863.

Tallahassee Screw steamer: 500 tons. **D.** 220' x 24'. **A.** 1 84-pdr, 2 24-pdr, 2 32-pdr. **S.** 17 knots. Purchased 1864. Seized in England April 1865. She was formerly the blockade runner *Atlanta*. Name changed to *Olustee* and *Chameleon*. (See p.130)

Talomico Sidewheel steamer. **A.** 2 guns. Stationed at Savannah. Accidentally sunk in 1863.

Teaser Screw tug: 64 tons. **D.** 80' x 18' x 4'. **A.** 1 32-pdr R, 1 12-pdr R. Purchased 1861. Abandoned in James River after boiler explosion, July 4, 1862, and captured by Union forces. *Teaser* was an aviation pioneer as she was an early carrier of balloons. When captured she had a balloon on board.

Teaser Cutter. Served at Mobile 1863.

Tennessee Ironclad. **D.** 165' x 35' x 11' 6". **A.** 6 guns. **S.** 8 knots. **C.** 200. Begun at Memphis, Tenn., by John Shirley and Co. in 1862, but never completed. Burnt on stocks to prevent capture, June 5, 1862. Contract price was $76,920.

Tennessee Ironclad: 1273 tons. **D.** 209' x 48' x 146'. **A.** 2 7-in R, 4 6.4-in R. **C.** 133. Built 1863. Surrendered at Mobile, August 5, 1864. (See p.44)

Tennessee Sidewheel steamer: 1149 tons. Built 1856. Seized 1862. Captured at New Orleans, April 1862. Sold 1865.

Texas Steamer. Seized 1861. Used as transport. Destroyed on Red River 1863.

Texas Sidewheel steamer: 800 tons. **A.** 8 guns. Used as privateer January 1863.

Texas Steam corvette: 1500 tons. **D.** 220' x 30' x 16'. Never saw service in war. Sold to Peru and renamed *America*. (See p.116)

Texas Screw steamer: 1000 tons. **D.** 230' x 32'. Built 1863. Known as *Pampero*. (See p.131)

Texas Ironclad. **D.** 217' x 50' 4" x 13' 6". **A.** 6 guns. Built 1864. Captured incomplete April 1865. Sold 1867. (See p.34)

Texas Sidewheel steamer: 1223 tons. Built 1852, seized 1862. Used as transport.

Theodora Sidewheel steamer: 518 tons. **D.** 175' x 7' draft. **A.** 3 guns. Built 1852. Captured May 28, 1862.

Thomas Jefferson Sidewheel steamer. Seized 1861. Sunk as obstruction in James River, May 1862.

Thirty-Fifth Parallel Sidewheel steamer: 419 tons. Built 1859. Run ashore and burnt to prevent capture in the Tallahatchie River, March 1863.

Tiger Floating battery. **A.** 2 guns. Built 1861.

Time Steamer. Used as transport 1862.

Tom Sugg Sidewheel steamer: 62 tons. **D.** 90' x 22' x 4'. **A.** 2 guns. Captured in White River, August 14, 1863.

Torch Screw steamer. Built 1863. Served at Charleston as torpedo vessel.

Torpedo Screw steamer: 150 tons. **D.** 70' x 16' x 5'. **A.** 1 gun. Partly burnt and sunk to prevent capture at Richmond April 3, 1865, but later raised.

Towns Steamer. Sunk as obstruction in Warwick River, September 1861.

Transport Sidewheel steamer: 40 tons. Used as tug. Captured at Charleston, February 1865.

Treaty Steam tug. Captured on Sautee River, June 20 1862.

Trent Steamer. Used as transport on Red River.

Tropic Steamer.

Tural Steamer. Used as transport.

Tuscaloosa Bark: 500 tons. Captured by *Alabama*, June 1863. Later seized by British authorities.

Tuscaloosa Ironclad. **D.** 152' x 34' x 8'. **A.** 4 guns. Built 1862. Sunk to prevent capture on Spanish River, Mobile, April 12, 1865.

Tuscarora Sidewheel steamer. **A.** 1 8-in. 1 32-pdr. Accidentally burnt at New Orleans, November 23, 1861.

Twilight Steamer: 392 tons. Used as transport 1864–65. Served on Ouachita River.

Uncle Ben Steam tug: 155 tons. **A.** 1 gun. Captured by US government but forced to put into Wilmington during a severe storm in April 1861 and seized by the Confederates. Her machinery was recovered and used in the ironclad *North Carolina*. The engineless vessel was then rigged as a schooner and served as a privateer renamed *Retribution* and later *Etta*.

Uncle Ben Steamer. **A.** 2 12-pdr. Served with Texas Marine Dept.

United States Frigate: 1576 tons. **D.** 175' 10" x 44' 8". **A.** 44 guns. Built 1798. The decayed vessel was left at Gosport Navy Yard in 1861 and taken over by the Confederates, who used her as a receiving ship. She was sunk as an obstruction in the Elizabeth River, N.C., but later raised and broken up. She was also known as *Confederate States*.

Velocity Schooner: 87 tons. **A.** 2 12-pdr H. Captured by Union forces September 30, 1862. Recaptured at Sabine Pass, June 21, 1863.

Vicksburg Sidewheel steamer: 635 tons. Built 1857. After an inconclusive action with the Union ram *Queen of the West* in February 1863, *Vicksburg* was set on fire and only kept afloat by the coal barges serving alongside. Later used as a wharf boat at Vicksburg, her machinery was removed and used in a steamer then under construction.

Victoria Sidewheel steamer: 405 tons. **D.** 222' x 32' 6" x 5' 10". Built 1858. Used as transport. Captured at Memphis, Tenn., June 6, 1862.

Victoria Sidewheel steamer: 487 tons. Built 1859, lost at sea 1866.

Virginia Ironclad. Former frigate *Merrimac*.

Virginia II Ironclad. **D.** 197' x 47' 6" x 14'. **A.** 1 11-in pivot aft, 1 8-in Brooke rifle forward, 1 6.4-in Brooke rifle on each ironside. **S.** 10 knots. **C.** 150. Laid down at Richmond 1863, completed 1864. Blown up at Richmond to prevent capture, April 4, 1865. Porter's original plan of the superstructure was shortened to save material. Armor was 6" thick on ends and 5" on sides.

Volunteer Sidewheel steamer: 209 tons. Used as transport. Captured off Natchez Island, Miss., November 25, 1863.

W. Burton Sidewheel steamer: 253 tons. **D.** 151' x 25' x 5' 6". Built 1857. Served as tender at New Orleans. Surrendered April 28, 1862.

W.W. Crawford Sidewheel steamer: 123 tons. Built 1861, captured 1863.

Waccamaw (See p.122)

Wade Water Belle Steamer. Captured September 1862.

Warrior Sidewheel tug. **A.** 1 32-pdr. Driven ashore and set on fire below New Orleans, April 25, 1862.

Washington Schooner. **A.** 1 42-pdr. Former US revenue cutter. Seized January 1861.

Wasp Screw steamer. **D.** 46' x 6' 3". **A.** 1 spar torpedo. Built 1864. Served on James River.

Water Witch Sidewheel steamer: 379 tons. **D.** 150' x 23' x 8' 2". **A.** 1 32-pdr R, 1 12-pdr R, 1 12-pdr H. Built 1852. Captured by Confederates in Ossabaw Sound, Ga., June 3, 1864. Burnt to prevent recapture at White Bluff, Ga., December 19, 1864.

Wave Sidewheel steamer: 229 tons. Built 1863. Captured by Confederates at Calcasieu Pass, Texas, May 6, 1864.

Webb Sidewheel tug: 655 tons. **D.** 206' x 32' x 9' 6". **A.** 1 30-pdr R, 2 12-pdr H. Built 1856. Run ashore and set on fire below New Orleans after a desperate race from the Red River, April 24, 1865.

Weldon N. Edwards Steamer. Noted as unfit for service in 1861.

White Cloud Steamer. Used as transport. Captured near Island No, 10, February 13, 1863.

Widgeon Sidewheel steamer: 645 tons. **D.** 225' x 24' x 6'. Blockade runner. Built 1865, but saw no active service as completed too late.

William B. King Schooner. Used on coastguard duties at Berwick, La., 1861.

William Bagley Sidewheel steamer: 396 tons.

William G. Hewes Sidewheel steamer: 767 tons. **D.** 258' x 34'. Built 1860. Renamed *Ella and Anne* in 1863 and served as blockade runner. Captured November 9, 1863. Sold 1865.

William H. Young Sidewheel steamer: 179 tons. Built 1860. Seized by Union forces June 1865.

Wilmington Ironclad. **D.** 224' x 42' 6" x 9' 6". **A.** 2 guns. Destroyed on building slip to prevent capture when the city of Wilmington was captured. (See p.61)

Wilson Sidewheel steamer: 58 tons. Built 1856. Used as transport. Captured on Roanoke River at Hamilton, N.C., July 9, 1862.

Winslow Sidewheel steamer: 207 tons. **A.** 1 32-pdr, 1 6-pdr R. Struck a sunken wreck near Ocracoke Inlet and set on fire to prevent capture, November 7, 1861.

Yadkin Screw steamer: 300 tons. Built 1863–64. Burnt at Wilmington to prevent capture, February 1865.

Yazoo Sidewheel steamer: 371 tons. Used as transport. Abandoned at Island No. 10, April 7, 1862 and seized by Union forces.

York Schooner: 68 tons. **A.** 1 18-pdr R. Privateer, former pilot boat. Burnt to prevent capture off new Inlet, N.C., August 9, 1861.

Young America Steam tug: 173 tons. Captured off Fortress Monroe while going to the aid of an endangered vessel, April 24, 1861.

INDEX